Political Essays On the Nature and Operation of Money, Public Finances, and Other Subjects

POLITICAL ESSAYS

ON THE

NATURE and OPERATION

OF

MONEY, PUBLIC FINANCES,

AND

OTHER SUBJECTS:

Published during the AMERICAN WAR, and continued up to the present Year, 1791.

By *PELATIAH WEBSTER*, A. M.

PHILADELPHIA:

PRINTED AND SOLD BY *JOSEPH CRUKSHANK*, NO. 91, HIGH STREET.

M DCC XCI.

PREFACE

Of the Author.

THE first thirty years of my life were spent in the *literary way*, and generally employed in a course of hard study, and close attention to some subject or other; after which, by a turn in my private affairs, I went into a course of *mercantile business*, which was indeed more a matter of necessity than inclination. My old habits of reading and thinking could not easily be shaken off, and I was scarce ever without either a book or some subject of discussion ready prepared, to which I could resort, the moment I found myself at leisure from other business.

My usual method of discussing any subjects which I undertook to examine, was, as far as possible, to find out and define the *original, natural principles* of them, and to suffer my mind to be drawn on without *bias or any incidental prejudice*, to such conclusions as those original principles would naturally *lead to* and *demonstrate*, i. e. I endeavoured, as far as I could, to make myself *my own original*, and draw all my knowledge from the *original and natural sources* or *first principles* of it.

The powerful pressures of the *British* force during the war, and the obstinate and determined defence of the *Americans*, soon threw every thing into disorder, and produced every day *new occurrences* and *new problems*, which America had never seen before, and, of course, knew not how either to obviate or solve them.

The first operations of the war affected my connexions in trade so much, that it threw me out of my usual course of business, and left me at leisure to contemplate *those occurrences;* and I thought I might render an essential service to my country by examining them, reducing them to *their original principles*, explaining their *nature*, and pointing out their *natural operation and probable effects.*

I conceived that the most important and alarming of these events and questions were those which respected *our resources*, and especially the *state of the Continental money*, which was the *sole supply* of the public treasury at that time.

time. This induced me to turn my attention very seriously to the *nature and operation of MONEY and finance;* a subject which I had never before examined, further than daily practice and private economy made necessary.

Some *reasonings and conclusions* on this subject were published under the signature of *A Financier* in 1776, and make the first of the following Essays; all the rest were published successively (as dated) under the signature of *A Citizen of Philadelphia.*

Whilst I reasoned on the great subjects of the *natural operation of money* and of *national finances,* and drew such theorems and conclusions as appeared to me to result from their natural, original *principles,* I had an opportunity to compare those *conclusions* with real *fact,* and to judge of their truth by *experiment of their actual effects;* and in this I was rarely mistaken. The effects or consequences which I inferred from the principles on which I reasoned, scarcely in one instance *failed to follow* in the *kind,* tho' not always in the *degree,* which I expected, *e. g.* the strength of the States, and the patriotism, the patience, the firmness, and steady virtue of our people, were *greater* than I could expect, whilst I reasoned on human nature and human passions, as exhibited in the example of other nations, *especially in the instance of unpaid armies.* From these sprang resources for continuing the war, beyond my sanguine calculations, whilst *national ruin* appeared to me more near and certain than it really was.

Again, the obstinate perseverance of the *British nation* in continuing the *American* war was *less* than I computed on. I believe, the *American independence* was the only point which that nation ever yielded, after exerting every nerve of their strength to carry their purpose.

Further, I had no idea that the *Continental money* could be made to pass at all *as a medium of trade* at a depreciation even of 50 or 100, much less of 500, for 1.

It may be worth notice here, that these Essays exhibit not only a discussion of the *principles and nature of money* and *national finances,* but contain also a kind of *history* of these principles *compared* with *facts* or their *real operation,* during the convulsions of *America* thro' a seven years' war, when the dangers, the distresses, the firmness, the terrors, the wisdom, the folly, the expedients, the exertions, the resources, the strength and the weakness, the successes and the disappointments, which appeared under all modes and forms, put every *principle* into *operation,* and every *conclusion*

PREFACE.

sion and *theorem to the test*, and left no room for *false reasonings* or *idle projections*, because their *fallacy* was sure to be *detected very soon* by a *failure* or *deficiency* of their *effects*.

These Essays were all written at the times in which the several subjects of them were *fresh*, and *strongly impressed* on every *American* mind, and the *feelings* of every body were *alive* and *wound up* to the highest pitch of anxiety, and an asylum of even safety was eagerly sought. It may, therefore, be agreeable to my *fellow-citizens* to *revise these distressing scenes*, as people sometimes have pleasure in viewing *places* in which they have passed thro' *sorrows* and *calamities* that are now over and past.

A review of arguments and reasonings on the abstruse subject of money and finance, *connected with fact*, i. e. with the *actual effects and consequences* of them, may afford some *gratification* and *amusement* to *speculative* people, who are disposed to examine and explore those *difficult*, but very *interesting matters*, errors and mistakes in which have tript up the heels of, and brought by the board, very many statesmen in every nation.

For this reason it is probable that *politicians* and *statesmen* who may happen to be involved in these inquiries, may find *benefit* in an attention to *American experience*.

Such a connexion of *principles*, *theorems*, and *facts*, in the great subject of *money* and *finance*, is a *phenomenon* rarely to be found in any nation so clearly exhibited, as in the history of money and finances in our States during the war and its consequences.

In short, in the history of *American* distresses, *perfect wisdom* is not to be expected; but we have an opportunity of *learning wisdom* from it. Many *projects*, *plans*, *schemes*, and *manœuvres*, some of them *hurtful*, and others *vain* and *ridiculous* enough, were set on foot, and some of them pushed into execution with great severity, which either *died soon* without effect, or were *marked with calamity* during their continuance.

Many others more *wise* and *judicious* were also proposed, and *sooner or later* adopted with *success and great benefit*.

We have now an opportunity of *distinguishing* the *wise* from the *foolish*, the *good* from the *bad*, by their effects, which may help us much to wisdom in our future counsels.

We are now *at leisure for consideration*, and cannot plead *pressures* and *distresses* in excuse for any mistakes; and we have the effects of former errors, like beacons of caution set up before our eyes to guard us against repeating them.

Some

PREFACE.

Some Essays on different subjects are introduced here, which I leave, with all the rest, to make their way in the world, *according to their merits.*

In these Essays Continental money is often considered; to understand the arguments it may often be necessary to recur to the value of that money at the date of each Essay: I have, for this purpose, added at the end of this book four *scales of depreciation,* viz. the scale of *Congress,* that of the State of *Pennsylvania,* established by law, *April* 3, 1781, and two others, one for *Philadelphia,* the other for *Virginia,* taken from the *merchants' books.*

The two first, for political reasons, vary from the *true exchange* part of the time; the other two, taken from the merchants' books, are as *near the true and actual exchange,* as a thing of such a fluctuating and variable nature can be expected to be.

I have also added a chronology of remarkable events, as people generally connect the occurrences of these times with some or other of those events.

I cannot say I had all the success in these publications which I wished.

In some cases, they crossed the favorite *plans* proposed by influential men, which, like their children, they could not bear to see *killed,* or even *corrected.*

In some cases they opposed some great and strong *interests,* which bore them down.

In some cases, they stood opposed to *general opinion* in point of real propriety. The subjects were new, and the public mind had not time to fix itself on the ground of *experience;* many errors prevailed at that time.

In fine, most people at the time were wrought up to such a *passionate attachment* to the *American cause,* that they had not patience to examine and consider *coolly* the *means necessary* to support it.

But all men have now an opportunity to compare the various *plans and projects* of those times with the *facts* which followed, and doubtless will have pleasure in distinguishing the *wise and prudent* from the *wild and idle,* by their *actual effects.*

In this view, I here present my Essays all together to the reader's perusal and censure.

Philadelphia, February 22, 1791.

CONTENTS.

CONTENTS.

AN Essay on the Danger of too much circulating Cash in a State, the ill Consequences thence arising, and the necessary Remedies, - Page 1
An Essay on Free Trade and Finance, - 9
A Second Essay on Free Trade and Finance, - 27
A Third Essay on Free Trade and Finance, - 50
A Fourth Essay on Free Trade and Finance, - 74
A Fifth Essay on Free Trade and Finance, - 97
Strictures on Tender-Acts, - - 128
An Essay or humble Attempt to examine and state the true Interest of Pennsylvania with Respect to the Paper Currency, - - - - 139
An Essay on the Economy, Policy, and Resources of the Thirteen States, and the Means of their Preservation, - - - - 152
A Dissertation on the Nature, Authority, and Uses of the Office of a Financier-General or Superintendant of the Finances, - - - 162
Remarks on the Resolution of Council, of the 2d of May, 1781, for raising the Exchange to 175 Continental Dollars for 1 hard, - - 172
Strictures on a Publication in the Freeman's Journal of May 16, 1781, signed *Timoleon*, - 181
Strictures on two Publications in the Freeman's Journal of May 30, 1781, signed, *Phocion*, and *Impartial*, 191
A Dissertation on the Political Union and Constitution of the Thirteen United States of *North-America*, which is necessary to their Preservation and Happiness, - - - - - 198
A Sixth Essay on Free Trade and Finance, particularly showing what Supplies of Public Revenue may be drawn from *Merchandise*, without injuring our Trade, or burdening our People, - 230
A Seventh Essay on Free Trade and Finance, in which the Expediency of *funding* the Public Securities, striking further Sums of *Paper Money*, and other important Matters, are considered, - 269
A Plea for the Poor Soldiers; or, an Essay to demonstrate that the Soldiers and other Public Creditors,

who

CONTENTS.

who *really and actually* supported the Burden of the late War, have not been paid, ought to be paid, can be paid, and muſt be paid, - - 306

A Review of the Principles and Arguments of the two foregoing Eſſays, viz. The Seventh Eſſay on Finance, and The Plea for the Poor Soldiers; with ſome Obſervations on the Finances of the Union, - 344

An Eſſay on the *Seat* of the Federal Government, and the Excluſive Juriſdiction of Congreſs over a *Ten Miles* Diſtrict; with Obſervations on the Economy and delicate Morals neceſſary to be obſerved in infant States, - - - 376

Remarks on the Addreſs of Sixteen Members of the Aſſembly of *Pennſylvania* to their Conſtituents, dated Sept. 29, 1787; with ſome Strictures on their Objections to the *Conſtitution* recommended by the late Federal Convention, - - 403

The Weakneſſes of *Brutus* expoſed: or, ſome Remarks In Vindication of the Conſtitution propoſed by the late Federal Convention, againſt the Objections and gloomy Fears of that Writer, - - 413

An Eſſay on Credit: in which the Doctrine of *Banks* is conſidered, and ſome Remarks are made on the preſent State of the *Bank of North-America*, - 427

Strictures on the Net Produce of the Taxes of *Great-Britain* in the Year 1784, as publiſhed by Order of their Houſe of Commons, - - 464

An Eſſay on *Teſt-Acts* impoſed with Penalties, - 471

An Eſſay on the Extent and Value of our Weſtern Unlocated Lands, and the Proper Method of diſpoſing of them, ſo as to gain the greateſt poſſible Advantage from them, - - - 485

Scales of Depreciation of Continental Money, - 501

A Chronological Table of Remarkable Events, - 503

AN ESSAY

On the Danger of too much circulating Cash in a State, the ill Consequences thence arising, and the Necessary Remedies.

[*Published in the Pennsylvania Evening Post of Oct. 5, 1776, under the signature of A Financier.*]

THE computations of the value of the Free States of America by *Conti*— and *Doria*, in the Evening Post of Sept. 21, rather prove that value to be immense than reduce it to a certainty. Perhaps another method of computation might be admitted, viz. from the quantity of land within the present inhabited part of those states, which is at least two hundred millions of acres, and worth a dollar per acre I should think at least, some say two or three dollars, and perhaps the personal estate may be computed at as much more, which I do not think is reckoning high, and will make the amount four hundred millions of dollars. All these computations prove with certainty enough that the funds, on which the Continental money depends, are sufficiently great to support a very much larger quantity than is already emitted. (*a*) I would farther observe that the American States owe nothing to any body but themselves, and employ no ships, soldiers, &c. but their own, so that they contract no foreign debt; and I take it

---

(*a*) The first emission of Continental money was dated May 10, 1775, but was not really issued into actual circulation till some months afterwards, but the quantity multiplied so fast that it became somewhat alarming at the time when this essay was written.

to be a clear maxim, that no state can be ruined, bankrupted, or indeed much endangered, by any debt due to itself only; nor can it ever be much impoverished by any war, if the war and other casualties do not destroy mankind faster than the women produce them, and the people that are left at home can furnish the provisions, clothing, &c. necessary for themselves and the soldiery, together with all other necessary stores and implements of the war.

There requires no more to preserve such a state in a war of any length of time than good economy in bringing the burden equally on all, in proportion to their abilities; but then I think it very necessary that they should *pay as they go*, as near as may be. The *soldier* renders his personal services down on the spot, the *farmer* his provisions, the *tradesman* his fabrics, and why should not the *monied man* pay his money down too? Why should the soldier, tradesman, farmer, &c. be paid in promises, which are not so good as money, if the fulfilment is at a distance?

Payment in promises or bills of credit is a temporary expedient, and will always be dangerous, where the quantity increases too much, at least it will always have the consequences of a medium increased beyond the necessities of trade; and whenever that happens, a speedy remedy is necessary, or the ill effects will soon be alarming, and, if long neglected, will not be easily remedied. The remedy or rather prevention of this evil I take to be very easy at present.

If the *quantity of Continental currency is greater than is necessary for a medium of trade*, it will appear by a number of very perceptible effects, each of which point out and facilitate the remedy. *One effect* will be, that people will choose to have their estates vested in any goods of intrinsic value rather than in money, and of course there will be a quick demand for every kind of goods, and consequently a high price for them; *another effect* will be discouragement of industry, for people will not work hard to procure goods for sale, while the medium for which they must sell them is supposed to be worse than the goods; and of course, *another effect* will be a discouragement of trade, for nobody will

will import goods, and fell them, when imported, for a medium that is worfe than the goods themfelves; for in that cafe, though the profits may be *nominal*, the lofs will be *real*.

Thefe effects all point out their only remedy, viz. leffening the quantity of the circulating medium, and this can be done by but three ways that I know of; Firft, the *deftruction of it* by fome cafualty, as fire, fhipwreck, &c. or fecondly, *exportation* of it, which cannot happen in our cafe, becaufe our medium has no currency abroad, and I think it very well for us that it has not; for in that cafe our debt would foon become due to people without ourfelves, and of courfe lefs fenfible, more difficult to be paid, and more dangerous; the third, and, in my opinion, the only practicable way of leffening the quantity is *by a tax*, which never can be paid fo eafy as when money is more plenty than goods, and of courfe, the very caufe which makes a tax neceffary, facilitates the payment of it.

The tax ought to be *equal to the excefs of the currency*, fo as to leffen the currency down to that quantity which is neceffary for a medium of trade, and this, in my opinion, ought to be done by every ftate, whether money is immediately wanted in the public treafury or not, for it is better for any ftate to have their excefs of money, tho' it were all gold and filver, *hoarded* in a public treafury or, bank, than *circulated* among the people, for nothing can have worfe effects on any ftate than an excefs of money. The poverty of the ftates of Holland, where nobody can have money who does not firft earn it, has produced induftry, frugality, economy, good habits of body and mind, and durable and well-eftablifhed riches, whilft the excefs of money has produced the contrary in Spain, i. e. has ruined their induftry and economy, and filled them with pride and poverty.

But there is, befides this general principle, a fpecial reafon in our cafe, why we fhould pay a large part of our Continental debt by a prefent tax; the great confumption of our armies, and ftoppage of our imports, make a great demand for the produce of our lands, the fabrics of our tradefmen,

tradefmen, and the labor of our people, and of courfe raifes the prices of all thefe much higher than ufual, fo that the hufbandman, tradefman, and laborer get money much fafter and eafier than they ufed to do, and it is a plain maxim, that people fhould always pay their debts when they have a good run of bufinefs, and have money plenty; many a man has been *diftreffed* for a debt when bufinefs and money were fcarce, which he had *neglected* to pay when he could have done it with great eafe to himfelf, had he attended to it in its proper feafon; this applies to a community or ftate as well as to a private perfon.

Thefe laft obfervations will apply with great exactnefs to thofe parts of the Continent which lie neareft to the great fcenes of the war, and have fuffered moft by it; and if they can bear the tax, I think thofe who lie at a diftance from thofe horrors, and have felt little more than a fympathy of the diftrefs of their brethren, can have no reafon to complain, if they are called on for their fhare of the expenfe.

The Continental money is to be confidered as a debt faftened on the perfon and eftate of every member of the United States, a debt of great honor and juftice, of national honor and juftice, not barely *empty honor*, but that *effential honor and credit* in which the fafety of the ftate is comprifed, and therefore by confeffion of every body muft be punctually and honorably paid in due time; otherwife all fecurity arifing from public credit muft be loft, all confidence of individuals in our public councils muft be deftroyed, and great injuftice muft be done to every poffeffor of our public currency, to the *detriment* of all, and ruin of many who have placed moft confidence in our public adminiftration: and nothing but fhame, fcandal, and contempt can enfue, for which nothing but moft inevitable neceffity can be any reafonable excufe. (*b*)

And in this great argument is every individual of our United States fo deeply interefted, that I cannot conceive
one

(*b*) The citizen, at the time of writing this, had no conception that the continental money could continue to be a quick currency at 500 for 1, and finally run itfelf out to nothing, and die, not only without *any tumult*, but with the general *fatisfaction* of the people.

one sensible person can be persuaded to risk these consequences for the sake of a little delay of payment of that which must one day be paid, or we must all be ruined together. The Continental debt is already a heavy one, and there is no way of sinking it but by paying it while we can; it is still increasing fast; and without a speedy tax, and a very sufficient one, it will grow upon us beyond any possibility of payment. If a man only suffers his rents, butcher's and tradesman's bills, &c. to be unpaid a number of years, it will endanger his whole fortune. An expense account ought always to be paid up as soon as it becomes due; these are accumulating sums, and it is dangerous to neglect them.

I have heard some people say, it is no matter for the present payment of the Continental debt, we are a country of rapid increase, and what is contracted by three millions of people, will soon be paid by six. But how unfatherly and ungenerous is it to load posterity with an immense debt, which we have an advantage in sinking a good part of ourselves; besides, it will be a great discouragement to foreign emigrants to settle in this country, to be told that the country is loaded with an immense debt, and their first title to an enfranchisement will be by beginning to pay it.

We are engaged in a cause which, in all annals of time, has ever been deemed most honorable and glorious, and most characteristic of noble and generous minds, viz. spurning off slavery, and asserting our liberty. As things now stand, the most hardened, impudent Tory does not pretend that if we fail of supporting our cause, we have any other chance but that of absolute submission and pardon, and even that pardon, doubtless, with numerous exceptions. Good GOD! Who can bear the thought of absolute *submission and pardon?* *Pardon!* for the greatest virtue of a civil nature that the human mind is capable of! Who can think, without distraction, of coming under the domination of tories, and suing to them for favors and intercessions? Tories! with standing armies at their heels, and soldiers with bayonets ready to enforce all the respect and submission they may claim.

This

This dreadful apprehension introduces, with great force on my mind, another reason why we ought to sink, by a sufficient tax, as much as we can of the continental debt, viz. That without this it is not possible to continue the war, and avoid absolute submission.

I conceive the *value of the currency* of any state has a *limit*, a *ne plus ultra*, beyond which it cannot go, and if the *nominal sum* is extended beyond that *limit*, the *value* will not follow. No human wisdom, or authority, can be able to stretch the nominal currency beyond such real value. The consequence of any attempt to extend such nominal addition, must depreciate the value of the whole, till it is reduced within said limit.

I will explain my meaning thus; (*c*) Suppose that thirty millions of dollars was the utmost limit of currency to which the United States of America could give real, effectual value, and they should emit thirty millions more; I say the last thirty millions would add nothing to the value of the whole, but would sink the value of the whole sixty millions down to its limit, viz. thirty millions; i. e. the whole sixty millions in that case would not purchase more real, substantial goods, than the thirty millions would have done, before the other thirty millions were added to it.

It follows from this, that any attempt to continue the war, by increasing the currency beyond the abovesaid limit, is vain, and must fail of the effect intended, and ruin all those who possess the currency already emitted. Whether the currency already emitted rises to the said limit, is a question of fact that may admit some doubt, but that it is not greatly within it, I think can be no doubt with people well acquainted with the nature and circumstances of this great subject; and be that as it may, I think every inconvenience arising from it is easily remedied by a sufficient tax. I do not apprehend we have yet suffered by a depreciation

---

(*c*) No estimate of the current cash of the Thirteen States had been made on any sure data when this essay was published, but it was generally computed at about 30,000,000 of dollars, which is somewhat less than one third of the current cash of Great Britain; but on a more critical examination of the subject, this computation appeared much too high: perhaps, about 12,000,000 of dollars may be near the truth.

ciation of the currency, becaufe I cannot obferve that the general prices of goods are more raifed than the circumftances of the war would make neceffary, were our money all gold and filver, and farther extremities may produce farther effects of the fame kind, without depreciating the currency at all.

No kind of neceffaries have rifen to the excefs of price given laft winter in Bofton for frefh provifions, tho' their currency was all gold and filver, increafe of rifk muft raife the price of all imported goods, fcarcity of laborers muft raife the price of labor, and of confequence the price of every thing produced by labor, fcarcity of tradefmen (many of whom are gone into the war) and demand for tradefmen's fabrics, muft raife the price of them; befides, many raw materials ufed by the tradefmen, muft be imported at great rifk, and I do not fee that the prices of moft or all thefe are greater than they would be, if every Continental dollar was a filver one.

But fhould we admit that we are on the verge of a depreciation, or that our currency hath fuffered fome little already in its value, two confequences will follow, which deferve great and immediate confideration.

Firft, That a *speedy remedy* is immediately neceffary, which fhall operate effectually, and prevent the ruin of our currency; and the fecond is, that the remedy by this very means becomes more *eafy and practicable* than otherwife it could be, becaufe a tax will be paid much more eafily in this cafe than it could be, if money was in credit enough to be avariciously hoarded, and this holds, let the tax be of any nature, fuch as general affeffment of polls and eftates, excifes, impofts, or duties on goods, lotteries, &c. &c. in any or all thefe ways, our currency may be leffened much eafier, when its credit is a little doubted, than when it is at its higheft. (d)

What

(d) However plain the neceffity of a tax at that time to prevent the exceffive increafe of the continental money, may appear to us *now*, it was *then* not fo clear; for after many debates in Congrefs, that meafure was not adopted for a long time. I am told, one member of Congrefs rofe during
thofe

What contributes not a little to this facility is, that it may be done by general consent, without public uneasiness and disturbance, for a depreciation of currency can be wished for by nobody, but those who are deeply in debt, the weight or numbers of whom I have reason to believe is not great at present in these States; it is the mighty interest of all the rest of the inhabitants to prevent a depreciation, and I conceive every man of estate who has cash in hand, or due to him, would be willing to contribute his share to the lessening our currency, and so preserving its credit. Yea, would eagerly choose this, rather than risk his own loss by a depreciation of the cash he has in hand, and in debts due.

In this time of distress the public has a right to every man's best thoughts. I have not the vanity to think I can exhaust the subject, but I have said so much on it, as I hope will set abler heads and pens on a thorough disquisition of it, for I think all will agree, that the subject is a very important one, and deserves most immediate and most serious attention.

those debates with this exclamation, " Do you think, Gentlemen, that I
" will consent to load my constituents with taxes, when we can send to our
" printer, and get a waggon-load of money, one quire of which will pay
" for the whole?"

A N

AN ESSAY ON FREE TRADE and FINANCE.

First published in Philadelphia, July 1779, and dedicated to CONGRESS.

FREEDOM of trade, or unrestrained liberty of the subject to *hold or dispose of* his property as he pleases, is absolutely necessary to the prosperity of every community, and to the happiness of all individuals who compose it: this liberty will produce the following effects:

1. Every industrious man will procure *all the goods* he can for sale; this is the way to get most money; and gain is the soul of industry, the hope of reward sweetens labor, and the most righteous have respect to the recompence of reward.

2. Every man will make his goods for market of the *best quality* he can, because they will bring more money and quicker sale than goods of mean quality.

3. Every man will endeavour to carry to market the *most scarce goods* because there is the greatest demand and best price for them. All experience shews, that the most effectual way to turn a scarcity into a plenty, is to raise the price of the articles wanted: witness, among other instances, the most alarming scarcity of saltpetre and gunpowder, in the beginning of the present war, succeeded by the most abundant plenty in less than one year, effected altogether by the high price and premiums set on them.

4. Every man will go to market and return in *good humor* and full satisfaction, even though he may be disappointed of the high price he expected, becaufe he has had the full chance of the market, and can blame nobody; and fhould he indulge fretting on the occafion, he would be the more ridiculed, and lefs pitied by his neighbours: and good humor and fatisfaction contribute not a little to the happinefs and profperity of communities, as well as individuals; and therefore this is an article by no means to be left out or overlooked in the adminiftration of either public or private œconomy.

5. In times of danger, diftrefs, and difficulty, every man will ufe *ftrong endeavours* to get his goods to market, in proportion to the neceffity and great demand for them; becaufe they will then bring the beft price, and every man is fond of embracing golden opportunities and favorable chances.

6. When things grow fcarce and dear, every man will ufe them with the *beft œconomy*, and make the ftock on hand go as far and laft as long as poffible; or if he is deftitute, will buy as little as will juft ferve his neceffity. This naturally preferves the ftock on hand from needlefs profufion and wafte, and converts it to the beft and moft prudent ufe for the benefit of the community, and naturally tends to ward off high diftrefs or total want, till the high price and great demand, by their natural operation, will bring further fupplies to market.

7. In times of fcarcity, every man will have ftrong inducements to bring *all he can fpare* to market, becaufe it will then bring the higheft price he can ever expect, and confequently the community will have the benefit of all that exifts among them, in a much furer manner than any degree of force could extort it, and all to the entire fatisfaction of buyer and feller; by which the numberlefs feuds, riots, refentments, and mifchiefs which ufually attend forced markets, would be entirely avoided; and the market be fupplied with all there is to be had. For no principle can draw into market, all the fupplies which are attainable,

so effectually, as the cheerful good-will and interest of the owners.

8. In times of scarcity, when all the goods that are to be had, are exposed to sale, it is not possible the prices should *exceed the degree of scarcity*, for when the prices rise very high, they will soon determine whether the scarcity is real or not; for *if not real* the high price will bring such quantity to market as will soon lower the price; but *if real*, it is necessary for the above reasons, that the prices should continue high till supplies are produced.

Restraint of property or * *limitation of prices* will hurt any community, and will probably produce the following effects, contrary to the above.

1. Every man will have as *little to do* with the market, and bring as few goods there as he can; for the less goods he has for sale, the less mortification and loss he sustains.

2. Every man will make his goods for market of a *bad quality*, or at least not the best; for they must all go at the limited price, and he therefore gets nothing for any special care or skill he may bestow on his goods to meliorate or perfect their quality: for the same reason, every man will expose his worst goods to market, and keep the best out of sight; for example, musty tea, stale flour, black heavy bread, &c.

3. Every man is induced to keep such goods as are *most scarce* from market; for if he carries them there, he can get no more than the limited price, and stands a chance of a bad hustling in the crowd into the bargain. Whereas, if he can keep his goods from market, the scarcity will soon force a great price, and he has a chance of great profits.

4. If

---

* The pressures of the war, together with the vast increase of Continental money had for a considerable time before this Essay was wrote, raised the nominal price of all goods, to a most alarming degree; to remedy which the most unhappy expedient had been adopted in most of the states, of *regulating* or *limiting the prices* at which goods should be sold, with high penalties on those who should sell at higher prices than those limited; and those ordinances were carried into such rigid execution, that many stores were forced open, and the goods sold at the limited prices, by committees, &c. when the owners refused to sell them at those prices; and much pains was taken to load the merchants with scandal and obloquy for combinations to raise the price of goods, depreciate the currency, &c. they were called Tories, Speculators, and many other hard names, &c. &c.

4. If prices are limited, and the owner is compelled to sell at the prices limited, he considers himself *injured* by every sale he makes for less than he supposes he could have obtained in a free market; that his liberty is taken from him, and he can no longer call his property his own. These are hard feelings to one born to freedom almost perfect, and raised to the expectations of enjoying it in future time, in its highest perfection. These feelings fill the mind with anxiety and resentment, and when instances of this become numerous among the merchants, tradesmen, and farmers, small accidents may blow up the concealed coal, and most fatal effects may easily be supposed to ensue. This is a danger of no small magnitude, for the real strength and establishment of every government consists in the hearty union and satisfaction of the individuals that compose it.

5. In times of danger, distress, and difficulty, no man will be induced to any *great efforts* to supply the market; for an additional danger makes an additional expense upon the goods; but he must take the limited price and no more; he will not consequently combat or risk an increase of danger and expense without any chance of compensation.

6. When things grow scarce, every man will endeavour to lay in *great stores* if he can do it without an increase of price, and will not think it necessary to retrench his expenses, whilst he thinks his stock will last through the scarcity; the consequence of which is, that all the scarce articles at market will be scrambled up by a few hands, who will have no inducement to parsimony in the expenditure of them, by which the scarcity and distress are increased, and many must be wholly destitute; and as far as this respects the necessaries of life, the consequences must be dreadful.

7. Add to the above, that in times of scarcity and great demand, every man who can possibly *conceal* his goods will be tempted to do it, in expectation that the great demand will soon break through the unnatural restraint of the limitation, and he shall be able to obtain a great profit in the future sale; and in spite of all the vigilance and force that can be used, many will be able to do this; which I

take

take to be one of the natural effects of any unnatural restraint of trade, which cannot be avoided.

8. In addition to all these, the *difficulties* which must attend the execution of such an act of limitation, may perhaps furnish not the least objection to it. Must the owner be obliged to sell to every person who applies to purchase, without knowing whether he wants for use or sale? Must he forego previous engagements of his goods in favor of the present demandant? Must he be obliged to sell to every knave and litigious fellow, with whom he would not chuse to be at all concerned in any dealing? Who shall judge how much he may reserve for his own use, and whether he may give corn to his cattle and hogs, and how much, and how many of each he may keep, &c. &c. &c. Must he have his house searched from top to bottom for concealments? Even the lodging-rooms of his wife and daughters! I must beg to be excused from any further description of these horrors, which too many know are not mere creatures of the imagination.

9. It is not possible to form a limitation of prices which shall *be just*, and therefore the whole scheme necessarily implies injustice. The principles on which the just prices of goods are fixed, are in a constant state of fluctuation, and therefore the prices must rise and fall with their causes: all experience proves this, and it holds true in the most excessive degree, in times of such public distress and convulsion as we now experience. And as it is much safer to bind a man in health than a man in convulsions, so it will be safer to limit trade in peaceable than convulsed times. It is not more absurd to limit the precise height to which a ship shall be fixed at a wharf, where the tide is constantly ebbing and flowing. A great force will be requisite to keep the ship from rising or falling with the tide, and a mighty little use to pay for the trouble; besides the probability of very essential damage which the ship must incur by the application of the necessary force: but indiscreet as this would be judged, it is less dangerous in a calm than in a stormy season.

10. Another

10. Another mischievous consequence of this fatal measure, and not the least, I conceive to be its unhappy tendency to *corrupt the morals and integrity* of the people. To escape the ruinous consequences of loosing in their sales, they are in a manner compelled, but to say the least, they have very strong temptation, either by downright lying, or using little arts, shifts, and cheats, to avoid the sale of their goods to disadvantage. *This* naturally brings them into the habit, and gives them a facility of inventing and practising *low methods* of shamming Abraham, which they never would otherwise have thought of, and which it is infinitely detrimental to the public, they ever should learn; instances of this sort might be enumerated without end. But it is needless to give examples, it were better they and their causes should be removed, than that they should be repeated. But after all, it is said that a limitation of prices is necessary to *appreciate the currency*, and *supply the army*. Two very great objects indeed: I will attend to both.

I. I do not conceive that a limitation of prices can possibly *appreciate the currency* or prevent a further depreciation.

1. The value of money is nothing in itself, it is a *mere relation*, it is the proportion between the medium of trade and the objects of trade; these two will always be in balance: Therefore, if the medium of trade be increased, whilst the objects of trade continue the same, the money must depreciate; if the medium of trade increases, and the objects of trade decrease, the proportion will alter fast, and the depreciation will increase in a double proportion, which I take to be the case at present. Money will therefore increase or decrease its value according to the increase or decrease of its quantity, and the increase or decrease of the quantity of goods, or the objects of trade. This principle is grounded on the nature of the thing, and can never be altered, and consequently any attempt to oppose it must be equally vain, as opposing any other law of nature whatever. It follows from this, that nothing can ever appreciate the money, but lessening its quantity, or increasing the quantity of goods or objects of trade, and all attempts to
do

do this in any other method, will prove vain and fruitless in the end.

2. It follows, that the price that any article of trade will bring in a free, open market, is the only *measure of the value* of that article at that time, and if this is warped from the truth, by any artifices of the merchant, or force of power, it cannot hold; but the error will soon discover itself, and the correction of it will be compelled by the irresistible force of natural principles, *i. e.* it is not possible for merchants to raise goods too high, or the force of power to depress them too low, and make them keep so. Both these may be done for a short time, but neither can last long.

3. It follows that any limitation of prices, however strongly enforced, if below the rates required by this great natural proportion, is but *temporary injustice*, cannot be of long continuance, will tend daily to lessen the quantity of goods in market, and so will increase the mischief it was designed to prevent, and bring with it a large train of evils besides, which will require much time and wisdom to remedy, and many that will be utterly remediless, examples of which are obvious.

4. Money is made only for a medium of trade, and must be kept in *circulation and use*, or it perishes; for to stop the circulation of money and to kill it is the same thing, stop its course and it dies, give it circulation again and it revives, or comes to life again; therefore, the price of goods for sale, or objects of trade (*i. e.* every thing for which money is paid) must always be so high, as to require all the money there is to purchase them, otherwise the sum remaining cannot circulate, *i. e.* there will be nothing to lay it out upon, and so the owner must keep it by him, dead and useless: so that let what sums of money soever be in circulation, the objects of trade must either increase in quantity, or rise in price so high as to take all the money there is in circulation to purchase them, and as this natural law cannot be restrained, so neither can it be exceeded by any degree of artifice or force for any long time, for if the objects of trade rise so high that all the money in circula-

tion

tion will not purchafe them, the overplus muft remain dead and unfaleable in the hands of the owner, which will foon reduce the price; for goods which cannot be fold, are as ufelefs in the hands of the merchant, as money which cannot be circulated.

5. Every limitation of prices below their due proportion, *checks the circulation* of money, than which nothing can be more dangerous, when money is over plenty; this has been the conftant effect of every limitation of prices which has been tried in America. Bufinefs immediately ftagnates, goods cannot be had, people cannot purchafe with their money the neceffaries they want, they begin of courfe to think that their money is good for nothing, and refufe to take any more of it, and grow willing to part with what they have on hand at a depreciated value; fo that the certain operation of a limitation of prices is a further depreciation of the money inftead of the contrary. Inftead of this, it is of the laft neceffity in a plenty of money, that a free circulation be kept up, people will readily and even greedily take any money which they can readily pafs again. And as long as this lafts, there can be no danger of the money's ftopping; whereas, the contrary chills it at once, and in a fhort time muft chill it into a torpor, incapable of cure. Much in this cafe depends on opinion, which is foon formed by people in general, when they find they cannot buy neceffaries with their money. Specious reafonings, warm harrangues, declarations of Congrefs, or even the force of power operate little againft this; it is a glaring intuitive proof of the badnefs of money, when it will not purchafe neceffaries, and as glaring and ftrong a proof that it is good, when it will buy any thing in market. Hence appears the neceffity of keeping up a high and brifk circulation of money, and the folly and danger of limitations, or any other meafures which prevent a circulation and obftruct trade. Thefe are arguments grounded on plain fact, they have their foundation in the laws of nature, and no artifice or force of man can prevent, elude, or avoid their effects; their operation is uncontrolable, and therefore I conceive all oppofition to them is the height

abfurdity

absurdity, and dangerous in the highest degree.——For ten months before the late limitations, we had a trade perfectly free, on which two observations are obvious.

1. That any goods at market might be bought for continental money, the Speculators especially (as they are called) were fond of receiving it, and no person could be at any loss for any thing at market, if he had that money to purchase the goods he needed.

2. That imported goods on an average (which were the only articles Speculators dealt in) were 50 per cent. cheaper on the 25th of May last, than on the 25th of July preceding, i. e. any given quantity of imported goods would buy 50 per cent. more articles of country produce, or hard money, on the 25th of July, than on the 25th of May last; and for the truth of this, I refer to the merchants' books; from which it follows that the Speculators (however numerous and however censured) have not raised the price of the goods they have principally dealt it :—Indeed all experience teaches, that the more hands the goods in market are held by, the cheaper they will be, and the more difficult to raise the price; and therefore, if the merchants ever think of raising the price of any article, they never fail to say, We must wait till these goods are drained out of the small stores and get them into few hands. In July 25, 1778, price current of imported goods, at Philadelphia, was as follows, West-India rum 3l. 15s. Muscovado sugars 30l. molasses 40s. pepper 17s. 6d. coffee 9s. cotton 15s. bohea tea 60s. Madeira wine 400l. dry goods about 8 to 1 old prices, and hard money 4 to 1, and price current of country produce, was as follows, for Indian corn 15s. oats 12s. flour 60s. bar iron 100l. consequently on July 25, 1778, one gallon of West-India rum would bring 5 bushels of Indian corn, 6 bushels of oats, 1¼ hundred of flour, and ⅔ of a *hundred of iron*, or 18s. 9d. hard money; any body may easily compare the rest, and they will find enough to, prove my assertion with large allowance. Price current 25th May last was, rum 7l. sugars 130l. iron 860l. tea 6l. 10s. &c. Indian corn 7l. 10s. oats 90s. flour 30l. (hard money 20 to 1) and consequently one gallon of rum would buy no

more than one bushel of Indian corn, 1¼ bushel of oats, ¼ hundred flour, and ¾ hundred iron or 7s. hard money, &c. These computations are made in the face of the world, and grounded on facts which any body may disprove if they are not true, or correct the reasoning if it is not just. Now I have only to add; let any body who is disposed to see, open their eyes, and see who it is that has raised our prices, or *which is the same thing*, depreciated our money. Is it the Speculators who deal only in imported articles? Or the farmers, among whom no kind of dangerous speculation does or can exist? Perhaps it may be replied here, that the articles of country produce are extremely scarce, which raises their price beyond the due proportion of other things: if you say this, you say every thing and yield every thing, viz. that the plenty and scarcity of goods will govern the price. You must admit too, that the plenty and scarcity of money will determine the value of that also. Why then will any one pretend to limit either, against the operation of this great principle? It is easy, in addition to all this, to prove that the price of imported articles in general does not exceed the value of them, if computed on the expense of acquirement: but this I mean only to hint, and wave it for the present; and only wish some merchants of experience and reputation would take it up, and publish the needful essay on it.

Nor do I think that the scheme of loans can give establishment to the currency, or prevent its depreciation.—For

1. All loans increase the public debt, and the immensity of the sum is one cause of the depreciation, as it induces people to think it never will be paid, or the payment will necessarily be delayed to such a distant period, as in point of use to the present possessor *is nearly* equal to total failure.

2. If the credit of the Loan-Office is well supported (as it must be to give it any good effect) the Loan-Office certificates themselves will pass in payment, and so become an addition to the currency which they are designed to lessen.

3. If foreign loans are negotiated, and bills sold here, drawn on the loaned bank in Europe, those very bills will become a currency here, and so add to the mischief.

4. The

4. The difcount on all European bills, is not lefs than 50 per cent. which lofs muft immediately be fuftained by the Continent on the firft fale of them.

5. If hard money, borrowed in Europe, fhould be imported and fold here, the infurance, which is more than 50 per cent. muft be loft, nor can any man tell the mifchief which would attend any attempt to import hard money, and open offices for the fale of it for continental bills: but a large group of thefe prefent themfelves too plainly to need enumeration.

6. Nor do I think the * fcheme adopted by *our Committee* promifes better fuccefs; for that propofes Loaning without inducement; and if it fhould fucceed to the utmoft expectation, it would drain the beft friends to our caufe of their money, whilft our internal enemies would pay nothing, for no compulfion is propofed, and after all, it will be at beft but an anticipation of the revenue, very dangerous in the end; for the very *worst* thing that can be done refpecting a revenue, is to *deftroy it all*, principal and ufe, and the *next worst* thing is to *anticipate it*, i. e. to fpend this year the rent and proceeds which will become due and payable next year, and thefe two are fo connected, that the latter generally brings on the former fooner or later.

After all thefe objections to the various methods that have been propofed, it may be expected that I fhould propofe fome method that will be practicable and effectual to fix the value of our currency; and this I cannot think very difficult, either in theory or practice, though I have not one new thought to offer the public on the fubject. We are now on the brink of ruin, and the worft difgrace, in danger of lofs of liberty hitherto nobly afferted, and fubjection to fhameful flavery to enemies moft cruel and infulting in themfelves, and all that heightened in them to madnefs by the determined oppofition we have given to their fcheme of tyranny over us. All this danger arifes not from our *poverty or want*, for we have officers and foldiers enough, ftores

---

* This was a propofal for a fubfcription and immediate advance of money, to be difcounted on their future taxes of the fubfcribers.

of every kind enough, and zeal, union, and virtue sufficient to insure success; our difficulties arise only from our having *too much money*, and the lessening that quantity would relieve us at once from every difficulty, and dissipate the thickest clouds that hang over us.

In matters of difficulty and importance, all wise counsellors compare well the *end* and the *means*, on which two very weighty matters always present themselves.

1. Whether the means are sufficient to secure and effect the end proposed.——And

2. Whether the end is worth the means necessary to effect it. When these two points are settled, there remains no more room for consultation or debate, the rest is all vigorous action, strenuous exertion to put the means into such effectual execution as to obtain the end. This is a wise method of planning, which no man will have any objection to. We will then adopt it in the consideration of the weighty subject now in view.

1. The end is fixing our currency and preventing any future depreciation, and so putting an effectual end to all the cheats, delusions, disappointments, and ruinous losses, which every one who has been concerned in it hath hitherto felt, and giving every one a sure and well grounded confidence in it in future. This is an end, an object of such vast, such weighty consequence, and so confessed and acknowledged by all, that no arguments or illustrations are necessary to be added here.

2. The *only means* I conceive possible to obtain this end, are to call in such sums annually by taxes, as shall be equal to the annual expenditures; this will prevent the increase of the money, will make a great demand for it through the Thirteen United States, will give it a brisk circulation, will exhibit a most convincing proof that it may be all called in and redeemed, and that it is the real design of Congress to do this. * Nothing helps the credit of a large debtor
like

---

* No taxes had hitherto been collected, or other funds but Continental money and loans, provided for supporting the war, which had lasted four years, nor had any methods been adopted either to *lessen the quantity* of that money, or
even

like making ample provision for actual payments; he may promise till he is grey without this, and all in vain; the larger his promises, the lefs are they credited, and the more ridiculous does he become: the cry againſt him is, Where is the money to come from? let us ſee a ſample of it: but the cry is altered when large payments are actually made, and ſufficient proviſion making for the diſcharge of the whole debt. Let people ſee the money collecting through the Continent, and the ſources of revenue actually opened, and the whole matter in train, there can remain no doubt but the whole of the Continental money will be redeemed, and every one will venture to truſt the credit of it; and in this confidence it will be ſoon ſought after and graſped with greedineſs, and hugged and hoarded with avidity.

This will put life into all our public meaſures, civil and military, will give our government the command of the fulleſt ſupplies of *men*, *money*, and *ſtores* that are in the country, and that can be made or procured, will give *ſpirit* to our people, will animate *induſtry*, and will be a total cure of the *miſchiefs* we now feel from the low credit of our currency. Here is an object highly worthy of our attention, as every one will admit without heſitation: the only thing then that remains, is *whether it be practicable*: I ſuppoſe the outcry againſt it will be, that the people will not bear ſuch enormous taxes, that they would *ſink the poor* and *diſtreſs the rich* far beyond what they will ever conſent to bear, &c. &c. I conceive a vein of converſation of this ſort not at all founded in truth, for ſeveral reaſons.

1. It

even to prevent the *increaſe of it*, except the inſtitution of the Loan-Office, October 3, 1776, which proved a remedy altogether inadequate to the purpoſe, and of courſe the emiſſions of that paper were multiplied, which together with the emiſſions of the particular ſtates, ſwelled the quantity ſo much that the depreciation at that time (July 24, 1779) became very alarming; it was about 20 to 1, *i. e.* one dollar hard money would buy 20 dollars continental: the annual expenſe of ſupporting an army of 50,000 men and a ſmall navy, amounted to at leaſt ten millions of Mexican dollars. That Congreſs ſhould ever *think* of ſupporting that expenſe with *ſuch funds*, or that it ſhould be *poſſible* to do it, may ſeem ſtrange to foreigners, and will appear ſo to our own poſterity; but the univerſal rage and zeal of the people through all the ſtates, for an emancipation from a power that claimed a right *to bind them in all caſes whatſoever*, ſupplied all defects, and made *apparent* impoſſibilities, *really* practicable.

1. It is rare that the people refuse burdens or even grumble under them, when, by general conviction, they are necessary for the public good. And I dare say, that the absolute necessity of fixing and establishing our currency is become obvious to almost every individual on this Continent, and the real necessity of taxes for this purpose clearly seen by all.

2. As far as my acquaintance with people of middling rank extends, they have been generally in favor of taxing for three years past; they say this money must be paid first or last, and we can better pay it now whilst we have little use for our money, whilst it is plenty and easy to be got, than in future time, when we can perhaps not so well spare it, and when the getting it will be much more difficult.

3. The *enormity of the sum* required for this purpose consists much more in *sound* than *substance;* a quarterly tax of one bushel of wheat, or two bushels of Indian corn per head, on all persons in the Thirteen States, would be amply sufficient. The number of souls are computed at 3,000,000, in all the States, and of course this would produce 12,000,000 bushels of wheat, which at 20 dollars per bushel (the lowest present price) will be 240,000,000 millions of dollars, a sum greatly exceeding any annual exigence of these States; each State might apportion this as they pleased, so as to relieve the poor, and increase the share of the rich, but the middling farmer, who has ten in family, would have 40 bushels of wheat or its value, to pay in a year.

I admit this would be a high tax; but is there any thing impossible or ruinous in this. In the best of times, it would have been 40 dollars or 15l. and the same sum of hard money will probably now pay it, it is to be observed this is not the tax of a poor man or a new beginner, but of a middling farmer, with ten in family; such are spread over the face of this fertile country, and few of them so poor, that such a sum would distress them to any great degree.—It is to be observed further this is not a tax to *last always*, but to be paid only for *a short time,* during our

strong

strong exertions for the liberty of ourselves and our posterity;—again, this sum is not all to be paid *at once*, but at *four quarterly payments;*—again this is not a tax which demands *wheat* in kind, *hard money*, or any thing else that is *scarce* and *hard to be obtained*, but for *Continental money*, which is so *plenty* as to become the great burden of the country, and the *source* of most of our public calamities, and which any valuable commodity will procure in plenty, and with little trouble; and for which any man may sell any thing he can best spare without difficulty;—again, this is a *sure method* to overcome our capital difficulties, and fix the currency, whereas all others are *precarious and uncertain* in their effect. This is a *durable*, a *finished* remedy; all others that have been proposed are at best but *temporary*, and should they succeed, would involve us and our posterity in great difficulties, involve us in a vast debt, which would lie so heavy on the country as would greatly check our future prosperity, and discourage foreigners from coming to settle with us. For nobody likes to move into a country where taxes are very high and burdensome.

I submit it to every man, whether it will not be much easier for us by a spirited exertion, for a short time, to collect large sums of our present currency, and pay our expenses as fast as they arise, than if a foreign loan could be obtained, to pay a *vast debt* of hard money with interest to *foreigners* in future time, when every dollar we pay, must *go out of the country* never to return again. Every man ought to consider that his proportion of the public debt is as much a debt *fastened on his estate*, and becomes to all intents and purposes as much a *burden* and *charge on it*, as any of his private debts of the same amount, and must as surely one day be paid; is it not better then to pay it now than to have it lie a burden on him, to be paid in in future time, which may be called for when he may not be in condition to pay it so easy as now. Every prudent man does this with respect to his private debts, and what reason can be given why the same prudence should not extend to the debt which he owes the public? Can any reason be assigned why the States should not imitate the prudence

dence and economy of a private man, who happens to be involved for a time in great expenditures, which is, to pay up and discharge as much as possible as he goes, and leave as little as possible to be settled in future time.

To facilitate this, I humbly propose one thing more; viz. To take off every restraint and limitation from our commerce. Let *trade be as free as air*. Let every man make the most of his goods and in his own way, and then he will be satisfied. Let every man taste and enjoy the sweets of that liberty of person and property, which was highly expected under an independent government. It is a sad omen to find among the first effects of independence, greater restraints and abridgments of natural liberty, than ever we felt under the government we have lately renounced and shaken off. Let the laws point out the *duty*, and be the bulwark of *security* of every man.

Nothing gives the people such high satisfaction with any system of government they live under, as the actual enjoyment of the inestimable blessings of perfect liberty and full security under it; this will most effectually induce them cheerfully to support it. No burdens will be thought heavy, or difficulties discouraging, which the exigencies of government may require, when every man finds his own *happiness* involved in the *establishment* of the State.

If, on the freedom of trade, any articles should rise in their price, the mischief facilitates this remedy, it makes the payment of the taxes more easy and tolerable. Whereas, if the taxes were collected during the limitation of the market and stagnation of business, the payment would be extremely difficult, and the murmurs high and reasonable; it would be almost like the Egyptians demanding brick without straw. But when the circulation of money is brisk, and the price and demand for goods high, every one knows that money may be raised and taxes may be paid much more easily than in dull times of stagnated business. And this ought to be noticed on another account.

It is necessary our *first taxes* should be rendered as *easy* as possible to the people; for tho' high in nominal sum, if they find them easily paid, the terror and uneasiness which

high

high taxes generally raise, will mostly vanish, and the payment will be made without endangering the peace of the State, and these things all considered together naturally lead us to the true answer to the second great question to be solved, viz.

II. *How is the army to be supplied?* The method I propose, if it can be adopted, will undoubtedly fix the currency and create a great demand for money, and a quick circulation of it; this will of course open all the stores in the State to any purchasers that may offer, and a *little prudence* used in purchasing, may supply the army to the full, at reasonable prices. Indeed I am rather afraid of *overdoing* the thing in this way, so far as to cause an *appreciation* of the money, which I do not think ought ever to be done, for I see no reason why the States should be taxed to raise the money in my pocket to twenty times the current value of it; but this is a great argument, and may be the subject of future discussion.

I must add here, that this method will not only fix our currency and support our army, but will afford another advantage of no small moment: it will take away the *capital hope* and *assurance* of our enemies of conquering us; for they depend more on the *failure* of our funds than on their *own force*, for this purpose; they count high on the quarrels, contention, oppressions, and mischiefs that will arise from the low, sinking credit of our money; and by this are encouraged to continue the war, which they would relinquish as desperate without it.

I will just note here, that however intolerable the means I propose may appear at first sight, I cannot think them impracticable; the tax I propose is not more than two thirds of the annual taxes in Great Britain; the whole revenue raised every year there is about 12,500,000l. sterling, which is somewhat more than 55,000,000 dollars, reckoning them at 4s. 6d. a-piece; divide this by the number of souls in Great Britain, which are computed at 9,000,000, and we have the sum of somewhat more than 6 dollars per head on each of the inhabitants or living persons there; but, be this as it may, to balance the argument fairly,

fairly, I think it stands thus: on the one side *certain destruction*, and on the other a *tax* so heavy, that a middling farmer's share annually, will be 40 bushels of wheat, 40 dollars hard money, or the value of it in any thing he chooses to sell, to be paid in four quarterly payments. This, if it can be done, will undoubtedly save us, restore our finances thoroughly, fix our currency, and supply our army; without this, I do not see how these great objects can be effected. If any other method can be devised, it is more than all the united wisdom of America has yet been able to find and accomplish, nor do I conceive we have any long time to hesitate; something speedy and decisive must avert our fate.

Thus I have offered my best thoughts freely to the public, and with most upright intentions; I hope they may be received with candour. The facts and reasonings are all open to the examination of every one; if they do not convince, I hope at least they may induce some abler person to sketch out something more perfect and adequate to the great subject.

A
SECOND
ESSAY
ON
FREE TRADE and FINANCE.

First published in Philadelphia, August 1779, *and dedicated to the several Legislatures of the American Union.*

IN my last ESSAY I observed, that the value of money was nothing in itself, it was a mere relation, it was the proportion between the medium of trade and the objects of trade, which two will be for ever in balance, or equal the one to the other; therefore, if the money or medium of trade be increased, whilst the objects of trade or occasions of money continue the same, the value of the money must depreciate or lessen; and this depreciation must and will be *(cæteris paribus)* according to the increase of the quantity.

It follows hence, *that the value of the current money in any country, cannot be increased by any additions made to its quantity.* I do not pretend that these propositions are absolutely universal—I know that money may be so lessened in its quantity, as to be inadequate to the purposes of trade; in which case, an addition to its quantity would doubtless add to its value and use. It is equally true, that the quantity of money may be increased to such an immensity of excess, that the very bulk or enormous mass would render it inconvenient for a medium of trade. I do not mean, nor does my argument require, that my propositions should be applied

plied to either of these extremes; it is sufficient for my purpose, that they hold true in any country where the money or medium of trade is so duly adapted and proportioned to the objects of trade, that the one is found adequate and sufficient for the other; in which case, any departure from the said due proportion, either by increasing or decreasing the medium, must verge either towards one or the other of these extremes, and partake more or less of their disadvantages.

It follows from the above, that *our national debt of Continental money has not increased in value for three years past, notwithstanding the vast increase of the bulk or nominal sum:* and this proposition is proved from fact (which is the best possible proof of any principle advanced in theory) for it is evident that it would not require one farthing more *real value*, say country produce or hard money, to buy up every Continental dollar *now* in circulation, than would have been necessary *three years ago*, to purchase all that was then in circulation; *i. e.* the depreciation has kept full pace with its increase of quantity. Indeed, I am of opinion, it rather *exceeds* this proportion, *i. e.* that the money has depreciated faster than the increase of its quantity would require, and that it would of course require a less real value to purchase it all now, than would have bought it all three years ago. I think the enormity of the sum has carried it within the sensible influence of that *fatal extreme* which must finally destroy its whole value and use, if the quantity continues to increase.

It appears then that we do not owe a shilling more of *real value* than we owed three years ago, except the debt abroad and the loans at home which have been contracted since; so that our finances are not in so deplorable a state as they seem to be, and a remedy is much more in our power than would be imagined on the first view of the matter, and may be adopted for three years to come, if the war should continue so long, with less *burden, hardship, oppression, danger, damage,* and *loss* than we have, to our sorrow, experienced for three years past.

It

It follows then, that *all the expenditures of the war for three years paſt except the foreign debts and internal loans* (in which laſt I include the monies due for lottery prizes) *have been actually paid in depreciation of our currency*, which is perhaps the moſt inconvenient method of levying public taxes that could be invented.

As this propoſition may be new to ſome people, I only beg they would not be ſtartled too much at it, but have patience to read a few lines further, in which I ſhall conſider both parts of it.

Without going into minute calculations of the depreciation, or determining with preciſion the preſent exchange, I imagine it will not be diſputed that the depreciation for three years paſt has been at leaſt *fifty per cent.* per ann. *i. e.* that *one hundred pounds* at the end of the year, would not buy more goods than *fifty pounds* would have purchaſed at the beginning of the year. Try it for the year paſt: in Auguſt 1778, fifty pounds would have purchaſed ſixteen hundred of flour, fifty buſhels of Indian corn, five hundred of bar iron, one and an half hundred of ſugar, twelve pounds of hard money, &c. See if one hundred pounds will buy as much now.

This is arguing on fact, which is ſtubborn and yields to the prejudice of no man. It appears then that a man who has kept one hundred pounds by him for the ſpace of one year, is to all intents in the ſame condition he would have been in, if the hundred pounds had kept its value undepreciated, and he had paid one half of it in a tax, *i. e.* in both caſes he would have had fifty pounds and no more left. He has then, to all intents and purpoſes, paid a tax of fifty pounds for the year towards the depreciation, and has now fifty pounds leſs money than he would have had if no depreciation had taken place, as much in every reſpect as his caſh would have leſſened fifty pounds by paying a tax of that ſum.

I have heard that this plea was made uſe of by the Agents of the *New-England* colonies, when the matter of reimburſements to thoſe colonies, for their great expenditures in the two laſt wars, was debated and granted in the

Britiſh

British Parliament, and the argument allowed to be a good one. The question was, what sums those colonies had emitted for the service of the wars, and what was the value of the bills to be redeemed? the Agents pleaded, that the value was to be estimated at the *time of emission*, not at the *time of redemption* of those bills; for when bills of credit depreciate in any country, *the depreciation is as much a tax on the inhabitants as the depreciated sum would be, if levied in the usual way of assessment on polls and estates.* The argument is indeed a demonstrable one, and supported and justified by plain fact in every view; yet there is such a *subtle and strong delusion* in the depreciation as obscures the subject, and will almost cheat a man who views it under full conviction, and feels the effects of it; and this tends to render the *mischief more ruinous* than otherwise it would be, because people who feel it, often *mistake the cause*, and adopt from thence remedies altogether *ineffectual*, and sometimes very *hurtful*, and which often tend rather to *increase* than *cure* the evil.

Of this sort, I take to be the whole torrent of *censure and abuse* which has been thrown out and kept up against the merchants, farmers, and tradesmen, for raising the prices of their several fabrics and goods. Of this sort likewise, I consider the absurd scheme of *limitation of prices*, which never fails to limit goods out of the market, at least out of sight; prevents importations and manufactures, discourages the adventures of the most patriotic merchants, who keep their money in trade through all risks, in order to produce foreign goods, without which, neither the country could be supplied, nor the war be supported; checks the industry of the farmers and tradesmen, without which all internal supplies must fail; fills the minds of all with ill humor, and raises the country into factions and heated parties, zealous to devour one another, &c. &c.

These are only a few of the evils which arise from mistaken causes of the depreciation of our currency, and the consequent improper methods adopted for its remedy, all which prove the absurdity as well as the reality of defraying the expenditures of the war in that way, which naturally

brings

brings on the confideration of the fecond part of my propofition, viz. this method of paying the expenfes of the war is very inconvenient.

1. Becaufe this method brings the burden beyond due proportion, on the moft *virtuous and ufeful* of our people, fuch as by prudence and economy have made money and got a good command of cafh, lying in debts due on mortgages, bonds, book-debts, &c. and at the fame time operates in favor of the moft *worthlefs men* amongft us, the *diffipating, flack, lazy,* and *dilatory* fort, who commonly keep themfelves in debt, and live on the fortunes of others. Thefe contemptible, ufelefs characters are enabled hereby, after keeping a creditor years out of his juft due, to pay him off with one *fourth*, yea, one *eighth*, yea, one *fixteenth*, yea, one *twentieth* part of the value of the debt when it was contracted, by which the frugal and induftrious are compelled to pay a very heavy tax to thofe ufelefs, idle men, by which many of them have acquired great fortunes, and of courfe great weight among us, to the manifeft damage of the public; for the weight and influence of this fort of men, ought never to be increafed in any community, for wherever we fee one of them taking the lead among the people, we have reafon to believe that mifchief is a brewing, and that the public peace and fecurity is more or lefs in danger. For the truth of this, I appeal to the experience and obfervation of all wife and good men.

2. In this way the burden comes very heavy on the moft *helplefs part of our people*, who are moft entitled to the protection of the ftate, and ought not to have their burdens increafed; fuch as widows, orphans, and old men, whofe principal dependence is on legacies, money at intereft, &c.

3. It oppreffes the *falary-men* and *all public officers*, both in church and ftate, whofe fees and falaries are reduced to almoft nothing, and any applications for relief are apt to raife an unreafonable clamor againft them, as if avarice and greedinefs of money was their principal paffion. This prejudices the public fervice, in which they are employed, and difcourages men of abilities from feeking or accepting fuch public

public offices, and lessens the weight and influence of those who hold them.

4. This discourages *industry and trade;* for if the profits obtained by these waste in the desk, there is little inducement to increase the stock.

5. This defrauds the *army of their pay* and appointments, and *discourages inlistments,* and promotes desertions, &c. Many would like the army very well, if they could live by the profession; but few are so attached to it as to be willing to be ruined there.

6. It makes *supplies for the army difficult* to be obtained; because few men are fond of carrying the fruits of their year's labor to the army, to be sold for a perishing medium, which every day grows worse and worse.

7. The whole system is grounded *in injustice, is contrary to the first maxims of upright dealing, and corrupts the whole course of trade and commutative justice,* and of course will soon *destroy* all principles of *morality* and *honesty* in trade, among the people; for here it is to be considered, that money is not only the *instrument or means* by which trade is carried on, but becomes a sort of *common measure of the value of all articles of trade;* and therefore I should conceive it would be as dangerous to adopt any measures which would alter its value and render it fluctuating, as to alter the *standard weights* and *measures,* by which the quantity of goods sold in market is usually ascertained:—as for example, to shorten the standard *yard,* lessen the standard *bushel,* or diminish the standard *pound* weight, or adopt any measures that tend to this, and will probably effect it. We easily see the dangerous consequences, nor can there be any necessity to expose here the absurdities and mischiefs which must follow.

Enough has been said on this dreary subject; the mischiefs are too glaring to need further proof; a remedy is the great thing now to be sought: ought we then to attempt a remedy of the mischiefs of *depreciation,* by any endeavour to *appreciate* our currency? I think not.

1. Because the sum depreciated has been *paid by the country once already,* by the depreciation itself in their hands, and

and there is no reason why the same country should be taxed to pay it over again: *i. e.* every man who has had a hundred pounds in his pocket a month, has paid four per cent. *i. e.* four pounds of tax for it at least; but this is not the worst of it, for he has likewise paid four per cent. per month on all the monies that were due to him during the whole time (by which the public were not benefited.) But execrable as this method of supplying the public exigencies may be, it has had its *full effect*, and therefore there can be no reason that payment should be made over again.

2. *The evil arises from the fluctuation and changeable state of the currency.* It matters little to the community whether it *rises* or *falls*; the fall of it has hurt the rich, the rise of it will ruin the poor; but to continue the fluctuation by appreciating it, is to continue the whole evil in all its destructive force and ruinous effects.

3. The mischief *is done*, and ought by no means *to be repeated*, the widows and orphans are already ruined, and I think it needs no proof that almost all the money is now possessed by people who have bought it at the present value, and shall the widows and orphans, with the rest of the sufferers, be taxed to raise or appreciate the money in the coffers of the rich, up to *twenty times* the present value of it? Verily I trow not.

4. *Any* PROBABLE *attempt to raise or appreciate the value of the money, would hoard it immediately,* and

5. *Destroy our trade;* for the rise of money in the desk would be better than the profits of any trade it can be employed in.—And

6. The scarcity would soon make *the payment of taxes impracticable.*—And

7. Every *poor man would lie perfectly at the mercy of the rich*, who alone would be benefited by his distress; for if the poor should run in debt to the rich in the beginning of the year, the debt would be much increased by the appreciation at the end of the year, and so from year to year, till the sum would rise beyond the utmost abilities of the poor man to pay it, and he must of course be perfectly at the mercy of his rich creditor.—Hence

8. *Popular*

8. *Popular discontents*, and perhaps *insurrections* would probaby be the consequence, and after all

9. *This plan of appreciation would not be any remedy to the principal sufferers by the depreciation;* for not one tenth part of the appreciated currency would probably be found in the same hands that suffered by the depreciation; the increase of tax would be more to the greatest part of the people, than all the profits they would gain by the appreciation.

10. It is not supposable that *thirteen General Assemblies would concur in voting and levying* such a useless, burdensome, and pernicious tax:—nor if they would, is it likely that the people either *could* or *would* pay it.—Therefore,

11. It appears that these reasons, which prove that this *ought not* to be done, all tend to prove that it *cannot* be done, and this is a good reason why it ought not to be *attempted*. But to sum up the whole argument in one word,

12. All the mischiefs arising from a *depreciation*, would equally arise from an *appreciation;* but in an *inversed order,* and I think it will appear plain to any person of discernment, who duly and attentively considers it, that inversing the order, will infer many mischiefs *more ruinous* to the community, than those we have already felt from the depreciation: but in any view, the very idea that we are to live under the curse of a fluctuating currency eighteen years longer is intolerable.

Therefore I humbly propose, that the foolish method of *denying* the depreciation or *lowering* it below what it really is, may be wholly discontinued, and that as soon as the value of the currency is fixed, there may be a * *scale* or *table* of exchange established as near as may be to its then present true value, and that hard money be received and paid in the Continental Treasury according to it: this will effectually prevent its appreciation, and if means can be found to collect monies sufficient for future expenditures, which

---

* This idea of forming a scale of depreciation, I believe was the first ever proposed in *America*, and was much censured and even reprobated at first, but soon afterwards was adopted by Congress and all the States.

I do not think difficult, no further depreciation need be apprehended, the currency will become fixed, which is all that the safety of the state requires, and all that we can reasonably hope for, or even wish to accomplish.

I beg leave to insert here one proposition more, which I think deducible from the foregoing ones, viz. that if any country which had a medium of trade properly balanced and adapted to the purposes of trade, should by any means receive a large *addition of money* without an *increase of the objects* of money, it would be more the interest of that country to *call in*, and *destroy* that additional quantity by taxes (if it could not be drained off speedily some other way) than *to let it circulate* among them; for example, if by opening mines, by large treasure trove, by large success and captures in war, or by too many presses the money should be increased beyond the due quantity necessary for the purposes of a medium of trade: in such case, I give my opinion, that it would be more for the benefit of such country, to call in and destroy *such surplusage* of cash, by taxes equally levied on all, than to *permit it to circulate* among them.—For

1. This *increased* quantity of money, if suffered to circulate, would *depreciate* till it had duly diffused itself over the country, when it would acquire a *certain rate* of exchange, and its value would become fixed in such a manner, that *the value of the whole* would be just equal to the *value of the money which was in circulation before the increase happened*, and consequently the country would gain nothing by it, but an increased *nominal sum;* just as if the *standard yard* should be *shortened* one half, and thereby increase the number of yards of cloth in the country to double the former number, but would not add *one inch of new cloth*, or enable the owners of all the cloth to make *one garment more* than before. But

2. While this was doing, *vast mischief* would arise from the depreciation; the *legacies* of the widow and orphans, the *salaries* and *fees* of public officers of church and state, the *pay of the army*, the value of all *debts due*, the *standard* of all contracts for money, &c. would be *lessened* to the most manifest injury of the creditors. Examples of
which

which dreadful effects we see daily before our eyes—this must surely force the most striking conviction.

3. I conceive these mischiefs would prove a much *heavier burden* on the country, and would have *much worse effects*, than could arise from *a tax to amount of the increased quantity* of money levied on the inhabitants.—For

4. The inhabitants could *not be impoverished by such a tax*, as there would be as much value of money, and as much goods and other estate in the country after the tax was levied as before, and all the loss to the country would be the time and charges spent in collecting it; for all the goods sold for the payment of this tax, would still remain in the country, and continue as valuable as they were before they were sold.

5. The *contentions, resentments, and ill-humor*, which a depreciation naturally generates, would by this method *be prevented*, which alone, in my opinion would, if not prevented, impoverish the country *more than the whole tax*, even if the money was all borrowed from abroad to pay it. Only observe two neighbours inflamed with rage and resentment against each other, and see what time, money, and labor they will spend, and how much they will engage their several friends in their quarrel, and how all kind offices of friendship and mutual assistance are totally lost between them during their anger. By this we may form some guess at the degree of impoverishment which a country must suffer by general discontents, and numberless instances of personal injuries and consequent resentments.

Hence it follows clearly, in my opinion, that it would be more for the interest of the Thirteen United States to *call in and sink* their Continental bills as fast as they issue, than to receive *a sum of gold* every year equal to the money issued, from some foreign power, as a perfect gift never to be repaid, *i. e.* we had better pay every year, by taxes, the whole expenditures of the year, than to receive the amount of those expenditures in cash from *Spain* as a free gift. Tho' I introduce this proposition as a corollary, yet as it is of some consequence, we will, if you please, view it awhile, and consider the operation and effects of its two

parts,

parts, and we fhall be better able to judge which of the two would contribute moft to the real welfare and happinefs of the country.

1. The tax would *fix the currency,* and thereby give eftablifhment to every branch and department of *bufinefs, trade, war, civil police, and religion,* which has any connexion with money; but the gift would make fuch an increafe of the circulating cafh as would depreciate it (for hard money can and will depreciate as well as paper bills, if increafed too much) and thereby every department of *bufinefs, trade, war, civil police, and religion* which has any connexion with money, muft languifh and be enervated.

2. The tax will *promote the induftry, prudence, and economy* of the people, but the *gift* would naturally introduce and encourage *idlenefs* and *diffipation*. Few men will rife early and eat the bread of carefulnefs, when money flows in upon them without their own anxious care. A man, preffed with a demand for money for a tax or any other debt, does not yield to his own appetite, or the requeft of his wife or child for a luxury, fo eafily as the fame man would do, with plenty of money, and no preffing demand: for the truth of this I appeal to the feelings of every man.

No virtue is fo fixed in the human mind as to continue long undiminifhed without its ufual motives and inducements, and it requires no great experience in the world to fhow us the danger of leffening any of thefe; the very beginning of remiffnefs of virtuous habits ought to be as alarming as the fwallowing of a flow poifon; and this, as applied to my fubject, is demonftrated by a very common obfervation, that fortunes fuddenly acquired without the *induftry* of the poffeffor, rarely ever increafe his happinefs and welfare, help his virtuous habits, or continue long with him; they moft commonly ruin him. Money in a ftate is like falt in cookery; fome of it is very neceffary, but too much of it fpoils every difh, and renders the whole dinner unfavory to the tafte, and hurtful to the health.

3. The tax will operate in *a way of juftice* to all, and therefore will give *general peace and fatisfaction to all good men,*

men, to all genuine Whigs and well-difpofed people, and will filence the clamors and difappoint the hopes of the Tories, which are grounded principally on the uneafinefs and jealoufies, injuries and refentments which wrong fteps will raife among the people. The operation of the tax would be juft this; it would compel the man who ftays at home and renders no actual fervice, and furnifhes no fupplies to the war, to pay as much as thofe do, who render the actual fervice and furnifh the fupplies: thofe who render perfonal fervice and furnifh fupplies, contribute thofe great aids in folid fubftance within the year; and therefore thofe who ftay at home ought to pay their quotas of folid fubftance alfo within the year. There can be no reafon given why thofe that go into the war fhould render their fervice within the year, and thofe who ftay at home fhould pay nothing, or be trufted to fome future day.

This method is grounded on fuch manifeft juftice, that no Tory, however litigious, can with any good face object to it; and therefore, however chagrined at heart he may be, he muft keep his mouth fhut, or look out for fome other fubject of complaint to make a noife about; but the natural operation of the gift would be very contrary to this; there would be fo many fchemes and pretences fet on foot to draw for the money before it could leave *Spain*; fo many hungry favorites crowding round every office of diftribution in every department, and in fhort, fuch a fcramble for the biggeft fhare of it; and fo much chagrin, difappointment, and mortification occafioned; and fo many jealoufies, quarrels, and refentments excited by it, as would, in my opinion, injure and impoverifh the States much more than the tax would do. But all this I fubmit to thofe who have been beft acquainted with public boards and offices.

4. The moft of the above arguments have been *confirmed by facts* in many notorious inftances, which are the beft proofs in matters of this fort which can be advanced: the fpoils and luxuries of *Capua* ruined *Hannibal*'s army; the fack of *Carthage* and plunder of the rich, eaftern, conquered provinces corrupted the morals of the *Romans*, deftroyed

stroyed their economy, brought in luxurious excesses, bred the most mortal quarrels, overturned the commonwealth, introduced tyranny, and ended in the most tragical destruction of the *Roman* Empire; the *Portuguese* (who were once most untainted in morals and most intrepid in war) it is said, were ruined by the mines of the *Brasils*, and are now an enervated people, without manufactures and internal supplies, a nation of Lords, poor in the midst of money, and proud in the midst of want, and are scarce a shadow of their ancestors.

And to come nearer home, the successes and spoils of the last war ruined the *English nation*; they are no longer that wise, that faithful, that benevolent, humane nation which we were ever taught to esteem them, but rude, faithless, cruel, savage, avaricious, sordid, &c. with scarce a single virtue left in their character; the principal remains of our ancestors is their prowess in war; but even this is perverted: this, which was heroism in them, is inhumanity in the present generation; the sword, which was the terror of their *enemies*, is by the present race sheathed in the bowels of their *brethren*.

It follows hence, I conceive, very clearly, that the riches of a nation do not consist in the abundance of money, but in number of people, in supplies and resources, in the necessaries and conveniencies of life, in good laws, good public officers, in virtuous citizens, in strength and concord, in wisdom, in justice, in wise counsels, and manly force.

From all these considerations, it appears plain to me, that sudden acquisitions of money are dangerous to any country, and have in many instances proved very ruinous and fatal to states and kingdoms as well as individuals; from hence I think we may fairly and strongly conclude, that it is not the wisdom of *America* to attempt by any means of gift or loan, an acquisition of money from any foreign powers, but by strong exertions of our own to furnish our own supplies. We have money enough for our own purposes, and as good as any in the world, if we can be wise and firm enough, by proper measures to fix its value, and preserve it from future fluctuation.

But

But if these arguments should not be convincing, I will venture to add one more, which with me has great weight.

5. By a tax we shall furnish *our own supplies* in a *sure* way, not liable to *disappointment* by any caprices of *others*, nor subjecting us to any sort of *dependence on foreigners*; we shall work out our own salvation without dependence on any power but Divine Providence, which we may ever acknowledge without danger of insult; but if we receive aids from foreign states by loan or gift, the obligation conferred on us will be ever great in their opinion, and should we ever have occasion in future time to adopt any measures not perfectly consistent with their views and demands, we must be insulted with large exhibitions of the present favors, and as large and plentiful accusations of ingratitude, and it may be long before we hear the last of it.

As it is more reputable for a man to acquire a fortune by his own industry, than by heirship, favor of friends, or sudden accidents, so I think our own deliverance and establishment, wrought out by our own strong exertions and virtuous efforts, will be more honorable and safe for us, than to receive these great blessings from the gift of a neighbour, were he willing to bestow them. The *English* never will have done holding up to the view of the *Dutch* the supplies and aids they received from the *English* in Queen *Elizabeth*'s time, and the *Portuguese* are obliged to hear a great deal of the same sort of language, on the score of assistances received by them from the *English* in the late wars.

Indeed I know not how we can call ourselves independent, if we are to lie under such sort of debts to our neighbours, especially if to the obligations of gratitude, we are to be loaded with the additional one of large sums of hard money, with a corroding, annual interest to devour the proceeds of our labors and trade for ages to come.

I would sooner consent to bear any present burden, not absolutely intolerable, than find myself and posterity loaded with such a heavy, galling debt, to last, as other national debts most commonly do, *for ever*, and the States so

oppressed

oppreffed and drained by it, as to have fcarce fpirits or ftrength left to refent any infults or injuries that may be offered in future time; or repel any invafions that may be attempted.

Indeed the alliance we have formed with *France*, is grounded on fuch generous principles of *juftice, mutual intereft*, and *independence*, as plainly demonftrate that it is not the wifh of *France* that our minds ever fhould be difturbed by any of thefe painful feelings; and I think it would be very mean in us to abufe their generofity, and we might *be afhamed to worry them* for fupplies, which we could *better furnifh* ourfelves than receive from them, efpecially to folicit *France* for money to pay the *intereft of loans* from our own people, certainly has a bad look. If a fon fhould demand fecurity of a ftranger for monies lent to his father, people would certainly fay fomething.———

We hope to form an alliance with *Spain* on principles of equal juftice and mutual benefit, but we fhall foon leffen our character in their eyes, if we improve our firft acquaintance in begging aids, which, with proper application and induftry, we could well do without. But whenever real neceffity does prefs us beyond our own powers of relief, we may then, without humiliation, apply for help to our friends; and I do not doubt but they would give with pleafure to our real neceffity, what they would either deny or grudgingly fpare to our lazinefs or needlefs folicitations.

I prefume it is needlefs to add any more arguments to prove the neceffity or expediency of taxing equal to our expenditures, but the great groan ftill is, that *this is impracticable*, it cannot be done. To all I have faid before, I beg leave here to add fome further arguments to prove the *practicability* of this method; three years ago, it was faid, *there is no danger yet*, it will be time enough to tax fome time hence; it is now faid, *it is too late*, we are involved fo much that a tax adequate to our prefent occafions for money is impoffible; had we begun fooner, it might have been done, but now it is too late. I take it that all this talk arifes from an improper view of the fubject.

F   1. We

1. We are under as good *advantages* to relieve ourselves by taxes *now* as we were *three years ago*, to all intents and purposes, and in some respects better; we are involved in no more debt, except the foreign and home loans, than we were then; the circulating cash is no more in value now than it was then, the increase of nominal sum makes no difference; and therefore, if it was necessary to call it all in (which, I conceive, is by no means the case) it might be done at the same expense now as then, *i. e.* it would not require *any more hard money* or *country produce* to purchase it all in *now*, than it would have required *three years ago ;* and we have sundry advantages in favor of taxing now, which we had not then, viz. 1st. A general conviction of the *absolute necessity* of taxing. 2d. *Established legislatures* to levy the tax; both which were wanting three years ago. 3d. The money to be collected by the tax is more *equably diffused* or spread thro' the Thirteen States than it was three years ago, and therefore the people in the remotest parts, as well as those who live near the seat of war, are enabled to pay their tax. 4th. People are *more settled in business* than they were three years ago; the violent shock of the war threw very many people *out of their common course of business*, or at least much incommoded them; but they are now *more settled*, either in new branches of business, in public employments, or find the profits of their former business in some measure restored. 5th. The farmer and most tradesmen can pay their taxes much easier than they could three years ago, because there is much *greater demand and price* for the *fabrics* of the one and the *produce* of the other, than there was three years ago. To these many other reasons might be added, all grounded on facts of public notoriety, and therefore are freely submitted to every person who has resided three years among us.

2. All the services and supplies for which the tax is wanted, *are actually furnished every year* by the Thirteen States, and have been for four years past; now is it more possible, more reasonable, or more easy *to compel a few* individuals to furnish these services and supplies *without payment*, than *to lay the burden* in proper proportion on all,

all, and *to compel every individual* to furnish his part? *i. e.* I do contend it is more easy, more reasonable, and therefore more practicable, and of course very possible to compel *those that stay at home* and render neither personal services nor supplies to the war, to pay *as much real value or substance* in money as those do who *render the services* or furnish the supplies; and if any of these stayers at home think this comes too hard on them, let them change places awhile with those that do render the services or furnish the supplies, *i. e.* let them go into the army in person, or send their corn, their beef, or other supplies, and when they have tried both, they will know which is easiest, and will always have their option to take the one or the other, and will be convinced that both are possible and practicable.

Can any man make any reasonable and weighty objection to this? Yet this is all that is required; for when the services are rendered, and the supplies are furnished, and both are paid for, the whole business is done, and the tax has had its full effect.

I will venture to add my opinion, that this reasoning will be verified in fact to very good purpose, viz. that when it is observed that the man who *renders the actual service* is paid fully for it, and the man who *stays at home* must pay his full quota towards it, many who now stay at home, will be induced to go and render the actual service, and thereby avoid making the payment at home, and become entitled to receive it in the army, which will greatly facilitate the recruiting service. An object of no small magnitude.

3. The tax which I propose, collected in quarterly or monthly payments, will occasion such *a quick circulation of money*, that every bill will probably pay its value *many times over* in a year, as it must do every time it passes from hand to hand; it will fly from the Commissary to the farmer, from him to the Collector; from him to the Treasurer, from him to the Commissary, from him to the farmer again, &c. in a circle often repeated in a year; consequently it would be possible to levy a Sum in a year by

taxes,

taxes, much exceeding the whole sum of current cash; it would render the whole Thirteen States like a full market, where all persons are eager to sell all they have for sale, and as eager to buy all which they have need of, and if this circle of business was permitted to run without any restraints, it would render the procurement and payment of money as easy as the nature of the thing admits, would vastly lighten the burden of taxes, and would give such great advantages, both to the farmer, mechanic, and trader, as would in good measure reimburse the tax itself.

4. Some peculiar circumstances of this country much contribute to make the payment of taxes practicable and easy. Those places which have *suffered* most by the war, lie *nearest* to the seat of it, and of course have the *greatest plenty* of money, and have the benefit of the *quickest demand* and *highest price* for every thing they have for sale, whilst it happily falls out, that those towns and counties that lie most remote from the seat of the war, and have the greatest scarcity of money, yet have been *least impoverished* by the war, and are almost every one of them fine, grazing, fruitful countries, which produce great quantities of beef, mutton, and pork, which may be easily conveyed to the army on foot, and thereby facilitate the payment of taxes and supply of the army at the same time.

Another favorable circumstance is this, the enemy cannot supply themselves, especially with those articles we most want, otherwise than by importing them; and as their vessels cannot always go under convoy, they often become a prey to our ships of war and privateers, by which we gain a supply of foreign necessaries, without contracting a foreign debt; those concerned are enriched, the objects of trade are increased, and the payment of taxes and supply of the army greatly facilitated.

The benefits of this we have often experienced, and perhaps might increase them, if our cruising business was *more properly conducted*, and *more liberally encouraged*. Upon the whole matter, I beg leave to close this Essay with a short view of the present state of our finances, then

to

to offer my propositions of trade and finance, and lastly, point out the effects and operations which I conceive these will have on our trade, currency, and army.

I. Our present debt is *what we owe abroad, all our domestic loans,* and all the *paper currency* now in circulation, with enough more (if more is necessary) to balance our public accounts.

II. The currency I rate at its present value; and admitting the nominal sum to be about 160,000,000 of dollars, the real value may be 8 or 9,000,000 of dollars, and which I conceive is not a larger sum than is at all times necessary for a medium of trade in the Thirteen States.

III. The great interest of these States, I take to be, *fixing* the value of the currency, and preventing the *further fluctuation* of it, either by *depreciation* or *appreciation;* for I conceive these to be equally destructive, or if there is any difference, the latter is the worst of the two.———
For this purpose,

IV. I think the *further increase* of the currency should *be prevented,* and the *presses stopped* as soon as may be, and this I think may take place on *January* next, nor do I see how it can be done sooner. What the further fluctuation of the currency will be in the mean time, is uncertain; but the two most powerful means I know of, to prevent the future depreciation, are, the *heavy tax* to be collected in this time, and *taking off all restraints from trade;* if this last is not done, the scarcity of goods will be so great, and the objects of trade so few, that no wisdom can prevent, or force suppress, the exorbitant rise of goods before that time, especially of salt, rum, coffee, tea, and other articles of great consumption, that have been *limited much below* the cost and charges of importation.

V. I propose that a *course of taxes* be instituted, to be paid monthly or quarterly, *equal to the public expenditures.*

VI. When the presses are stopped, and an effectual method of supplying the Treasury by taxes is well secured, the *Continental money* will in a short time make *for itself an exchange,* or gain a fixed value; it is impossible now to say
what

what that value will be, but however it fixes, it will be right, and then I propose,

VII. To fix the exchange according to that value, by directing that *hard money* shall be paid and received in the Treasury *at that exchange*, which will effectually prevent its appreciation; and if an adequate tax is well paid, the depreciation also will be effectually stopped: *e. g.* if the exchange should be fixed at 20 for 1, and any person is disposed to pay his tax in hard money, let 1 dollar be received in full for 20 paper ones, and let all payments be made from the Treasury by the same exchange.

But you will say, what is to *become of the public faith?* and I say, what *is become of it already?* I *leave* it where I *found* it, I do not make it any *worse*, but endeavour to preserve it from *further decays*. If *nineteen parts* out of twenty are dead already, I am for preserving the *twentieth part* which remains alive; perhaps by good management and proper nursing, it may grow into full magnitude; but to effect this, it appears to me very necessary to purge it of all those deadly mixtures and bad adherents which have already brought it within an ace of total destruction.

However this may be, I think it appears very plain, from what has been before advanced in this Essay, that continuing the dreadful mischiefs and injuries of a fluctuating currency for *eighteen years* * to come, will no how atone for the wrongs, or compensate the damages, incurred by that destructive delusion in four years past, and I cannot conceive on what principles any man could wish to purchase such a deadly evil for many years to come, at the expense of heavy, galling taxes, almost as useless, difficult, and desperate, as the rolling of *Sisyphus*'s stone.

VIII. And for the same reason, *all debts* due from or to the Treasury, ought to be paid *at the exchange* which existed at the *time they were contracted;* and therefore, I think it necessary to form a *table* or *rate* of exchange, to be continued from the first depreciation of Continental bills

up

---

* Congress, about this time, published a sort of funding system, in which they proposed *(and plighted the public faith with solemnity enough too, for)* the payment of the public debt in *eighteen years*.

up to the aforesaid period, when they shall become of fixed value; and that all *Loan-Office certificates* be paid according to the *exchange which exifted* at the time in which the certificates were dated, and that all other debts be paid at *the exchange* which exifted when *they were contracted*, and all *intereft* due ought to be paid at the *fame exchange* as the *debt* out of which it grows.

This appears to me fo manifeftly juft and reafonable, that I cannot think any objection can be made to it, and therefore to offer any arguments in fupport of it, would feem to call into doubt the juftice of my country; I have only to obferve, that great judgment and accuracy will be required in forming thofe rates of exchange, as any error in thefe would introduce an error into the adjuftment of all contracts for money, which yet remain unfettled.

9. The currency fixed as above, will be *juft fufficient* for a medium of trade and *no more*, and if we can by firm and proper, fteady conduct, keep it fixed, it will anfwer all the ends of a medium of trade, without any inconveniency, for no one can fuppofe it is of any confequence, whether we eftimate a dollar at three pence, or fix pence, or nine pence, or ninety pence, if it continues the fame at all times, with no more variation than is ever incident to the nature of money.—Therefore

10. There will be no immediate occafion for *further taxes* for finking any part of the bills, which are or fhall be in circulation on the 1ft of *January* next, for no reafon can be affigned why the country fhould be taxed to leffen the quantity of money in circulation, when there is no more in being than is neceffary for a medium of trade.

11. The method I propofe will, by its natural operation, keep the *army full of men* and *well fupplied*, and we may be in good condition to carry on the war any length of time that may be neceffary, till it can be clofed by a fafe and honorable peace.

12. And this method will alfo, by its natural operation, *fix our finances* on the beft and fureft footing that can be wifhed, our currency will be *as good as any on earth*, and all the refources of a moft plentiful country will be properly

ly and effectually opened for the use of the public, at whatever time and to whatever amount the public exigence and necessity may require.

13. When the war shall cease, it will leave us in a manner *free of debt and little impoverished;* we may easily, when the war is over, pay our foreign and domestic loans, and whenever we find it necessary, sink the whole current bills, all which may be done in a short time, and without any burdens so heavy as to endanger the peace or prosperity of the States. Every other scheme which I have heard proposed, leaves us subject to two dreadful calamities: 1st. The *danger of sinking under the weight of the war.* 2d. If we get through that, yet we shall be left *under such a load of debt,* which must be sunk by such long and galling taxes, as will almost make our *lives a burden* and our *liberty a dear purchase,* yea, the weight of the debt will *abridge* our liberty itself, for I know not how any persons or states can be called entirely free, who are deeply involved in debt beyond their present powers of payment.

14. This method will be a good criterion by which we may *distinguish the Whigs from the Tories,* this scheme touches the present cash, it compels the present and actual contributions of every one to the great cause of *American* liberty, this will rouse the feelings of every Tory, partly because his present cash is called for, and partly because it establishes the system of liberty which he wishes to see destroyed. And as we have reason to suppose that much *English* gold is spread among us, for the purpose of bribing our most popular and able men, it will be of great consequence to discover who they are that may be thus engaged to destroy us, and as they probably will assume the character of zealous Whigs, they cannot be better distinguished than by the temper in which they receive such propositions, as promise an effectual remedy of the mischiefs and dangers which most threaten our destruction, and at the same time blast the surest hopes and confidence of our enemies.

Thus I have a second time given my thoughts, with the greatest freedom, on the great subject of free trade and finance, a subject perhaps as difficult and intricate as any whatever.

whatever. A good *financier* is as rare as a *phœnix*, there is but here and there one appears in an age, yet in our present circumstances, a good financier is as necessary as a general, for the one cannot be supported without the other. I do not pretend to be equal to this great subject, I know I am not, but in these times of distress, every one ought to contribute what he can, and my fortunes are so impaired by the depredations of the enemy, and my health and constitution so broken by their insult and cruelty, that I have little left but sentiments and kind wishes to bestow, and as the widow's mite was of great account in heaven, I hope my mite may be candidly received, as it is most uprightly intended.

I know the *limitation* of trade, the doctrine of *loans*, and *appreciation* of our currency are ideas much favored by very many zealous people; my Essays are directly opposed to them all, and I have only to say in excuse, that I should not venture to face the censure of such characters, if I were not really convinced of the high impropriety of all the three mentioned doctrines, and the absolute necessity of adopting sentiments and measures the most *opposed* to them.

It is with great pain I differ in sentiments from many gentlemen of shining abilities, great experience, and most undoubted integrity; and was the importance of the subject at the present crisis less, I should not obtrude my thoughts on the public, nor have I the vanity to imagine that the feeble Essays of an obscure individual can correct the errors of a Continent; I only hope my publications may be so far regarded, as to bring on a most serious inquiry and thorough discussion of the weighty subject, by men of genius and abilities, equal to the mighty task, that so the real source of our calamities and their proper remedies may be discovered, and the wisest measures may be adopted and pursued with diligence, spirit, and decision.

For however weak or ridiculous my Essays may be deemed, the subject of them will be acknowledged of sufficient weight to engage the attention of the most able and respectable characters among us.———*Si nôsti rectius istis, candidus imperti, si non, his utere mecum.*

A THIRD ESSAY

ON

FREE TRADE and FINANCE.

[*Published in Philadelphia, January 8th, 1780.*]

CREDIT, either public or private, may always be kept good, where there is a sufficient estate to support it. Therefore, if private persons, a company of merchants, or a State, suffer their credit to decay, when they have a sufficient stock to support it, their management must be *bad*, but their affairs can never be *desperate* so long as their stock or estate continues sufficient to discharge all demands on them; their *bad management* only need be corrected, and *a good one* adopted, and their affairs may be retrieved, and their credit restored. Therefore, the Thirteen United States are not bankrupt, nor are their affairs desperate, tho' their credit runs very low, and their finances are in the worst condition. We have men enough for every purpose—We have provisions and stores enough. Our houses, lands, and stock on the lands, are little diminished, and in many places increased, since the war began; yet our credit runs so low, that it is with great difficulty sufficient supplies can be obtained.

The error lies in our *finances*, or *management of the public stock*, and must be mended, or we are ruined. In the
midst

midſt of full plenty we already ſuffer the want of all things.

The firſt thing neceſſary to correcting an error, is to *diſcover* it, the next is to *confeſs* it, and the laſt to *avoid* it. Perhaps neither of theſe three things are eaſy in the preſent caſe. An error in finances, like a leak in a ſhip, may be obvious in the *fact*, alarming in its *effects*, but difficult *to find*. The fact in view affords perhaps the ſtrongeſt proof of this. Our finances have, for five years paſt, been under the management of fifty men, of the beſt abilities and moſt ſpotleſs integrity, that could be elected out of the Thirteen States; yet they are in a ruined condition. We have ſuffered *more* from this than from *every other* cauſe of calamity : it has killed *more* men, pervaded and corrupted the choiceſt intereſts of our country *more*, and done *more* injuſtice, than even the arms and artifices of our enemies; ſtill the fatal error continues unmended, and perhaps unexplored.

Our admiration and cenſure will be greatly diminiſhed here, when we conſider that the doctrine of finance, or the *nature*, *effects*, and *operation* of money may be placed among the moſt *abſtruſe and intricate ſubjects,* which we ever have occaſion to examine. Not one in ten thouſand is capable of underſtanding it, and perhaps not one man in the world was ever complete maſter of it.

As a full proof of this, I adduce the many fruitleſs attempts to ſtop the depreciation of our currency, which have been adopted both in and out of Congreſs; all of which have failed of the expected ſucceſs, and many of them have greatly *increaſed* the miſchief they were intended to *remedy*. The *various ſchemes* and plans for the ſame purpoſe, which have been formed and propoſed by many men of moſt acknowledged abilities, warmly *adopted* by ſome, and as warmly *oppoſed* by others, are a further proof of the great difficulty and abſtruſe nature of the ſubject.

The univerſal *diſtreſs* of the country, ariſing from this *error* in our finances, makes it a ſubject of the moſt intereſting importance, and the moſt univerſal inquiry, yet the intellectual powers of the Continent, tho' wound up to

the

the highest pitch of attention, have not yet been able to find a remedy. The evil still continues as unchecked as ever. It seems impossible to control or compute its force; it baffles all calculation. Yet so are we situated, and so critical is the present moment, that a remedy must be found, or we perish.

The *morality* and *industry* of our people are declining fast. Our *laws* become iniquitous, and the worst of all sin is that iniquity which *is framed by a law*, for it fixes the *mischief* in the very place where a *remedy* ought always to be sought and found. The confidence of our people in the *government* is lessened, our *army suffers*, and our *credit* and *character abroad* is in danger of contempt. All these, and no man can tell how many more, evils, hang like a thick cloud over us, the bursting of which will overwhelm us. But this is no time or place for declamation; a *remedy* is the thing to be sought; a *remedy* or *ruin* are the only two alternatives before us.

I have twice essayed to throw some light on this dark subject, with very little effect; my system, however some of its parts were approved, has not been adopted. My arguments, perhaps, were not thought conclusive, or were not sufficiently clear, and therefore were little attended to; I will, nevertheless, once more attempt to lay before the public, some principles and propositions which appear to me to have great weight, and which I shall ground on fact as much as I can; for in this, as in natural philosophy, *one experiment* I conceive to be better, and stronger proof than an *hundred theorems*.

I. In every State where the occasions of money continue unvaried, the *incomes* and *expenditures* ought to be kept equal, otherwise the *value* of money will *fluctuate*, i. e. increase or decrease; by which every money-contract, as well as all legacies, salaries, fees of public offices, rents, &c. will be altered, and the money, when paid, will be either more or less than was intended in the contract, in the law, &c. In this case, it matters little whether the increase of money proceeds from foreign loans or gifts, from opening mines, or presses; an increase of money in any of these or any other way, will, with great injustice, alter the value of the payment, to the manifest wrong and injury of the receiver; by which the law itself, as well as the contract or donation, becomes perverted and corrupted, and is made to enure contrary to the original intention of all the parties concerned; this is proved by very sad experiment among ourselves.

Hence it appears from plain experiment, that any method that tends to increase or decrease the quantity of circulating cash, will not prove a remedy, but will increase the evil, or run us into the contrary extreme, equally unjust and mischievous, or perhaps more fatal. Hence it follows, that our true remedy, must, in the nature of the thing, lie, not *in appreciating*, more than *in depreciating*, the currency, but *in fixing* the value of it where it is, and keeping it so fixed, that any man who makes a money-contract, may find, when the day of payment comes, that the money paid is just the same as it was at the time of contract, that so the money paid may exactly correspond with the intention of the contract, and be of course a just fulfilment of it without increase or decrease; which cannot possibly happen where there is any fluctuation of its value between the times of contract and payment.

Hence, when the value of money is fixed and can be kept so, it is in the *most perfect state* its nature is capable of, and does, in the *most perfect manner*, answer all the purposes and uses which are desired or expected from it; for it is impossible that money should exist in higher perfection, than when it is of such fixed and certain value that all other articles may be compared with it, and their value safely estimated from that comparison.

Hence it follows clearly, that as far as money deviates from a fixed value, and becomes fluctuating, it loses its use, and becomes dangerous to the possessor, and this will of course, without any regard to its quantity, lessen its value, or increase its depreciation; and this may be assigned as one great cause of the present depreciation of our currency beyond what its quantity would require.

Hence

Hence it follows, that if money can obtain a fixed value, it is of no manner of consequence what the quantity is, for its value will ever fix at that rate or proportion to the occasions for money, which will make the one equal to the other, and of course our Continental money will have just the same use, if the value of it fixes at two pence the dollar, as at any other sum that can be named; but if that value of two pence is variable and like to be reduced to a penny, every man would prefer two pence of fixed money to it; but if that value of two pence is fixed, it will be considered by every man just as good, and no better than two pence of any other sort of fixed money.

II. As the use and design of money is to be a medium of all trade, it is necessary that the *demand for money* should be at least equal to the *demand for every thing else* which is to be bought or sold, for if there is one thing to be sold, which money will not purchase, the use of money is not so great as it would be if it would buy every thing, and therefore its value is so far depreciated. Trade is carried on by the medium of money easier than in any other way, and for that reason it was introduced. An over plenty or scarcity of money introduces barter, which takes away the use of money so far as it extends, and consequently depreciates it, and perhaps the great practice of *bartering one scarce article for another*, which has been introduced by the great plenty of money among us, may be assigned as one great cause of the depreciation of our currency beyond what the quantity would require.

Hence it follows that the only possible way to restore our money to its true value and use, is to *increase the demand* for it; but this cannot be done by opening *mines* or *presses*, by *foreign loans* or *importations of money*, but may be done by *taxes*, which make a demand for money all over the Thirteen States, and from every taxable in it. In this every one is agreed. The only question is, How far this demand is to be increased? The answer is easy, viz. Till all supplies which we need can be purchased for money, which will certainly be the case, when the demand for money is sufficiently great.

This

This demand may be raised at any time, and to any pitch we please, by taxes; so that the true and only possible remedy of the great mischief lies constantly *in our power,* and may be put in practice whenever *we please.* But it must be put into *actual practice; talking* about it, *voting* about it, making *assessments* and *tax bills,* will not do without an *actual* and *seasonable collection and payment* into the treasury.

That this may be done, so as to give a fixed and established permanancy to our currency; and thereby save the States, and at the same time relieve every individual from the danger, damage, and anxiety he now suffers from the deficiency of our currency; and avoid oppression of individuals, and thereby put an end to all uneasinesses in the government: that this may be done, I say, the several things following must be strictly attended to.

1. That the taxation be *fair and equitable,* so as to bring the burden equally or in due proportion on each State, and on the *individuals* of each State. The first is the business of Congress, the second of every particular State. As to the first, it is absolutely necessary that there be an estimate made of the abilities of each State, on which the quotas are to be grounded; and this I think cannot be done better than by making the *number of souls* in each State the rule of it. * This can easily be obtained with exactness and certainty, and will be as just and true a measure of the abilities of each State as can be obtained. If more need to be said on this, it may be deferred to another time.

2. It

---

* It is to be observed here that it was not the practice of Congress under the old confederation, to institute taxes by any direct acts of their own, but they calculated the sums wanted, and made requisitions of them from the several States, in such proportions or quotas as were made *pro re nata,* as no established quotas, or rules of forming them, were settled. There was much conversation about this time and many debates in Congress, concerning the rule or principle on which the estimates of the quotas of each State should be fixed; and sundry modes of this estimation were adopted by Congress, with various alterations and amendments, till at last the long debated matter was settled by the new Constitution (article I.) on the principle here proposed, with a small variation respecting Negroes and Indians.

N. B. This matter was taken up again, and the principle or rule of estimation here proposed, discussed and proved more fully in a future Dissertation.

2. It is further absolutely neceffary, that the *quotas* of each State be eftimated *in hard money*, payable in Continental money *at the exchange* which exifts in each particular State at the time they pay their tax into the Continental Treafury: hard money is a fixed ftandard of value, and can never vary much here from its value in *Europe*, and therefore fixing the quotas by this ftandard, will prevent any irregularities which will arife from depreciation of our currency between the time of the *demand* of the quotas, and the time of *payment* by each State; without this the depreciation might afford an inducement, tho' a *very wicked one*, to fome States, to make their *collections and payments dilatory*, for there would be an advantage in delaying payment of taxes, as well as of every other debt, if the fum fhould *leffen* every day, and it has been found in fact, tho' little to the honor of the tardy States, that *fome States* have paid their quotas, when the exchange was *four to one*, whilft *others* have paid their quotas of the fame tax at the exchange of *twenty for one*, i. e. juft one fifth part of the juft debt.

I faid that the payments ought to be made at the exchange that fubfifts in the State that pays the money, at the time of payment, for all fupplies which are purchafed for the ufe of the public in that State, are purchafed at that exchange, and therefore it is reafonable that their quotas of taxes fhould be paid at the fame exchange, whether it be higher or lower than that which exifts in the other States at the fame time.

Befides, if the quotas demanded of each State be not made in fixed money, it is not at all certain they will be fufficient when paid; for if the eftimates of expenditures were made in money at twenty for one, and the tax demanded be made out accordingly, it is very certain if it fhould be paid at forty for one, it would not fatisfy more than half the eftimate, and therefore muft be deficient by one half, and the work is all to do over again to get the other half collected and paid, befides all the dangers and damages which may arife from the delay.

Nor

Nor do I fee that any reasonable objection could be made to the justice of *crediting* the States for their past payments *by the same rule;* for it is surely wrong that a dilatory State that has really paid but one fifth part of the value of her quota, should have credit for the whole: but whatever may be thought proper with respect to the time *past*, I think there can be no doubt that such scandalous and dangerous mischiefs should be well guarded against in *time to come*. To all this it ought to be further added, that when any State delays to collect their taxes, the money will accumulate, and consequently depreciate faster in it than in other States where the tax is quickly collected; and no reason can be given, why any State should take advantage of that depreciation which their own iniquitous delay has occasioned.

It is further necessary that each delinquent State should be charged with *the interest* of all such parts of their several quotas which shall be unpaid at the time prescribed by Congress, till payment be made; and for the same reason they should be allowed interest on all such sums as may be paid before the said time of payment, till such time of payment comes; and if all this, together with the honor and zeal of the several States, should be insufficient to prevent *deficiencies*, further methods should be adopted and effectually executed, till such deficiencies shall be prevented; for the very idea of supporting the union, dignity, public faith, and even safety of the Thirteen States, without *good punctuality* in each State, is most manifestly chimerical, vain, and ridiculous; for there can never be any *confidence* placed in our administration, if their *counsels, covenants, and measures*, must be ever liable to be rendered fruitless or impracticable by the deficiencies of one or two of those States.

3. On the part of the particular States, it is necessary that each of them at the beginning of each year should have a list or assessment of all taxables completed, and all appeals adjusted, and good collectors appointed, that as soon as any tax is granted by their Legislature, it may be put immediately into the collectors' hands, and the collection be finished and the money paid into the Continental Treasury,

H without

without lofs of time. If matters were once put into this train, any neceffary fum demanded by Congrefs might be collected, and ready for ufe in a very fhort time; and this will fully obviate the great objection, that taxes, tho' acknowledged to be the only fure and final remedy, are yet too flow in their operation to be depended on.

It appears from this view, that taxes are a much more *certain and fpeedy* fupply, and may be depended on with much greater fafety than any other method which has been pointed out to me, and they are a final, *a finifhed remedy;* whereas loans, lotteries, annuities, and every other method which I have heard of, are no more than temporary expedients, are but plaufible anticipations of our revenue, and all look forward to a burden to be impofed in future time, which had better be borne now, and be finally done with.

And as I propofe that all the eftimates of Congrefs, and all the quotas demanded of the States, fhould be made out in hard money, fo I alfo propofe that the taxes may be made out in the fame money, payable either in hard money or Continental, at the option of the perfon who pays the tax. Sundry material advantages I conceive will arife from this:

1. Many perfons out of trade have no money but hard, and when called on for the tax, may be compelled to part with their hard money, at an unreafonable exchange, which will be avoided if hard money itfelf will pay the tax.

2. This will preferve the tax from any poffibility of fluctuation, by the depreciation or appreciation of the currency, for if any perfon thinks the exchange demanded unreafonable, he may pay it in hard money, and then he is fure not to pay either too much or too little.

3. This will gradually bring fums of hard money, perhaps not inconfiderable, into the Continental Treafury, which may be fo ufed as to prevent drawing on *Europe*, and thereby increafing our foreign debt, which I conceive an object greatly worth attention.

4. This will exhibit the tax to view in its real value, and prevent the terrors which may arife from the enormous found in Continental money.

5. This

5. This would greatly tend in a short course of time to reduce all our private contracts to the fixed standard of hard money, by which we should avoid that vortex of fluctuation and uncertainty, which has rendered all our private dealings precarious, and made even our profits rather the effect of chance, than of wise calculation and industry. Nor do I think that this would at all prejudice the real use of the Continental money, for it would still pass at its exchange or value.

Indeed I do not see that the depreciation of the money would have been in itself a calamity half so ruinous as it has proved, if it had *operated only on the cash in being;* it would have been a tax upon every possessor of it, and would have lessened the public debt, for it is manifest that the public debt at the exchange of forty for one, is but half what it was when the exchange was twenty for one; and as that money was perhaps as equally diffused over the Thirteen States, as any other property, the tax might have operated with a tolerable degree of justice; but the case was altered when the depreciation was not confined to the Continental money only, but drew every thing else after it: when it came to operate on *every debt and money-contract,* on every *legacy, salary, public fee* and *fine,* yea, on the *finances* of the States, so as to destroy all *calculation of both supplies and expenditures,* the mischief became infinite: we were both in our private affairs and public councils, thrown into confusion inextricable.

New objects, new effects, started up to view in every quarter, which no *discernment* could foresee, nor *wisdom* obviate, and like an inchantment of fairy visions, bewildered us all in such a maze of errors, interwoven with such subtilty into every branch of our movements, that no one department was free of them; and we all stand trembling this moment before this monster of depreciation, like bewildered travellers in a giant's castle, where the *bones* of broken fortunes are every where in sight, with the *spectres of widows and fatherless,* and a thousand others, which the monster has devoured, and *is still* devouring as greedy as ever.

This

This mischief will be greatly lessened, if, by reducing all our debts and demands, public and private, to the standard of hard money, we can confine the depreciation of the money to itself, and prevent its operation on all other money-contracts and securities, and this will, in my opinion, greatly tend to cure the depreciation itself, because in that case no man can gain any thing by the depreciation, but every man who has any cash must lose by it; and when private interest is brought into a coincidence with the public good, they will greatly help each other.

But be all this as it may, let us not lose sight of the principal argument, viz. that no project or scheme to stop the depreciation can have the desired effect, if it does not *increase the demand* for our currency; and on the contrary, any scheme whatever that will increase the demand for our currency, will *lessen or check the depreciation*. Hence we see how vain all propositions must be, which, by their natural operation, will increase cash among us, and thereby lessen the demand for it, or increase the national debt beyond all probability of payment, and thereby lessen the public credit, and of course lessen also the demand for the currency which depends on it. Of this sort are all *loans, foreign and domestic;* for as long as people can get money without *earning it*, without actually raising and paying it, it will not appear so precious, nor can the demand be so great, as when these great and necessary conditions are the *only terms* of acquiring it. Hence also, every project which lessens the use of our currency, lessens also the demand for it, and cannot possibly help, but will hurt, it; such as barter in trade or levying taxes *in kind* * in finance.

My great proposition is, that *by taxes* we have it always in our power to *fix our currency at any value we please;* because, by this way, we may raise the demand for money just *as high* as we please, and, if we have not great prudence, *much higher* than the public good requires; and if the method and train proposed, be adopted, the operation of

---

* Taxes in kind are taxes to be paid, not in cash, but in necessaries for the army, such as flour, beef, rum, clothing, &c. &c. A scheme of this sort was brisk a-foot, among other wild projects, about this time.

of taxes may be made more quick and more sure, than in any other I know of. This is dealing in *realities*. We have dealt in *shadows and delusions* too long already for our *honor*, too long for our *safety*. It is not only wicked, dishonorable, and dangerous, but it is weak and absurd, to suppose that we can any longer produce our public supplies out of shadows and visionary projects; the baseless fabric will vanish; our resources consist in *real substance* only, and from thence alone can our supplies be produced, and let them be collected by an equable tax, and the burden on the public will not be any thing near so heavy and ruinous, as the numberless mischiefs of the depreciation have proved for four years past.

But it may be asked, What is to be done in the present distress? How are our present, immediate wants to be relieved? The answer must lie in a pretty narrow compass. I know of but three things that can be done in the case: 1. To *borrow money*, which is fatal in its operation, and uncertain in its effects. 2. To set the *presses* a going again, which will not only increase the mischief, but destroy the operation of any remedy. Or, 3. do without supplies awhile. If the crows cannot be killed, nor the carcass be removed out of their reach, the sure way is to let them eat it all up to the very bones, and then they will go away of their own accord; and this is better than to have *Tityus*'s vulture for ever gnawing on our liver, and our liver growing at the same time as fast as he eats it. Here is indeed a notable difficulty which would vanish into nothing, if there was a proper connexion formed between the *great resources* of the Thirteen States, the real substance, the mighty wealth which they contain, and *the credit of the States*, necessary to collect them, and bring them to public use, when the public safety or convenience requires them. The credit of our currrency is too lax, too enervated, and feeble for this; people have more of it already than they have use for, and the depreciation makes it a dangerous article to keep on hand: it is like perishable goods, which are lost in the keeping. In the nature of the thing there is nor can be no remedy for this, but increasing the demands mand for the currency, and this can be done in no other way than by an univerfal tax, which alone can create an univerfal demand, and this demand muft operate on thofe perfons who have the neceffary fupplies, fo as to make their neceffity for money equal to the neceffity of the purchafer of the fupplies.

This will put the contracting parties on a par of equal neceffity on each fide, which alone can ever produce an equal bargain, and is the real, natural fource of all trade. Filling the Treafury never fo full of money by Loans or any other way, will not effect the purpofe, unlefs demanded of the very perfons who have the fupplies in their hands, for in any other way, their neceffity for money will not be increafed, and of courfe they will withhold the fupplies, or demand an unreafonable price, when they fee a great neceffity on the purchafer, and none on themfelves.

I appeal to every perfon who deals, whether this is not the true fact. Let a perfon who is under neceffity of an article, apply to one who has it, but is under no neceffity to fell it, he muft give any price that is afked. Let a man who is under neceffity of felling an article, apply to one to purchafe, who is under no neceffity of buying, he muft take what is offered. This may be thought a refinement of argument, but I appeal to every man, the leaft or the moft verfed in trade, if this is not the univerfal principle of all trade, and if it is not the univerfal practice of all wife traders, if they are under a neceffity of buying or felling, to conceal that neceffity as far as they can, left it fhould put them under difadvantage in making their bargain.

It is further to be obferved, that an increafed demand for money is the only thing which will naturally excite great diligence and pains in procuring fuch articles as will bring it; therefore, it appears that this is the only true means of reftoring the *decayed induftry* of our people, without which we fhall foon have no fupplies raifed, and then we muft be deftitute indeed, for no demand for money can produce fupplies which are not in exiftence, which to me appears to be a matter worthy of very great attention.

Every idea of a *loan* either at home or abroad, operates directly against thefe great principles, and directly tends to increafe our diftrefs.*

I *abhor* and *execrate* every idea of a *foreign loan* to purchafe neceffaries produced among ourfelves; it may be neceffary to borrow in *Europe* money fufficient to purchafe what we muft export from thence, and enough to make former contracts punctually and honeftly good; but to borrow money in *Europe* to pay for fupplies produced here among ourfelves, appears to me the height of abfurdity: this expofes our weaknefs to all the world; not our *weaknefs* in point of *fupplies*; not the exhaufted ftate of our country, for that is full of every thing we want, clothing and military ftores excepted; but the weaknefs of our *counfels* and *adminiftration*, that our *domeftic economy* fhould be fo bad, that we fhould not be able to call into public ufe the very fupplies in which the country abounds, is *fhameful*: fuch an imbecility of counfels, I imagine, will hold us up in fo very contemptible a light in *Europe* as will effectually deftroy all our *credit there*, and thereby put it out of our power to *deftroy ourfelves*; but if this fhould not be the cafe, I do not fee but our independence, with all the bleffings refulting from it, is in danger: for I really fear that fome among us would, without concern, mortgage the Thirteen States up to the value of every acre they contain, to any foreign power that will truft us.

It is as neceffary that we preferve ourfelves independent of *France*, *Spain*, and *Holland*, as of *England*. It is manifeft beyond any need of proof, that the nation who is in debt to a fuperior power, cannot be free and independent, but is ever liable to demands the moft infulting and inconfiftent with freedom and fafety.

But

---

* A fmall loan had been negotiated a little before this time in *France*, and further loans in *France*, *Spain*, and *Holland* were propofed, and urged in and out of Congrefs with great earneftnefs and zeal. This feems to have been a period of diftrefs and madnefs.

But if after all, nothing can stop the career of this fatal measure of contracting a further foreign debt, I beg, at least, that the monies necessary be borrowed at home on yearly interest, payable in bills on *Europe*, or in hard money at home, and let the delinquent States be charged with this interest, for if there was no delinquency, there would be no need of a loan: my reasons are,

1. If interest of hard money or bills must be paid, I think it better that our own people should have it than strangers, that the yearly profits of the loan should lie among ourselves, and not go out of the country, never to return.

2. It is less dangerous to contract a foreign debt, sufficient for the yearly interest of this loan, than for the principal and interest too.

3. This method will have one absurdity less than the other, for if bills are to issue for the money to be loaned in *Europe* (for our necessities are so pressing, it is said we cannot wait till the advices arrive that the loan is completed) they must be drawn on funds of mere imagination, for not one shilling of the fund on which they are to be drawn, is yet procured, nor do we know that the loan can be obtained at all; and therefore every bill is liable to come back protested, to the utter ruin, and most laughable contempt of the credit of the States. And

4. The uncertainty of the payment of the bills will certainly operate on the sale of them. I believe nobody expects they can be sold at a loss of less than 20 or 30 per cent. The present exchange of the currency is 40 to 1; but I have not heard any body propose selling the bills at more than 30 for 1.

5. The very idea of drawing bills or loaning at a loss of 20, 30, or 40 per cent. appears to me so very ruinous and absurd, and the fact stands in so glaring and striking a light, that I do not know how to form one argument for the conviction of such as are willing to adopt either. The great, sure, and only supply of all our wants, and remedy of our distress, lies in taxes. Justice requires that this remedy should be effectually adopted: public burdens ought

to

to reſt in due proportion on all, which can be effected in no other way.* This alone will create an univerſal demand for our currency; and bring it into ſuch repute, that every neceſſary article in the country may be readily purchaſed with it; this ſettles and finiſhes the matter as we go, and relieves us at once from the anxious terrors of an unſupportable debt, and all future demands and inſults from any power on earth.

Say, *Americans*, if this freedom and independence, for which you have bled and nobly dared every danger, and for which you have ſet at defiance, and incurred the vengeance of, the mighteſt power on earth, is not ſtill worth your moſt capital attention: it avails little to *change our maſters;* to have *none* is our object, which can never be our caſe, if we are in debt to foreign powers.

III. I beg leave here to propoſe one thing more, viz. to *take off every reſtraint from our trade.* Let every man be at liberty to get money as faſt as he can; and let the public call for it as faſt as the public exigence requires. Limitations of our trade have been ſo often tried, ſo ſtrongly enforced, and have ſo conſtantly failed of the intended effect, and have, in every inſtance, produced ſo much injuſtice and oppreſſion in our dealings, and excited ſo many quarrels, ſo much ill-will and chagrin among our people, that they have, in every inſtance, after ſome time of moſt pernicious continuance, been laid aſide by a kind of general conſent, and even moſt of their advocates have been convinced of their hurtful tendency, as well as utter impracticability.

As experiment is the ſureſt proof of the natural effects of all ſpeculations of this kind, and as this proof of fact has ever appeared in the ſtrongeſt manner, againſt the practicability and ſucceſs of all reſtraints of this ſort, and as every ſeeming, temporary advantage that has reſulted from them, has conſtantly been followed by effects ſo very pernicious and alarming, it is *ſtrange*, it is *marvellous* to me, that any perſon of common diſcernment, who has been acquainted with all the above-mentioned trials and effects,

effects, should entertain any idea of the expediency of trying any such method again.

Not less absurd should I conceive a number of adepts in *Barclay*'s system of ideas, driving their heads ten times going against a wall, and still preparing to try it again with greater force than before, because they could not believe there was the *substance* of a wall, but an *idea* only there; equally in both cases must the career of the zealots be stopped in hard fact, and their skulls, if not exceeding thick, must be greatly wounded.

Liberty and property are the most tender interests of mankind; any kind of abridgment, restraint, or control of these is ever sensibly felt and borne with impatience; and the natural course of things seems so adapted to those two great and favorite rights, that any violations of them will, by their most natural operation, produce effects very unsalutary, if not fatal. Indeed, this mischief may at any time be increased till the effects are tragical. Trade, if let alone, will ever make its own way best, and, like an irresistible river, will ever run safest, do least mischief and most good, when suffered to run without obstruction in its own natural channel.

IV. I humbly propose further, that *no private property may ever be taken for public use, against the consent of the owner, without the most manifest necessity*, and in that case, not without paying the *full value*. If the public wants any man's property, they are certainly better able to pay for it, than an individual is to lose it. Paying half or any thing less than the whole value, is a scurvy and evasive way of robbing the owner, and infinitely unworthy of the justice and dignity of a State. There has been so much of this iniquity committed either with or without pretext of Law, that it has been really dangerous for a man to possess an article of capital demand; he has been in danger of having the article torn from him, not only without due payment, but with insult and abuse; and this wicked and shameful practice has really discouraged many persons of great ability and industry, from procuring articles of great demand, lest they should be thereby subjected to the mor-

tification

tification of having them torn away with violence and disgrace.

Many great necessaries have been rendered scarce by these means, and thereby the price has become enormous, and the procurement difficult. Instances in flour, salt, &c. are most notorious and obvious. This greatly destroys the confidence of the holders of the great necessaries, in the officers of government, and lessens their assiduity and zeal in procuring or bringing their goods to the public stores. The consequences of this shameful iniquity are most fatal in their nature, and tho' slow and not immediately perceptible, yet most certain in their operation, and most sure of effects.

V. I propose further that there be the greatest care and attention in the *appointment of the men* who are to fill all *places* of public trust, and especially such as are employed in the *revenue* and *expenditures* of the public monies and supplies. I should conceive the following qualifications so necessary as to admit of no dispensation:

1. That the candidate for any place of public trust have sufficient *knowledge and ability* to discharge the duties of the office proposed for him. A public officer, like St. *Paul*'s bishop, ought to be a workman that needs not to be ashamed. But I am sure any *person needs to be ashamed*, who appears in a public office without understanding the *duties of it*, and therefore utterly incapable of discharging them properly: and the *persons who appointed* him ought to be ashamed of him too, and he certainly will prove a *shame to the public*; for the public, *i. e.* a kingdom, a state, a country, or a city, always shine thro' the medium of their *public men*; if they mean to have their weight, dignity, character, and interest well supported in a treaty, a Congress, a General Assembly, or a Court of Justice, they must appoint *sufficient men* to represent them and act for them; if they would have their most public and important counsels, their laws, the administration of public justice and civil policy, or their revenue *well conducted*, they must appoint *men of knowledge* ane *abilities* sufficient for these great purposes, to conduct them; these are all objects of such magnitude,

magnitude, such general importance, and pervade with such subtilty every interest of the community, that they reach and deeply affect every individual, and prescribe the degree of security, honor, and peace which he is to enjoy.

How mad and execrable then must be that elector, or person concerned in the appointment of a public officer, who, from motives of party, personal friendship, or any worse inducement, will give his vote for a person, who, he knows, is deficient in the knowledge and abilities requisite to the proper discharge of the office? Let a man's virtue and integrity be never so great, if he wants knowledge and ability, he never can shine, he never can serve with honor or advantage in the office, but must be a shame to himself and to his constituents, and most probably a damage, and may be a ruin into the bargain. But

2. Knowledge and abilities, tho' essential, are not the only requisites in a public man; *integrity and prudence* are also most necessary. The true character of the heart cannot be certainly known indeed, but is best judged of by his general deportment; therefore the character which a man obtains among his neighbours, and those who best know him, is the surest rule by which he can be estimated, and will be most likely to pre-engage the public confidence in his favor; and it is necessary, not only that a public man should be upright, but also that he should be generally esteemed so. The wife of *Cæsar* ought not to be suspected; therefore it must be the height of folly (to say no worse) to appoint a man to public station, whose private character for integrity and prudence is not good.

3. *Sound judgment and rational discretion* is a most essential part of necessary character *in a public man*, especially one who is concerned in the public councils, or important offices of any sort. Nothing can scarcely be conceived more dangerous to the public, than to have its great arrangements subject to the influence of a man of *wild projection, and extravagant conceits;* such a person, especially if he has a good address and copious invention, is enough to *make errors faster* than twenty men of the best wisdom

can

can *mend*. It is not strange, to find men, who have great talents at discovering valuable mines, who, at the same time, have no knowledge in essaying the ore, or making the proper use of it. But to come more immediately to the point in view,

4. In the appointment of an officer of the revenue, or expenditures of the public monies, *i. e.* one through whose hands the public monies or supplies are to pass, it is necessary, most essentially necessary, that he should be a man of known *industry, economy, and thriftiness in his own private affairs*. If a man's *regard to his own character, fortune, and family*, is not a sufficient inducement to make him *careful, industrious*, and *thrifty* in his own affairs, it is not to be presumed, that any regard he may have to the public *can make* him so; a man's own interest always lies nearest his heart, *i. e.* self-love is the strongest of all passions and motives. It was hardly ever known, that raising a man into public office, *mended his private vices*, but *they* most commonly like a pervading poison, get incorporated into the department, in which he officiates, and greatly corrupt and injure the administration of it.

Therefore to appoint a *bankrupt*, a man of *dissipation, idleness*, and *prodigality*, to an office, through which the public *monies* and *supplies* are to pass, is a sure way to have them *wasted* or *purloined*, in which the riches, strength, and blood of the States are exhausted; not to answer *the great ends* of goverment, the *safety, security*, and *peace* of the great whole, but to gratify the *extravagance, dissipation*, and *debauchery* of an individual; it would be much better, if a man has such a friend, that must be served, to *give him a few thousands*, to spend in his own way, than to admit him into the important *offices of revenue*, and thereby corrupt its course and use.

Perhaps some errors of this sort may have occasioned a profusion of expense, a neglect and loss of public stores, and a failure of distribution, all which tend to increase our distress, and accelerate the decays of our finances; for as in private affairs, *prudence* in expense is as necessary to a fortune as the *acquirement of money*, so in our public administration, niftration, I conceive *economy* in expenditures, as neceffary a part of financiering, as the *acquirement* of a revenue: and I conceive in this, as in all other parts of public adminiftration, good government depends more on the *men who adminifter*, than on the fyftem or form of the conftitution, the wifdom of the laws, or prudence of the general orders; for let all thefe be ever fo good, if the executive part is not committed to induftrious, wife, and faithful *men*, there will be a great failure of *juftice, fecurity*, and *peace*.

VI. I propofe a review of all our departments, and *reducing all unneceffary expenditures* in them, as far as poffible. It is better to leffen the expenfes, where it can be done with fafety, than to increafe the revenue; the one leffens, the other increafes the public burden. I am told there are 9000 rations iffued daily in this city, where there is not the leaft appearance of any military movements, except a few invalids, and fick in the hofpital, and the prifoners, all which do not amount to one third of the aforefaid number of rations.

I am told there are pofts of commiffioners, quarter-mafters, purchafers, &c. fixed at about 10 or 15 miles diftance from each other thro' this State, and fome fay thro' the whole Thirteen States; if they were all fent out of the way, all the fupplies within reach of our market, would come of courfe to this city, and might be all purchafed here by one man, much cheaper, and at lefs expenfe, than by all thofe pofts; fpreading them about thro' the country anfwers the fame end, as if a private man fhould fend a fervant ten miles out of town to buy his marketing; he muft folicit more, pay a higher price, and have a worfe choice than if he ftayed at home, and bought in market. But I cannot pretend to go into the minutiæ of thefe matters; I can only obferve, that people out of doors cannot at all conceive the reafon or ufe of thefe multiplied officers of fo many different names, that one has need of a dictionary to underftand them; I am apt to wifh they were all ftruck off the lift, by one dafh of the pen, at leaft that their rations and clothing might be ftopped, and fent to camp for the ufe of our foldiers in real fervice.

I would

I would add to my wish also, that their horses might be taken away from them, that they might not be able to parade it thro' the country on horseback, or in carriages, as they now do with a gaiety of dress, importance of air, and grandeur of equipage, very chagrining to the impoverished inhabitants who maintain them: I conceive this method would supply our camp very comfortably for several months, till our finances might be recruited by the numerous taxes which are coming in, and in this way the necessity of Loans might be prevented, or at least lessened.

If it should not be thought expedient to send *their wines* to camp, as I do not know that an abundance of liquors do soldiers or any body else any good, I propose to send them to vendue, as they have much engrossed that article of late, it is become very scarce and dear, and would probably bring a great price, and the proceeds of them might be a seasonable supply to the Continental Treasury, and further lessen the necessity of loaning.

In fine, my great object is to get our *revenue fixed* on a sure and sufficient foundation, and our *expenditures reduced within the bounds of use, necessary to the safety and benefit of the community*. In this case our people will all be willing to contribute the aids necessary; for the intentions of the people at large are *ever upright*, and it is rare that there is any difficulty with them in this respect, when they are convinced that the public monies are all *prudently expended* for necessary uses.

I further conceive that taxes are absolutely necessary, not only to supply the public treasury, but to reduce our money to a fixed standard, and restore it to its natural and necessary use, which no other method of supplying the treasury can do, and which yet must be done, in order to deliver us from the most dreadful calamity of a fluctuating currency. This I consider as of the most weighty importance, and at the same time of so critical, difficult, and intricate a nature, that it will require the utmost attention to the means of it, and the highest prudence and care to watch their operations, and add to or diminish their force as occasion may require.

For

For if the money should appreciate, it will, over and above all private wrong, increase the national debt. An appreciation of only 10 per cent. which may be done almost imperceptibly, will add 20,000,000 to that debt, which must be paid, not in shadows, but by the hard labor of our people. Such is the *subtile nature* and *imperceptible operation of this mighty error*, that no degree of attention to it can be deemed unneceffary. To mend this, I conceive to be the great work before us, *hic labor, hoc opus est*.

I am but little concerned or alarmed at the present pinch of the treasury. Our resources are too great to permit such a temporary, such a momentary distress to be fatal; a proper reduction of our expenditures, or a small anticipation of our revenue in any way, will remedy it. If the great springs of our revenue can be put in motion, we may be easily saved, otherwise we must perish.

I beg leave here to add, that the attention of Congress, however sufficient, if it were not unavoidably drawn off by an infinity of other objects that constantly crowd upon them, is not and cannot be practicable in a degree adequate to this great object. Nor indeed do I think that any board of numbers or aggregate body would be likely to form a system so exact, and bestow an attention so accurate and uniform as would be necessary in this case. I conceive it must be the work of *one mind*, which ever could investigate and superintend matters of an abstruse nature and critical movements better alone than with company; and therefore,

VII. * I propose, that a *financier or comptroller of finances*, be appointed, whose sole object and business should be to superintend the finances, *i. e.* the *revenues and expenditures* of the States, the state of the *currency*, and all the *funds* in which we are concerned, and in short, our whole *resources* and *expenditures;* and keep the one well in balance with

---

* I believe this was the first proposal made in *America*, for the appointment of such an officer; I was so much convinced of the importance of such an appointment, that I repeated the proposal in several subsequent publications, and about a year after this, at the particular desire of some members of Congress, published an essay on the nature, authority, and uses of this office.

with the other, all under the authority of Congress, and in every thing subject to their control. The Congress would then have the subject examined and formed to their hand, and would have nothing more to do than correct and approve it.

If a man adequate to this business could be found, I conceive his appointment would be of the highest utility to the States, as we may easily conceive only by imagining the benefits which might have resulted from such an appointment, had such an one been made five years ago.

However, I do but propose this with the same simplicity of mind as I express my other thoughts; if it is not approved, it may be easily rejected, with any other of my propositions, and I have only to desire this one favor of my indulgent reader, that if he does not like this, or any other part of my Essays, that he would lay them by, and read them again a year or two hence, after which he has my leave to do what he pleases with them.

Time is the *surest expositor and best judge* of all plans and speculations of this sort; the *vain and vicious* will either *vanish* or stand *condemned* before him; the *useful and good* only can be *approved* and *preserved* by him: and while I make this appeal, every body will allow that I refer myself to a most equitable and reasonable arbiter, and I hope all my readers will candidly wait this decision with me, without censuring too bitterly sentiments on which time has not yet decided.

—*Quod optanti Divûm promittere nemo,*
Auderet, Volvenda Dies en attulit ultro.——VIRGIL.

A FOURTH ESSAY

ON

FREE TRADE and FINANCE.

First published in Philadelphia, February 10, 1780.

THE system of taxation equal to the public expenditures, adopted and recommended by Congress,* is grounded on the most solid and demonstrable principles, and, if there is no error or defect in the execution of it, cannot fail of producing the two great ends expected from it, viz. *Supplying the expenses of the States,* and *reducing our currency to a fixed and permanent value.* These two effects will be produced by the natural operation of this system, without any force or extraneous helps.

Yet

---

* The first recommendation of Congress to the States *to raise money by a tax* (which I recollect) was on *Jan.* 14, 1777; but this was done in *so indefinite* a manner, *without any sums or quotas specified*, that little or nothing came of it.

In *Nov.* 22, 1777, Congress recommended to the States *to raise 5,000,000 of dollars* in the course of the year 1778, in quarterly payments, *with the quotas of each State annexed*, &c. but this had little effect; *small sums* were raised and paid by *some of the States*, within the year 1778; others made some remittances *long afterwards*, when the money was 20 for 1, or more, &c. but great part was never paid at all.———In the address of Congress to the people of the United States, *May* 8, 1778, is this expression: " What are the reasons that your *money is depreciated*? Because *no taxes have been imposed* to carry on the war."

Jan. 2, 1779, Congress resolved, that the States be called on for their quotas of 15,000,000 *of dollars*, to be raised by taxes for the year 1779,

and

Yet it is to be noted here with care and concern, that when these great and steady principles come to operate on the present distracted state of our currency and finances, very *sad* and perhaps *fatal effects* will be produced, and infinite injustice done, even by this forcible remedy, tho' the most salutary and only effectual one, if some care is not taken to *direct* its force and *limit* its first effects. The *appreciation* of our currency is among the first of these ill consequences which I fear, and would guard against. The evils of this I have considered in my Second Essay; but as what I there urged either has not been understood or regarded, I think it necessary here to resume the subject, which certainly merits the highest attention of every *American*.

The value of Continental money is what it *is now* worth to the possessor. The *present exchange* of Continental money is

---

and of 6,000,000 *of dollars* to be raised *annually* for 18 *years*, commencing with the year 1780; as a *fund* for sinking *loans* and *emissions*, paying *interest*, &c.

May 21, 1779, Congress resolved, that the States should be called on for their quotas of the *further* sum of 45,000,000 *of dollars*, to be paid into the Continental Treasury before the 1*st of Jan.* 1780.

Oct. 6, 1779, they further resolved, that the States be called on to raise their respective quotas of 15,000,000 *of dollars, monthly*; to be paid into the Continental Treasury on the 1*st day of Feb.* 1780, and on the 1st day of *each following* month up to *Oct.* 1st, inclusive; *i. e.* 15,000,000 of dollars *per month* for 9 months successively, beginning with *Feb.* 1780.

This provision for the year 1780, *if continued thro' the year*, would have amounted to 180,000,000 *of dollars*; to which if we add, the annual 6,000,000 for that year, it would raise the sum to 186,000,000 of dollars; which, had it been *rigidly and effectually collected* (as might be expected; for *every body by this time*, both in and out of Congress, *seemed pretty much in earnest for effectual taxes*) I say, had this sum been *rigidly collected*, it would doubtless have produced a *very destructive* and *very useless appreciation* of the currency, which it was my object in this Essay to prevent and avoid.

For, by *fixing* the money at 40 for 1 (which was the *true exchange* at that time) and directing the *taxes* to be paid either *in hard money* or *Continental bills at that exchange*, it would be manifestly impossible to *raise* or *depress* the Continental money *above* or *below* that exchange, let the *demand for it be increased* ever so much. A *want of demand* might have *reduced* the value of the Continental money (as was afterwards in fact the case) but an *increase of demand* never could *raise* the value of it *above* that exchange.

Nor could such a regulation be *oppressive* or *burdensome* to the States, as hard money was at that time *extremely plenty*; which was occasioned by large sums by various means *coming from the English army at New-York*, and spreading thro' the States; also by large sums remitted by *France to their army and navy then here*; also by *large importations* of hard money from the *Havannah* and other places abroad; so that hard money was never more plenty or more easily collected than at that time.

is to hard money at the rate of about 40 to 1, tho' it is very fluctuating; at this exchange of 40 to 1, which is very near the truth, and for which I appeal to the merchants' and goldsmiths' books, I say, at this exchange, our debt of continental money, *i. e.* all the continental money in circulation, is worth 5,000,000 *of dollars in hard money*. For the reader need not be told that that value is found by dividing the whole sum of our currency, viz. 200,000,000 *of dollars*, by the exchange, viz. 40, which will make a quotient of 5,000,000 of dollars of hard money.

If this exchange is reduced, say to 20 for 1, it will increase this public debt to 10,000,000 of hard dollars. Therefore, it follows, that *every appreciation* of the money *increases* the public debt, and to an amazing degree, by movements, indeed almost imperceptible, yet certain, and to an amount almost beyond belief. For if the exchange should fall to 10 for 1, the debt would rise to 20,000,000; an exchange of 5 to 1 would raise the debt to 40,000,000 of hard dollars, and so on till the debt would rise to 200,000,000 of hard dollars, and all this *without the least benefit to the public*, but in every view to its *detriment*. For, over and above the vast increase of taxes necessary to pay this increased debt, many other evils still worse than the tax would follow, to which I must beg the reader's most serious attention; for however out of sight and distant it may appear, the mischief is infinite, and must be fatal, if not prevented.

1. *This appreciation will raise the value of the money in the chests of the possessors, in proportion as it increases the public debt.* This will raise the *great* money-holders into nabobs, so rich there will be no living with them. They have already, it is generally thought, much more than their share. Men of *overgrown riches*, especially of sudden acquirement, are *dangerous* to any community. They are not generally people of the *best refinement of manners* or *wisest discretion*, and therefore, their influence in the community (which will ever be, *cæteris paribus*, in proportion to their wealth) will be dangerous; but were they all the best of men, such amazing and sudden acquisitions of wealth would be enough

to spoil them. We find, by long and various experience, that human nature cannot bear, without corruption, such sudden leaps into the heights of greatness, prosperity, wealth, and influence.

2. *This same cause will induce all men to hoard their money, when they find it grows better and better daily in their chests.* Money will soon become so scarce, as not to be obtained without great difficulty, and this will increase the value or appreciation of it; for the value of money will ever be in proportion to its scarcity and demand. Thus every stage of this mischief will tend to increase the evil, and lead on to further stages of the same calamity and distress. This is obvious to every one.

3. *This same cause will ruin our trade and manufactures;* for the rise of money in the desk will be more profitable than any trade or branch of manufacture. This will *ruin all industry;* for the rich will not go into business, and the poor will not find employers, and this will produce scarcity of all goods, both home produced and imported, and of course general distress and want must follow.

4. *This same appreciation will increase the public debt, and consequently will increase the taxes by which it must be paid, and that in proportion to the value or amount of the appreciation.* The appreciation of money is like an account in a merchant's book; there must be a *debtor* and *creditor* to it. It is not possible that one shilling should be *gained* by one person in this way, which is not *lost* by somebody. If you make the money more valuable in my pocket, it will cost the public more to redeem it; and therefore, if it was to be appreciated up to its original value, every man's tax must be multiplied by the present exchange, *i. e.* made about 40 times greater than it need be, to redeem all the money at the present value; and therefore it is probable those who think the present taxes are not more than the fortieth part of what they should be, will be zealous promoters of the scheme of appreciation.

5. *This same thing will increase every private debt.* For nothing is plainer than this, viz. if the money is more valuable at the time of payment than it was at the time of contract,

contract, the debt is thereby increased, *i. e.* it will take more hard money, or more wheat to pay the debt, than would have paid it at the time of contract. This brings on the inevitable ruin of many poor people, who cannot avoid being more or less in debt for rent or some other necessary thing. It is hard enough for them to pay their debts at their just value; but when the sum comes to be increased, perhaps doubled or trebled in a few months, the payment becomes either extremely difficult or impossible. This might at first please the rich pretty well, but they would find their mistake, for they would be obliged soon to accept a notice of bankruptcy, instead of payment from their debtors.

6. The great cry for appreciation is, that those who have suffered by depreciation ought to have the benefit of a compensation by the appreciation of the currency; but this is nugatory, and will prove in the end a perfect deception. *For not one tenth part, perhaps not an hundredth part of the money, when it shall appreciate, will be found in the hands of those who have suffered by the depreciation.* It will be no adequate remedy to any of them, but will be an increase of distress and injury to far the greatest part of them.

Those persons who have suffered by the depreciation, but by the chance of the times have been able to make it up some other way, so as to be able to hoard up sufficient sums of money to take advantage of the appreciation, those, I say, are not the great objects of my concern; but the helpless widow, the fatherless infant, and a thousand others, who have been obliged, thro' the deficiency of their interest, to spend on the principal, till it is all or mostly gone, those, I say, are the *great objects of pity;* their *cries for justice* and *compensation* ought to be heard; the appreciation does them no good, for they have not cash on which it can operate; for nobody can take any benefit of the appreciation, but such as have more cash on hand than all their taxes will amount to; but the aforesaid widows, &c. are by the appreciation plunged into an increased distress and injury; for if they have an acre of land, or a horse or cow left, they must be loaded with a vast increase of taxes, in order to appreciate the money which *they have loft*, and which now lies hoarded in the coffers of their *rich neighbours*, who have gotten it from them.

From this view of the matter, it appears that many people may imagine that they shall receive an advantage from the appreciation, and therefore cry loudly for it, who will, in the end, be greatly hurt by it. It seems they ask *they know not what*, like the mother of *Zebedee*'s children, who, in the ardency of maternal affection, petitioned our Saviour that her two sons might sit, the one on his *right* hand, and the other on his *left*, not considering that the purport of her petition was, that one of her sons might be *saved* and the other *damned*.

7. The appreciation *of the Continental bills* will continue thro' the *whole course of it, all the mischiefs of a fluctuating currency.* This destroys or varies the *standard* or *common measure of value* of all things bought or sold; renders all *money-contracts* and *debts uncertain; corrupts the equity* and *alters the force of our laws*, by varying the *fines, forfeitures*, and *fees* limited by them; and in short, throws both the *private man in his dealings*, and the *judge on the bench*, into such perplexity and confusion, that neither can have due *knowledge of right*, even when they may be disposed to do it, whilst the *wicked* have the greatest latitude in which they may practise *shocking wrongs*, and that in the *face of the sun*, and *with impunity*. This suspends the *rewards of virtue* and the *punishment of vice, corrupts the morals* of the people, and in the end *produces every evil work*. Surely this picture is dreary.

8. *From all these mischiefs no one benefit can arise to the public.* Every *advantage* of the appreciation goes to the *rich men* who have got the money hoarded, and to them *alone*. Why then all this more than *Herculean labor* of appreciating the money? why all these risks and public dangers? why all this multiplied *burden and distress* on our people? The uses of the currency are to every purpose as great to the public, if fixed at the present value, at two pence or three pence the dollar, as at any *other value* that can be named.

9. The

9. *The appreciation of the currency will destroy the equity of the taxation itself,* according to the known and received principles of it, viz. that all estates ought to be taxed in proportion *to their value*, in such manner that every man's estate, after the tax is paid, shall bear the *same proportion* to his neighbour's as before, *i. e.* so that no man should be *enriched* or *impoverished* by the tax more than his neighbour.

But if the money is appreciated, the tax will have a very different effect, as will be obvious at first sight, only by viewing its operation in one very familiar instance, viz. Suppose two brothers have each a plantation of equal value, say worth 1000*l.* hard money each, and one of them sells his plantation for 1000*l.* hard money, and changes that money into 40,000*l.* continental money, and the tax comes on; and we will further suppose they are both taxed according to the value of their estates, *i. e.* equally, and that the tax necessary to appretiate the money be 20 per cent. on the whole value; it appears then plain that the tax of *the one*, who keeps his plantation, will be 200*l.* hard money, and the tax of *the other*, who has 40,000*l.* continental money, will be 8000*l.* of that money; consequently, the first will have a clear estate left of 800*l.* hard money value, but the other will have an estate worth 32,000*l.* hard money, for by the supposition all the money he has left will be *appreciated* up to its original value, *i. e.* to the value of hard money, and will be worth 40 times as much as his brother's estate. But if all these arguments do not convince, I have one more, which, I think, must do for the hardiest opponent; it is this:—

10. *The scheme of appreciation will destroy itself; it is in its nature impracticable, and its own operation will work its destruction.* For the appreciation of the currency will increase the *taxes* and *public burdens* to such an enormous and *insupportable amount,* that the people neither *can*, or *will*, or *ought to bear them*. When they come to be told that all their taxes are not at all for the benefit of the public, but are for no other purpose than to increase the value of the money hoarded by their rich neighbours (and *they certainly will*

will find this out) they will join in one general cry against the oppression, with one voice damn the taxes, and swear they will not pay them.

Then the mighty bubble will sink into nothing, and with it will go all our *revenue, public faith, defense, honor,* and *political existence.*

Very many things more might be added on this fertile subject; but if what I have said in my Second Essay on this subject, and what I have repeated and added here, is not sufficient for conviction, it is vain and useless in my opinion to add more, and shall only here beg my reader's patience and attention a moment to an affair of my own.

I do here, as an individual, *enter my protest* most solemnly against this most fatal, useless, and chimerical scheme of appreciating the currency, and am determined to leave a copy of my Essays with my children, that my posterity may know that in 1780 there was, at least, *one citizen* of Philadelphia who was not totally distracted, and that they may have the honor and consolation of being descended from a man, who was able to keep *in his senses* in times of the greatest *infatuation.*

But all this notwithstanding, and altho' appearances are strong against me, I will still hope that there yet is a judicious majority on my side, who are thoroughly sick of all *visionary projects,* and wish to adopt the *substantial and sure* remedies which still remain in our power. With such as these I will most cheerfully join in company, and sit down with them with great pleasure, and unite in farther consultation on the important subject, begging this favor at the same time of the rest, who do not like our employment, that they would not come into the room to interrupt us; and this they cannot think a hardship, as they certainly can lose nothing by it, for I really have not one word more to say to them.

If it is granted that the currency ought not to be appreciated up to its original value, *I cannot see a shadow of reason why it should be appreciated at all, and not be fixed at its present value.* The *truth* is always better than *any thing near it,* altho' ever so near. Every shilling that it may be appreciated

ciated is added to the public debt, for which the public receives not the *least advantage*, but all the *profit* goes to the *great hoarders* of our currency; for those who have no more on hand than just the amount of their whole tax get nothing by it. There remain then but two things to be considered: 1st. *What the present exchange of the currency is;* and 2dly. *How to fix it to that exchange or value.*

I. As to the first of these there is a difficulty, principally arising from this, viz. that the exchange is not the *same* in all the States, but *different* in the different States, and this difference is not fixed in the different States, but sometimes varies in the several parts of the same State. But it is here to be observed, that the exchange of the several parts of the State differs very little from that which prevails in the great capitals nearest to them, and what little variation there is, most generally appears to lie in this, viz. that the exchange rises *first in the great capitals,* and the *out towns,* of less trade, follow pretty *quickly* after them; so that the exchange of each State may be pretty safely taken from that of its capital, or the great capital to which it is most contiguous.

The rule by which I find the true exchange at any given time is, to take the exchange which prevailed at the given time in each State, and add them all together and divide the sum by 13, and the quotient will be the mean exchange or value of the currency. For instance, by the best advice I can collect, the exchange *last Christmas,* or *December* 25, 1779, was, in the four *New-England* States, *New-York, North* and *South Carolina,* and *Georgia, i. e.* in eight States, at 35 for 1, and in *New-Jersey, Pennsylvania, Delaware, Maryland,* and *Virginia, i. e.* in five States, at 40 for 1, their sums will stand thus,—

$$8 \text{ into } 35 \text{ is } - - - 280$$
$$\text{And } 5 \text{ into } 40 \text{ is } - - - 200$$
$$\text{Sum, } 480$$

which sum divided by 13 gives a quotient of $36\frac{12}{13}$ or 37 nearly, which I suppose to be the true mean exchange or

averaged

averaged value of the currency, through all the Thirteen States, at that time.

The present exchange in this city is 45 to 1, and the exchange was rising both to the eastward and southward when the last advices came away, so that I suppose the present mean exchange may safely and truly be fixed at 40 for 1, but our future advices will soon determine this beyond all doubt. This is throwing aside all theory and speculation, and grounding my computation entirely on fact, and is a method which I expect will be allowed to be fair, true, and unexceptionable; *and at this value I propose that the currency should be fixed at present, and be finally redeemed at the same.* Both these I conceive very just and practicable.

I do not think there is any justice in taxing the public to appreciate any man's money in his chest beyond the present value. This would be burdening the public, merely for the benefit of a few individuals of monied men; for I before observed that no person could take benefit of such an appreciation, but such as have more money on hand than all their taxes for redeeming the whole currency will amount to; and those few among us who have such a surplus of money are the men who have the least occasion of assistance from the public, and in general have the least right to expect or even to wish it. For a further consideration of this I refer back to all the reasons I have given against an appreciation.

On the other hand, it will be readily granted that every principle of justice requires that any further depreciation of our currency should, if possible, be prevented. The *practicability* of both these, *i. e. of fixing the currency*, deserves our most serious consideration; and here, notwithstanding the unaccountable and seemingly capricious fluctuation of the exchange, both in progressive and retrograde motion (for we have frequently seen both) yet I say, this notwithstanding, I do contend *there are great natural principles, which, if properly applied, will confine this slippery subject, fix it to a point, and prevent such fluctuation as will greatly prejudice its use.*——To prevent an APPRECIATION,

I. As

I. As the currency has no real fixed value in itself, it is necessary that *it should be connected, tied, or fastened firmly to something that is fixed, which may hold it steady,* as an anchor does a ship, which keeps its place by that connection, let the wind or tide set either way. Such a fixed medium is hard money, the value of which cannot vary much from its value in *Europe*, and therefore its permanency may be safely depended on. To this end I propose,

1. *That an order of Congress be passed, that hard money shall be received for taxes and all other payments into the Continental Treasury, at the present value or fixed exchange;* say 40 for 1. For as the demand for taxes will be very great and universal; if the present system of taxation be carried into effectual execution, as it doubtless will be, it will not be possible for any man to get a better exchange than is received in the public treasury.

2. *I propose that a resolution pass to redeem the whole currency finally at the present value;* say 40 for 1. This will effectually take away all inducement to raise the value of it beyond the exchange which can finally be obtained for it, when it shall be redeemed. I do apprehend that my reasons before assigned against the appreciation will prove the justice, good policy, and necessity of these resolutions, to which I therefore refer.

3. *I propose that all public estimates, quotas, payments, &c. be made in hard money, or Continental equal to it at the current exchange,* and also *that all judgments of courts, fees, salaries, &c. should be made up in the same manner,* that so no public community or private person should receive either injury or benefit from any future fluctuation of the currency, either up or down, if such should happen, any farther than his cash on hand might be affected by it. This would not only be an effectual remedy of the crying injustice, both public and private, which has too long prevailed among us, but will also take away the principal inducement and temptation to attempt any fluctuation of the currency.

4. I propose, for the more effectual operation of this remedy, *that all the tender acts, all laws against dealing in hard money, and every other of that nature which now subsist*

in any of the States, may be repealed. As those acts were mostly made on the recommendation of Congress, I apprehend a recommendation of that honorable body to the several States for such repeal might be necessary.—It appears to me that these propositions will most effectually prevent any future *appreciation* of our currency.

But it may be said here, we are sufficiently out of danger of that, the present labor is stop the *depreciation*. But I do not know all this. I have many reasons to fear an appreciation, which would be a very ruinous calamity if it should happen, and I think we may do well to use precautions against a possible evil; and I have at least the common argument of quacks in favor of my propositions, " that they are innocent, they can do no hurt, and they " may do good." If the event to which they are designed to be applied should happen, they will be of the utmost use and benefit; if that event should not happen, their operation will be prevented, and no bad effects can proceed from them. I am as sensible as any man of the urgent necessity of preventing a farther depreciation, and therefore recur to such great natural principles as I think will most effectually and assuredly remedy the mischief; and here I hope it will not be taken amiss, if I repeat some things I have heretofore advanced; for great truths, and weighty principles of decisive importance, ought often to be repeated, that they may be better kept in mind. I proceed then, to prevent DEPRECIATION,

II. To observe, that *one great cause of depreciation is the increase of the quantity of our currency, and therefore the quantity must by no means be increased.* For it is not possible to prevent the operation of such increase on the depreciation. It matters not in what shape such an increase may appear, whether *of Continental bills, certificates, bills on* Europe, *or bills of particular States. If the quantity in circulation is increased, it is not in the nature of the thing possible to prevent the effect of depreciation, which must and will flow from that increase.* Therefore, *the incomes must be made equal to the expenditures.* This will give the currency a quick circulation, sufficient for every purpose, without any increase of
its

its quantity, will raise that demand for it, which is essential to its nature and use, and from its natural operation will prevent any possibility of depreciation, if the confidence of the public in its final redemption can be made entire and free of doubt.

And this brings me to the consideration of another great principle, on which the credit of all bills must depend, viz. *the final redemption of the bills must be made certain, and the value or exchange at which they shall be finally paid or redeemed must be certainly known.* If there is any doubt of either of these in the minds of the people, that doubt will lessen the value of the bills; for a certainty will always be better than an uncertainty, i. e. the credit of the States must stand so firmly connected with their real substance, that there can be no doubt but the one will be supported by the other. The life and use of money lies in a quick and ready circulation; yet, although this circulation should be ever so brisk, if it passes from hand to hand, like *Robin's alive*, in constant danger of *dying in the last hand*, it must, notwithstanding all its signs of life and vigor, depreciate fast; and *I conceive a general confidence or doubt of this kind has operated more on our currency than people are generally aware of.*

In the gloomy aspect of our affairs in the winter of 1778, when the *British* army had possession of *Philadelphia*, the exchange rose to 6, 7, and 8 *for* 1. In the summer and fall of the same year, when we began to feel the great effects of General *Gates*'s *success*, the *English* sued for peace and their army left *Philadelphia*, our alliance with *France* was formed, with a prospect of the accession of *Spain*, and a powerful *French* fleet was on our coast, the exchange fell to 4 *for* 1, and kept down for many months together.

But when our sanguine expectations began to abate, new difficulties arose, and the multiplied emissions had swelled the quantity of our currency to an enormous amount, beyond any probability or even possibility of payment *at full value*, there ensued a *great abatement of the general confidence*, and mighty doubts arose whether it would ever be redeemed at all, or, if it was, at what value; and these doubts increased with the increase of the quantity, and some other causes,

causes, till the exchange rose up to the enormous height which now exists. The principal causes of these doubts, and consequently of the depreciation, I take it, have been *the uncertainty of the fate of the war, or support of our Independence, and the increasing enormous sum of our currency.* I conceive all doubts arising from the first of these causes are pretty well done away.

I think it is so far from remaining a doubt whether we shall support our Independence, that *I do not apprehend it is in our power to give it up if we were willing,* and to fall back into the dominion of *Great-Britain.* I am of opinion that *France* and *Spain,* and perhaps some other powers, must be conquered, before the *trade* or *government of America* can be permitted to be monopolized and controlled by *Great-Britain.* The vast *extent* of our country, the *fertility* of our soil, *salubrity* of our climates, with other natural advantages, together with the *rapid increase* of our people, agriculture, and arts, make us an object of vast importance, expectation, and attention with every trading country of *Europe,* and they will not easily give up the share of profit which they expect to derive from us.

If we continue to increase as we have done in time past, that is, to *double every* 25 *years,* the Thirteen States will contain more people at the end of the next century, than *France, Spain,* and *Great-Britain* together all contain at present. All *Europe* gaze with attention on our rising greatness, and it is a pity that *America,* like some *careless beauty,* should be the only person in the company, *insensible of her charms.* It is time for us to know our own importance, and not throw ourselves away in a needless despondency.

As to the doubts arising from the great quantity of our currency, and the consequent uncertainty of its redemption, I conceive they will be effectually removed by the foregoing propositions. The present debt of Continental money ceases to appear enormous; it does not exceed 5,000,000 *of hard dollars,* which is less than 2 dollars per head on the inhabitants; a light burden! a trifle! not adequate to the abilities of the poorest town in the Thirteen States. The only remaining doubt is, whether the States *will in fact pay*

pay this sum, small as it is. This doubt appears to me ridiculous; for were we to suppose there was not a grain of *honor* or *honesty* left in the Thirteen States, on which we could depend for the payment of their debts, yet they have suffered so much by the depreciation of their currency, that they will, from a principle of *self-preservation*, remedy the mischief, and prevent it in future. A burnt child dreads the fire, and certainly we have not lost all the feelings of human nature, however callous we may be to the inducements of moral principles.

But *my confidence, even in the morality of the States, is not shaken, it is entire.* It is my opinion our people are able and willing to do all that is necessary to be done in the present crisis. Nothing more is or can be necessary, than to put the matter in a *proper train of operation*.

Let the people see the *expenditures* made with *prudence and economy;* that the *demand* of public money is grounded on *public necessity only;* let them see men acting in the offices, through which the public monies are to pass, in whom they can have *confidence;* let them see a *system of finance* formed, which shall appear both *practicable and sufficient,* and put under *such direction* as shall afford a good probability of *prudent management and effectual execution;* let these things be done (and I do not take them to be mountains impracticable) and I conceive our public faith will be effectually restored, and rise to such a degree of respectability, that no branch of the revenue will dare to defraud the treasury, or withhold the supplies necessary to the public safety; nor, on the other hand, will our public faith prove a ruinous and infamous trap to those who have trusted their fortunes to its security.

I do not pretend these are light matters and without difficulty. *The forming a system of finance is an arduous work, fully equal to the abilities of a person of the strongest intellects, steady attention, and aptitude to the subject. It must be the work of* ONE MIND, *capable of the necessary attention to all the parts, and able so to comprehend and arrange the whole, as to form a system both practicable and sufficient. I do not think any aggregate body of men on earth able to do this.*

this. I am of opinion, that we might as well expect that a *General Assembly*, a *Parliament*, a *Diet* of an Empire, or a *Congress*, could describe and demonstrate the properties of the sphere, compute the force of falling bodies, define the laws of hydrostatics, or make an almanac, as form a system of finance.

The power of *superintendence* and *legal sanction* is theirs; but the *calculation and execution* of the system is not, in my humble opinion, compatible to the senatorial body. The *British* Parliament, some years ago, abolished the *Julian style*, and adopted the *Gregorian*, and gave it legal sanction, to the great satisfaction and benefit of the kingdom; but I never heard any man suppose that that Parliament was ever capable of *calculating or demonstrating* either of the styles; yet I do not apprehend that it is any reflection on the dignity, abilities, or competency of that Parliament to suppose, that, if nobody could have calculated styles better than they could, we might have done without any till this time, and computed the advance of the spring by the budding of white-oak trees, as the *Indians* do.

The consequence from all this is, in my opinion, that if a senatorial body want styles, systems, of finance, or any things else which require peculiar abilities, such as by common probability cannot be presumed to exist in such a body, they can only manifest their wisdom and employ their authority in appointing men of proper abilities to make them; then the Senate can *examine* and *correct* them, and *add their sanction* and authority, put the *execution of them* under a proper direction, and keep the *superintendence only* in themselves. I think it may easily appear, that *the nature of the subject limits the powers of a Senate to this line of conduct.*

But were it not so, good policy would prescribe this method; for *the ground of finance is, every step of it, most dangerous ground*. Errors are at first imperceptible and easily made, but soon shoot up into capital importance, and often assume a most hideous and ghastly appearance; all which is apt to throw disgrace and censure, and sometimes contempt, on the authors. That which proceeded from *ignorance* may be attributed to *bad design*. In any view, mistakes and disappointments prove the ignorance or imperfection of the managers, and there will always be some degree of *contempt due to persons* who undertake things which they *know not how* to perform.

Bodies of *supreme dignity ought never to incur censures or aspersions of this sort. The public always suffer, when the wisdom or integrity of their supreme power is called at all into question*. They ought, therefore, in all good policy, to appoint proper persons to do all business of this sort, were it only that they might have a *scape-goat* to bear away from themselves the censure, disgrace, and contempt which any errors might occasion, when they came to be discovered; for it is very observable, that when any error or misconduct happens in any great department of the State, the blame always falls on the *officer under whose direction it was made*. No part of the censure ever falls on the supreme power, unless it is that of making a *corrupt or injudicious appointment* of the officer, or taking the *management of the matter out of his hands* by too particular instructions.

On the whole matter, our country *abounds* with *men* and every sort of *supplies* which we need *(military stores and clothing* excepted, which are easily attainable from abroad). Our public counsels and measures are very little obstructed by *disputes* or *parties in opposition*. The great thing wanted is, to put our finances into such a *train, order*, or *system*, as will revive the public credit, bring our currency into such an established value and demand, as is necessary to its nature and use, and enable the public to call into use such services and supplies as are necessary to the public safety.

The abilities requisite to form and execute such a system are not to be found or expected in any *senatorial body; i. e.* by common probability it cannot be presumed, that the component members of such a body should be possessed of the rare and peculiar abilities requisite for this great purpose.

It remains then a matter of the highest and most urgent necessity, that a suitable person for the great office of *Financier-General*, or *Superintendent of Finance*, should be looked

looked up, and *appointed* as soon as may be, whose sole business should be to inspect and control our whole *revenue and expenditures*, and keep them in balance with each other.

I imagine this high office will not be very greedily sought or eagerly accepted by any person *capable* of it. It will require the most unwearied, unremitted application, the most intense and fixed attention to a subject of a most *intricate* nature and *great extent;* the *heart-felt interests*, the *loss or gain, the injury or benefit of millions*, will stand closely connected with his conclusions and management, and of course his errors, if he makes any (as from the intricacy and vast extent of the subject he undoubtedly must) his errors, I say, will incur the *severe resentment*, and raise the *merciless cry* of the inconsiderate and ill-natured, which make a considerable part of the world; and after all, if he conducts with success, he will get *little praise;* for every thing in his way will go smoothly on in a regular train, which will soon grow *familiar*, and of course *unnoticed*, and not *one in a thousand* will know to whom they are indebted for *their tranquillity*.

Besides, I do not know that the present *confusions* of our revenue are capable of being speedily reduced to *order* by any address of wisdom, skill, and diligence; and should he fail, the weighty burden might crush him in an instant, and he may fall, like *Phaëton*, ridiculous and unpitied, for undertaking a work for which, perhaps any degree of human wisdom or ability may prove insufficient. Be this as it may, much will depend on the *choice of this officer*. Should an insufficient man be appointed, his defects or mismanagement will not only be *severely felt* while he is in office, but most probably his *successor* may find a more difficult task to *correct* his errors, than to have taken up the matter *new*, and set out *right* at first.

But to return to the main point; the great question seems now to be, whether, in any practicable train or method, *it would be possible to raise money among ourselves equal to the necessary expenditures, i. e.* whether the people could pay such a large sum. To this I answer, the best method of judging of the mighty wealth and abilities of the States is, by reflecting

flecting on what they have paid in times paſt. The expenſes of the war for 5 years paſt have been about 11,000,000 of hard dollars per annum, beſides the loans, as will eaſily appear by computing the value of the bills emitted each year; and this has been all paid, except 5,000,000, and that in the *worſt*, moſt *diſtreſſing* and *oppreſſive* method that could be deviſed, viz. by the *depreciation* of the currency.

The payments of the laſt year, 1779, which were *actually made*, were much more than the ſaid ſum, for on the laſt day of the year 1778, the whole currency was ſomewhat more than 90,000,000, and the exchange was 6 to 1; conſequently, 90,000,000, divided by 6, will give in hard money the amount of our debt of continental money, viz. 15,000,000 of hard dollars, to which add the expenditures of the year 1779, viz. about 140,000,000 of dollars,* which is ſomewhat leſs than was emitted in that year. To find the value of this, we muſt divide it by the mean exchange of the year, which I conceive may be found by multiplying the exchange at the end of the year 1778, viz. 6 for 1, by the exchange at the end of the year 1779, viz. 40, which makes a product of 240, the ſquare-root of which, viz. 15½, nearly, is the mean exchange, and the ſum of expenditures of 1779, viz. 140,000,000, divided by ſaid mean exchange. viz. 15½, gives for quotient 9,000,000 of hard dollars, which, added to the amount of the debt at the end of the year 1778, viz. 15,000,000, makes ſomewhat

---

* It may be objected to this calculation, that 33,000,000 of the 140,000,000 of dollars emitted in 1779, were for exchanging the *emiſſions* of *May* 20, 1777 (8,000,000 of dollars) *and of April* 11, 1778 (25,000,000) which were called *out of circulation*; but this does not *diminiſh* but *increaſes* the *loſs* by depreciation, *which the States ſuffered in that year;* for the *whole* 140,000,000 were *really emitted* (it matters not on what occaſion) and all that the bills *ſunk in value* by depreciation from the time of *emiſſion* to the *end* of that year, was *loſt* by the States.

And as to the 33,000,000 of the ſaid *two emiſſions called in*, it is to be obſerved, that on the *laſt* day of the year 1778, they were worth at 6 for 1 (which was the exchange at that time) 5,500,000 of hard dollars; but on *Aug.* 1, 1779 (the *day appointed* by Congreſs for their *redemption)* the exchange was 20 *for* 1, and of courſe they *were worth but about* 1,700,000, which, ſubtracted from *their value* on the *laſt* of the year 1778 (5,500,000 hard dollars) leaves a *loſs of* 3,800,000 *of hard dollars*, which the States ſuffered that year by the depreciation of the ſaid *two emiſſions* only.

what more than 24,000,000; out of which subtract the debt now remaining, viz. 5,000,000, there remain 19,000,000 of hard dollars, which have been *actually paid* by the Thirteen States in the year 1779.*

The

* This proves the prodigious *strength* of the *American* States, and the very *great burdens* they *can* bear, as well as their *firmness* and *patience* in bearing them.

Indeed in the above calculations a very heavy, impoverishing part of their burdens was not brought into the account, viz. over and above what is there mentioned, they had to support *a tax* which the war itself imposed, more than *four times* as heavy as all the present duties of impost, with all the new additions, which the States now support, *i. e.* multiply the present impost laid on every article of imported goods by 4, and add the product to the old price-current of the same goods in 1774, and it will not raise them so high as the average price at which the same imported goods were sold thro' the war.

Add to this the losses which were sustained by the *extreme scarcity and want* of some necessary articles, *e. g.* much meat was *spoiled* and lost for *want of salt* to preserve it; many *trades* and *manufactures* were either wholly *stopped* or greatly *diminished* for *want of materials*, &c.

To all this may be added the *dire effects* of the depreciation of the currency on all *debts* and *money-contracts*, all *fees, salaries, taxes, fines*, &c. &c. Also the *distresses* and *losses* arising from the *limitations of the market*, the ruinous effects of which were *innumerable*, and in many instances *shocking* and almost *tragical*.

Another hardship very sensibly felt, was the *force* which was used with all descriptions of men in *seizing their goods, waggons, stock, grain, cattle, timber*, and *every thing else* which was wanted for the public service; most of which, if ever paid for, were paid in certificates, or depreciated money, the real value or exchange of which at the time bore but small proportion to the value of the supplies for which they were given.

The *bad management* of the *finances*, and of course their *deficiency*, made *some* of these methods indeed necessary to carry on the war; but at the same time they operated not only by way of great *injury* and *oppression* of individuals, but as a very *heavy tax* on the States.

Under all the forementioned pressures, a *murmur* at the *expense* of the war was scarcely heard, but the last mentioned *incidental evils* and *hardships* were matters of very *great* and *universal complaint*.

To all these direful sufferings may be added the *captures*, the *ravages* and *depredations*, the *burnings* and *plunders* of the *enemy*, which were very *terrible* and *extensive*; they had possession first or last, in the course of the war, of *eleven of the capitals* of the Thirteen States, pervaded the country in every part, and left dreadful *tracks of their marches* behind them; burned in *cool blood* a great number, not only of *houses, barns, mills*, &c. but also of most *capital towns* and *villages*.

The losses arising from all these, which were *really sustained* by the *American* States, must be *immense*.

Yet all this notwithstanding, such are the *riches, strength*, and *resources* of the States, that had any prudence in their *finances* and *police* been adopted and practised from *even the close of the war*, our country would by this time have recovered itself, and might have possessed and enjoyed all the blessings of general prosperity and full supplies.

But

The question is then reduced to this, viz. Whether it is not only possible, but much easier to pay 11,000,000 of hard dollars in some equitable mode, which distributes the burden on all in due proportion to their abilities, than it was last year to pay almost *double that sum* in the most unequal and oppressive way imaginable. I know it will require strong exertions, but we began the war with this expectation and resolution, and I do not think our people will shrink or give back under the burden when it comes.

Besides, it does not appear to me possible to increase our circulating cash in any way, without further depreciating it, which at once destroys its use, and the very end we should have in view by increasing it. Loans will do this; for every loan makes a new certificate or bill of some sort, and all these will flow into circulation as soon as they gain that established value which they ought to have, and which they must have, before we can borrow without a loss or discount.

I think it manifestly reasonable, *that all loan-office certificates should be redeemed at the exchange which existed at their dates,* and that there should be a rate of exchange from the first depreciation down to the present time made, to ascertain the exchange at the time when each bill was dated, and a sure *interest,* in proportion to the value of the principal, should be secured to the possessor, until the certificate shall be paid. If this was done, we might borrow, perhaps, without a discount or loss, and keep our debt at home, which would be much better than drawing bills on *Europe* at a loss of 30 or 40 per cent. and contracting a hard money debt abroad. But this is digression. To return to my subject.

I do not really see but that general and heavy *taxes* are most absolutely necessary to *give demand* to our *currency,* animate the *industry* of our people, and *banish idleness, speculation,* and a thousand *visionary projects,* which prevail to
an

But whilst we rejoice in the riches and strength of our country, we have reason to lament, with tears of the deepest regret, the most pernicious shift of property which the above mentioned irregularities of our finances introduced, and the many thousands of fortunes which were ruined by it; the *generous, patriotic spirits* suffered the *injury;* the *avaricious* and *idle* derived *benefit* from the said confusion.

an alarming degree, and which muft *vanifh* into nothing *foon*, and therefore the *fooner the better*. Taxes will increafe the circulation of our currency, which will increafe its ufe quite up to the full amount neceffary to all our needs, nor can I fee any other way in which we can carry on the war, without incurring fuch an enormous debt at the end of it, as will mix the very *joys* of eftablifhed *liberty* with *bitternefs*, and even endanger that very *liberty* itfelf, for which we have fo ftrenuoufly *contended*, and for which *the debt itfelf* was contracted. *The writer* of *three letters on appreciation*, has advifed us to fet the *preffes a going again*, and in the *plenitude of calculation* made out that the depreciation or exchange, at the end of the year 1780, would in that cafe be about 68 *to* 1; but had he founded his calculation on fact (on the fuppofition that the depreciation would be no greater this year than it was laft, which is not true) he would have found the depreciation or exchange, at the end of the year 1780, at leaft 260 *to* 1, and probably it would be more than *double*, perhaps the *treble* of that exchange, if it fhould continue to *pafs at all* thro' the year, which is far from a certainty. This method then will not do.*

From all which it appears pretty plain we have but two things before us, viz. to raife as much money as will be fufficient to *pay* our expenditures *as we go;* or, if we cannot do this, to *reduce* our expenditures to the fum which we *can pay*. For to talk of keeping up a greater expenfe than we *can pay* any how, is abfurd and ridiculous to a very contemptible degree. To borrow abroad is ruinous, and nothing is plainer than that we cannot hold it out long in this way; and what is worfe, our enemies muft know this, and thereby be encouraged to continue the war againft us.

To

---

* The exchange of the currency at the end of the year 1780, *without the preffes, or additional emiffions*, was *up to* 75 *to* 1; but no man can tell what it would have been, had the *preffes kept going* thro' that year.
  Indeed the final redemption of the Continental money began to be much doubted, or rather confidered *defperate*, about that time, which increafed the depreciation far beyond what the *quantity* only in circulation would have produced, for the value of the whole of it at the end of the year 1780 (when the exchange was 75 for 1) was lefs than 3,000,000 of hard dollars, which is not more than one fourth part of the current cafh of the States.

To borrow at home destroys the very end and use of the loan as it goes. The great purpose cannot be served in this way. *What we can raise among ourselves is all that we can pay, and we cannot attempt expenditures beyond this without bankruptcy.*

A peace cannot be expected till the end of the great contest between *three* of the greatest powers of *Europe*, which may involve more powers in the dispute. It is a matter of such high point of honor, pride, and interest with them all, especially *Great-Britain*, that they will strain the last nerve for superiority before they will yield an ace, and the war may last many years; the consequence of all this is, that *we must take up the matter as we can hold out.*

A man who has a long race before him is mad, if he *exhausts* all his strength *in the first mile*. A certain degree of exertion we are capable of, beyond which we cannot go; within this we must keep and confine ourselves. This degree ought to be calculated *with great judgment*, and used with *great economy*, and with the *most effect* it will bear, but it cannot be exceeded without the mighty and tremendous danger of *final ruin*.

These are my best thoughts, the subject is too vast, too unexplored for my comprehension. This is my fourth address to the public on this weighty theme. I am obliged for the favorable reception of the other three, hope the same candor will be extended to this. My thoughts are free, the nature and incidents of the subject dictate my argument. Great *natural principles* will always *make their own way* in the end; and if they are ever *rejected*, it is because they are not rightly *apprehended*, and any *departure* from them will be *checked* and *reformed* by *dear experience.*

My close attention to this great and intricate subject has taught me that it baffles all speculative theory and calculation. The only safe basis of every principle of reasoning on it must be fact or experiment. Here I drop my pen, ready to stand corrected by the better thoughts and more useful discoveries of any superior genius.

A

A FIFTH ESSAY

ON

FREE TRADE and FINANCE.

First published in Philadelphia, March 30, 1780.

THE expenditures of the present year 1780, are estimated (as I am told) at about 10,000,000 of dollars hard money. This sum must be raised and paid, or our defence must be discontinued; we must lose our liberties and probably many of our heads too; our struggles must vanish into smoke and disgrace; and our glorious *revolution* must be dubbed *rebellion*, and punished as such, and how much more God knows. The said *sum* must be *raised*, or *these miseries must ensue*. We have no other alternative, and it is vain and idle to amuse ourselves with any hopes or even shadows of any other. Our *defence* cannot be continued without the *necessary money*; if that ceases, we instantly lie open to the full power of our enemies, and must submit to any conditions they may prescribe.

This I take to be the plain state of the facts; stubborn facts, which can neither be removed, eluded, or softened, by any possible *finesse*, *coloring*, or *evasions*. We may as well keep them in *sight* as to *shut our eyes* against them; for *facts they are, and will have their operation, which we must feel, whether we will see them or not*. If the expenditures, on which the estimates are made, can be reduced, doubtless every possible attention will be paid to such an object, but we cannot flatter ourselves that any very considerable savings can be made in this way; it only remains then that we set ourselves *immediately* to raise the money, or give up the cause in despair. I say IMMEDIATELY, for it will soon be too late; every department will be so involved in debt, and the difficulties, disappointments, and confusions thence arising will multiply so fast, that no remedy can be admitted.*

In a crisis of danger, when the most spirited and resolute efforts are called for, to see *men* like children stand with one hand in their eyes, and the other in their mouths, blubbering out with voices half assured, *I cannot! I cannot! I dare not! I dare not!* is ridiculous, argues such meanness of spirit, such heartless cowardice, I am ashamed of it. If I really thought the people of *America* capable of this, I would not move a finger to save them from that slavery and subjection for which they must, in that case, be so well fitted by nature; it would not move my pity to see them *lashed* by their masters into that *severity* of effort, which their cowardly souls had not *animation* enough to *exert* in defence of their own liberties.

The very *taxes* which we now hesitate to *impose on ourselves* to defend and secure our liberties, will, I dare say, be

---

* To this Essay, when first published, the following preface was prefixed, viz. " The urging taxes, I know very well, is an unpopular task, and generally meets a *sour reception* and very *little thanks;* but the *belly* must be fed, or all the *members* must perish, and it is not possible it should *convey* nutriment which it does not *receive.* When we find a general decay and weakness spreading into every limb and nerve of the body, it is time to attend very seriously to the *malady*, and every other consideration must give place to the *remedy.* If there is a disorder or worm in the bowels which devours much of the food, it is a sad circumstance indeed, but still the belly must be fed, while we are taking every method in our power to extract or kill the worm. *Truth,* however disagreeable, *will force itself* into notice and attention, and *to know it is always* safer than *to be deceived;* our *deception or ignorance* will not retard the hasty steps *of ruin.* The man who *points out* the real distresses and dangers or errors of the State, does not *make* them; the knowledge of them tends to a remedy. I therefore hope my humble attempt may be received with candour, however disagreeable the subject, a present and diligent attention to which, I conceive absolutely necessary to the public safety. man can *avoid* my propositions, or *substitute better*, he may *serve* the and *will not disoblige* me."

be *impofed* and *rigidly extorted* by our enemies, whenever they fhall get their yoke on our necks: the price which they will make us pay for our *chains*, will be greater than that which is now neceffary to pay for our *liberty*: the *temporary* burdens which are now demanded to fecure the well-being of ourfelves and pofterity, will be made *perpetual* on us and them by our enemies, when they fhall find it neceffary to fecure *our* flavery and *their* luxury: for did any man ever know or read the hiftory of any country, governed as an appendage of a diftant empire, that was not fleeced, if not fkinned and peeled to the bone, by their diftant, unfeeling, unfympathizing defpots. Such countries are never, in fuch cafe, eftimated by any other fcale, than the amount of the revenue and other advantages that can be drawn from them.

I do not really think that the people of the United States are at all the proper fubjects of this kind of government; I do not think a meannefs of fpirit, a grofs ftupidity, or cowardly diffidence makes any part of their character; they have, in fact, refented injuries, afferted their liberties, and nobly dared to defend them, with a degree of exertion, perfeverance, and firmnefs, unparalleled and almoft beyond belief. It is my opinion that we may fafely depend on any *degree of exertion* and *fpirit* in our people, which is neceffary to their fafety; and if this is not all called out and put in force, when and to any degree the public fafety may require it, the fault will lie in the *rulers*, not in the *people*.

Indeed I am of opinion, there are few inftances of any countries over-run or enflaved, thro' any *defect of virtue* in the *people*, which does not originate in their *rulers*; the natural and common fource of remedies lies in the rulers, and if they are good, they will fee the mifchief, and apply the remedy, before it rifes to fuch force as to endanger the liberties of a country. If vice or corruption gets ground in any popular ftate, it generally difcovers itfelf pretty early in the appointment of *officers of notorious improper character*, or infufficient abilities, to fill and manage the important departments of the ftate; for where any corruption or prejudice prevails in any state, they will generally endeavour to get into place, such officers as are likely to *support such corruption or prejudice*.

In this case, the mischief is carried into the very *source of remedy*, and corruption gets a whip-row, which gains by every movement; and if this whip-row cannot be broken, the game must soon be up, and there remains nothing to do, but to set again, and try a new game. But as all that is *not our case*, this may be deemed a needless digression: we will come then directly to what *is our case*, which I will here endeavour to state as it stands in fact, which no fretting, or jesting, or shrugging can alter.

I. The estimates of the present year amount to about 10,000,000 of hard dollars, or the value of them, which must *be paid* by somebody, or *our defence cannot be continued*. If this ceases, our country must lie open to the unrestrained ravages and plunders of our enemies, and every obnoxious individual be exposed to their vengeance, and we have seen enough of them to know that their tender mercies are cruelty. And the only question I conceive that can arise here is this, Whether this heavy burden shall be laid on a *part only* of our people, and crush them into ruin; or whether it shall be laid *equably on all?* In the latter case, heavy as it is, it may be borne; it will not amount to more than 4 dollars on each person, or 20 dollars on a middling family of 5 persons. If there is a beggar in the Thirteen States who cannot pay this, he must have some rich neighbours who can pay it for him; and it lies with each State to *apportion* their taxes in such manner as to *ease the poor*, and *increase the share of the rich*, so as to bring the burden on all in due proportion to their abilities.

If, instead of this, the whole weight must lie on a few, viz. such as happen to have the supplies necessary for public use; if the wheat, hay, &c. must be *torn from the farmer;* the rum, salt, &c. from the *merchant;* the services of the *soldiers, waggoners,* &c. be *compelled by force;* if in this way our supplies and services are to be *extorted from a few,* whilst the *rest* bear nothing, the community must

must suffer much more than it would do, were the burden equally proportioned on all.

For to say nothing about the *execrable injustice and wickedness* of this method, the *resentment and rage* it will excite, the *discouragement to the future industry* of the farmer, or *adventure* of the merchant, the *reluctant recruits* of the army, hereby occasioned; to say nothing of these, it is as manifest that a heavy burden may be borne by a whole community with more convenience than the same can be borne by a part only; as that a large beam of timber can be borne by 20 men, each bearing in proportion to his strength, better than by 10 only who are crushed by the weight, whilst the other 10 bear nothing, or perhaps some of them *hang on and increase* the weight. The 10 who are crushed and overstrained will be rendered unfit *to bear any burden* in future time, and of course their future services will be *lost* to the community; whereas if the whole 20 bore each his due proportion, it might be a heavy lift indeed, but none of them would be *overstrained*, and they would all be *fit* for future service.

II. *Our currency is in such a feeble* and *fluctuating state, that the ends and uses of it are much decayed, and in a manner lost; it ceases* to be a certain *security* to the possessor of any *determinate value,* and of course cannot be a common measure of value for other things; so that it becomes impossible to calculate or carry on our *private business* or *public operations* with this medium, and of course both must cease, or be greatly impaired by this mischief.

This may be easily and speedily remedied by taxes; for if every bill of our currency was a *Turkish turban*, we might easily set any price on it we pleased, and make the demand quick at that price, in this way; for was an adequate tax made, and speedily and rigidly pressed, obliging every man to pay a turban or 10 dollars into the public treasury, it is manifest the price of a *turban* would immediately be 10 *dollars*, and the demand quick at that price. For the same reason, we may raise the value and demand for our currency to any pitch or degree we please, in the same way, viz. by making a tax for any sufficient sum of

continental

continental dollars, or the value in hard money, at any exchange we please to fix. This would immediately raise the continental money up to that exchange, if the tax was large enough, and sufficiently pressed.

Indeed we manifestly have it in our power to increase the demand and value of our currency to a much *higher degree* in this way, than either the fixing the currency or the *public exigencies* require. This is a matter that requires great judgment and nicety of observation. Some may think there may be danger of oppression here; but I answer there is neither danger nor possibility of oppression, if the exchange is not fixed higher or lower than the current exchange or *real present* value, nor more money required than is necessary for the public use, and the States apportion the tax on their people properly according to their several abilities; all which ought to be very carefully attended to; and if any part is not *done right*, the fault will lie on *those that do it*, but not at all on *the principle* here advanced.

But before we quit this idea, I beg leave to add one observation more here, viz. every honest individual, I conceive, *loses more* in a year by the present fluctuating state of our currency, and the present mode of procuring the public supplies, than his *whole tax* would amount to; he *loses his business* on which the support of himself and family depends, and must live on his dead stock, or at least is subjected to most material disadvantage and discouragement; for I submit it to every man to judge, whether any man, either in the occupation of *husbandry, mechanic arts, or merchandise*, can compute his business in such a manner, as to make it safe to put his *whole stock in action* in any of these ways, while he has no *reasonable assurance* what the produce of his diligence may be, or whether he may have *the selling* his produce, fabrics, or merchandise, when he has procured them.

The *occupations of life* are of such *great* importance to every man, that it is manifest that even small embarrassments in them, involve a *damage much greater* than any man's *tax would be* to the whole expenditures of the war.

This

This opens to our view another actual circumstance, another fact, which is too obvious to be overlooked, and too serious and interesting to be neglected, viz.

III. *The whole sources of our supplies are dying away fast, are lessening to an alarming degree, and threaten not a mere scarcity, but universal famine, want, and deficiency in a short time.* Most people are *lessening the business* of their several occupations down to a pitch just sufficient for their present occasions and necessities, and many have wholly *thrown up* their occupations, and live on their *dead stock*, and very few are calculating their business on any *large scale*. I submit the truth of this to common observation. The present *great demand* for merchandise, fabrics, and the farmers' produce, which would be the *sharpest spur* of industry, were our public counsels wise, and our currency good, now becomes the *terror of the possessors*, and induces them to *hide and conceal* their effects, instead of *exposing them in open market:* our public acts (for taking supplies by *force*) demonstrate this, for such acts are always supposed to *be suited to the circumstances of the times.*

This is a direct and manifest consequence of the numberless instances of *force* and *fraud* which have been practised to *rob* and *cheat* the possessors out of their goods. These methods are in every view mad, wicked, and absurd; *mad* in those who do not see the consequences of them; *wicked* in those who do see them; and *absurd* in both, because by their natural operation they soon *defeat and destroy the very ends* for which they are adopted, viz. *mending the currency,* and *procuring supplies.*

The great Creator has not given to all men equal discernment; some politicians are short-sighted, and cannot see the *distant* ill consequences of measures which yield a *present advantage,* but he must be a *stupid blockhead* who cannot see such effects when they *stare him in the face,* and stand in full fact *before his eyes.*

The proper remedy of these terrible mischiefs is to lay the public burden equally on all by taxes; this is easier, more reasonable, and more safe for the community, than to suffer it to rest upon a few. The burden must be borne
by

by the community in some way; the supplies and services cannot be procured for nothing; we have too lately tried it out and out, and have full proof that *something* cannot be paid for with *nothing*, and therefore if something is to be paid for, it is vain and ridiculous to be casting about, and starting and chasing one *visionary project* after another, of *new emissions and better emissions*, of *loans foreign and domestic*, &c. We must recur to *solid wealth* to pay for all our *solid supplies*. The nature of the subject will drive us to this at last, and the longer we put it off, the longer our miseries will increase; and God grant that we may not put it off till all remedy is desperate.

We must at last have recourse to the solid wealth of the States, and every individual must be called on for his share. In this there can be no reason of complaint; the *cry of oppression* will cease; that *demand* will be given to our currency which *is essential to its nature and use;* and every possessor of supplies will hasten to offer them: this will stimulate the industry of men of all occupations, and fill our country with virtue and plenty. But it may be objected here,

1. That our old currency is got so much out of repute, that it cannot be reformed, but may be *called in*, and replaced with a *new and better one*. I answer, all that ails the old currency is, that it is not, it carries not in it, a sufficient *certain security* of any determinate value to the possessor; and this same thing will ail the *new currency* or *any currency* we can make, unless we can *mend the public faith* on which it depends, and *connect* it so manifestly and firmly with the *real wealth* of the States, that the *security may be undoubted*. It is impossible this can be done by any thing but payment, either present or so secured, that there will remain no doubt in the mind of the possessor that it will be *bona fide* made. If this can be done, there is no doubt but we may make our currency good, yea, better than hard money, because it is *sooner counted*, and more *easily conveyed*.

There is indeed one reason for calling in the old currency, and issuing a new one, which appears to me to have real and great weight, viz. Many of the bills of the present

sent currency are *counterfeited*, and it is very neceffary the public should be freed from these impositions; and to this another may be added, viz. It would be very desirable to have a currency which should *express the true value* of the bills in *the face of them*. The present bills carry but a *fortieth part* of the value expressed *in their face;* and this holds out the *feeble, enervated,* and *debilitated state of our public credit* in so glaring a light, and publishes our *shame* and *distress* so very undeniably and universally, that I should be willing to have them out of sight; as people generally endeavour to keep out of view, *brands* and *marks* which indicate the *disgrace* of their families.

Besides, there is a sort of deception in the bills, which I conceive to be hurtful; when a man gets a great bundle of them, he is apt to be cheated in spite of the convictions of his own heart, into an opinion that he is *richer* than he is, and of course to *abate* a little of that *economy* which he would think neceffary if his mind was not *dilated* by that delusion; whilst, on the other hand, the taxes appear more *heavy* and *terrible* when heightened under the enormous denomination of the currency, than they would do were they offered and demanded in *a shape* that corresponded to their real value.

These may perhaps by general consent be allowed good reasons for calling in the present bills and issuing new ones, and this may be well enough, if the mode and regulations of the measure are limited to its uses.

But the *substance is yet wanting*, every thing neceffary to give *fixture* to the currency is *still to be done*, and *all* remains to be done, and will remain so, till we can *fix the funds* of our currency so sure as to make it a *certain security of real value* to the possessor, and call it in so fast by taxes as to *limit its quantity* within the uses of circulation, and prevent its increasing to such amount as to render the *final redemption difficult, improbable*, or *uncertain*. This is the grand gift of the whole matter; this will effectually *save us;* lefs than this *will not;* all the *rest* is but shifting the weights in the scale, without adding a single ounce to help a balance or preponderation; this therefore is our great object, from which

which our attention must *not be diverted*, no, not *for a moment;* on this our *fate* depends.

2. It may be further objected, that no nation of *Europe* can carry on a war without loans, or some way anticipating their revenue, and running in debt, and how can it be supposed that we can do it otherwise? I answer, their case differs from ours very materially.

1. They have *credit to borrow on*, which we have not, unless we allow such a ruinous discount as makes our affairs desperate, and must soon put it out of our power to preserve our liberty.

2. Our country is *richer*, more full of *men and stores* necessary in war, than those of *Europe* in general, and of course the carrying on the war without running in debt is more practicable by us, than by them.

3. They have such sure and established *systems of finance fixed and settled,* on which they can issue internal bills, as furnish a *certain security* to the possessor, of payment; their treasuries are the safest repositories of their nation's wealth; we have not these advantages, our treasury has hitherto proved the *destruction of the wealth* that has been *trusted to it,* and of course every body is afraid of it, and therefore loaning at home to any great amount is impracticable, and what *cannot be done* need not be urged as *politic, eligible* or *salutary.*

4. If any nation of *Europe* borrows specie, and thereby *increases* and of course *depreciates* their cash but 2 or 3 per cent. that discount is enough *to spread it all over Europe,* by which the balance is soon restored, and the depreciation is checked; or if any nation, as *Spain,* imports money from *Peru,* and makes it over plenty and of reduced value, it spreads over *Europe* directly; and so by covering a larger surface the depreciation becomes insensible, and the inconvenience little felt: but this is not the case with us; *our currency cannot be exported,* were it ever so good, therefore, any increase of quantity must have its full effect by way of depreciation among ourselves; and of course any *increase of the quantity* destroys at once the very end and use of such increase, as the *value* cannot be thereby *increased,*

but

but instead of this, the whole deluge of mischiefs arising from a fluctuating currency must flow in upon us.

5. The very *operation of this method of loaning, and anticipating* of the revenue, adopted and practised by the nations of *Europe*, is in itself enough, were it ever so practicable by us, to deter us from following so *fatal an example*. See *Great-Britain* enervated and benumbed under the pressure of an enormous debt, the very interest of which consumes the best part of the richest revenue which the wealth, industry, and oppression of the nation can produce. How disheartening must it be for that people to struggle thro' the year merely to pay a corroding interest, which brings them *not the nearer* to the end of their misery, but only *keeps alive that gnawing vulture* that must *for ever* feed on their very entrails. I cannot but wonder that any man in his senses should hold up such a sad spectacle for an example to the *Americans*.

6. The nations of *Europe* never attempt to borrow money, till they have first *raised all the revenue they can within themselves,* and find it not sufficient; but this is so far from our case, that we have *never yet taxed half enough* to drain off that surplusage of money which the war has occasioned, and our capital distresses and difficulties have all along arisen from that *flood of money* which made it *too plenty* for use; even *hard money* will buy little more *than half* so much country produce as it would purchase before the war.

This mischief cannot be remedied by *increase of the quantity*, by loans or any other way, but must in its nature be checked by *draining off* and *lessening that quantity*, and thereby raising the demand for it which is essential to its use. From all this it appears to be weak and silly as well as absurd, to urge for our imitation the example of other nations, the very convenience, necessity, or even practicability of which depends on circumstances which do not apply at all to our case.

It is not the least danger of this practice that it *operates insensibly*, saps and mortgages our wealth before we know it; it operates like a *slow poison*, which is certain death, and more painful, tho' more slow and lingering, than the

sudden

sudden execution of the ball or sword. Indeed I look on all *insensible taxes* to be highly dangerous; a fatal *instance of which* we have in the *depreciation* of our own currency. I think it necessary that the people should *see and feel* what they pay, should earn the money before it is spent; this would prevent a thousand *stupid, foolish,* and *needless ways of spending the public money;* this would make the rulers careful how they adopt any *expensive operations,* and attentive to the strictest *economy* in the expenditure.

Insensible taxes are like *insensible perspiration,* which *weakens* the body, and *wastes* the constitution before the patient knows he is sick. Nature generally marks places of danger with signals of notice, and every mariner looks on one sunken rock as more dangerous than twenty that are above water; for this reason I think that every branch of the revenue should originate in such sensible and visible demands on the wealth of the people, that they may all feel and know *what they pay,* and what they *pay it for;* and this is, in my opinion, the surest way to keep a *treasury always supplied* with enough by the cheerful contributions of the people, when the public safety or convenience requires it, and to prevent *more than enough* being ever demanded or granted: a due attention to both these I take to be no small *branch* or even *pillar of policy* in every state. The foregoing survey of our mischiefs and remedies brings up to view another circumstance which appears to me a very plain fact, viz.

IV. Our distresses, dangers, and difficulties do not consist in a *want of any thing,* but in *over plenty,* in surplusage of cash, which is become so common and easy of acquirement, that it is slighted, it is little thought of, it is scarce an object of *desire,* much less of *animation;* our burdens are burdens *of cash,* that which is the *wish* and *want* of most other distressed people is *our misery;* like plethoric constitutions, whose *stamina are all good,* but are *overloaded* with too much blood. A sufficient bleeding, a proper *draining off* of this superfluous matter, would set us all right in a short time, and every part of the constitution would find *ease, relief,* and a *speedy return of life* and *vigor*

from

from the fimple operation of this moft obvious, natural remedy. On the whole matter, I think that one more fact offers itfelf to view, which were we in a *lefs torpid ftate*, might animate us to fome fpirited efforts, fome lively exertions to extricate ourfelves from diftrefs and danger, viz.

V. Every circumftance confpires to demonftrate that the *moft fure and effectual remedies are in our own power*, are *very practicable*, and the prefent time is the *moft fuitable for the application of them* that any nation in diftrefs ever had or could wifh. We are *free of debt*, at leaft of the *preffures* of debt; the whole public debt at home and abroad does not exceed our abilities, and may be paid in two or three years without any painful exertions. We are yet *on this fide of that bottomlefs abyfs of debt*, into which our enemies find themfelves plunged; that infupportable but everlafting burden that preffes and exhaufts them in fo fatal a manner, that they are become the fport of their enemies and neglect of their friends; none appears for them in this their day of diftrefs.

This *enervating, difheartening circumftance we are yet free of*; our ftrength is *our own*, and in proper condition for ufe; we are yet to receive the fruits of our own labors; none of our crops are mortgaged or fold before they are reaped; our wealth is entire; our country abounds with moft of the fupplies and ftores we need; we have no difficulty but in the *diforders of our finances*, and they are not only *capable of being reftored*, but *felf-prefervation will compel us to it*. We are like a ftrong man who is obliged to labor, but the labor required is but juft enough to afford that degree of exercife which is abfolutely neceffary *to his health*, and which he muft practife or *be fick*.

The fame *kind and degree of exertion* neceffary to reftore our *currency*, reinftate our *finances*, eftablifh our *credit*, and animate the *induftry* of our people, will at the fame time pay our *civil lift*, and *carry on the war*. Our enemies are in a declining ftate, under great degrees of embarraffment, and have their hands full in every quarter, and every body *againft them*; whilft we *are courted*, like the rifing fun, by every

every body; our alliances and connexions are of the surest and best kind, grounded on *such interests* as cannot deceive us; a general *union* prevails among ourselves; our public *counsels* are all dictated by the *same views* and ends, and if ever we differ, it is only about the *means* of obtaining the *same end;* our relief indeed requires the animated exertions of our people, but the very distress they all feel, makes them willing to put into vigorous practice, any efforts which tend to their deliverance.

Here I beg leave to call the reader's attention to the *act of Congress of the 18th of March* 1780, respecting our finances, that we may, on the best examination, judge how far that important act, if duly executed, will reduce our finances into such method, and give them such establishment as the public safety requires. It is necessary that the nature, design, and use of that act should be thoroughly discussed, because the efforts for its execution will probably take their tone from the degree of conviction which generally prevails of its utility.*

I do

---

* The substance of said act is as follows, viz.

1. The monthly tax of 15,000,000 of dollars, from *Feb.* to *Aug.* 1780 (recommended to the States, *Oct.* 7, 1779) is continued to the 1st of *April*, 1781, inclusive.

2. That hard money be receivable in payment of said tax, at the rate of 1 *Mexican* dollar in lieu of 40 Continental dollars.

3. That the Continental bills paid in for said tax, except for the months of *Jan.* and *Feb.* 1779, be not *re-issued*, but *destroyed*.

4. That as fast as those bills shall be brought in to be *destroyed* (and other *funds* shall be established *for other bills)* other bills be issued, not to exceed on any account one twentieth part *of the nominal sum of the bills brought in to be destroyed.*

5. That the new bills which shall be issued, be *redeemable in specie* within 6 years from *Jan.* 1, 1781, and bear an *interest* of 6 per cent. to be paid *in specie* at the *redemption* of the bills, or, at the election of the holders, *in sterling bills of exchange*, at *4s.* 6d. *sterling per dollar.*

6. That the said new bills issue on the *funds* of individual States to be established for that purpose, and be *signed by persons appointed by them.*

7. That the United States *be likewise* pledged for the payment *of such of said* bills, as shall be signed by *those States*, who, by the *events* of the war, shall be *rendered incapable to redeem* them; which *undertaking of Congress* shall be *endorsed* on said bills, and be *signed by a commissioner of Congress.*

8. That the several States shall receive 6 *tenths of the bills which they sign,* for their own use, and that the remaining 4 *tenths* shall be subject to the *orders of Congress*, but shall *be credited* to the several States who signed them.

9. That

I do not pretend to be adequate to such a discussion, and shall only beg leave to make a few remarks on it; and this I am induced to do at this time, because the act is but lately published, and our people have not had time to make up their minds on it, and I conceive many persons misapprehend the real design and true construction of it.

1. I take it that the design of the act *is not to be a substitute for taxes;* our public *credit or finances* want the same *support and supplies from our real substance, our material wealth, as they did before the act.* If the *new bills* are no better supported than the *old ones* were, they will *depreciate* as fast, become as *useless* and more *ruinous* than those, as these involve us in a vast debt of *interest*, which those did not. The past error of our finances is clearly seen, and the deluge of mischiefs resulting from it is severely felt, and the design of this act is not to *continue* but *prevent* those mischiefs in future, not to *repeat* our former error, but to *mend* it.

2. The act contains in it *a declaration or fixture of the present value* or *exchange* of the *public bills,* making them redeemable at *40 for* 1, or *6d.* in the pound, and this on the *highest reason,* grounded on such *rigid facts,* such real change of circumstances, as render the *fulfilment of the promises* contained in *the old bills, impracticable, injurious* to the public, *absurd,* and *useless,* as I think I have fully proved in my Fourth Essay; and all *clamor* and exclamation on this subject is as *idle* and *void of reason and sentiment,* as a clamor against any other promise, which, however properly made at first, is become, by a change of circumstances, either *impossible* or *highly improper to be performed,* of which we have daily instances in every part of human experience.

We

---

9. That the said new bills be *received in taxes* at the same rate *as specie.*
10. That the several States be called on to provide *effectual funds* to sink 1 *sixth part* of their respective quotas, annually, after *Jan.* 1, 1781.
11. That this act be despatched to the Executive of the several States, to be laid before their Assemblies, who are requested, as *soon as possible to provide certain* funds for the purposes of it, and take every *other measure* to carry it into *full and vigorous effect.*

We are to consider *the depreciation* of our currency as a *public calamity*, like a *blast*, a *deluge*, a *drought*, or *ravages* of an enemy, which affect every man as he happens to *stand* in their way, and to become their object; in all these cases the *mischief must lie where it lights*; it is doubtless so directed by Divine Providence, that each individual receives that degree of correction from it, which is suited to his own particular case.

In point of remedy, it is vain to inquire whether this *calamity arose from the public necessity*, or from the *fault* of any *individuals* or *boards* of our policy; for could we *find* and *punish* the faulty delinquents, their *heads or gibbets* might hang up *in terrorem*, as monuments of caution to *future financiers*, but can *avail nothing to the easement* of the calamity; our duty at present, and all we can do is, to *correct* the mischief in time, and *prevent* it in future.

3. It is objected to this act, that it *doubles the quantity* of circulating bills, because it issues 2 *dollars out* for 1 that *is brought in*, for 10,000,000 *of the new bills* are equal to 400,000,000 *of the old ones*, at the exchange of 40 for 1, prescribed in the act itself; that this will *clash with a former resolution* (of Sept. 1, 1779) "that the quantity of bills should not be increased *beyond* 200,000,000;" will tend to a *depreciation;* and render the *fixing* the medium more difficult, if not impossible. But I beg leave to observe here, that few laws would be salutary, or even tolerable, if they were executed up to the height of their letter; and I conceive that a prudent execution of this act will obviate all the ill effects arising from the above objections.

I do not conceive it to be the design of Congress that any part of the *new bills shall issue at all;* if it shall be found that it cannot be done *at their full value*, without any *depreciation;* or that they shall issue *any faster*, or to any *larger amount* than can be done, without any *depreciation;* for I can by no means admit the supposition, that the new bills are to be issued in *a depreciated state*, because that very depreciation *defeats their use*, renders them insufficient for the procurement of supplies, and involves us over again in the *miseries of a fluctuating currency*, whilst we are at the

same

same time loaded with a vast debt of hard money *to pay the interest of them.* I never doubted the integrity of Congress, and therefore cannot attribute to them such absurdity of design, even tho' the letter of their act might admit such a ruinous and absurd construction.

They reserve, in their act, 4 *tenths of the new bills for their own disposal,* which they will doubtless *issue in a manner safe* and *useful* to the States; whilst the other 6 *tenths* are left to the discretion of the States, who have every inducement to a *prudent issue of them,* as each state will stand bound to redeem both principal and interest of all they shall issue.

I am further told, that the Congress have it in contemplation *to appoint a Financier-General, of known gravity, judgment, and economy,* to *superintend* this great department, who can either *let out* or *withhold* the issues in such manner as to give the bills all the *effect* and *use* their nature will admit, without *overloading* the public credit, or *increasing the quantity* so far as to *lessen their demand,* and, by that means, *lose the whole benefit* by grasping at too much. This error is so fatal and recent, and the apprehensions of the people *wound up to such a pitch of alarm,* that I much doubt if *half* the proposed quantity of the new bills can be issued *without a sensible depreciation;* but experience will best show this, and prudence at the time must dictate the *practicable degree* which may be ventured on; and it is my opinion, that no possible height of public necessity can *justify exceeding such degree,* because that excess is a sure way to defeat the uses of the currency, and of course to increase the public necessities, let them be ever so high before.

The exchange is a sure barometer of the public credit, as it is of the trade, and will always serve as a safe monitor and guide to our counsels of revenue. It is the *vainest of all vanities* to imagine that a public bill is *worth a dollar* when it *will not bring it,* or that it is *worth any more than it will bring.* If it shall be found on trial that any larger sum than I have supposed, or that the whole 10,000,000 can be issued without depreciation, the public may safely receive the benefit of the whole; and the addition of the interest,

P

interest, which will be received by every individual that holds the bills, will compensate for the increase of his taxes to pay it.

This matter cannot be computed on with any exactness, without knowing the *whole amount of the current cash of the Thirteen States,* which I have not yet seen any where ascertained. I have heretofore on a few data made a sort of loose, rough computation of it, to be about 12,000,000 *of hard dollars;* but I have of late been collecting documents for a more exact calculation, and on a nearer view am induced to believe the amount will rather fall *short of that sum,* and perhaps very considerably; and I think farther, it is very manifest that we must have a *promiscuous circulation* of both *hard money* and *paper,* in order to keep the *exchange of them equal:* but this by the bye.

4. It may be further objected to this act, that we can have no security that *some necessity or other* will not be urged next year to make a *further addition to the emissions* of circulating bills, till they *will depreciate.*

But in answer to this, I am clearly of opinion, Congress will not be able to issue *the whole* 10,000,000 already voted *without a depreciation;* and also, that they will not dare to issue *any of it in a depreciated state;* this will so manifestly and immediately *ruin the use of the whole,* and defeat its *whole purpose,* and bring on afresh the mischiefs of a *fluctuating currency,* that I can have no idea that any men in their senses can think of adopting it.

But if we are to suppose our wisest men capable of such *idle frenzy,* it is needless to reason any further about it, we may as well give up *all use of our intellects,* and follow where wild distraction roves, and take the fate which a concourse of *whim and accident* shall provide for us: but I augur better things; I am full of expectation that before our affairs come to this pass, our wisest men, both in Congress and State-Assemblies, will be convinced of one great truth, dictated by nature and our present circumstances, viz. *that we must pay our expenditures as we go:* and this is the only practicable method before us; this will make any scheme good, which is not wretched indeed, and without this, every devisable scheme is but whim, vision, and frenzy.

5. The sum of 10,000,000 is not more than the States are able to make *the most sufficient* and *undoubted security for,* if they please. But let that security be ever so good; to give it a currency, and prevent a depreciation, they must raise a demand for it by general taxes. These are recommended by Congress in their act of the 18th instant, and others foregoing; and were they put under rigid collection by all the States, we might judge whether the demand thereby raised was sufficient to give life and use to the currency; if it should not be so, it is necessary that the taxes be still increased till that effect shall appear, at which time, and not before, the grand point will be gained, viz. that of fixing our currency. We shall then have the two great things necessary to fix any paper currency, viz. *good funds,* which may give the possessor a certain security; and a *quick demand* and circulation of the currency itself.

6. It appears then, that if the said act was put into proper and wise execution, duly limited and sufficiently vigorous, it will answer the great and important ends expected from it; and tho' it may not be thought the *best possible,* yet as it appears to be sufficient for its purpose, were it duly put into operation, and properly supported, I think it clear that the States ought not to *hesitate adopting* it, nor *starve* it by too languid and dilatory movements; the best plan possible may be rendered useless and ineffectual this way; wisdom and decision in counsel are not more necessary in any important plans of this sort, than vigor in execution.

I do not consider the act so much a scheme of increasing the revenue as of fixing the currency; but if it is to include both, the first certainly depends on the *last,* and *is limited by it;* for Congress cannot think of issuing any part of the new bills in a depreciated state; they must fix their value, or it is idle, dangerous, and ineffectual to the last degree to issue them; if they can be issued in a fixed state, yet no more of them can be issued than can be kept in a fixed state; for to exceed this limit, will be to destroy their whole use at once, and involve us in more distress than before. I look on it a *very bold step* to put the revenue on such *a risk*; but I suppose the public necessities require it; and of this the Congress are the best judges, and doubtless acted on more reasons than we out of doors can see.

The fixing the currency, and *incomes of revenue* are of of the last consequence to us all in the present crisis; and therefore it appears to me absolutely necessary that every State should exert themselves in the most speedy and effectual manner to give sanction and force to this act, lest, by their defect, the important chance should turn against us, and we should be left without revenue or currency at this critical time, when our *political existence*, as well as the *occupation* and *means of living* of every individual, *depend on both.**

To

---

* In my Fourth Essay on Trade and Finance, published *Feb.* 10, 1780, I calculated the exchange of Continental money at that time to be 40 for 1, and strongly urged the *fixture* of it at that exchange, that the fatal mischiefs of a *fluctuating* currency, either by appreciation or depreciation, might be avoided.

From this I suppose that some people have surmised that the *first idea and original plan* of this act was *formed* by me and *suggested* to Congress, and my opinion here expressed, " that the States ought to adopt it without hesitation," confirms their conjecture: this induces me to observe some things on this matter, viz.

1. This act was not the absurd, inefficient, and ridiculous thing, which some people have represented it to be; there was *no error in its principle*; it wanted nothing to complete its purposes but *decided support* and *effectual execution*. The *taxes then instituted* by Congress, with the arrearages of former requisitions, would have been (if punctually paid) sufficient to *call in every bill* of the old money, and a *large sum* of the *new bills*, in the course of one year, and would doubtless have raised such a demand for what remained, as would have *kept up its value*, and prevented any depreciation.

Yet, 2d, I did *not approve* of it, but in all conversations I had with Members of Congress, whilst it was under debate, I constantly *opposed it*; principally because I did not expect, as the state of things then was, that it would receive that *support and vigorous execution* which was necessary to give it a due effect.

The people of the States at that time had been worried and fretted, disappointed and put out of humor by so many *tender-acts, limitations of prices*, and other *compulsory methods to force value into paper money*, and *compel the circulation of it*, and by so many vain *funding schemes, declarations*, and *promises*, all which issued from Congress, but *died under the most zealous efforts to put them into operation* and *effect*, that their patience was all exhausted; I say, these

To have a currency of fixed value, and the same as is expressed in the face of the bills, is an object most important and desirable, but can be obtained in no other way than by keeping the quantity within due bounds, and ascertaining its value, by such connexion with our real substance as will make it a certain security to the possessor. The value of money being wholly grounded in the proportion of two objects, viz. the quantity of money, and the objects of money, it is demonstrable that if either varies, whilst the other continues the same, the proportion must vary likewise, and of course the value of the money must fluctuate, as appears most plain to any person who has the least knowledge of the nature of proportion.

All experience justifies and confirms this reasoning, and puts the truth of it beyond all doubt; yet so strongly does the

---

these *irritations* and *disappointments* had so destroyed the *courage* and *confidence* of the people, that they appeared *heartless* and almost *stupid* when their attention was called to any *new propositions*.

Besides all this, I had objections to several clauses of the act, viz. our people were pretty well accustomed to the old bills (bad as they were) but to *call them all in*, and substitute *a new sort* in their stead, I thought would be a *novelty* that might have danger in it; at least, it would require great *expense*, *time*, &c. and all to very little use or benefit; for the *same energy of taxation* absolutely necessary to *support the credit of the new bills*, would be quite sufficient to make *such demands for the old ones* as would prevent their further *depreciation*, and receiving hard money in their stead at 40 for 1, would prevent their *appreciation*.

I could not see any benefit in *the signature of the States*, and feared this might bring *into doubt* the full *powers* of Congress to issue bills, or do any other like acts under their *own signature*.

Nor could I see any advantage arising from the *interest* annexed to the bills; it being payable *six years afterwards* would create mighty little inducement to their *present* circulation; but if the bills succeeded, this would greatly *increase the price of* their *final* redemption.

But I had another material objection to the act; for when I calculated the exchange, *Feb.* 10, 1780, it was really 40 to 1; but when this act passed, viz. the 18th of *March* following, the exchange had increased to 60 for 1, and consequently, all the provisions of the act which related to the exchange, became essentially wrong, and of course rendered the act itself utterly impracticable, without new provisions conformable to the exchange which really existed at the time, or making all the requisitions of the act in hard money or Continental bills of the same value, *i. e.* at any exchange that should exist at the time of payment.

But notwithstanding all this, when the bill was actually *past*, and the *revenues and supplies* of the year depended on its *success*, I readily offered my little mite of aid to give it an effectual operation, as I suppose any Member of Congress would and ought to do, *when it was past*, tho' he opposed it in every stage, *whilst under debate*.

the *infatuating bias*, like some darling, favorite lust, work itself into our *public counsels*, that after the longest and gravest consideration of the subject, they will, in the face of the clearest demonstration, in spite of repeated experience and the fullest proof of fact, still work up their deliberations into the vain issue, the fruitless resolution of *trying new methods*, adopting *new plans of increasing the currency*, and thereby defeat their own purposes, render their counsels ridiculous, and leave us all *without remedy*. The mischief lies in the *nature*, not in the *modification* of this fatal charm; there is *too much* already, and it is not possible that any *increase of quantity*, however modified, should help the matter, nor is it possible to *fix the value* in this way; for the increase of the quantity will for ever render the punctual redemption of it *more difficult*, and therefore more *uncertain*, and of course of *less* credibility or credit.

The nature of money is such, that its quantity cannot be increased beyond a certain degree, without losing its use; this has already been far exceeded, and it is not therefore possible that our remedy should lie in further increases of it, however modified. I have known people try to fatten their hogs with *pumkins*, *turnips*, and *bran*, to save *corn*, but without success; I have known people who had *not milk* enough, add *water* to it, but the nutritious particles of milk were *not increased* thereby; I have known children change their *pistereens* into *coppers*, and gain a *greater heap* of *money*; in all these cases the *substance was wanting*; the *show*, tho' increased, *was delusive*; and the *counsels puerile* and *without effect*, to say no worse of them.

Impending destruction is no longer a matter of empty declamation. All *occupations of town and country* are embarrassed and near to a full stop. Our public debts are every where increasing, and supplies failing. Famine, want, and total enervation of all strength and effort must be the speedy consequence. When the *springs*, the fountains, the resources are dried up, it is not possible but the *streams* must fail soon. We are in every respect *well and safe*, except in the article of *finances*. Were they restored, every
thing

thing else would immediately flourish and gain vigor sufficient for every purpose of safety and happiness.

There is in nature but one way to restore these, viz. *by immediate recourse to our solid substance, by taxing equal to our expenditures.* This I have often urged in vain; whenever it comes in view every countenance gathers paleness. *True, but it is impossible,* is the cry. Had it been a *spectre,* or *goblin* of terror, it could not have been *started from* and *avoided* with more precipitation. People will even take *fatal leaps into certain destruction,* to get away from it.

Pray, my countrymen, let us muster up a little courage and firmness of mind, and not, like a distempered imagination or guilty conscience, start with terror at a distant movement of we know not what. Let us compose ourselves, and take a little nearer view of this dreadful expedient; it is not so frightful in *near view* as in *distant apprehension.* There is such a thing as being penny wise and pound foolish. We may lose the *ship* for fear of hurting the *sails.*

Presence of mind and courage in distress,
Are more than armies to procure success.

A cool and careful examination of the subject will at least let us into the truth of it; and be that truth ever so hard and dreadful, our knowing *the worst* of it, is preferable to *suspense.*

Many things which strike us at first as intolerable or impossible, lose much of their difficulty and terror by growing familiar to us. Could we have thought it possible to support the dreadful war which we have hitherto *sustained,* had it been *held up* to our view five years ago? The remedy now proposed is but *trifling* in comparison of what we *have suffered.* And shall we sink disheartened in sight of a desirable shore, after we have surpassed the tempests and billows of the ocean thro' the voyage? The remedy I propose, is allowed by all to be *effectual and sufficient,* if it can be practised; and we shall find it the only one that can save us from ruin; at least this is my opinion, after

more

more than six months' close attention to the subject, and viewing it in every light in which I can consider it.

I conceive, if it should appear that each industrious individual *loses more for want of the tax*, than his tax *would amount to*, that every doubt of the expediency of the tax would instantly be removed and vanish at once; and I think this may be made very clear and plain. I shall attempt to prove this.

I. The tax demanded will amount to about 4 *hard dollars* in a year to each person in the States, or 20 such dollars, or the value of them, to a middling family of 5 persons; and this will, by the due apportionment of the tax, be *lessened* to the *poor* and *increased* to the *rich*, in proportion to their abilities. This is the *height* of it; this is the worst that can happen; this is the *dreadful price* demanded for our *salvation*, to save us from sure destruction, and which the Thirteen States are deeply *hesitating* and *contemplating* whether they *will pay or no*: at least this tax is what the *Congress* are hesitating to *recommend*, and the *States* to *levy* and *collect*, tho' I doubt if the people would hesitate a moment to pay it, if it was put under collection, especially if it was demanded in monthly rates, which would render the payment much more practicable than it would be, if it was all called for at one payment. Now we will consider what is lost for want of this tax.

1. Every industrious man loses his *business*, his *occupation*, or at least finds it *greatly embarrassed*, and subjected to great difficulty and discouragement: for, I submit it to every man to judge, whether, in the present *fluctuating state of the currency* and mode of *procuring the public supplies*, whether, I say, it can be *safe or prudent* for any man to lay out any business of husbandry, mechanic arts, or merchandise, *on any large scale*, whilst he knows not *what he must sell his proceeds for* when he has got them, or whether he may *have the selling of them at all or not?* These embarrassments are very *sensibly felt* thro' the States, but would all vanish, if our finances were restored. And I think it very plain, that a man's occupation must be very poor indeed,

if

if thefe embarraffments are not more *damage* to him, than his *whole tax would amount to*.

2. For want of the tax, *the fupplies of the country are daily leffening, our plenty waftes away faft*, and *fcarcity* and *want* are fucceeding in the place of them. This makes every man's eftate in the country *lefs valuable*, as it is apparent that an eftate in a country of *poverty and want*, is not fo good, or worth fo much money, as the fame eftate would be in a country *full of riches and plentiful fupplies*. *All means of living* will of courfe become harder to be obtained, as it is more difficult procuring fupplies in a country where *they are fcarce*, than in one where they *are plenty*. What may be the amount of *lofs* to each individual from thefe caufes, is not eafy to calculate; but as they affect the *whole bulk of eftates*, and operate on the *whole means of livelihood*, they cannot be fuppofed *fmall*, and I think will readily be allowed to *exceed* any man's *fhare* of the *tax* neceffary to *prevent them*.

3. For want of the tax, *the morality and induftry of the people are greatly diminifhed*. *Frauds, cheats*, and *grofs difhonefty* are introduced, and a thoufand *idle ways of living* are attempted in the room of that honeft *induftry, economy,* and *diligence* which heretofore *bleffed* and *enriched* this country. And as an eftate in a country of *honeft*, induftrious people, is better than in one filled with *idle rogues*; and as all property is hereby rendered more unfafe and lefs valuable; it is very eafy to fee, that the *lofs* of each individual in this refpect, will be very confiderable, and muft, on a very moderate computation, much *exceed the tax* required to *remedy the whole mifchief*.

4. For want of the tax, our *trade is decaying faft*; and this not only ruins the merchant, and renders the procurement of fuch neceffaries as are ufually fupplied by our trade, more dear and difficult, but it *enervates the whole fyftem both of hufbandry* and *mechanic arts*, as thefe can never flourifh *without a market*, where the produce of the farmer and the fabrics of the mechanic may be fold, when ready for fale. This affects the whole country in a moft material manner, and muft at leaft involve each individual in

a *lofs*

a *loss* of more than his *tax would amount to*, sufficient to give a fixed value and use to our currency, and thereby restore our trade and husbandry to their former vigor.

5. For want of the tax our *defence must cease*, and we must *lie open to the ravages* and *plunders of our enemies;* the very risk and danger of which involves many distresses that must occasion *loss* to every individual, far greater than the whole amount of his tax would be towards such defence as would render the country quite safe and secure. Add to this, the danger of being finally *overrun* and *conquered* by our enemies, and falling under their unrestrained power; in which case, they would doubtless extort *perpetual taxes* from us, to as great amount as are now required for *a short time* to secure us against their power.

6. The want of this tax *enervates our laws*, renders their fines, penalties, and forfeitures uncertain and ineffectual; destroys the salaries, fees, and rewards of our civil and religious officers, and of course prevents men of abilities from serving in the character of judge, sheriff, gospel-minister, schoolmaster, &c. and of course the whole *system of our civil and religious polity, and education of youth is clearly on the decline* to a very dangerous degree; but as all these institutions tend much to the happiness of society, any decline of them must greatly *prejudice the value of every estate*, and the prospects of happiness and utility arising from it, to an amount greatly *beyond the tax required* to secure all these wholesome institutions in their fullest use, respectability, and general influence.

I might add here more instances of loss incurred by individuals from the fluctuating state of our currency and disorders of our finances, which would be all remedied by the tax I recommend; but it appears to me, those already adduced are grounded on such obvious and notorious facts, are of such interesting concern, and of such forcible conclusion, that if they do not convince, it is needless to offer more on the subject; it is vain to *offer arguments* to people who will not give a *shilling to save a pound;* and yet this is much more than the tax I propose, requires, however it may be *aggravated and heightened* by stingy, timorous,

or

or corrupted men, into an *exorbitancy* utterly infupportable.

II. As the money collected by taxes, or other money to the amount will be conftantly iffuing, the payment of heavy taxes will be rendered as eafy as the nature of the cafe admits; while at the fame time the great demand for money occafioned by the tax, will be fufficient to keep its value fixed, and its ufes well fecured and preferved. The facility of raifing fums of money when the circulation is brifk, and the demand quick for goods on hand, is eafily conceived, by any perfon in the leaft acquainted with trade. This mightily leffens the burden of the tax below what it would be, if collected in a dull time of bufinefs, and fcarcity of cafh, and confequently the tax itfelf becomes lefs fenfibly felt under thefe favorable circumftances of eafy procurement, than the fame would be, if deferred to fome future time, when there might be lefs demand for goods, and greater fcarcity of cafh; therefore it is the intereft of every individual to pay his dues to the public whilft he can do it with the greateft eafe, rather than defer it to fome future time, when he may happen to be called on for it at a juncture when the payment will be more difficult and diftreffing than now.

III. The price of moft kinds of country produce is *much higher* than it is ufually in times of general quiet, and therefore *the tax may be paid* much *eafier* now than then; as a bufhel of wheat, a cow, a fheep, &c. will bring *much more* now than it will do when quiet is again reftored, and of courfe ought to be fold now, that the payment may be made whilft it can be done with moft eafe and advantage; for *what is not paid* now *muft lie as a debt* to be paid in future time, when it will probably take near a *double quantity* of wheat, beef, mutton, pork, &c. to pay it, as would now be fufficient.

IV. Further, a prudent man will never let a demand *lie againft him* when he can *conveniently fatisfy it;* and a public debt is the worft of all kind of demands, when a man is not ready for them; for I fubmit it to every man if he would not fee *any fort of creditor* come to him when he was

unprepared

unprepared to pay, rather than *a public collector*. *Present payment* avoids all this trouble and mortification, as well as *saves much* by the high price which that produce will now bring, which must be sold to pay the tax.

V. The tax will procure a good market, and sure, sufficient payment to individuals who have such articles for sale as are needed by the public; whereas for want of the tax, thousands who have sold their goods to the public, have been paid in a useless currency, or have not been able to get any payment at all, to their great disappointment and damage. This is a consideration of great importance to most people in the States, as there are few who would not choose to supply the public with some kind of goods or services in their power, if they could be sure of punctual and sufficient payment. The having a quick and profitable market for what is made ready for sale, is no small advantage to every individual; for without this all his goods which he does not need for his own consumption, lie useless on his hands, or his time may be lost for want of an employer, who would pay him for his services.

The *advantages* resulting from this *one circumstance* would be equal to the tax to many thousands of individuals; as the goods or time they would *lose* for want of a market or employers, would be more than equal to the *tax*, as they have experienced to their sorrow, who have lost their goods for want of a market, or sold them where they could not get their payment either in due time, or in currency of certain value.

VI. The tax would remove all cause of complaint, and put an end to the great oppression which has taken place much too long; for if the burden is laid equally on all, no one can have any cause to complain of oppression when his share is demanded; but without this the supplies wanted for the public must be taken by force or fraud from the owners, without payment, to their great oppression and injury. Indeed if supplies are not procured and sent to the army, these oppressions must be multiplied to a very tragical degree; for to disband the army and send them home, when their present supplies are spent, will not probably be

either

either safe for the country, or agreeable to them; they must therefore live in free quarters; they will probably be directed to march into such States and towns as have been most deficient in furnishing their quotas: but even in that case, thousands of individuals will suffer, who have not been guilty of any deficiency or delays; for in cases of such extremity, the innocent must be involved with the guilty, and of course oppressions must be infinite, and very terrible. The burden of the tax bears no proportion to the ruinous and most dreadful effects resulting in this one instance from the want of it.

VII. The tax in a few months will *restore our finances, fix our currency*, and put us in condition *to unite* our force with every *possible advantage;* and this will so clearly demonstrate our unbroken strength, union, and firmness, that the *hearts* of our enemies *will die* within them, and they will soon break up and leave us in despair. Their *only hope* of conquest has long been from the *confusions of our finances;* they have not attempted for two years past *to oppose their capital force to ours*, but have hung on us in hopes that we should *soon sink under the pressure of our own expenses*, and so fall an easy prey into their hands; and they will continue in this hope as long as they see us *ringing the changes on visionary schemes*, and trying in *new shapes and attitudes* an *old delusion*, that always *has deceived* us in every shape, and probably *always will.**

VIII. This same thing will show *to foreign powers our unbroken strength, great resources, wisdom of policy, and vigor in execution*, give us great *respectability* in their eyes, and enable us to *demand and expect any aids from them* which we

---

* *Nov.* 19, 1779, Congress earnestly recommended to the several States, "forthwith to *enact laws* for a *general limitation of prices*, to commence from the 1*st day of Feb.* (then) next," on the principle of *the exchange of the currency being at* 20 *for* 1.

The *real* exchange when this resolution passed, was 38 *for* 1; and on *Feb.* (when their limitation was to commence) the *real* exchange was 47 *for* 1.

Various *other* methods *equally idle and visionary* were set on foot about this time to *fix* the currency, such as, modifying the loan-office with many proposals of supposed advantage, *exclamations* and *threats* against such as refused to sell their property for *Continental money*, setting on foot *subscriptions* for supplying the Treasury, &c. vide Journal of Congress.

we may need; for the state of human nature is such, that those can get *least help* who *need it most*, and those can procure *most friends* who need them *least*; and the *best way* for a man or a nation to *get assistance from his neighbours* is to be *able to do without it*.

On the whole, I do not see that any thing more is necessary, than wise, decisive counsels, put into action with spirit and resolution. We have enough to do with, if we had but spirit and wisdom to call it into use; and I think *this spirit* is much more wanting in our *rulers* than in the *people*. In old times of distress among *the Israelites*, it was a sign of approaching deliverance when the *Spirit of the Lord came on their great men*, i. e. in the *Hebrew* dialect, a *great spirit*, *great courage*, and *resolution*, adequate to the work; as the *trees of the Lord* mean *great trees*; the *sons of God* were their *great men*, and *thunder* is called the *voice* of the Lord, because it is *greatest of voices* in the natural world. The *Romans*, without inspiration, somehow catched the same idea. *Audentes fortuna juvat*. They esteemed *Fortune* a divinity, ready *to help those* who had spirit and courage *to help themselves*. Little is to be expected from *languid counsels, half assured resolutions, plans* that want *extent adequate to their purpose*, and *vigor* of execution equal to their *extent*. If I could see a little more of that *Spirit of the Lord* which animated the brave old worthies, I should soon expect to see the *sword of the Lord* follow, and our *troubles* and *troublers* all melting away before us.

But before I quit this subject, I beg leave to add one thought more, which appears to me of the most capital importance, viz. *that no plan of taxation*, or any thing else, can be of *any good effect*, if there is not *some method adopted* to bring all the States into *an union and punctuality of execution*. The least company of men, who have a common concern, if it is but in a ship or piece of banked meadow, find it absolutely and essentially necessary to have some way *to compel their partners* into a punctual *discharge of their quotas*. The very existence of our union requires this. If one State *hangs back*, another *will*, and the best concerted *plan* possible may be rendered ineffectual by *delays and defects* in the execution.

It

It is essential to the very being of any independent community, that it has in it *all the powers* necessary to its *own preservation*. These powers doubtless *exist* in the Thirteen States, *as perfectly* as in any other community in the world. And tho' I do not pretend to understand the constitution of our union well enough to decide *where these powers lie*, yet I should suppose they must be *vested in the Congress*, as I know of no powers which extend *over the whole*, but theirs. But if it is thought that these powers are not sufficiently *explicit and declared* to be in them, it is necessary that this *declaration* should be made *without delay*, and put into such force as is absolutely necessary to give effect to our public counsels, preserve the union, and concentre the force of the whole, and prevent that destruction which may ensue for want of such union of effort for the common safety.

If it was possible for the tardy States to go to destruction *alone, without dragging the rest after them*, it might be best to dismiss them from the union with contempt. But as this cannot be done, it is necessary to the preservation of the whole, that some means be found *to compel* such States to keep pace with their neighbours, and bear their *due proportion of the burden and duty*, as well as receive their share of *protection* and *benefit*.

In fine, we want nothing but *united and spirited efforts* for a short time, to restore our *finances*, establish our *currency*, retrieve our *honor*, secure our *safety*, give *vigor to every kind of business and occupation*, recover our *virtue*, and make ourselves the *laudable* and *envied example of wisdom and happiness to all the world*. Our *posterity* expect and have a right to demand this from us. The eager eyes of all *Europe* are on us, ready to give their *plaudit to our virtue*, decision, and success. Our enemies *tremble*, for fear we should *grow wise and virtuous;* and *Heaven opens the scene favorably*, and has given us the *lucky cards*, and we have nothing to do but to *play them out well*.

Et dubitamus adhuc virtutem extendere factis,
Aut metus, hac libera, prohibet consistere terra.

STRIC-

STRICTURES

ON

TENDER-ACTS.*

[*First published in Philadelphia, Dec. 13, 1780.*]

THE Tender-Act of *November* 29, 1780, is published by order of the Assembly of *Pennsylvania* for public confideration, and therefore the duty and respect due to the Assembly and the Public obliges every one to confider it, and offer such remarks on it as deserve public notice. In compliance with this duty, I have confidered the said act, and the following Strictures appear to me of importance sufficient to engage the public attention.

The *nature of a Tender-Act* is no more or lefs than *establishing by law the standard value of money*, and has the fame use with respect to the *currency*, that the legal standard *pound, bushel, yard,* or *gallon* has to *those goods,* the quantities of which are usually ascertained by those weights and measures; therefore to call any thing a *pound or shilling,* which *really is not so,* and *make it a legal standard,* is an error of the fame nature as *diminishing* the *standard bushel, yard, gallon,* &c. or making a law that a *foot* shall be the *legal yard,* an *ounce* the *legal pound,* a *peck* the *legal bushel,*
or

---

* The fatal error, that *the credit and currency of the Continental money could be kept up and supported by acts of compulsion,* entered so deep into the mind of Congress and of all departments of administration thro' the States, that no confiderations of justice, religion, or policy, or even experience of its utter
inefficacy,

or a *quart* the *legal gallon*, and compelling every body to receive all *goods due to them* by such deficient measures.

Further, to make any thing the *legal standard* of any of these, which is not of *fixed* but *variable nature*, is an error of the same kind and mischief as the other; *e. g.* to make a *turnip* the standard pound weight, which may dry up in the course of a year to a *pith* of not more than *two or three ounces*, or to make a *flannel string* the standard *yard*, which will shrink in using to half its length. The absurdity of this is too glaring to need any thing further said on it.

But to come to the matter now in question.

The first observation which occurs to me is, that the bills, which are made a tender, contain a *public promise of money to be paid in six years*. On which I beg leave to remark,

R that

---

inefficacy, could eradicate it; it seemed to be a kind of obstinate delirium, totally deaf to every argument drawn from justice and right, from its natural tendency and mischief, from common sense, and even common safety.

Congress began, as early as *Jan.* 11, 1776, to hold up and recommend this *maxim of maniasm*, when Continental money was but 5 months old (for its actual circulation commenced the beginning of *August* 1775, tho' the bills were dated *May* 10, preceding, that being the first day of that session of Congress) Congress then resolved, that " whoever *should refuse to receive in payment, Continental bills*, &c. should be *deemed* and *treated as an enemy of his country*, and be precluded from all *trade* and *intercourse* with the inhabitants," &c. *i. e.* should be *outlawed*; which is the *severest penalty* (except of life and limb) known in our laws.

This ruinous principle was continued in practice for *five successive years*, and appeared in all *shapes* and *forms*, i. e. in *tender-acts*, in *limitations* of prices, in *awful* and *threatening declarations*, in *penal laws* with dreadful and ruinous *punishments*, and in every *other way* that could be devised, and all *executed* with a *relentless severity*, by the *highest authorities* then in being, viz: by *Congress*, by *Assemblies* and *Conventions* of the States, by *committees of inspection* (whose powers in those days were nearly sovereign) and even by *military force*; and tho' men of all descriptions stood trembling before this monster of force, without daring to lift a hand against it, during all this period, yet its unrestrained energy ever proved ineffectual to its purposes, but in every instance increased the *evils* it was designed to remedy, and destroyed the *benefits* it was intended to promote; at best its utmost effect was like that of water sprinkled on a blacksmith's forge, which indeed deadens the flame for a moment, but never fails to increase the *heat and force* of the internal fire. Many *thousand families* of full and easy fortune were *ruined* by these *fatal measures*, and he in *ruins to this day*, without the least *benefit* to the *country*, or to the great and noble *cause* in which we were then engaged.

I do not mention these things from any pleasure I have in opening the wounds of my country, or exposing its errors, but with a hope that our *fatal mistakes* may be a caution and warning to future financiers, who may live and act in any country which may happen to be in circumstances similar to ours at that time.

N. B. The act of *Nov.* 29, 1780, herein referred to, was passed into a law, *Dec.* 19, 1780.

that the best and most indubitable security of money to be paid in *six years*, or any *future time*, is not so good or valuable as ready cash. The truth of this proposition is so evident and obvious to every body, that it cannot need proof.

Therefore the law, which obliges a man to accept these bills instead of ready cash, obliges him to receive a *less* valuable thing in full payment of a *more* valuable one, and injures him to amount of the difference; and is so far a direct violation of the *laws of commutative justice—laws* grounded in the nature of *human rights*, supported by the most necessary *natural principles*, and enjoined by the most express authority *of God Almighty*, and which it is not possible that any legislature on earth should *have right* to infringe or abrogate.

Again, the security arising from the public promise is not generally deemed *certain*. The public *faith* has been *so often violated*, and the *sufferings* of individuals thence arising have been so *multiplied and extensive*, that the general confidence of our people in that security is much *lessened*; and as a chance or *uncertainty* can never be so valuable as a *certainty*, those bills must and will be considered as less valuable than they would be, was the security on which they depended, free of all doubt or uncertainty; and consequently, the discount of their value will always be estimated by, and of course be equal to, this difference. Therefore, the injustice of forcing them on the subject at *full value* of present cash, is greatly increased.

These positions and reasonings are grounded on such notoriety of fact, that any explanation or proof is needless; and I hope an objection against a law, drawn from the most manifest and acknowledged injustice of its operation and effect, will not be deemed trivial, or be easily set aside or got over.

Naked facts are *powerful* things, and arguments sometimes do best, and have the greatest effect, when addressed to the *feelings* of mankind; and that I may press the matter as close as I can, I beg leave to propose the following case, viz.

Suppose a man of grave phiz and character should, *in distress*, apply to his neighbour for the loan of 1000 *silver*

silver dollars, with solemn promise on his *honor* and *truth* to repay them in a month, and in the mean time the tender-act under consideration should pass into a law, and the borrower, at the month's end, should tender 1000 of the *new* paper dollars in payment.

I beg leave here to propose to every *Member* of the Assembly who voted for that law, and to every *other* man, who is a *member of this State*, what their sentiments of that action would be, and in what light they would view the *borrower*, who tendered the *paper* dollars (*i. e.* ⅔ of the debt) in payment of the silver ones he had received; *i. e.* would they consider him as an *upright, honest man*, or a *shameless rascal?*

In whichever of the two characters they may choose to consider such a man, it may be proper to note, that the *act* in question, if passed into a law, would *protect* him, and not only so, but would subject the lender to the *loss* of the *whole money* if he refused to receive it. This is a somewhat delicate matter, which it is painful to dwell long upon. I will therefore close what I have to say on it with a few very serious remarks, the truth, justice, and propriety of which I humbly submit to the reader.

1. The worst kind of evil, and that which corrupts and endangers any community most, is that *iniquity which is framed by a law;* for this places the mischief in the very spot, on the very seat, to which every one ought to look and apply for a remedy.

2. It cannot be consistent with the honor, the policy, the interest, or character of an Assembly of *Pennsylvania*, to make a law, which, by its natural operation, shall afford *protection* to manifest injustice, deliberate knavery, and known wrong.

3. No cause or end can be so good, *i. e.* so *heavenly* in its origin, so *excellent* in its nature, so *perfect* in its principles, and so *useful* in its operation, as to require or justify *infernal means* to promote it. By *infernal means* I mean such as are most *opposed to Heaven and its laws;* most repugnant to natural principles of *equity*, which are all derived from *Heaven;* and most destructive of the *rights* of human nature, which are essential to the happiness of society, the laws of

which

which are *engraven by Heaven* on the heart of every man; some wicked men have formerly said, " let us do *evil*, that *good* may come, whose *damnation* is just."

But perhaps this *sort* of argument may not have all the effect I could wish on the mind of *every* reader. I therefore proceed to another argument, which goes to the nature and principle of the act itself, viz. that the *credit or value of money* cannot, in the very nature of the thing, be supplied, preserved, or restored by *penal laws*, or any *coercive* methods. The subject is *incompatible to force*, it is put of its reach, and never can be made susceptible of it, or controllable by it. The thing which makes money an object of desire, which gives it strength of motive on the hearts of all men, is the general *confidence*, the *opinion* which it gains, as a sovereign *means* of obtaining every thing needful. This confidence, this opinion, exists in the mind only, and is not *compellable* or *assailable by force*, but must be grounded on that evidence and reason which the mind can see and believe; and is no more subject to the action of force, than any other passion, sentiment, or affection of the mind; any more than faith, love, or esteem.

It is not more absurd to attempt to *impel faith* into the heart of an unbeliever by *fire* and *faggot*, or to *whip* love into your mistress with a *cowskin*, than to force *value* or *credit* into your money by *penal laws*.

You may, indeed, by force compel a man to deliver his goods for *money* which he does not *esteem*, and the same force may compel him to deliver his goods without any *money* at all; but the credit or value of the money cannot be helped by all this, as appears by numberless examples. Plain facts are stubborn and undeniable proofs of this. Indeed, this has been tried among ourselves in such extent of places and variety of shapes, and in every instance been found ineffectual, that I am amazed to see any attempt to revive it, under any devisable form whatsoever. Numberless are the instances of flagrant oppression and wrong, and even ruin, which have been the sad effects of these dreadful experiments, with infinite detriment to the community in general, without effecting in any one inſtance the *ends intended*. The facts on which this argument depends, are freſh in every one's memory.

I could wiſh, for the honor of my country, to draw a veil over what is paſt, and that wiſdom might be derived from paſt errors, ſufficient to induce every one to avoid them in future. In fine, from the contemplation of the nature of the thing, and of the facts and experiments which have been made in every variety of mode, and ſupported by every degree of power and exertion, it appears as plain and undeniable as intuitive proof, that the credit or value of money is not in its nature controllable by force, and therefore, any attempt to reach it in that way, muſt end in diſappointment, and the greater the efforts, and the higher the authority which may be exerted in that way, the greater muſt be the chagrin, ſhame, and mortification, when the baſeleſs fabric ſhall vaniſh into ſmoke.

The only poſſible method then of giving value or credit to money is, to give it ſuch qualities, and clothe it with ſuch circumſtances, as ſhall make it a ſure means of procuring every needful thing; for money that will not anſwer all things, is defective, and has not in it the full nature and qualities of money. In this way only it will grow faſt enough into eſteem, and become a ſufficient object of deſire, to anſwer every end and uſe of money. Therefore, when the queſtion is propoſed, how ſhall we give credit or value to our money? the anſwer, the only true anſwer, is, bring it into demand, make it neceſſary to every one, make it a high means of happineſs, and a ſure remedy of miſery. To attempt this in any other way is to go out of nature, and of courſe into difficulty, only to obtain ſhameful diſappointment in the end.

There is nothing better than to take things in their natural way. A *great and difficult work* may be accompliſhed by eaſy diligence, if a good method and a wiſe choice of means are adopted; but a *ſmall work* may be made difficult, very ſoon, if taken at the wrong end, and purſued by unnatural means. There is a *right* and a *wrong method* of doing every thing. You may lead with a *thread* what you cannot

cannot drive with *whips* and *scorpions*. The *Britons* have found this to their coft, in the unnatural means they have purfued to preferve and recover their dominions in *America*. I wifh we might be made wife by their errors.

Felix quem faciunt aliena pericula cautum.

I would be willing to learn wifdom from *Great Britain*. *Fas eft ab hofte doceri.* Amidft all their madnefs, and in all their diftreffes for money, they never once thought of making their bank or exchequer bills a tender, or fupporting their currency by penal laws. But thefe confiderations may have little effect on *fome minds*, who are not very delicate in their choice of means, but feem refolved to carry their point, *volente nolente Deo*.

I therefore haften to another topic of argument, viz. It appears to me the act is founded in miftaken and very bad policy, and by its natural operation muft produce many effects extremely prejudicial to our great and moft important interefts.

1. It feems plain to me, that the act has a fatal tendency to deftroy the great motives of *induftry*, and to difhearten and difcourage men of every profeffion and occupation from purfuing their bufinefs *on any large fcale* or to any *great effect*, and therefore will prevent the production of thofe fupplies derived from hufbandry and manufactures, which are effential to our fafety, fupport and comfort. Few men will beftow their labor, attention, and good money, with zeal, to procure goods and commodities for fale, which they know they muft fell for money which they efteem bad, or at beft doubtful. This propofition is fo obvious and natural, that it ftrikes the mind with conviction at firft fight without proof, and is fo amply confirmed by our paft experience, that it can admit no doubt as to its truth or confequence.

The extent and dreadful effects of this are *unavoidable and immenfe*. If the induftry of the farmer and tradefman is difcouraged, and they ceafe to lay themfelves out for large crops and fabrics, the confequence muft be an univerfal verſal diminution and ſcarcity of the produce of the country and moſt important articles of living; as well as commerce. The general induſtry of the country is of ſuch vaſt importance, is an object of ſuch magnitude, that to check it, is to bring on ruin, poverty, famine, and diſtreſs, with idleneſs, vice, corruption of morals, and every ſpecies of evil; but enumeration or enlargement is unneceſſary here.

As money is the ſinews of every buſineſs, the introducing a doubtful medium, and forcing it into currency by penal laws, muſt weaken and leſſen every branch of buſineſs, in proportion to the diminution of inducement found in the money.

2. The ſame thing will *render the procurement of ſupplies for the army difficult*, if not utterly *impracticable*. Moſt men will hold back their goods from the market, rather than ſell them for money of a doubtful credit; and there will be no poſſible way of collecting them, but to ſend a *ſuperior force* into the country, and there take them by *violence* from the owner, which will occaſion ſuch an expenſe as will *double the coſt* of the ſupplies by the time they get to the army, be ſubject to a thouſand *frauds*, &c. &c. &c. This is the moſt obvious and ntural operation of the act, if we conſider its own nature only, and is confirmed by ſuch ample experience, recent in the memory of every man, that it can leave no doubt but all this train of michiefs muſt follow the act from its firſt operation.

3. I apprehend the act will, by its natural operation, tend to *corrupt the morality of the people*, *ſap* the ſupport, if not the very foundation, of our *independence*, leſſen the reſpect due to our *Legiſlature*, and deſtroy that *reverence for our laws*, which is abſolutely neceſſary to their proper operation, and the peace and protection of ſociety. Many people will be ſo terrified with the apprehenſion of ſeeing their real ſubſtance, the fruit of their labor and anxious attention, converted into a bundle of paper bills of uneertain value, that, to avoid this evil, they will have ſtrong inducements to rack their invention for all deviſable ways and methods of avoiding it; and this will give riſe to ſuch

numberleſs

numberless *frauds*, *ambiguities*, *lies*, *quibbles*, and *shams*, as will introduce the habit and give a kind of facility to the practice of such guile and feats of art, as will endanger the *uprightness*, *plain honesty*, and *noble sincerity*, which ever *mark* the character of a happy and virtuous people.

Many, who wish well to our independence, and have many necessaries for our army which they would wish to supply, will be yet held back from offering their goods, from the sole consideration of the doubtful value of the bills in which those supplies must be paid for; and instances of this sort I conceive will be so numerous, as greatly to affect the supplies of our army, and of course the support of our independence. The injuries and sufferings of people, who are compelled to take said bills in satisfaction of contracts for real money, will induce them in their rage to use the legislature, who formed the act, with great liberty, and perhaps gross disrespect; whilst the habit of reproaching the legislature, and eluding the injurious act, will become general, and pave the way to an habitual and universal abhorrence of our legislature and contempt of our laws, with a kind of facility and artful dexterity in eluding the force of the whole code.

I freely submit it to my reader, if these consequences are at all unnatural or ill-drawn, if the surmises are at all groundless, or the painting a whit too strong. No art of government is more necessary, than that of keeping up the dignity and respectability of the legislatures, and all courts and officers of government, and exciting and preserving in the hearts of the people a high reverence for the laws; and any thing which endangers these great supports of the state ought to be avoided as a deadly evil.

4. The act, I apprehend, will give a bad appearance to our *credit*, *honor*, and *respectability*, in the eyes of our neighbours on this continent, and the nations of *Europe*, and other more distant parts of the world. For when they come to be informed that our *own people must be compelled*, by the loss of half their estates and imprisonment of their persons, *to trust the public faith*, they will at once conclude there must be some great danger, some shocking mischief
dormant

dormant there, which the people nearest to and best acquainted with it, abhor so much; and of course, as they are out of the reach of our *confiscations and imprisonments*, will have little inducement to trust or esteem us. And

5. Will give great *exultation and encouragement* to *our enemies*, and induce them to *prolong the war*, and thereby increase the horrid penalty of imprisonment, which is to last during the war. When they see that our money is become so detestable, that it requires such an act as this to compel our own people to take it, they must at least be convinced that its nature is greatly corrupted, and its efficacy and use nearly at an end. When we see the passionate *admirers* of a great beauty *forced* by lashes and tortures into her embraces, we at once conclude that she has lost *her charms*, and is become *dangerous and loathsome*.

It cannot be fairly objected to these Strictures, that they suppose the bills funded by this act are of less value than hard money. The act itself implies this. The Assembly never thought of wasting time in framing an act to compel people to take guineas, joes, and *Spanish* dollars, under penalty of confiscation and imprisonment. Besides, the fact stands in such glaring light in the eyes of all men, that it is mere trifling to dispute it.

I dare think that there is not a man to be found, either in the Assembly or out of it, that would esteem himself so rich and safe in the possession of 1000 of these dollars, as of 1000 *Spanish* ones; and the most effectual way to impress a sense of the deficiency of the act on the minds of all men, and even discover the idea which the Assembly themselves have of it, is to enforce it by penalties of extreme severity; for were there no deficiency in the act, it could not possibly require such penalties to give it all necessary effect, nor is it supposable that the Assembly would add the sanction of horrid penalties to any of their acts, unless they thought there was need of them.

The enormity of the penalty deserves remark. The penalty for *refusing* a dollar of these bills is greater than for *stealing ten times the sum*.

S   Further

Further, the act alters, and of course destroys, the nature and value of public and private contracts, and of consequence strikes at the root of all public and private credit. Who can lend money with any security, and of course who can borrow, let his necessity and distress be ever so great? who can purchase on credit, or make any contract for future payment? in very deed all confidence of our fellow-citizens in one another is hereby destroyed, as well as all faith of individuals in the public credit.

Upon the whole matter, the bills must rest on the *credit of their funds*, their *quantity*, and other *circumstances*. If these are sufficient to give them a currency at full value, they will pass readily enough without the help of penal laws. If these are not sufficient, they must and will depreciate, and thereby destroy the end of their own creation; and this will proceed from such strong natural principles, such physical causes, as cannot, in the nature of the thing, be checked or controlled by *penal laws*, or any other *application of force*.

These Strictures are humbly offered to public consideration. The facts alleged are all open to view, and well understood. If the remarks and reasonings are just, they will carry conviction; if they are not so, they are liable to any one's correction.

AN ESSAY

OR

Humble Attempt to examine and state the

TRUE INTEREST

Of PENNSYLVANIA *with Respect to the Paper Currency.*

[*First published in Philadelphia, Dec.* 13, 1780.]

I PROPOSE, first, some remarks on the *subject of paper money*, and, secondly, some particular consideration of the *Acts of our Assembly for issuing the new Continental bills*, with some reasons why I think the true interest of *Pennsylvania* requires that *those acts should be repealed*, and the issuing of those bills should be stopped or suspended for the present, and I hope to do this without offence; for the great interests of a State, in which 400,000 *citizens* are concerned, cannot be too well understood, nor the utility of its laws be too carefully examined, or the errors of them be discovered and amended too soon.

Two things are *essentially necessary to give paper bills a credit and currency equal to hard money*. 1. Such certainty of HONEST *and* PUNCTUAL REDEMPTION, as shall fully satisfy the mind of the possessor. 2. *That the* CREDIT *and* DEMAND *for said bills should be so constantly kept up, from the time of their* EMISSION *to that of their* REDEMPTION, *that the possessor may be able, at any time, to pass them at hard money value.* The first of these is provided for by

the

the Affembly, if their act shall produce the *certainty* of redemption required, which I am not here to difpute: but the fecond is equally neceffary; for fhould the bills pafs from their emiffion to their redemption, or any part of that intermediate time, at a depreciated value, fay 2, 3, or 4 for 1, tho' they fhould be redeemed at full value at the *expiration* of their currency in the moft punctual manner, yet the *mifchiefs* they would occafion *in the mean time* would be infinite.

One of which would be, that the depreciation itfelf would render the final redemption of the bills at full value both unjuft and pernicious, as well as very hard and oppreffive to the body of the people; for, in this cafe, the people muft be taxed, fay *two, three,* or *four times* the value or current exchange of the bills; not to the *public benefit,* but folely to increafe the wealth of thofe *rich people,* who will hoard up the bills, and have them in poffeffion at the time of their redemption. From which it appears (and indeed I think it may be demonftrated from the plaineft principles) *that public bills ought always to be redeemed at that value or current exchange, at which they ufually pafs at the time of redemption, let their nominal value be whatever it may.* Indeed, the infinite and ruinous mifchiefs of a fluctuating currency are fo generally felt and well underftood, that I conceive there is no need of proof, that it is equally neceffary to keep the value or exchange of bills ftable and unvarying thro' the *whole time of their currency,* as to provide fure funds for their *final redemption,* and that the *firft* of thefe does not depend folely on the *laft.* The *firft* of thefe depends on opinion, perfuafion, and general practice; the *laft* on the ability and integrity of the redeemer.

If you offer a bill to a ftranger, he never thinks of afking when, by whom, or how certainly that bill is to be redeemed, but his only queftion is, whether he can *pafs it again?* Not one in a thoufand who takes a public bill, takes it with a defign to lay it up five or fix years, tho' its redemption be ever fo fure at that time, but his object is immediate ufe, to ferve his prefent occafions by inftantly paffing it again, or at leaft having it in his power to do it whenever occasion may offer. I take it that these principles and reasonings are perfectly plain and clear, and will afford, by the clearest inference, the following consequence, viz. *That no public bills ought ever to be issued, which have not these two great and essential supports,* 1. *a* CERTAINTY *of final redemption;* and, 2. *such general confidence and demand, as will insure their currency at full value without depreciation, during the whole time of their circulation.*

Indeed, it appears to me, that to issue public bills without these supports is the plainest folly, bordering on insanity, and must be very *criminal*, when done in the face of clear evidence and conviction. It further appears to me, that the *new Continental bills have not these supports at present, and therefore ought not to be issued till these supports can be obtained,* and of consequence, that the great interest of the State requires that the laws for issuing them should be repealed; or at least that the issuing them should be suspended till these supports can be obtained; for which I offer the following reasons, which seem to me to be of weight and force sufficient to engage the most serious attention of the public.

1. The quantity (viz. 10,000,000 of dollars) is at least *four times as much in value as all the old Continental bills*, and therefore must, from the nature of the thing, depreciate it, were its funds ever so indubitable, and the public confidence in it ever so great.—I conceive the present mean exchange of the Continental bills is about 100 for 1, at least they cannot be set at less than 80 for 1, on any sure facts, which makes the whole quantity (viz. 200,000,000) worth 2,500,000 of hard dollars, which is but one fourth of 10,000,000;—and further, that increasing the quantity of money will *(cæteris paribus)* decrease its value. This will always be a natural truth, as long as the value of money is nothing but the proportion between the quantity of circulating money and the *occasions* of money (as I think I have demonstrated in my *Essays* on Free Trade and Finance, and especially in the *Second* Essay) and which now

is

is become such a received truth, that it cannot need further proof here.

2. The sum of 10,000,000 of dollars, added to the other bills which will continue circulating, such as State money, and certificates of various kinds, &c. *is much more paper money than the Thirteen States ever did or can bear.* The whole circulating cash of the Thirteen States, on the best calculation I have been able to make, never did exceed 12,000,000, I rather think it not more than 10,000,000 of hard dollars in value, and not more than half, or at most three fifths, of the circulating cash in this State was paper in 1774; and I am convinced, by very good documents, that that proportion was not exceeded in the other States, where paper money was circulated; and as most of the trade and business that requires stock or cash, is now in stagnation, there cannot be occasion for so much circulating cash as in 1774, when every business, trade, and occupation was in full vigor.

Indeed, it is easy to make a pretty just estimate of the quantity of circulating paper which the country can now bear, from fact, viz. from the value of the present circulating paper, of which the Continental bills are much the greatest part; by which it will appear, that the present circulating paper cannot exceed *four* millions of *Spanish* dollars in value,—and that it is as much as the Thirteen States can bear, or rather more, is plain from this,—viz. that the paper of all sorts continues to depreciate. Now, in these circumstances, to pour on 3 or 4 times as much new paper as we are found, by experiment, by plain fact, able to bear, is in my opinion a sure way to depreciate it. I think it is not more certain, if you pour three or four buckets of water into one that is already full, that some of it must run over; yea, I think that the whole quantity you pour in must all run over.

3. We have *already too much money circulating among us,* for it is certain that even hard money will not purchase more than two thirds as much labor, country produce, or other necessaries, which are not heightened in their price by the extraordinary expense of importation, as the same
would

would have purchased in 1774. Hence it follows, that the quantity of money has increased beyond the occasions of money in that proportion. This is reasoning on sure principles, which any body may disprove that can; the price of market, rents, and even real estates, afford a most plain and striking proof of this; it is further to be noted here, that the *French* and *British* armies import much money, which they are daily spreading among us, and thereby rapidly increase our circulating cash. It follows then, that our best policy is to reduce the quantity of our circulating medium, especially that dangerous part of it which consists in paper, that we may avoid, as far as possible, the further horrors and mischiefs of a depreciating currency, rather than to increase the evil by pouring in immense additions.

4. The present Continental money *passes at its exchange* thro' all the Thirteen States readily enough; any thing, even hard money, may be purchased with it; therefore it answers well the ends and uses of a circulating medium. But the new bills, however well established their funds may be, *have not the confidence* of the public in general, nor will they be readily *received*. They are a *new thing*, and their fate uncertain. This will naturally depreciate them in the first beginning of their circulation, by which the whole *commerce* of the Thirteen States, as well as the *public finance and expenditures*, will receive the most essential injury. Now *to call in a currency that is well received, and which answers well the ends and uses of a circulating medium, and issue instead of it one of doubtful credit, which will probably be received with diffidence, if not disgust, appears to me the height of absurdity.*

5. The *new bills*, however funded, must stand on the *same basis as the old*, viz. the PUBLIC FAITH, which, however modified, is neither better nor worse in the one case than the other, and therefore the new bills will depend on no better supports than the old ones, and of consequence nothing can be gained by the exchange, the trouble, risk, and expense of which must therefore be wholly lost.

6. If

6. If the old bills should depreciate, the public will *gain* the depreciation; but if the new bills should depreciate, the public must *lose* the depreciation, or must suffer a second bankruptcy to avoid the loss.

7. *If the new bills should be emitted, they will not answer the purpose of a* GENERAL CURRENCY, *which is one principal end of their creation; but, like the State money, will be confined to the State that signs them.* For it is very certain, that one State will no sooner take the new bills signed by another State, than they will take any other bills signed by the same State; for the Continental security, added to the new bills, is neither expressed nor intended to mend the credit or make good the *deficiencies* of any of the States, but such as are rendered *incapable of* payment by the *power or possession of the enemy.* The present Continental bills have a general currency, and therefore ought to be kept in circulation in preference to the new bills, if no other reason could be given for it.

8. Most of the other States who have emitted the new bills, have issued them at 40 for 1, *i. e.* at about half their nominal value, and it is in my opinion pretty much in vain for us to attempt to give our bills a better exchange or value than theirs have, in as much as their funds of redemption and means of intermediate circulation are as good as ours; besides, to attempt this would be to introduce such a variety, such a jargon of exchanges, as would defeat every purpose of a general currency of those bills.

9. If the new bills should be issued *at half value*, or should speedily *depreciate to 2 for* 1 (and I think on every natural principle they must depreciate to 3 or 4 for 1 by the time they are all out) I say, at 2 for 1 the States will not only—1. give 40*s.* for every 20*s.* which they issue; and, 2. give 10 *per cent. interest* in hard money for it all; but, 3. when they have issued it all, it will pay *but half the expenditures of the year*, if those expenditures are 10,000,000 of hard dollars, as they are generally computed; for it is plain that 10,000,000 *at 2 for* 1, will pay but 5,000,000 real money; and if the whole 10,000,000 should be called in by taxes within the year, yet at the end of the

year,

year, the States would find themselves in debt 5,000,000 of hard dollars, over and above the heavy balance now against them, and the annual increase of the public debt abroad.

But if (as will most likely be the case) most of the new bills should be outstanding at the end of the year, we must add to the aforesaid 5,000,000 of hard dollars debt, the amount of all the outstanding bills, with one year's hard money interest on them all——a vast chaos this, equal to the dreary regions of ancient night! My reader may think my reasoning is sanguine, and expression strong, but both proceed from the real convictions of my own mind, from the force of truth.

If I have discovered and described properly these operations of the new bills on the Thirteen States, it follows that *this State must take its share* of *these consequences* if they issue *their quota* of them.

What I would humbly propose, instead of this measure, is, *to repeal the acts for issuing the new bills, or suspend their execution till we are in condition to give them a currency truly and really equal to hard money, and keep them so; and in the mean time to continue the circulation of the present Continental or State bills, or both, till we can get hard money enough for a currency*, or till time and wisdom shall discover some other resource, less fraught with dishonor, disappointment, and ruin.

In fine, *taxation equal to the public expenditures* is, in my opinion, the only method in nature by which our *defence* can be continued, our *independence* be preserved, a destructive *increase of the public debt* be avoided, *our currency* (hard or paper) be kept in a state of *fixed value*, the natural springs of *industry* be given to every profession of men, our *supplies* made plentiful, the public *confidence* be restored to the *public counsels*, the *morality* of our people be revived, and the *blessings* of heaven be secured to ourselves and our posterity. All this, I conceive, is proved fully in my five Essays, especially the Fifth, to which I refer every one who is not already weary of my thoughts, and would wish to be further acquainted with my sentiments on this subject.

T

Upon

Upon the whole matter, I conceive that *union in counsels, uniformity of method* in our finances, and the benefits of a *general currency*, were the principal *objects* of the resolution of Congress of the 18th of March, 1780 (tho' I confess I never could see the advantages of that resolution.) I further conceive *these objects are already lost;* for the different exchange at which the different States issue and pass the bills, and the want of confidence of the States in each other (for one State will not take the bills of the other *States*, as we find by experiment) together with the deficient and dilatory supports given to those resolutions, I say, all these together destroy the intended union of counsels and uniformity of finances, and render a general currency of the bills impracticable.

Indeed, I ever considered the *enormous quantity of bills proposed for emission in the said resolution*, to be a seed of mischief, which would grow up with force in the course of its operation, and defeat its effects; the ill consequences of which could no otherwise be avoided, than by the most strenuous and united efforts of the States in its support, and using the greatest prudence and caution as to the quantity issued; all which I noticed with great freedom in my strictures on said resolution, in my *Fifth Essay*, published ten months ago. It now appears that the efforts of the States in support of said resolution have been very dilatory, far from decisive, and widely differing in the manner of exertion; that the general confidence of the public in the success of the bills is greatly shaken; and that the general currency of them is rendered impracticable, and not to be expected, and of course that the great design, and benefits of the measure are already become desperate.

I cannot see that it would be wise in our Assembly further to pursue a *scheme, the principal objects of which are already defeated,* and which, of course, has already *lost its capital uses;* especially when there are so many and important objections lying in the way of its operation: to suppose that we can *cut our way* thro' all these difficulties, and force the bills into circulation by *penal laws* is an idea which I cannot think admissible, for the reasons I alleged in my

Strictures

Strictures on the Tender-Act, whilst it was under consideration; at least this dependence is dangerous to a great degree, for should it fail, we shall be left dreadfully destitute, without any cash at command, and without time or means of recurring in season to our more sure resources.

If the emission of the new Continental bills should be laid aside, we may be able well to support our new emission of state bills; *if* the *demand* for them is sufficiently increased by taxes which is very practicable; and *if* the legislature could be prevailed on to take off *the penalties* of the tender-act, which were designed to enforce their circulation, but which, in my opinion, add *horror* to the currency itself, and raise *doubts and fears* which otherwise would not be thought of; and, in any view, stand as a monument of the *weakness* of our public credit, which requires such *unnatural supports* to keep it in exiſtence, and will be a monument of our *folly, shame, and inadequate policy*, if it should fail of producing the effects intended.

I apprehend it would be much more sure, natural, and advisable, if we need money for any use, *e. g.* to pay and feed the army, &c. to lay a tax on our people for it, and *solemnly appropriate* it to that purpose ONLY, and tell them so. I am of opinion such a tax would be speedily and cheerfully paid, and let the same be done for every other branch of expenditure. This will be *settling and finishing the matter as we go along*, and will keep our State and counsels free from the confusion of *perplexed finances*, the endless *labor of settling public accounts*, the *pressure* of a public debt, and the disheartening *horrors of future endless taxes*, to discharge the Lord knows what of interest and principal, which will remain to be paid in future time.

If other States are disposed to involve themselves and posterity in an *endless labyrinth* of confused accounts, fluctuating currency, and immensity of debt, it does not follow that it is either prudent or necessary that we should imitate their example. If we satisfy the quotas (demanded by Congress) as well as they, we do our duty as well; and if this be done in a way of more ease and safety to our own people, the other States cannot be prejudiced by it; and if they should apprehend that our method has more advantages in it than theirs, instead of blaming us, they may, if they please, follow our example. If this should not suit them, they will be at liberty to load themselves with *paper*, whilst we shall draw their *hard money* to ourselves, which will be the natural and unavoidable consequence of *their continuing*, and *our restraining*, the emissions of paper money.

The same thing will fill our *State* with the best inhabitants; for it is plain that every sensible man would choose to settle himself in a State free of debt, rather than in one loaded with a debt which would require the galling taxes of an age to discharge it.

But, all this aside, I would rather discharge the expenditures as we go, tho' it should prove heavy, than to leave a *legacy of debt on posterity*, which will mix bitterness with the sweets of that liberty which we are endeavouring to procure for them, and induce them to censure the humanity of our counsels, and lessen their gratitude to us for a most valuable blessing secured to them, because they will find themselves charged with the expense of it.

But still I expect to hear the old cry against my principles, that they are good, *in theory*, but not admissible, because *impracticable*; that taxing equal to the expenditures is impossible, because the people cannot bear such weight of taxes; but there is no disputing against *necessity*, I therefore beg the reader's patient attention to the following short propositions.

1. Taxing equal to the expenditures is the only possible *method of keeping our currency to a fixed value;* for if there is more money in any country issued into currency, than is taken out during the year, there must be more money in circulation at the end of the year than there was in the beginning of it, and an increase of quantity will depreciate the value of any currency (hard or paper:) this depends on principles as natural and unalterable as the laws of *gravitation,* or powers of the *magnet.*

2. A

2. A fluctuating currency is by all men confessed to be a *calamity*, much more dreadful and ruinous than *any degree of taxation* necessary to prevent it.

3. The *mischief* of a fluctuating currency is dreadfully increased by all *regulations*, *tender-acts*, and every other application of *force* made use of to prevent it; the noise, force, and devastation of an irresistible current are dreadfully increased by *obstacles* thrown in its way, beyond what would happen, if it was suffered to take its natural course without interruption; for a practical proof of these two last propositions, I appeal to the experience of every man of any business, with this plain question, " *Sir, would you not rather pay your share of the whole expenditures of the year in monthly or quarterly taxes, than suffer, thro' the year, the pains, injuries, and inconveniences of a fluctuating currency, with regulations, committees, tender-acts, and penalties in force?*" I dare believe that scarce a man of business and character can be found in this State, who would not readily answer, and from full conviction, that the tax would be much the least burdensome of the two.—I will then state my propositions with freedom, and submit them to the candid examination and censure of the public. I propose,

1. To *repeal the acts for issuing the new Continental bills*, of *March* 18th, 1780; and

2. All the *tender-acts;* and

3. To let the laws have their *free course* to oblige every man to fulfil his contracts as plain justice requires; in order to this, a *scale of depreciation* * for some time past may be easily made for the government of the courts; or the court and jury may be empowered to give judgment for what appears to be in justice due, on the full hearing the case; *i. e.* I humbly propose to be *honest once more*, to revive our *old notions and practice of justice and equity; i. e.* to suffer *justice and judgment to run down our streets, and overflow our land.* My reason for this proposal is, because I really

---

* The Assembly of *Pennsylvania*, by their act of *April* 3, 1781, made a scale of depreciation, by which all debts, accounts, contracts, &c. were to be adjusted and settled.

really believe it is both a natural and revealed truth, that *"righteousness exalteth a nation,* but SIN is a reproach to any people."

4. To *issue a tax* for whatever money we want for public use, which will lay the public burden on all *equally,* in proportion to every one's ability, and cannot wrong or ruin any body.

5. To continue the *new State money,* or *old Continental bills, or both,* in circulation. I do not think that Congress will object to this, on a review of the case; for the old Continental bills are the only paper money among us, which has any chance of a *general currency* thro' the Thirteen States, and I look on a *general currency* to be an object of such indispensable necessity, such vast magnitude, that Congress will rather choose to relinquish an old resolution already *in ruins,* than attempt to support the vast expenses of the Thirteen States, without any general currency at all.

6. I propose *to call in the old State money (i. e.* all the old State money made since the last bills under the crown) at its present exchange or current value,* which may be easily done by a tax made for hard money, or that money at the present exchange. We shall then have no bills to redeem, but the *new State bills,*† and *our share of the old continental ones.*———These things I conceive to be more practicable and less burdensome than the omission of them would be, and will be a good introduction to our reinstating our public finances, and restoring the industry and morality of our people, and of course recovering our trade, manufactures, and husbandry.

The whole is freely submitted to the consideration of the public.—It is undoubtedly mine as an individual to examine,

---

* The money here meant is resolve-money, shilling-money, and in short, all bills of this State, dated prior to 1778; the nominal amount was great indeed, but the value was so reduced by the depreciation (the exchange being at about 100 for 1) that a small tax of hard money would have sunk or redeemed it all.

† The new State bills were such as were dated since 1778, of which the Island money (100,000*l.*) was the principal emission then extant; but an addition of 500,000*l.* more was made afterwards with tender, *April* 7, 1781.

mine, remark, and propose; it is the public that must adopt or reject, and may God give the wisdom necessary to the due exercise of this great privilege.

I beg leave to conclude, by observing that this State, and our posterity, born and unborn, are yet *on this side the bottomless gulf of infinite debt,** *shame, and slavery*, but they stand trembling on the *brink* of it, and it depends much on our present counsels, whether they shall be *pushed in or not.*

---

* Our circumstances were extremely dreary at this time; the *enemy pressed* us very hard; the *burden* of the war seemed insupportable; our *visionary revenues all failed;* and our public counsels (tho' all *firm and united* in the great idea of establishing our independence at all events, and of sacrificing every other consideration to this most capital object) yet, I say, our counsels were much *divided* in opinion with respect to the *means* of obtaining it.

Schemes and projects *various* enough, and some of them *wild enough*, were proposed and urged; the great difficulty lay in the *deficiency of the revenue;* ways and means *of procuring money* engrossed every one's attention.

Among other things the scheme of negotiating *immense loans in* Europe, had long been proposed and at this time began to gain ground in *Congress;* and the ruling powers of *Pennsylvania,* seemed disposed to adopt the same idea for the particular supplies of their own treasury.

This raised in every body the alarming idea of an immense foreign debt, which would drain the country for ages to pay the *interest,* with little hopes of getting clear of it, by ever paying the *principal.*

The horrors of this almost swallowed up the dreadful apprehensions of the domestic debt, for the *burden* of this still lay heavy on the public mind; for the idea of sinking it *by depreciation* had not yet gained establishment in the public opinion. The author of these Essays, from first to last, reprobated every idea of *foreign loans* beyond a sum sufficient to purchase such articles in *Europe,* as were essentially necessary for us, and which could not *be procured among ourselves.*

He thought the resources of the country were by no means exhausted, and that by proper *wisdom and exertion,* we could *much better* furnish all necessary supplies *within ourselves,* than *by loans* abroad.

This idea he not only adopted fully himself, but endeavoured to impress it on his countrymen to the utmost of his power, by every argument and means of conviction which he could possibly lay before them.

AN ESSAY

ON

The ECONOMY, POLICY, *and* RESOURCES *of the*

THIRTEEN STATES,

AND

The MEANS *of their* PRESERVATION.

[*First publifhed in Philadelphia, in January* 1781.]

THE exhaufted ftate of the public treafury, and the univerfal diforder of our finances, the prefling demand for fupplies for every department of the public fervice, the convulfions which begin to appear, and the general confufion that threatens us, are become very ferious and alarming, are become matters of very anxious concern, and even painful defpondency, in the minds of many very wife and good men; and the public neceffities are thence arifen to fuch a pitch of urgency, as muft convince every thinking man that a fpeedy remedy or ruin muft be the confequence. In this dreadful crifis, I will venture to lay before the public fome thoughts on the prefent ftate of our affairs, and the ways and means of deliverance, which appear to me moft wife, natural, and practicable; and this I propofe to do with the fame opennefs and freedom of mind and expreffion, which I have heretofore ufed, and hope for the fame candor and indulgence from the public which I have heretofore experienced.

1. Our

1. Our country is not exhausted; *it is full of supplies of every kind, which are needed for public service.* We have men enough who would wish to serve in the army, if they could be properly *supported and paid.* We have provisions and all other supplies enough in the hands of our own people, who wish to sell them to any body who would *pay for them.*

2. We have *unanimity and general zeal for the great cause of liberty,* for which we are contending. Neither our public counsels nor movements are obstructed or weakened by strong, *opposite factions,* wasting our wisdom or force in counter-working each other. The most dangerous and alarming *commotions* among us, show such firmness, zeal, and unshaken attachment to the great *American* cause, as plainly demonstrate that they do not at all arise from disaffection, but from *other real, distressing causes.*

3. We want nothing but *wisdom, to draw into use the force and supplies of which the country has sufficient plenty.* Like the foolish prodigal, we are feeding and starving on *busks,* while there is *bread* enough and to spare, within our reach; and if we fall at last under the power of our enemies, we shall fall a sacrifice to our *own folly,* not to *their wisdom or power;* to the *weakness* of our counsels, not to the *want* of sufficient strength; if we fall at last, no nation or people ever fell more despised, or less pitied. Our *absurdities of counsel* will be *topics of ridicule* and *by-words* of scorn, whilst our posterity will be noticed groaning under the iron rod of oppression, and lashed into that *effort* for the benefit of their masters, which would *now be sufficient* to secure their and our liberty; but which we have not now *wisdom and virtue* enough to call into use.

How will the by-standers *laugh,* and our poor posterity *groan,* at the absurdity of our plans of *appreciating* our currency *month by month,* whilst every cause of depreciation continues and *increases;*—of *lessening* the number of buyers, in order to *increase* the sellers;—of *limiting, forcing, and reducing* the market, in order to *increase* the quantity of goods brought for sale;—of *forcing credit, value,* and *desirableness* into our currency by *tender-acts* and *penal laws;*—and of

procuring

[154]

procuring the vaſt ſupplies for the public ſervice, by *taking away* every inducement of *induſtry*, and throwing every branch of our trade, mechanic arts, and huſbandry into ſtagnation;—and, which caps all the reſt, the ſacred ſcheme of *ſupporting* our government, and *ſecuring* all the bleſſings of liberty by a *ſhameleſs departure* from every principle of honeſty and juſtice, which is eſſential to the very exiſtence of civil ſociety.

Theſe are but few of the *abſurdities in politics* which we have ſeen adopted, and *forced* into practice by every application of compulſive methods, and with a *perſeverance incredible*. Nothing but the abſolute impoſſibility of the practice could compel the *chimerical zealots* to diſcontinue their mad career; but, however *laughable* to our enemies, and *diſtreſſing* to our poſterity, and *incredible* to both, theſe things may appear, they may be of *uſe to us*, as the dreadful and deſtructive conſequences, the ſhame, diſgrace, and ruin, which we have ſeen reſulting from them, and which now threaten us in a manner that makes every conſiderate face gather paleneſs; theſe, I ſay, all tend to work an univerſal conviction in the minds of all men, of their total inutility and the abſolute neceſſity of an immediate reformation.

And as a neceſſary means of it, to *reject for ever from our public counſels*, thoſe weak, unprincipled men of *wild projection and madneſs of deſign*, who have infatuated the land with their extravagant *chimeras*, and drawn many of the honeſt, unthinking, but too eaſy people into their methods of ſhame and ruin. A man will not *kill his own child*, tho' ever ſo monſtrous; nor is it to be ſuppoſed, that theſe authors of our preſent diſtreſs will ever heartily concur in the *rejection* and public *cenſure* of their *own darling ſchemes*, or that they are capable of that *wiſdom* neceſſary to bring about a total reformation.*

Here

---

* Tho' the *principle* of the *American* revolution was perfectly *juſt*, and the *neceſſity* of adopting it *unavoidable*, yet the ſame great evil and inconvenience happened in the courſe of it, which, I conceive, always did take place, more or leſs, in all public commotions and revolutions which have exiſted in all States in the world; viz. that many very *improper men* worked

themſelves,

Here I muſt ſtop a little, and obſerve that the thing which makes *one nation excel another* in glory, political prudence, and happineſs, is moſt commonly this, viz. That *men of genius, abilities, integrity, and induſtry, are placed at the head of their public departments.* The public will ever receive its *tone, in reſpect of its dignity, fame, good order, and happineſs, from the men who are intruſted with the management of the public affairs.* This obſervation is ſo manifeſtly true, that every man, in the ſmall circle of his own domeſtics or neighbours, can judge well *how any buſineſs will be done, if he knows who is to do it.* We cannot hope for reformation and good management of our public affairs, unleſs we ſee *judicious, upright,* and *ſteady* men in the ſeveral departments of the State; men *adequate* to the offices they fill, and *induſtrious* and *perſevering* in attending thereto. But to return,

I will ſuppoſe for once that every public department was filled with the beſt and moſt ſuitable men, and that every individual was willing to adopt and purſue the beſt methods of ſafety and deliverance which our caſe admits; what then can and ought to be done? I anſwer,

1. *Every man is to be called on for the debt which he owes the public.* Every man ſtands indebted to the public for his ſhare or proportion of all the money or ſupplies neceſſary to the public ſafety, and this debt muſt be paid, or the public ſafety muſt be inſecure, muſt be in danger. The public ſafety cannot be put off, as ſome people ſerve their Maker, *with empty prayers and good wiſhes.* This payment can *ruin nobody.*

---

themſelves ſomehow or other *into places of great truſt and importance,* both in the *legiſlative* and *executive* departments; by which the *vices,* the *whims,* the *wild projections,* and *viſionary plans* of individuals became diffuſed and almoſt incorporated into the *character, counſels, laws,* and *adminiſtration* of the States.

Such men are ever dangerous, but moſt peculiarly ſo in times of general *calamity and diſtreſs,* when wiſdom, fortitude, and prudence are moſt indiſpenſably neceſſary in rulers and leading men. But however unfortunate our States have been in that reſpect, they were ſtill happy in this, that the evil did not reach their moſt capital departments; the *army, foreign affairs,* and, in moſt inſtances, the *preſidency of Congreſs* were under the direction of men of moſt unblemiſhed *integrity, adequate abilities,* and moſt *conſummate prudence;* and had not our confuſions been in ſome degree under *their* check, it is hard to ſay to what lengths they might have extended.

nobody. It is manifest, that if any individual, even the least able to pay, should, by some accident, lose as much money or other estate as his share of this debt amounts to, it would not *ruin* him, it would not greatly distress him; for the truth of this I appeal to every man's knowledge of his own and his neighbour's circumstances; but on the other hand, how many thousands of individuals are *ruined for want of this payment?* Dreadful and swift witnesses of this are, all those who have suffered by the *violations of our public faith*, by the *depreciation* of our currency; all those who are *not paid* for the *produce of their lands*, or personal *services*, or *other fruits* of their labor, with which the public has been *furnished*.

The people of the Thirteen States are almost in the same condition which they would have been in, if they *had sold their principal produce to bankrupts* or broken merchants, who could not pay them. They, by this means, have not money *to pay* their debts, to *trade* with, to *buy* of the merchant, to *lay in their stock* for the ensuing year, to increase their *scale* of business, &c. &c. *One disappointment creates another;* an universal stagnation of business is the consequence; and all industry is checked even in its first principle, as well as in practice; and of course the produce of the lands, and the fabrics of the tradesman are daily lessened, and of course the *great stock for home consumption*, and the great *staples of trade*, are daily dwindling away. These are facts notorious to every body, and arise directly from this, viz. that there is not public money enough to pay the public creditors.

Whereas, if every man was called on for his share of the public debt, *there would be money enough to pay every body*, and all this dreadful deluge of calamity would be remedied at once, and every individual would be a gainer by the tax he would pay, because he loses more every year by the *confusions* and *disappointments* arising from *this want* of public monies, than his *tax* would amount to. This is all *mighty well* in THEORY, but *impossible enough* in PRACTICE. Do you say this in earnest? I do most seriously contend,

that

that it is very possible in *practice;* it is possible, it is practicable, it is necessary.

2. *To make out a true estimate of the public debts and demands, and issue a monthly tax* for the amount, in which every one shall be called on for his share, and no more than his share. The money which is collected in the first month's tax will go out again among the people, and help them to pay the next month's tax; that will go out again, to be again called in by the third tax, and so on; and the quickness of circulation hereby excited will supply the want of medium; for it is plain to every man, that *a guinea, which passes from hand to hand thirty times in one month, pays as much, and of course goes as far, as thirty guineas which are paid but once in a month.*

It is further manifest, that such an universal *demand* for money will give it *value,* will make it an object of universal *desire;* this will give *spring* to industry, *motion* to every method of obtaining money, and *security* to every man who has obtained it. It is necessary for us *to know the worst of the matter,* let that *worst be as bad as it will.* Let us know how much it will *cost* to *save* our country, to *restore our morality,* our *industry,* our *safety, and happiness.* The *profits of the year at most will do it,* because no more *is or can* be spent in the year than is raised or produced in the year; for we loan abroad enough to pay for all we import from abroad for the public use.

It is impossible indeed to *increase our husbandry or manufactures, without a free, open, and sufficient market.* Shut or diminish the market, and the supplies of it will soon lessen; open and increase the demand of the market, and all supplies of it will soon increase. All this is too manifest to need proof; therefore it is necessary to *remove wholly all obstructions* of our market, *all fetters, and restraints, and discouragements* of business, such as *embargoes, tender-acts, limitations, regulations,* &c. &c. Let every body be at liberty *to get money as fast as they can,* and be put under every natural advantage for doing it.

I am of opinion that our people would receive an *enfranchisement* of this sort with as much joy, as the inhabitants of *Greece* received the declaration of their liberties from the mouth of the *Roman* Ambaſſador. If premiums had been offered for *ſtupid plans* and *wild projections*, I think worſe could not have been offered than ſuch as we have ſeen, viz. *laying embargoes on the exports, to increaſe the produce of the country for the army; forcing people to ſell their goods below the market price, in order to induce them to bring more to market; offering money with horrid penalties, in order to make folks love and eſteem it; embarraſſing all buſineſs, to get the more of it done;* &c. &c.

Such wild, ſtupid, horrible, and unnatural projects, with the effects of them, diſcourage our people, and render the wheels of government heavy, and deſtroy all confidence of the people in the public counſels, much more than the real weight and burdens of the war. Theſe bear no ſort of proportion to the diſtreſſes which are produced by the madneſs of our counſels, and unnatural way of doing every thing. Laws ought to be *conformed to the natural courſe of things;* but we have been abſurdly endeavouring to *control* the natural courſe of things, and *bend it to our laws.*

I think it impoſſible that further arguments ſhould be neceſſary to prove the expediency, yea, the ſtrong propriety, and urgent reaſon of diſmiſſing at once all theſe moſt unnatural and deſtructive meaſures, theſe abſurd *ſcandals of human reaſon, and of* American *policy;* that ſo our minds may be open to impreſſions from the true ſtate of our caſe; open to the real difficulties we are under, and to the proper meaſures which will, by their natural operation, afford us relief. We ought to *ſtudy hard* for this. Perhaps we may by ſtrong exertion, by cloſe *attention,* and the *bleſſing of God*, be able to find out, *that means muſt be adequate to their ends; that the way to reſtore our credit is to pay our debts; that the way to pay our debts is to get money to pay them with; that any burden laid on the whole community is ſafer for the whole, than when the ſame burden is laid on a part only; that the only way to keep the members ſtrong and in health is, to keep the belly full of ſubſtantial food,* not of *huſks,* &c.

But

But the absurdity of our measures is not all the objection I have to them. They are *inadequate* to their own purposes. What can it signify to plague the continent, and exhaust all the patience of our people with difficult, *intricate plans* of raising money, when all the plans put together, and fully executed, would not produce *half*, *perhaps not a quarter*, *of the sum necessary to our preservation?* This is like bailing a leaky ship with a spoon, when buckets are necessary to keep her free. I think it would be far more *natural* and *satisfactory* to our people, to make out *estimates and demands equal to our necessities*, which will give this strong inducement to the efforts of each individual, viz. that it will be adequate to the purpose; that the *means, however difficult, will be sufficient to produce the great ends designed.* When the great demand is made known, the first question will be, *Is this enough? Will this be sufficient to the purpose?* An assured, affirmative answer will inspire great courage and effort, when the object is the *great wish*, the *passionate desire* of almost every individual, as is most manifestly the case with our people. It is a false delicacy, a shameful timidity, a dangerous injury to a nation, to keep them ignorant of their *true circumstances and real danger, and not give them an opportunity to put the means of their safety in practice.*

I am clearly of opinion, that scarce a man of any weight could be found in the Thirteen States, who would not readily and with joy pay a much larger sum than his tax would amount to, if he had reasonable hope that the *distresses, oppressions,* and *dangers* of the country could be thereby removed, a *free course of justice* be restored, every man's *person* and *property* be *protected*, and the *natural inducements of industry* be favored and encouraged, and our *insulting enemies be effectually opposed.*

The *yearly incomes of the country* are much more than sufficient to do all this, if properly called into use. We have two armies in the country to feed, and the produce of the country is amply sufficient for both. The supplies of the *one* we are paid for, it is only *the other* which must be supported from our own resources; and after supplying both
armies

armies (if our hufbandry and trade could be fuffered to take their natural courfe) we fhould have large produce to fpare for exportation.

In addition to all this, I am clearly of opinion that our refources are fo great, that with proper management (even tho' the war fhould continue feven years longer) *the treafury of the Thirteen States might be filled with filver and gold coin, and be made a BANK as fafe and ufeful as that of* Amfterdam *or* Venice; and all this within a very fhort time, as may be clearly demonftrated to any body who is acquainted with the nature and conftitution of this kind of fubject.

The *Dutch*, as foon as they found out the fecret of infpiring their people with the true fpirit of induftry and enterprife, foon recovered their national credit, and grew amazingly rich, long *before their wars with* Spain *ceafed*. We have vaftly greater means in our power than they had, and want nothing but *their wifdom* to improve them to as great advantage. I conceive it to be very certain and manifeft, that *our national character, honor, and fafety are yet in our own power*, and depend on nothing for their full and *perfect eftablifhment*, but our own *wifdom* and *effort*, and the *bleffing* of Divine Providence.

I will conclude this Effay with one propofition, which, however much like a paradox it may appear at firft fight, I think is very demonftrable, and I conceive will require little more than mere infpection for a fhort time, to convince every man of difcernment and ferious attention of its truth, viz. *it would be eafier and cheaper for every man of bufinefs, whether farmer, tradefman, or merchant, to pay his fhare of the whole annual expenditures of the public within the year, than not to pay it;* i. e. he would live more *eafy* thro' the year, and be *richer* at the end of it, by *paying* fuch tax, than by *not paying* it. This was the great Poftlethwait's grand doctrine in *England* thirty years ago, and every body now fees the great advantages which would have refulted from his advice, had it then been adopted and purfued.—

" Oh! that we could know *the things of our peace*, in this the day of them." God forbid they fhould be *hid* from
our

our eyes. Men often look abroad for things that are at home, and seek at a distance for things that are near. I apprehend that union of sentiment and effort, *in the practice of means*, which it does not require any great sagacity to discover, would be quite sufficient for our safety. A plain *simplicity* is more to our purpose, than any *depth of delusive policy.**

An honest *integrity* and natural *prudence* always create *dignity, confidence,* and *respect*. On these I would wish to build our national character, on these I would ground our defence, and in the practice of these I would hope for the divine blessing on ourselves and on our posterity.

* Every reader will easily observe, that the grand *principle of revenue* every where recommended in these Essays is this, viz. an actual recourse to the solid wealth of the States for the public supplies, *i. e.* a tax of sure product, payable in hard money or paper at the exchange which should be current at the time of payment; and this tax must be so really productive as to be equal to the expenditures. These are the MEANS here referred to, on which the States could *safely rest*, and all *visionary projects* (which multiplied in abundance at this time) would of course vanish before the *true means* of our deliverance, and become soon as *manifestly useless* as they were *really vain and ridiculous.*

A DIS-

A DISSERTATION

ON THE

Nature, Authority, and Uses of the Office of a

FINANCIER-GENERAL,

OR

SUPERINTENDANT *of the* FINANCES.

[*First published in Philadelphia, Jan.* 24, 1781.]

AS the appointment of a *Financier-General*, or *Superintendant of the finances* or *public revenues*, has been *some time* in contemplation, it may not be unacceptable to the public to see a dissertation on the *nature* of that high office, and the *duties, powers,* and *privileges* annexed to it, with some notes on its *importance, dignity, and uses*.

This is a new subject in *America*;[*] it may therefore be expected that the first essays on it will be imperfect. Nothing but experience in so immense a subject can give a full and comprehensive knowledge of all its parts, and of the duties, powers, and privileges necessary to the proper management and due execution of it. I have thought much on the subject, and find it greatly exceeds my comprehension. I can only give the public such thoughts as occur to me,

---

[*] The office of *Superintendant of finance* was first created by resolution of Congress, *Feb.* 7, 1781; and on the 20th of the same month, *Robert Morris, esq.* was appointed by vote of Congress to execute the office under the name of *Superintendant of finance*, tho' he was commonly called the *financier-general*, or simply the *financier*.

He

me, which, without further preface or apology, I shall do with freedom, and hope they may be received with candor.

The duty of a Financier-General, I humbly conceive, is,

I. To *inspect and take account of the whole finances or public revenues* of the States, and the whole *funds* or *stock* out of which they are to grow; *i. e.* every sort of public property, all sources of all kinds out of which public monies are to be derived to supply the public treasury, and superintend all these, *i. e.* take due care that they are *well kept*, free from waste, destruction, and embezzlement, and that they be *managed* and *improved* to the best advantage.

II. To inspect and point out, arrange and put into action, *the ways and means by which the necessary supplies of the public treasury* may be derived from all these *sources* or *funds*, that the same be done with most *ease* to the subject, and *safety* to the States, with all that *effect*, *decision*, and *expedition* necessary to all public movements, and at the *least expense* which can be adequate to these great ends; *i. e.* to make *estimates* of the yearly expenditures, and point out the *ways and means* of supplies, and to arrange both in so clear and particular a manner for the inspection of Congress, that they may have at once a view of the whole and all the parts, to the end that, having such a state of all the facts and materials before them, they may be able to form the most wise and proper resolutions thereon, which the safety and well-being of the States require.

It is further necessary that this be done in such *season*, as to give sufficient time for the deliberations of Congress, and carrying their resolutions into effect, in the most natural and easy way, that thereby the dangers, mischiefs, and

---

He continued in the office till *Nov.* 1, 1784, when he resigned, and *no successor* has been since appointed *under that name;* (the business of the treasury was put into commission afterwards, and continued so till the dissolution of the old Congress) but I take it that the same office is revived and continued by the present Congress under a *new name,* viz. that of *Secretary of the treasury;* which office is at present held by *Alexander Hamilton, esq.* and the appointment of this officer lies (among others) in the President of the United States, with the approbation of the Senate.

and confusion of precipitation, hurry, and extreme urgency of these very weighty matters, may be avoided.

III. To *inspect and control all officers* who have the *keeping, disposal,* or *management of each and all of said funds,* to the end they may be properly directed, encouraged, checked, and supported in the discharge of their several offices, in such manner that their management, accounts, and payments may be completed with least delay and most advantage to the States.

IV. *To call on the several States for such quotas as may be assessed by Congress,* and to keep them advised of every thing that the demands of Congress and the public exigencies may require of them, respecting the revenue.

V. *To inspect all the expenditures of the States,* of every kind, to the end they may be made with the *best economy,* and to the *utmost benefit* of the public.

VI. *To inspect and control all officers, concerned in the payment or expenditure of the public monies or revenues,* and to demand a return of all such expenditures from such officers, with the balance of all their accounts, that so he may be enabled to keep an exact balance of all the public revenues and expenditures, ready for the inspection or information of Congress, whenever they shall call for the same.

VII. *To inspect all debts due to and from the States, all bills of credit,* and *all treaties* and *contracts* relating to the revenue or public monies, to the end there may be collection and payment made, with that punctuality and decision necessary to the *support of the public faith,* that so the States may receive no detriment from any *failure or delay* in this delicate and important particular.

VIII. *To keep an account of the whole revenue,* and all its parts, and of the *whole expenditures,* and all their parts, in so clear and digested a manner, as to be able, on reasonable notice, to report to Congress the state and amount of each, with the *deficiency* or *surplusage* of the revenue for purposes of government.

IX. *To procure such certain documents of the whole funds or resources* of the public revenue, and all their parts, and

make

make himself so acquainted with the same, as to be able to point out the *best ways and means* of increasing the revenue, for any purposes of public safety and advantage, when Congress shall require such service from him.

X. *To make discovery and report to Congress* of any department of the expenditures, which are *more expensive than necessary*, and of any that *are starved* thro' want of such supplies and allowances as are necessary.

XI. To be in all things subject to the *control of Congress*, and to be *accountable to them only*.

This view of the extensive duty of a Financier clearly discovers the *nature, importance, and uses* of his office. The great design of it is, to range the several sources of the public revenue in order, that the *whole system* of it may be *clearly understood*, that any *part that is wanted* may be at hand, that the whole may be *raised* with the *least burden* possible to the people, and be made to go as *far, and produce as much benefit*, as possible.

The *invention of ways and means* of improving the revenue, or raising public money, is not a more necessary part of the business of finance, than *economy and prudence in the expenditures*. Perhaps the latter is the more important and difficult of the two. For I conceive there may be found *ten men* who know how to *get money*, to *one* who knows how to *keep it*, or *pay it away with proper economy and prudence;* and I apprehend that our present distresses, and the exhausted state of our revenues, arise more from defects in the *last* of these, than the *first*. The natural operation of this office discovers these errors, and leads to a remedy. For,

1. It is manifest that the man, whose duty it is to *find all the money* which is to pay every department, will be most likely to study and introduce *economy* in the expenditures, and to spy out and check any *excessive expense or waste*.

2. It is further very natural to suppose, that when the Congress are informed with certainty of the *extent of the revenue*, they will calculate their *expenditures within the limits of it;* so that this office becomes a restraint even
on

on Congress itself, if we can suppose them *capable of any want of due consideration or prudence* in this respect: And,

3. Every officer of expenditure will find himself under *some check* also, when he reflects that he must bear the *penetrating eye of the man* who finds all the money which he *spends or pays out* of his office. Further,

The *powers*, *rights*, and *privileges* of this great office are also obvious from the above survey of its nature and uses.

1. It appears that this office is of *great extent and importance*, and therefore ought to receive from every department of the States all such *suitable helps, countenance, and support*, as are necessary to procure and preserve its *uses, proper operation, authority, and dignity*.

2. That this officer ought to be *kept constantly advised by Congress, of all such resolutions* of that body as respect the public *revenues and expenditures*.

3. That he should have right to *demand all accounts*, and *inspection of all books*, which respect the public revenues and expenditures. And,

4. That he should be vested, by commission from Congress, with all *the authority* necessary to the full and perfect discharge of all the duties of his office, and be indulged with *all the privileges* necessary to the *success, use, and dignity* of it.

As this ground is all new and untrodden, it may be dangerous to define *too particularly* the *duties, rights, authority, and privileges* of this office. A little practice on the great and general principles on which it is founded will gradually open the particulars further necessary, which may be added by future provisions, if such shall be found expedient.

As I am ignorant of the present arrangement of the revenues and expenditures, I cannot tell how far any of the above particulars may fall within the departments already established, and have here only to add, that as far as any of them are provided for, *a return only* will be necessary from the subordinate officers, of such particulars as may be requisite to complete the accounts, and furnish the materials of this great office.

From

From which it appears, that this office does not interfere with any other offices of the revenue or expenditures; such as the office of *Treasurer or Treasury Board, Auditor of Accounts*, &c. &c. This office *begins* where they *end*. This office takes the state and balance of the accounts of all the other officers, as they make up and finish them. This office arranges and brings them all into one view, and states in order every branch both of revenue and expenditure, from the aggregate of which the amount of the whole is made.

This brings into distinct and plain view, the *whole stock, cash, credits*, and *incomes of the revenue* of every kind, and also all the *debts and expenses* which are to be provided for and paid.

With these documents, a man endowed with the proper *skill*, great *comprehension* of mind, and natural *aptitude* to the subject, necessary for this great work, will be able to see the *excesses* and *deficiencies* of each branch of revenue and expenditure, and to judge in what manner every error may be corrected and reformed; and what makes this reformation easier is, that the error may be soon discovered, and the particular branch or place in which it lies be pointed out, and the natural and proper means of amendment put into direct and speedy operation, which *nips the evil in the bud*, before it has *time* to grow into such *fatal magnitude*, as not only to *corrupt the department* in which it lies, but also to spread into other contiguous departments, so as to become *ruinous* in its continuance, and very *difficult* in the cure.

Further, this great officer, with such a comprehensive view of the whole stock and resources of the revenue, will be furnished with the best advantages to consider the nature and strength of each of them, and to *form such arrangements* and put them all into such *operation and effect*, as to produce the greatest supply with the least burden to the people.

This is of mighty importance. This may be done, and often is, *in such an injudicious and unnatural way, as to double the burden of the people, without increasing the supplies;* and the

the worſt way that perhaps ever was or could be thought of, is that which has been adopted for five years paſt, viz. *paying the expenditures by the depreciation of the currency.* This has done it indeed in ſome meaſure, but with ſuch an inundation of calamities as are enough to draw tears.

A good *Financier* is much the *rareſt character* to be found of any in the great departments of ſtate. *France* has had but *three* in 400 years, viz. the *Duke of Sully*, under *Henry IV. Colbert*, under *Louis XIV.* and Mr. *Neckar*. *England* has not had one ſince Queen *Elizabeth*'s time: perhaps Lord *North* is equal to any that have gone before him, but his whole talents at finance are all exhauſted in *running his nation in debt*, and contriving ways and means of paying the *intereſt* by the endleſs oppreſſion of his people.

The great *Poſtlethwait* indeed, about thirty years ago, had the true genius of financiering, as appears by his various treatiſes on that ſubject; but the ſtupid miniſtry of his time had ſo little conception of the matter, that they did *not know a Financier when they ſaw one*, or, like the cock in the fable, did not know the *value of the jewel* which *ſhined* in their ſight.

We rarely read in hiſtory of any wars, or other movements *of expenſe*, undertaken by any nation, but we find their *finances ſoon fail*, and then the movements (be they ever ſo important) muſt be *diſcontinued*, or *ſtarved* into very trivial effect. This generally happens becauſe they have not an *able financier*, who can calculate and balance the *expenſes* and *reſources*, and keep the latter in ſuch effectual operation, as will be ſufficient for the exigencies of the former. This calamity does not always ariſe from the *expenſes* being greater than the *reſources*; it more commonly takes its origin from ſome or all of the following capital errors of finance:

1. *In the aſſeſſment and collection;* as when the tax is not laid *in ſeaſon*, or is ſo laid that it does not operate by way of *equality* on every part of the community; when the tax is conſumed *in the collection of taxes;* by an over number of officers or other needleſs expenſe; by the *embezzlement* of the officers; &c. &c. Of this kind of error are, all free quarters of troops,

troops, all forcible impreffing of fupplies, or fervices for the public, &c. &c. becaufe thefe bring the public burden in an *over proportion on a few*, by which not only the *few* are oppreffed, but the *whole community* fuffers. Injuftice always carries *damage* with it; thofe who do *not fuffer*, fee they are *liable* to like injury, and of courfe are *in fear*—their peace and eafe are not *fecure*.

2. By *wafte or want of economy in the expenditure*; as where the money is paid for purpofes *diverfe* from thofe for which it was granted, and appropriated; when the public movements are fo ill contrived and managed, as to coft *more money* than is neceffary; when *ufelefs projects* are undertaken; when the public property is fuffered to *wafte, decay*, or *perifh* for want of *due care* and *proper difpofal* of it; want of difcernment and difcretion to pay the *moft preffing* demands *firft*, and let thofe debts lie unpaid, that can remain with the *leaft damage*, whenever it fo happens that there is not money on hand enough to fatisfy *all the demands*. A great deal depends on this kind of difcretion, when the demands may happen to *exceed* the fupplies, &c. &c.

3. *By fuffering the public credit to decay*; this is an amazing wafte of the public wealth; for when a man's credit runs low, he muft be in difficulty to find people that will *truft him at all*, cannot expect a *good choice*, or to be well ferved, and after all, over and above the *intereft and other douceurs*, he muft expect to pay heavily for the *rifk* of trufting him. When a prodigal's eftate comes to be devoured by *premiums, intereft, and difcount*, when he begins to receive 50*l*. or 80*l*. and give fecurity for 100*l*. his fortune muft grow *defperate* foon. It is the *fame cafe with the public;* and in this way no nation on earth can hold it out long. Every *degree* of this mifery brings an *increafe* with it, and if it cannot be ftopped, a bankruptcy muft enfue.

I mention thefe particulars only to fhow, that a *Financier* is the moft *natural and fure guard* againft thefe mifchiefs, as well as the moft able and likely perfon to *remedy* them. The man *who finds all the money* that is to be expended,

expended, is the most *likely man* on earth to spy out any errors in the *revenue* or *expenditures*, and to keep the public *faith sacred and inviolate;* as his own personal happiness, fortune, and character, will be immediately affected by these errors; and as he is supposed to be a man of the best abilities and strong attention to business, and that he devotes his whole time and powers to this branch or department only, he must be presumed to understand it *the best*, to inspect every part of it with the most *pervading eye*, to spy out the errors *soonest*, and to have the best ability and disposition to apply the most natural, speedy, and effectual *remedy*. That which is *every body's business* is commonly *nobody's*.

In all aggregate bodies, where *many men* make up a board, they can throw off the blame of any mismanagement from *one* to *another*, &c. which cannot be the case when the trust is committed to a single *person*. Besides, from the nature and duty, the design and uses of this office, it appears most plain and evident, that *it must be the work of* ONE MIND.

Its object is so *vast and complex*, and the action consists in *comparing, fitting, and balancing* so many different things to and with each other, that it cannot be otherwise done than by the attention of a *single mind*. In a state of quietude, when small expenditures are necessary, little experience, skill, or economy may do; but when the expenditures grow vast, and require a *strong draft* on every resource of the revenue, then *skill, attention, order, and method* become essentially necessary. A small shed may be built without skilful workmen, but in a building which requires a *thousand pieces* of timber to be framed together, a *head workman*, of skill and attention, becomes absolutely necessary to regulate and control the whole work; in the smallest frames indeed, such a workman is very desirable and useful, tho' not so *essentially* and *absolutely* necessary.

It follows then, that every community, every nation, every state, ought to have a *Financier to control the revenues and expenditures*, and preserve the *public faith* inviolate.

late. We have tried it on five years *without one*, I am fully of opinion that we cannot be worsted the five next years *with one;* and therefore, as the quacks say of their nostrums, it will do no *hurt*, there is a *probability* of success, the *expense* is small, it is at least worth a *trial*.

As this is the first essay of the kind that has appeared here, it cannot reasonably be supposed that it should *be perfect;* and I hope those who find *faults* in this, will mend them in *more perfect* exhibitions of their own, that our country may reap all advantage from the *best and most correct wisdom* of all its inhabitants.

REMARKS

ON THE

RESOLUTION OF COUNCIL,

Of the 2d of May, 1781, for raising the Exchange to 175 Continental dollars for 1 hard.

Humbly offered to the Public.

[*First published in Philadelphia, May 9, 1781.*]

I HAVE read President *Reed's* defence of the resolution of Council of the 2d instant, for raising the exchange of the Continental currency from 75 to 175 for 1 of specie, or State money; but am not convinced that that resolution was grounded on the interests of this State, much less, that it was *indispensably necessary* in our present circumstances.

I agree perfectly in his opinion, that it is not *beneath the dignity* of a government to explain any public measures which may be misunderstood thro' *ignorance;* but should they be misunderstood any *other way*, I do not pretend to say how far the dignity of government might suffer by an explanation.

I am also clearly of his opinion, that there has long been a number of persons in this city, who have fermented uneasiness, sparing neither *art, nor falsehood, nor violence*, to effect their purpose. We have seen uneasinesses, tumults, and ferments among our citizens rise even to the *shedding of blood*,[*] which doubtless originated with very *bad men*, and

---

[*] We had many tumults during mr. *Reed's* administration; the most memorable of which was, the riotous assault of mr. *Wilson's* house, *Oct.* 4, 1779.

and I could have wished that inquiries and profecutions might have gone on, till the *true, guilty authors* could have been difcovered, held up to public view, and punifhed; but government has found this inconvenient, fo I have no more to fay about it.

I will only obferve, that I do not think the character of our citizens is that of uneafinefs, tumult, and faction: I rather think they have exhibited an example of great meeknefs, of tame patience, almoft bordering on ftupidity. Nor am I at all convinced, that the objections that have been made to the abovefaid refolution of Council, arife at all from *faction*, or any difpofition to impofe on the unwary. When a man finds that *eleven fhillings out of every pound* of his cafh, is annihilated by a public refolution, we may allow him to be *uneafy*, without calling him *factious*.

I proceed, with all refpect due to the honorable Council, to make fome remarks on their defence. I have no pleafure in cavilling at the meafures of government, but only wifh to caft light on a fubject, in which our *whole State is interefted*. And, as I have never been concerned in factions, ferments, tumults, or riots, but ever have been a peaceable citizen, and hearty well-wifher to the true interefts of our State, I expect a candid attention of my fellow-citizens to the arguments I offer.*

1. The

1779, in which the mob proceeded from infulting language and violent abufe, to actual firing with mufkets, with which they were all armed.

A great number of moft refpectable citizens, who were in the houfe, returned the fire on the mob, and in fine, a number of lives were loft.

Many of thefe rioters were taken up, and held under legal profecution for their offence; but the Affembly, by their act of *March* 13th following, indemnified and pardoned them all.

* The facts referred to in thefe Effays were, at the time of their publication, frefh in every one's memory, and matters of general notoriety; but that is not the cafe with ftrangers, or even our own people, at this diftance of time; therefore a ftatement of thefe facts may be neceffary to enable the reader to underftand thefe remarks, and the reafonings on them.

The Affembly of *Pennfylvania*, 25th of *March*, 1780, iffued 100,000*l.* paper bills, funded on the *faith* of the State, fome *city lots*, and the Province *Ifland*, which at that time belonged to the State (hence this emiffion was called Ifland money:) they alfo iffued the bills on intereft at 5 *per cent. per annum*.

Thefe bills, thus propped up, were ufhered into the world with great confidence of the Affembly. They, however, paffed in a depreciated ftate, much

1. The firſt fact alleged by the Council is, "*that by the law of the State, and their own oaths, they are required to publiſh*

much below their nominal value: to remedy which, a ſubſequent act was paſſed,. *Dec.* 23, 1780, by which theſe bills were made " a legal tender; with penalties for *refuſing* to take them for goods, &c. viz. *forfeiture* of *double* the value offered; and for the ſecond offence, of *half* the offender's lands, goods, and chattels, and *impriſonment of his perſon* during the war."

This act had ſeveral uncommon clauſes inſerted in it, viz.

1. That agents for the public, collectors of taxes, &c. ſhould account to the treaſury for ſuch of theſe bills as they had received, at the price or rate at which they received them, *i. e.* at their depreciated value.

2. That the exchange, till *Feb.* 1, then next, between Continental currency and theſe bills, ſhould be 75 for 1; but the real exchange of Continental to hard money was 100 for 1, at that time.

3. The Executive Council were empowered and required to publiſh the rate of exchange between ſpecie and Continental money, in the firſt week of every month after ſaid *Feb.* 1: and

4. That exchange, ſo publiſhed, ſhould be the exchange between *Continental money and theſe bills*. On *May* 2, 1781, the current exchange of theſe bills to hard money was 3 for 1, and to Continental, was 75 for 1; but the exchange of hard money for Continental was about 220 or 225 for 1; and the practice was, to multiply the exchange of the State bills reduced to Continental, by their exchange with hard money, viz. 3; which gave 225 Continental for the value of one hard dollar.

At this time, the Council declared the rate of exchange of hard money for the month of *May*, to be 175 for 1, which was the ſame thing (according to the operation of the ſaid act of the 23d of *Dec.* 1780) as declaring the exchange of the State bills to Continental to be 175 for 1; and the practice ſtill continued of multiplying the State money reduced to Continental, which was now become 175 for 1, by its hard money exchange, viz. 3; which made the exchange of Continental money three times 175, viz. 525 for 1 of hard; a vaſt and ſudden leap indeed, and which became the *current exchange* in *leſs than a week* from the declaration of the exchange by the Council.

So that every perſon who had one week before given a hard dollar for 225 Continental ones, found that he had loſt *above half the value of his money*, as it would, at the end of the week, purchaſe but 3-7ths of a hard dollar.

This made a mighty noiſe, and deeply affected every body; as Continental money was then *the general currency*, and *all prices in market were ſet or eſtimated in it*, as much as they were in *old Tenor* at *Boſton,* at the cloſe of the *laſt French war* in 1763.

This rouſed the feelings of mr. *Reed*, who was Preſident of the State at that time, and was ſuppoſed to be the *prime mover*, not only of the ſaid *declaration of Council*, but of the *act* on which it was grounded, and induced him to publiſh his defence of ſaid declaration, on which theſe remarks were made.

The error really lay in the *abſurdity of the law itſelf*, which limited the State money to a certain exchange of Continental (viz. 75 to 1) with ſuch variations of exchange of hard money, as ſhould be publiſhed by Council the *firſt week in every month;* which exchange of *hard money, by the operation of the act*, became the legal exchange of the *State bills*, and of courſe raiſed their exchange 4-7ths higher than the *real, true exchange* of them was at that

publish the rate of exchange the *first week in every month.* This proves, I conceive, that the Council are required to

publish

that time, and made them bring indeed more than double the Continental money which they would have purchased before, but did not enable them to buy any more hard money than before.

Had the Council *pursued the act*, they might have *been excused;* but their *error* lay in declaring *a false exchange* of hard money, *much below* the true one, with design, by way *of trimming and bending facts*, to reduce a *little* the absurd effects of the act itself. The true exchange of Continental for hard money, the first week in *Feb.* 1781, was about 100 for 1, where it had stood several months; in *March* it was about 115 to 1, and in the beginning of *April*, 130; but rose fast thro' the month, and got up to 220, the first week in *May*.

These exchanges and the interesting effects of every variation of them, will appear to a stranger as *intricate and hard to understand* as the *price of stocks* in *Change-alley;* but they were perfectly understood by people of all ranks at that time, in as much as every variation of the exchange altered the value of all their cash on hand.

One thing makes these manœuvres very important, viz. they not only *raised the exchange* of Continental money up to 500 or 600 to 1, but in a few days *stopped the currency of the Continental bills intirely*, after which they never passed at all *as money;* or any otherwise than as an article of speculation, at most desultory and capricious exchanges from 400 to 1000 for 1.

The same cause so disgusted the minds of all men with paper bills of all sorts, that our State money (tho' undoubtedly well funded) depreciated in less than a month to 6 and 7 to 1: the final redemption of which, by a *future appreciation*, cost this State above 120,000*l.* tho' we never received more than 20, or at most, 30,000*l. real value* for it.

Perhaps this whole transaction affords the most striking proof conceivable, of the absurdity of all attempts to *fix the value of money by a law*, or any other methods of *compulsion*.

In this instance we see the Continental money *mortally wounded*, and our State money *debilitated and depreciated* down to a *seventh* part of its nominal value, by the *very ill-fated means* which were designed to *support both of them*.

Thus *fell, ended, and died*, the Continental currency, aged 6 *years;* the most *powerful state engine*, and the greatest *prodigy of revenue*, and of the most *mysterious, uncontrollable*, and almost *magical operation*, ever known or heard of in the *political* or *commercial* world; bubbles of a like sort which have happened in other countries, such as the *Mississippi scheme in France*, the *South-Sea in England*, &c. lasted but a few months, and then *burst* into nothing; but this held out much longer, and seemed to retain a *vigorous constitution* to its last, for its circulation was never more brisk and quick than when its exchange was 500 to 1; yet it *expired without one groan or struggle;* and I believe, of all things which ever suffered dissolution since life was first given to the creation, this *mighty monster died the least lamented*.

Yet I hear that some folks are preparing to dig the skeleton of it out of the grave where it has quietly rested 9 *years*, that we may have the pleasure of *wasting a million or two* upon its obsequies.

If it *saved the State;* it has also *polluted* the *equity of our laws;* turned them into *engines of oppression and wrong;* corrupted the *justice of our public administration;* destroyed the *fortunes* of thousands who had most *confidence in it;* enervated the *trade, husbandry, and manufactures* of our country; and went far to

destroy

publish the *true* exchange the first week in every month; but the whole city knows, that 175 for 1 was not the *true exchange* on the 2d instant; and the Council cannot be supposed to be *ignorant* of what is known to every other person in the city, and which the laws suppose them to be acquainted with, or it would be absurd to lodge the power of judgment with them.

So that their *variation from the true exchange* cannot be excused by any plea of *ignorance*. Therefore, when they say, " that they have not the same opportunity of *knowing* the current rate of exchange with accurate precision," as the merchants have, I think it follows, that they ought to have inquired of the merchants, and gained the most accurate information possible, in a matter of that consequence and delicacy, in which the *laws* of the State, their own *oaths*, and the *interests* of the whole State, were concerned; but not that they should adopt the *lowest* known rate, at which they could discover that any commercial transactions had been adjusted.

The *lowest rate* is never the *current* or *true* rate of exchange, any more than the *highest*. It essentially and most manifestly differs from the *true*, as far as the *extreme* differs from the *mean*; a difference which the Council, on their own principles, had no right to make, as it did not, in my opinion, comport with, or satisfy, either the *words* or *meaning of the law* under which they acted. But while the obligations of the *law*, and their *oaths*, are urged, and the *integrity* and *consciences* of the Council are deeply affected; would any one suppose that the Council would publish what all the world knows to be *false*, and that under the sanction of an *oath?* Could the Council, without violating every principle of truth and veracity, declare the exchange to be 175, when there was not one person in the city but must know the contrary; Indeed I think it is bad

enough

---

destroy the morality of our people; after all this, I wish it might be suffered to lie where it is, in a state of quiet *oblivion*, yea, *perfectly forgotten*; for I think that every *remembrance of it* must be mixed with *bitterness*.

I hope the reader will excuse this small digression; for when I came to the *spot* where the poor old CONTINENTAL died, I could not help stopping to mark *the place* with some little *signal of notice*.

enough when a Council, by any solemn act, violate their *faith;* but when they are hardy enough to violate their *oath* and " *veracity*" too, the matter must look very serious to all good men.

Further, while we are told so much about *laws* of the State and *oaths* of office, I am led to inquire where these *laws* and *oaths* have been for several months past, during which time the exchange was *constantly and gradually rising;* and the Council, in the first week in each month as constantly declaring and publishing the exchange to be 75 for 1, for three successive months past, when there was not a single person in the city but must have known the contrary? *Consistency* in the acts and declarations of public bodies, is of great use, and much to be desired; their *dignity* stands mightily tarnished, and nigh unto ridicule without it.

2. Another fact adduced by the Council, is, " that the rate of exchange has been, by common consent and usage of trade, *gradually rising* for some time past; so that no person, in his private dealing, pays or receives at the rate of 75 for 1;" and the whole city may add, *neither was it on the 2d inst.* (the date of their resolution) at 175 for 1; the current exchange was known to every one to be at least 220 for 1, at that time.

The Council go on to argue, " that the people have raised it (the exchange) by common consent, and Council have only followed them, by making a declaration of what *they* have done." If this allegation is *true*, it will justify the Council's conclusion; but if it *is not*, it may be deemed a provoking, insulting attempt to impose a *deception* on " *the unwary*" public, and beneath the *dignity* of Council to adduce it. I will examine it with confidence, because every merchant in the city knows whether it is true or not.

The resolution of Council declares (if not expressly, at least *in effect*, and all the effect that it could in reason be supposed to have) that the exchange of old Continental to State money is 175 for 1. Now the people, by common consent and usage of trade, have never done this; have not raised that exchange to 175 for 1; it had never

Z

exceeded

exceeded 75 at that time; therefore the refolution annihilated the difference between 175 and 75, *i. e.* 4-7ths, *i. e.* fomewhat more than eleven fhillings in the pound, of all the Continental money, which every man was poffeffed of at that time. The truth of thefe facts and obfervations are obvious to every *merchant*, and indeed to every *market-woman*; and I leave them to ftand on their own ground, having no difpofition to indulge a vein of farcafm or ridicule on this ferious fubject.

I would only obferve, that this fatal refolution has taken from thoufands their *daily bread*, and ruined the fortunes of many who had capital fums of that money on hand; that all the Continental money in the *treafury* of the State, or *due* in taxes, or any other way, is reduced more than half, to the great lofs and embarraffment of the public; and every man who has *not paid* his taxes, may now pay them with *lefs than* half the real value which thofe paid, whofe rates were collected one week before. " And is this reafonable? Is this juft?"

Further, the Council adduce this fact, viz. " that the rate of exchange has been *gradually rifing* for fome time paft:" and they might have added, that the people have been *gradually conforming* themfelves to that rife. But the cafe is widely different, when they make fuch a fhocking *ftart at once*, as from 75 to 175. A man may defcend from the *garret* to the *lower floor* by a flight of ftairs without any damage; but were he to defcend at *one leap*, he would probably break his neck. The feelings of too many make any further explanation of this matter quite unneceffary.

3. But the third fact adduced by the Council, and which, I fuppofe, is defigned for a clincher, and which is to afford an argument of *indifpenfable neceffity*, is this, viz. " that the State of *New-Jerfey* had, on the 27th ult. raifed their exchange to 150 for 1; and that the people of that State were pouring in their Continental money on us," &c.

I cannot but ftop here, to obferve how quick the old tone is changed. It has been a long time urged by people of great judgment, that the only natural and fure way to

prevent

prevent our being deluged by an inundation of Continental money, is, to keep the exchange of it somewhat higher here, than it was in the neighbouring States. Yet those very people who now, for this reason, force up the exchange, have, for years past, been in the bitterest manner raising an outcry against such as depreciated the currency.

It is true, indeed, that the *Jersey* people could bring their Continental money over *Delaware*, and purchase State money at 75 for 1; and it is as true, that our people could carry the *Jersey* money over the *Delaware*, and sell it at 150 for 1; and the advantage, on the whole, would be on our side; because all the Continental money which was in the *Jersies* at the date of their resolution, cost their people 75 for 1, and they get no more for it here. Whereas our people, who carry their State money to them, purchased it for 75, and got 150 for it.

But after all, it could be but the *bubble of a day;* it might furnish employment for stock-jobbers, schemers, and idle people a short time, but could not continue long; it is not possible that advantage could be taken long of different exchanges on the two sides of *Delaware*, whilst the communication is so very great; and after all, the difference could be but trifling.

For neither the resolution of the *Jersies*, nor of *our State*, can make the State money of either a whit more valuable, *i. e.* make it purchase any more hard money or any other valuable goods, than before; but the *violent shock* must depreciate both, as we find by experience, which is the surest evidence in matters of this nature.

But, *salus populi, suprema lex*. What is now to be done? Is it best to repeal the resolution? I think not. The mischief *is done*. A repeal will not *remedy it*. The *Continental money has received its mortal wound*. I do not think it advisable or possible to *heal* it. The State money follows fast after it. The exchange for hard money on the 2d instant was 3 for 1; it is now said to be 4 for 1 at least.

I think we have now no choice left, but to adopt my old doctrine, viz. " To recur to our solid substance, or real wealth,

wealth, bidding a *final* farewel to all bubbles, vain expedients, and shadows."

The present evil originates *in the law*, which the Council have undertaken to *execute*. If a law is so *absurdly* made as to be *incapable of execution*, nothing but absurdity and perplexity can arise out of it. It will lie with the Assembly in their approaching session, to repeal the law or not.

On the whole, if the Council have not increased the *esteem* of the public by their resolution, they are at least entitled to some *compassion*. They have undertaken a *task that is impossible;* and I imagine their difficulties would puzzle much *abler heads* than theirs. If a legislature should make a law that a *bar of iron* should be cut asunder with an *ax of wood*, the officer entrusted with the execution of it, might think it his duty to *try;* but he need not be surprised, after all his labor and chopping, to find the *iron bar intire*, and his *ax sadly bruised*.

The exchange, or operation of money, is a very nice, touchy, delicate subject; and no man can, by right or prudence, intermeddle with it, who does not *understand its nature and principles*. No *dignity* of station, or *reverence* of character, can secure a man against *ridicule* and *contempt*, when he comes to be knocked about by the *magical effects* of that all-powerful subject, when put into operation under the direction of *unskilful hands*.

STRIC-

STRICTURES

ON A

Publication in the FREEMAN's JOURNAL of May 16, 1781, *signed*

TIMOLEON.*

[*First published in Philadelphia, May 23, 1781.*]

IT is of no confequence to the public, whether TIMO-LEON or myfelf have the *blackeſt heart*, the *fouleſt mouth*, or the *moſt ſpiteful pen*. I yield to him the *palm* in every article of perſonal abufe, fly innuendo, or grofs ſcandal; I mean to confine myſelf to ſuch particulars as the public have an *intereſt* in.

In my Remarks on the Refolution for raifing the Exchange, I obferved that the Council, in their defence, had urged that both the *laws of the State*, and their *oaths of office*, required what they had done.

I replied, that the exchange which they had publifhed for ſeveral ſucceffive months, was not the *true exchange;* and therefore could not ſatisfy either the *law* or their *oaths of office*. Mr. T. ſeems to deny this, but ſays, the virtuous part of the community reprefented the exchange as various from 150 to 200 or 225. This I deny, and call on mr. T. to produce *one virtuous perſon* of the community, of

knowledge

---

* TIMOLEON was an angry writer, who appeared in the *Freeman's Journal* of *May* 16, 1781, in vindication of the *reſolve of Council* on which the foregoing Remarks *(of the Citizen)* were made.

I ever

knowledge fit to be confulted, who ever *told* the Council the exchange on the date of their refolution was 175; or one refpectable merchant (as he goes on to affert) who ever *faid* or *agreed* that the exchange in *March* or *April* laft, was 75 for 1. The *contrary of both* is well known to every body in this city. *Plain fact* is here notoriously againft mr. *T.*; for which I appeal to the *whole city*, who are the moft competent judges.

What mr. *T.* afferts, and I deny, is this, viz. that *the exchange of hard money was here in* February, March, *and* April *laft, at* 75 *for* 1, *and in* May 2*d, inftant, at* 175 *for* 1. I do not begrudge mr. *T.* the whole credit of his fetch, viz. " that the act of Affembly does not require the Council to publifh the moft *current rate*, but fimply *the rate of exchange;*" but whatever credit this precious fubtilty may give to his ingenuity, it can afford no help to his argument; becaufe *the exchange* does mean the *current* or ufual *exchange*, from the force of the particle *the*, for which I refer to the moft common *Englifh* Grammar of the fchools. The words are not *an exchange*, or *any exchange*, but *the exchange*, which cannot with any propriety mean any but that *particular one* which was moft *current* or ufual at the time.

But mr. *T.* cannot poffibly underftand this myftery, how a *buyer* can be a *lofer* by the Council's declaring the exchange 175. I can eafily explain this matter of fact; before the date of that declaration, with 220 dollars the buyer could purchafe candles or fifh to the value of one hard dollar;

I ever fuppofed the author to be Prefident *Reed*; but as he chofe to fhroud himfelf *in darknefs*, and the printer would not *give up his name*, I did not think myfelf under any obligation to addrefs him in a *ftyle or manner* due to the *firft officer* of the State; but, with the greateft freedom, treated the performance according *to the merit of it*.

But whoever was the author, the arguments (fuch as they were) are confidered in thefe Strictures; but where the author was mean enough to *leave* the merits of the matter, and *defcend* to low fcurrility and perfonal abufe, I paffed over it, as it was of no confequence to the public; and only remarked on one or two fcandalous perfonal imputations, which I never before heard of from any body but himfelf.

In fine, the *fatal importance of the facts*, not any *perfonal animofity*, was at that time my fole motive for making my Remarks and Strictures, and is now the fame for re-publifhing them.

dollar; but after that declaration, he must pay 500 of the same dollars for the same goods; his loss therefore is the difference between 220 and 500, *i. e.* 280, or *something more than eleven shillings in the pound.*

This is a computation grown very familiar in the city; and I cannot but wonder it should remain so long a mystery to mr. *T.;* for this same reason, or to use the numerical figures of the resolution (to make the matter plainer to mr. *T.* who discovers much mystery, and some *mystery of mysteries* in the matter) because that 175 dollars bring no more after the resolution, than 75 would bring before, every possessor of Continental money, and of course the public treasury, *loses 4-7ths of all they have on hand,* and all *debts due and payable* in that currency.

This he *confidently asserts to be a falsehood.* I think he might be ashamed to deny a *truth of public notoriety;* but if he is really so dull as not to be able to see this, it is manifest the Council see it very plain, as is very evident by their attempt (tho' a vain one) to obviate the mischiefs of it, in the payment of *taxes, fines,* &c.* and which, he says, is *the real and true cause of much of the clamor* against the Council's resolution.

But in this he is very much mistaken, because the remedy adopted by the Council is *void of effect,* as it does not reach or remedy the *mischief;* for tho' the tories and whigs too cannot pay their *State money* for taxes at more than 75, yet they can and daily do change their State money for *Continental,* and pay their taxes with much less than *half the real value* which those paid, who paid their taxes before the resolution was published, and this is publicly known to every body. Nor can I see any thing but personal honesty which prevents all our collectors from changing all the State money which they received before the resolution, for old Continental;

---

* By resolve of Council, *May* 4, 1781, collectors of taxes, fines, &c. are directed to receive them in the following manner, viz. when paid in old Continental money, they are to receive the same sum at which each person stands charged in the duplicate (or tax-book;) but if paid in specie, or State money, or new Continental *(i. e.* 40 for 1 money) they should receive it at the *former exchange* of 75 for 1, not according to the *new rate* of 175 for 1, published by Council, *May* 2d, *i. e.* two days before.

nental; and paying *that* into the treasury. This is the blessed way in which (it is the peculiar felicity of mr. T. to discover) our treasury has been enriched since the resolution.

If it still does not appear to mr. T. that the old Continental money, either in his own desk or in the treasury, is reduced to less than *half the value* it had before the resolution, the best way I know of to satisfy himself is, to take some of it to buy any necessaries, and he will, I doubt not, have a *practical proof* too strong to admit a doubt; and if in this or any other way he should happen to be *convinced*, I shall expect that he will *publicly acknowledge it*, for his own sake.

But to follow mr. T. a little further. I have said in my Remarks, that " the resolution of Council declares (if not expresly, at least *in effect*, and all the effect that it could in reason be supposed to have) that the exchange of old Continental to State money, is 175 for 1." This mr. T. denies with great triumph. I must beg the reader's attention here a moment; the words of the law are, that the Council are required to publish " the then rate of exchange between specie and Continental money, which exchange, so published, shall be *the exchange of the Continental money and the State money*," &c. in which it is manifest, that the most express design of publishing the exchange of *specie*, was thereby to fix the exchange of the *State money* on a par with it; this was the effect which the legislature intended, and the very effect which the Council intended, as appears by their provision *against* the effects of it, in the case of taxes, fines, &c.

Yet mr. T. with great assurance asks, " What has this to do with the Council's publication, which has not State money in contemplation?" His *law logic* helps him out but poorly here, viz. that the *operation of the law* on this publication, and not this *publication* itself, produced the effect: he might as well deny that a *miller* grinds wheat, because the *millstones* grind it; or that a *man* travels a journey on horseback, because the *horse* only travels; for it is very plain, that the law, without this publication, would no

more

more have raised the exchange of State money, than the mill would grind the whea . without the *miller* to set it a-going, or the horse perform the journey without the *rider* on his back. I therefore conclude, that every one will be convinced that my proposition is true; and if it is true, mr. *T.* acknowledges that " *my observation will apply.*"

Mr. *T.* among other reasons why the Council did not raise the exchange last month, gives this one, viz. the *speculation* at *Boston* and *Rhode-Island* improved the *credit* of the old Continental money here, and therefore was not to be interrupted by any *disadvantageous alteration* of the exchange.

This speculation was, to purchase Continental *here* at 220 for 1, and sell it at *Boston* for 75; but in the very next paragraph, he reprobates the same kind of *speculation to the Jerseys* very severely, I suppose, because it was not so *profitable*. " Is this," says he, " a traffic which public counsels are to promote and encourage?" I have no where said these speculations were *good*, I mentioned them as *bad* things; and all I said, and all my argument required, was, that they were but *bubbles of a day*, &c. and could not justify so *dangerous* and *ruinous* a measure, as raising the exchange to prevent their mischief, because this would make the remedy worse than the disease.

I did oppose the tender-act, which is the act in question *(see my Strictures on Tender-acts, p.* 128*)* whilst it was under consideration, with all the power I was able, and in the most public way; and therefore, in mr. *T.*'s opinion, my *indecency*,*

---

* This author is fond of finding fault with my manner of writing, complains of *indecency*, &c. the writings which excite his uneasiness are now before the reader, who will judge whether his censures are well or ill grounded.

I have only to observe for myself, that I ever meant, when writing on serious and grave subjects, to deal in *definite ideas and sentiments*, and to use *such words to express them*, as should convey my meaning with the greatest *clearness and ease* to the reader; *polish* of expression, or *grace* of period, is neither my *talent* nor *object*; and I suppose, the *plainness of my style*, especially when it happened to excite his *feelings strongly*, appeared to him like *indecency*; but if calling things by their *right names*, or, as the *Dutch* say, *calling a spade, a spade*, is *indecency*, I must bear it as well as I can; and I hope, the *clearness* of the sense will make amends for the *want of polish* in the expression with *such readers* as are more delighted with the *sentiments and ideas* of an author, than with the *turn of his periods*, or the *dress of his language*; and this is the sort of readers I most wish to please.

as he calls it, may have some palliation. But I can see no *indecency* in pointing out the evils or impracticabilities of a law, which the whole community must suffer; if this is done in such a way as tends to a remedy. *The numberless instances of private distress*, as well as the *starving condition* of all the public departments, and especially the *unprovided state of the army*, were my great inducements to write my Remarks, and thereby expose the errors which at least aggravated our calamities. I have no *ill will* to the *Council*, I have none to the *Assembly;* but I wish the wisdom of both may increase, and all their errors may be mended.

I cannot forbear animadverting a little on the rancorous, malignant conclusion of mr. *T.* in his invective against some of our citizens. I think a little *decency* to the place which gives him bread, might have induced him to spare his black epithets. It is a foul bird that besmears his own nest. But if he intends (as perhaps he does) to apply any of his detestable characters to me personally, I have only to aver, they are *sheer abuse, without the least foundation of truth*.

I did, indeed, on repeated advices of the great distress of *Boston*, for flour and iron, in 1777, load a vessel of my own with a cargo of both, and sailed for *Boston*, but was (on *April* 6) unfortunately taken on the passage, by the *Orpheus, English* frigate, and carried into *Rhode-Island*, where, after a month's imprisonment, I was released *on exchange*, having *lost my whole vessel and cargo*, to the amount of about 2000*l.* hard money; for which I *never had*, nor *do expect* ever to have, the *least compensation* from them.

I also did remain in the city when the *British* troops captured it, having, among other reasons, a child in the smallpox at the time, who could not be removed; but it is not true that I enjoyed the least *friendly or confidential intercourse* with them or their adherents.

I spent three months of the time in visiting the *American* prisoners in the gaols here, and procuring and carrying to their relief, such food and clothing as I could collect, at a time when their distresses were beyond all description, and when it was deemed *a crime* to show compassion to

them;

them; and on the 6th of *February*, 1778 (long before there was any probability of an evacuation of the city) I was committed to gaol, and suffered not a *collusive*, but a most severe, confinement of 132 days, without being able, by every possible application,* to obtain any knowledge of the cause of my confinement; but the presumption generally admitted was, that my *constant* and *careful attendance* on the *American prisoners* was thought to imply too strong an attachment to *Americans*, to be compatible with either the duty or protection of a *British* subject.

As to what mr. *T*. very malignantly suggests about *reviling government, evading resolutions of committees, and croaking discontent*, I beg leave to observe, that I never have opposed either *projects* of committees, or *measures* of government, except such as have since, on the fullest experiment, and the plainest demonstration of fact, been *reprobated*

---

* When the *British* troops under the command of general sir *William Howe* took possession of *Philadelphia*, *Sep*. 26, 1777, my whole family then in town was myself and two daughters, the one a little over, and the other under, twenty years of age, and were under such terrors, that I could scarce leave them an hour in the day-time.

On the 6th of *Feb*. 1778, I was taken out of bed at 11 o'clock at night, by orders (as was said) of general *Howe*, and confined in the public gaol of the city.

I was under great apprehensions that my daughters would go *out of their senses*, with the *fright* and their *unprotected condition*.

I represented my distress in sundry letters to general *Howe*, to his superintendant of police in the city, and to sundry other officers, with most earnest request that I might be informed of the cause of my imprisonment, and have an opportunity of a hearing before the general, or any court he might appoint; but never could get any answer or knowledge of any crime or fault charged to me, but was held in close confinement till the day preceding the evacuation of the city, 17th *June*, 1778.

My property to a large amount was likewise seized and conveyed into the king's stores; part of which I indeed recovered afterwards, but I sustained a final loss of about 500*l*. value, which I could never recover or obtain any compensation for.

And more than all this, my long and close confinement so injured my health, and impaired my constitution, that I am not yet, nor ever expect to be, restored to the state of sound health which I enjoyed before that grievous oppression.

From these circumstances (which were well known to President *Reed*, and the whole city) we may judge with what rancor and malignancy of heart it could be suggested by TIMOLEON, that *my intercourse with the British troops was friendly and confidential*, or *my confinement collusive*, and of my own seeking, that I might plead the merit of it with my countrymen after the *British* were gone.

bated by our graveſt counſels, and *condemned* by the general conſent of *Americans* as *bad policy;* ſuch as *limitations of prices, forcing ſales* of private property, *tender-acts,* emitting *deluges of paper currency, fixing* the value of paper currency *by law,* and other *abſurdities* which have involved *America* in *greater calamities* than the *Britiſh arms.*

And I freely ſubmit it to every ſound *American,* whether I may not, *with* good right, *and without* vanity, boaſt of it as an inſtance and proof of *ſound judgment* and moſt *genuine patriotiſm,* that I have *early* diſcovered and oppoſed thoſe *ill-judged* and *pernicious expedients,* which, by the general voice of *America,* are now *execrated* as the undoubted ſources and cauſes of our preſent *corrupted morality, enervated ſtate* of defence, *ruin* of *public faith, proſtitution* of *national character, loſs* of the *confidence* of our friends, *contempt* and *diſgrace abroad,* and *confuſion at home.*

I have, indeed, with great reluctance, *oppoſed* popular prejudices, when they were incapable of being *controlled.* But I freely ſubmit it to my fellow-citizens, whether time and fact have not ever juſtified my concluſions, with this only difference, that the conſequences have been verified in *fact* in a much *ſtronger degree,* and more *aggravated miſchief,* than I have *delineated.* If one material inſtance of my oppoſition to projects of committees, or meaſures of government, different from this, can be produced, I am content to ſtand corrected in the face of the public; and I am confident my fellow-citizens will not ſuffer me to be *oppreſſed,* becauſe I have told them the *truth before every one could ſee it.*

I never once expreſſed or felt any *diſſatisfaction* to the *great cauſe* of *American* liberty, but ever wiſhed and promoted its ſucceſs, as far as was in my power. The truth of every part of this declaration I do aver on *my honor,* and have the fulleſt proof of the facts, and doubt not my fellow-citizens will conſider me as a *much-injured man,* and give full credit to what I ſay.

I do at leaſt call on mr. *T.* to produce the leaſt ſpark of proof of the contrary. However injurious I conſider his malignity, I am yet leſs affected by his *publication,* than I
ſhould

should have been by his *secret whispers*, which I could have no opportunity to contradict.

I humbly beg leave to suggest further here, that out of these *very facts*, so spitefully misrepresented by mr. *T.* when they are candidly considered, arises a *stronger proof* of *my attachment* to the *American* cause, than most whigs are able to exhibit, and a much stronger proof than any which I even heard mr. *T.* ever has exhibited of *his* whiggism.

My writings on *finance* are open to every body, and have met the approbation of many of the *greatest men* in *America;* and I believe mr. *T.* begins to feel the *force* of them: for I find he begins to ' *hope* we shall have *spirit* enough to enforce *a hard money tax,*' which has long made *a part* of my scheme of finance, and which mr. *T.* has constantly *reprobated,* till now. But this does not flatter my vanity much; for I believe he might as well ' jump out of the garret into the street,' as write on the subject of finance at all.

I have only to beg the reader to keep his eye steadily on *the facts,* not on *the colorings,* of mr. *T.* or myself, and from those facts to form his judgment. Facts are hardy, stubborn things, which mr. *T.* or I may *color* indeed, but neither of us can *break* or *bend* them; such as follow, viz.

1. Was the current exchange of specie in *February, March,* and *April* last, 75 for 1; or was it 175 for 1 on the 2d instant, as declared by Council?

2. Was the exchange required by law to be published, *an* or *any exchange,* and not *the current exchange,* as mr. *T.* quibbles?

3. Did the Council's declaring the exchange of specie at 175, produce the same effect as declaring the exchange of State money at 175 would have done?

4. Did the Council's declaring the exchange of 75 in *February, March,* and *April,* and 175 in *May,* which was not the then current rate of exchange, satisfy either the words of the *law,* or *their oaths* of office?

5. Did

5. Did any respectable merchants, on consultation, inform the Council that the current exchange in *February*, *March*, and *April* last, was 75, or 175 on the 2d instant?

6. Did the declaration of the Council on the 2d instant so operate on the old Continental money, as to reduce the value of it to less than half, both in private hands and in the public treasury?

7. Did the raising the exchange in the *Jerseys* afford reasons by any means sufficient to justify our following so fatal an example?

These are some of the principal facts contested between mr. *T.* and myself. They are all matters of public notoriety. The public are not all beholden either to mr. *T.* or myself, for the knowledge of any of them, *except the 5th*, of which we must depend on mr. *T.* for the necessary proof.

If the above facts and reasonings are true, I think it will follow, that the *poison* which mr. *T.* is so much concerned to find an antidote for, will prove to be these *poison truths*, which he fears will have an operation to his disadvantage. I am sorry, too, that they ever were truths. I am quite of opinion they are a sort of *poison truths*, which have done, and I fear will do, much hurt; and therefore I hope I may be excused for putting my mark of disapprobation on them.

STRICTURES

ON

Two Publications in the FREEMAN'S JOURNAL *of May* 30, 1781, *signed*

PHOCION,

AND

IMPARTIAL.*

[*First published in Philadelphia, May* 23, 1781.]

THESE authors, together with TIMOLEON, are the *sons of darkness*. The printers are not at liberty to give up their names. I take PHOCION and TIMOLEON to be the same person. But as I suppose they are ashamed to be seen, I do not mean to disoblige them by hauling them *into light*, but hope, whilst it is impossible for me to know who they are, it will be deemed very absurd to suppose any thing I write, designed for a *personal application* to either of them. PHOCION says, that " the CITIZEN has insinuated that no merchant could *have advised the continuance* of the exchange at 75 in *April* last." This is *not true*, PHOCION; you do *depart from the fact*; and you *know you do*.

---

* PHOCION appeared in the *Freeman's Journal* of *May* 30, 1781, when, in answer to my challenge, he, with great triumph, produced *Robert Morris*, esq. who, he says, advised *publishing the exchange* at 75 for 1, in *April* last; which, *if true*, would have been *nothing to the purpose*.

But

do. Had you kept to the fact, your sentence would have stood thus, viz. *The* CITIZEN *denies that any respectable merchants ever informed the Council that the true or current exchange of specie was* 75 *in* April *last.*

On this I have challenged TIMOLEON, and now challenge PHOCION. It is mean for you, PHOCION, to sneak out from the point in question, by such an artful but pitiful evasion. A man of character would be ashamed of it; but it is easier to *blush in the dark* than before company.

You go on to mention mr. *Robert Morris,* as having given his opinion and advice to publish " the exchange in *April* at 75." I have reason to believe that this is *not true;* that mr. *Robert Morris* never was consulted in *April* last, nor did give any *opinion* or *advice about publishing the exchange* so late as *April* last; and that his opinion at that time was decidedly for publishing the exchange *as high as the truth,* if it was determined to publish it *at all.*

Mr. PHOCION has called up mr. *Morris*'s name, which obliges me to do the same. Mr. *Morris* is easily consulted, and will doubtless inform, if desired, what he did say on the subject to which I refer.

At an earlier period, say the beginning of *February* or *March,* when the exchange stood with little variation, and the subsequent rise of it was not foreseen; when the effects of the tender law could not be known; many merchants, and mr. *Morris* among them, might think it dangerous to shock the then state of our trade and currency by any unnatural and sudden start of the exchange, and might give it as their opinion and advice to publish it at 75. But if this is admitted ever so true, it does not follow that any of them ever meant to intimate thereby, that the *true exchange*

even

But he appeared again in the *Journal* of *June* 6, with a recantation of what he had published about mr. *Morris.*————IMPARTIAL appeared in the same paper of *May* 30, and is, I suppose, the same person with TIMOLEON and PHOCION, or, which comes to about the same thing, some heated partisan of the *same cast.*

He set out with blackening the CITIZEN and all the *Republican party* with rancor enough, and concludes with a labored panegyric of mr. *Reed's* government. Any body who wishes to see any of these pieces, may find them in the *Freeman's Journal,* as above quoted.

even in *February* or *March,* much less in *April* last, was 75.

Therefore, the whole matter does not contain any the least contradiction to any thing which I have asserted, is therefore a manifest departure from the fact in question, and of course is just so much foreign matter lugged in for the mere purpose of artful shuffle and deception.

Mr. PHOCION, you must stick better to the point; it is shameful to start, shuffle, and evade the true matter which labours at bar; you must keep to the fact; if you do not do this *for yourself,* I will do it *for you;* for I can and will hold you *so close,* that it shall not be in your power to *squirm out of the grasp* which pinches you. Farewell.

Now mr. IMPARTIAL calls for my attention a moment. It would be hard to take no notice of this man, who seems to be boiling over with gallish matter, and to have taken great pains to scrape together a considerable number of very hard, black words, suitable to express it. It is easy to see what sort of a blowing genius this is, by only casting an eye over his " *crude revilements, villanies, hollow principles, pestilent spirit, jaundiced eyes, feculencies of wealth, execrable characters, stream of discord, Sodom, false patriot,* BECAUSE JEALOUS, *sneer of the States, disappointment and malice,* which are IMMORTAL *with the wicked* AFTER THEIR DEATH," to which may be added his poor old hackneyed word, " *junto,*" which he has honored with large employment in this service.

But I must beg to be excused from following him thro' such a foul thicket of hard names, coarse scurrility, and low dirt. I can easily believe he is not acquainted with President *Reed,* tho' I cannot so easily admit that he is acquainted with *his government,* yet it is very clear he means to defend it; but as he seems to be very scant of matter, and barren of argument, it may be deemed a good-natured action to help him out a little. We generally judge of our governors as we do of our carpenters, *by the goodness of their work when it is done.*

I will therefore attempt to lay down some general rules, marks, or signs, by which a good or bad government may

B b

be distinguished; by the help of which mr. IMPARTIAL may, if he pleases, elucidate and embellish the government of his hero, and support it with *some kind of argument*, which will probably have more weight with the public, than any *loud-sounding*, *hollow* encomiums whatever.

1. When the *laws protect* the persons and property of the subject, the government is *good*: but it must be *weak* or *wicked*, when the laws are so framed, as in their operation to *injure* and *oppress* the subject in his person or estate.

2. When the laws are held in general *reverence* by the people, the government is *good*: but it must be bad, when the laws are generally considered as *iniquitous*, and *execrated* as such.

3. When the laws *restrain* wicked men, and support, *protect*, and encourage honesty, upright dealings, and industry, the government is *good*: but when the laws let all the *rogues* in the community *loose on the honest* and industrious citizen, the government must be very *weak* or *wicked*.

4. When men of grave *wisdom*, proper *abilities*, and known *integrity*, are put *into office*, the government is *good*: but when we see men of *wild projection*, doubtful *morals*, and inadequate *abilities*, crowding themselves by address and corruption into office, the *confidence* of the people in the government must be *lost*, and the *administration* itself must be *very weak*.

5. When the laws are made a *rule of duty*, and *bulwark of safety* and *protection* to the subject, the government is *good*: but when we see people imprisoned, persecuted, and ruined, *without trial*, *conviction*, or a *day* in *court*, the administration will be deemed *bad*. The *worst man* that ever lived has a *right to a day in court*, to a cool hearing, and an opportunity *to say*, by himself or counsel, all which he fairly can *for himself*.

6. When the laws are gravely administered by the proper officers, the government is *good*: but when *mobs*, *riots*, *and insurrections* infest the community, and disturb the public peace; when the force of the community is put under any *other direction* than that of the *law*; the government becomes *dangerous*, and all security is lost.

7. When

7. When the forces and resources of a State are so modelled, put into order, and under such control, that both may be called into action and use, when, and to such degree as the public safety requires, the government is *good:* but when the public debts are unliquidated or unpaid, the army ill-supplied or ill-paid, the force of the State dwindling away, and the means of preservation lost, the administration must be amazingly *bad*, and the State in a condition of most alarming danger.

8. When the trade, agriculture, and mechanic arts, those great sources of, not the wealth only, but even *morality*, of a country, are properly encouraged, the government is *good:* but when we see our merchants drove, by the *oppression* of the *laws*, or *absurdity of administration*, out of the State, and the farmers and tradesmen following them with their produce and fabrics, the government must be *bad* indeed.

9. When the *dignity* of public boards, and the *personal* respectability of public men, are well kept up in the minds of the people, the government is *good:* but when the public *boards* are execrated as wanting common honesty or prudence, and public *men* cursed, hated, and despised, as void of *honor*, *truth*, *skill*, and *uprightness*, the government must be *bad*.

10. When we see the officers of government carefully attending to the forms, decisions, and spirit of the laws, which secure the liberty of the subject, the government is *good:* but when we see officers in the great departments eagerly and impatiently grasping at *enormous*, *dangerous*, and *arbitrary powers*, attempting to deprive the subject of the *rights of a jury*, the *habeas corpus*, and other essential legal forms of process and trial, we have reason to apprehend the government is *bad*. These are the very *tyrannies* of the *British* court, and are ranked among the *capital articles* of complaint, on which we ground our *war* against them, and *separation* from them.

11. A good government is willing to come to the *light*, and to *explain* the *public movements* to the understandings of the subject: *bad governments* are more impatient of *examination*,

mination, are apt to complain of the *liberty of the press*, and when remarks are made on their measures with ever so much propriety, truth, and modesty, they rarely attend with candor, but endeavour to *divert* the attention of the public by *artful evasions* of the matter in question, and instead of answers, entertain their fellow-citizens either with fulsome *rapture* of *panegyric*, or declamations of *personal abuse*, or *foul scurrility*, neither of which has the most distant relation to the grievances complained of, and which require their explanation.

It may be objected that the above rules, as far as they relate to the laws, will not apply, because it *luckily* happens that our constitution does not vest the President with the power of legislation; it is equally true, that our constitution does not empower the President to *raise mobs*, and *appoint committees*, and therefore the objection may go to that part too. Upon this I have only to observe, that the whole management of the public affairs, which is supposed to be under the great influence of any *prime mover*, is commonly called the administration or government of such a minister.

But as I am not going to make use of any of these rules for myself, but wrote them solely for the benefit of mr. IMPARTIAL, he or any body else that reads them, may *leave out* all which he thinks *not for his purpose*, and make use of, and apply, such of them only as he thinks *apropos*.

On the whole I have to observe to TIMOLEON, PHOCION, IMPARTIAL, and every other writer, that if any of them are disposed to object to the truth of any fact or principle which I have advanced or may advance, and will state their objections fairly and candidly, I shall have pleasure in giving them all the information in my power; but if they are disposed to *run off in a tangent*, thro' the endless wilds of *abuse, personal reflection*, and *scurrility*, in which the public can have *no concern*, I must beg leave to inform them once for all, that I think it inconsistent with the *respect* I owe the public, and the *dignity of character* I mean to assume to myself, to follow them in such a *dirty career*. I have neither talents nor taste for that kind of writing.
I mean

I mean to addrefs the underftanding of my readers, not their paffions, their biaffes, much lefs their corrupt tafte. I mean to write on very ferious, important fubjects, and wifh to convince and inform ferious minds. I have no more ambition to be thought a *witling*, a *punfter*, or *fharp dealer* in *fquibs* or *innuendoes*, than I have to be reputed an *able bruifer*, a *fly ftabber*, or an *accomplifhed affaffin*.

Facts and principles are my only objects, and the public good the great end I have in view, and it is painful to me to be diverted from my courfe by objects of *low wit*, *fcurrility*, or *fcandal*, which can only raife a *laugh*, or a *grin*, without the leaft advantage to the public.

SINCE writing the above, I find mr. PHOCION begins to acknowledge and mend his errors. I doubt not he was compelled to this by force of very *ftrong conviction*. It is *human* to err, it is *honorable* to own and correct an error, it is *diabolical* to perfift in an error after conviction. I am rejoiced to fee fo honorable a motion in mr. PHOCION, and I hope he will go on in the good way, till all his errors and miftakes are corrected.*

---

* It may be worth notice here, that the tender-act which was to be fupported by the precious plan of *regulating the exchange month by month* by the *definitions* and *publications* of the Council, and the vain and ridiculous attempts of the Council to put the fame into execution (all which make the fubject of thefe remarks and publications) I fay, the faid tender-act and fubfequent refolutions produced fuch unexpected, wild, and pernicious effects, as not only gave a mortal wound to the Continental money, but proved alfo to be the *laft efforts*, the *dying ftruggles* of the whole *fyftem of tender-acts*, of *limitations of prices of goods*, of *regulating the market*, and *defining the value of money by laws* and *acts of force*.

For we find that the Affembly of *Pennfylvania*, with the recommendation of Congrefs, on *June* 2, 1781, repealed all the tender-acts then exifting in that State, and difcharged all penalties and forfeitures annexed to them, and the like was done about the fame time in all the other States.

And fo ftrongly is the injuftice of that wild fyftem impreffed on the general mind, that it is an article in moft of the conftitutions fince publifhed, that *all contracts fhall be fulfilled according to the true and honeft intention of them*.

A DISSERTATION

ON THE

POLITICAL UNION

AND

CONSTITUTION

OF THE

THIRTEEN UNITED STATES

OF

NORTH-AMERICA,

Which is necessary to their Preservation and Happiness; humbly offered to the Public.*

[*First published in Philadelphia*, 1783.]

I. THE *supreme authority of any State must have power enough to effect the ends of its appointment*, otherwise these ends cannot be answered, and *effectually secured;* at best they are precarious.—But at the same time,

II. The

---

* Forming a plan of *confederation*, or a *system of general government of the United States*, engrossed the attention of Congress from the declaration of independence, *July* 4, 1776, till the same was *completed by Congress, July* 9, 1778, and recommended to the several States for *ratification*, which finally took place, *March* 1, 1781; from which time the said confederation was considered as *the grand constitution of the general government*, and the whole administration was conformed to it.

And as it had stood the *test of discussion in Congress* for *two years*, before they completed and adopted it, and *in all the States* for *three years more*, before it was finally ratified, one would have thought that it must have been a very finished and perfect plan of government.

But

II. *The supreme authority ought to be so limited and checked, if possible, as to prevent the abuse of power, or the exercise of powers that are not necessary to the ends of its appointment.*

But on trial of it in practice, it was found to be extremely *weak, defective, totally inefficient, and altogether inadequate to its great ends and purposes.* For,

1. It *blended the legislative and executive powers* together in one body.
2. This body, viz. Congress, consisted of *but one house*, without any *check* upon their resolutions.
3. The powers of Congress in very few instances were *definitive and final;* in the most important articles of government they could do no more than *recommend* to the several States; the consent of *every one of which* was necessary to give *legal sanction* to any *act* so recommended.
4. They could *assess and levy no taxes.*
5. They could institute and execute *no punishments*, except in the military department.
6. They had no power of *deciding or controlling the contentions and disputes of different States* with each other.
7. They could not *regulate the general trade:* or,
8. Even make laws to secure either *public treaties* with foreign States, or the *persons of public ambassadors*, or to *punish violations or injuries* done to either of them.
9. They could institute no *general judiciary powers.*
10. They could *regulate no public roads, canals, or inland navigation*, &c. &c. &c.

And what caps all the rest was, that (whilst under such an inefficient political constitution, the *only chance* we had of any tolerable administration lay wholly in the *prudence* and *wisdom of the men* who happened to take *the lead* in our public councils) it was fatally provided by the absurd *doctrine of rotation*, that if any Member of Congress by *three years'* experience and application, had qualified himself to manage our public affairs with consistency and fitness, that he should be *constitutionally and absolutely rendered incapable of serving any longer*, till by *three years' discontinuance*, he had pretty well lost the cue or train of the public counsels, and forgot the ideas and plans which made his services useful and important; and, in the mean time, his place should be supplied by a *fresh man*, who had *the whole matter to learn*, and when he had *learned it*, was to give place to another *fresh man;* and so on to the end of the chapter.

The sensible mind of the United States, by long experience of the *fatal mischiefs of anarchy*, or (which is about the same thing) of this *ridiculous, inefficient form of government*, began to apprehend that there was *something wrong* in our policy, which ought to be redressed and mended; but nobody undertook to delineate the necessary amendments.

I was then pretty much at leisure, and was fully of opinion (tho' the sentiment at that time would not very well bear) that it would be ten times easier to *form a new constitution* than to *mend the old one.* I therefore sat myself down to sketch out the *leading principles* of that *political constitution*, which I thought necessary to the *preservation and happiness* of the United States of *America*, which are comprised in this Dissertation.

I hope the reader will please to consider, that these are the original thoughts of a private individual, dictated by the nature of the subject only, long before the important theme became the great object of discussion, in the most dignified and important assembly, which ever sat or decided in *America.*

pointment, but hurtful and oppressive to the subject;—but to limit a supreme authority so far as to diminish its dignity, or lessen its power of doing good, would be to destroy or at least to corrupt it, and render it *ineffectual* to its ends.

III. A number of sovereign States uniting into one Commonwealth, and appointing a supreme power to manage the affairs of the union, *do necessarily and unavoidably part with and transfer over to such supreme power, so much of their own sovereignty, as is necessary to render the ends of the union effectual*, otherwise their confederation will be an union without bands of union, like a cask without hoops, that may and probably will fall to pieces, as soon as it is put to any exercise which requires strength.

In like manner, every member of civil society parts with many of his natural rights, that he may enjoy the rest in greater security under the protection of society.

The UNION of the Thirteen States of *America* is of mighty consequence to the *security, sovereignty*, and even *liberty* of each of them, and of all the individuals who compose them; *united* under a natural, well adjusted, and effectual constitution, they are a strong, rich, growing power, with great resources and means of defence, which no foreign power will easily attempt to invade or insult; they may easily command respect.

As their exports are mostly either *raw materials* or *provisions*, and their imports mostly *finished goods*, their trade becomes a capital object with every manufacturing nation of *Europe*, and all the southern colonies of *America*; their friendship and trade will of course be courted, and each power in amity with them will contribute to their security.

Their *union* is of great moment in another respect; they thereby form a *superintending power among themselves*, that can moderate and terminate *disputes* that may arise between *different States*, restrain intestine violence, and prevent any recourse to the *dreadful decision* of the sword.

I do not mean here to go into a detail of all the advantages of our union; they offer themselves on every view,

and

and are important enough to engage every honest, prudent mind, to secure and establish that union by every possible method, that we may enjoy the full benefit of it, and be rendered happy and safe under the protection it affords.

This *union*, however important, cannot be supported without a *constitution founded on principles of natural truth, fitness*, and *utility*. If there is one article wrong in such constitution, it will discover itself in practice, by its baleful operation, and destroy or at least injure the union.

Many nations have been ruined by the *errors of their political constitutions*. Such errors first introduce wrongs and injuries, which soon breed discontents, which gradually work up into mortal hatred and resentments; hence inveterate parties are formed, which of course make the whole community a house divided against itself, which soon falls either a prey to some enemies without, who watch to devour them, or else crumble into their original constituent parts, and lose all respectability, strength, and security.

It is as physically impossible to secure to civil society, good *cement of union, duration, and security, without a constitution* founded on principles of natural fitness and right, as to raise timbers into a strong, compact building, which have not been framed upon true geometric principles; for if you cut one beam a *foot too long or too short*, not all the *authority* and all the *force* of all the carpenters can ever get it into its place, and make it fit with proper symmetry there.

As the fate then of all governments depends much on their political constitutions, they become an object of mighty moment to the happiness and well-being of society; and as the framing of such a constitution requires great knowledge of the rights of men and societies, as well as of the interests, circumstances, and even prejudices of the several parts of the community or commonwealth, for which it is intended; it becomes a very complex subject, and of course requires great steadiness and comprehension of thought, as well as great knowledge of men and things, to do it properly. I shall, however, attempt it with my best abilities, and hope from the candor of the public to escape censure, if I cannot merit praise.

I BEGIN with my first and great principle, viz. *That the constitution must vest powers in every department sufficient to secure and make effectual the ends of it.* The supreme authority must have the power of *making war* and *peace*—of *appointing armies* and *navies*—of appointing *officers both civil and military*—of making *contracts*—of *emitting, coining,* and *borrowing money*—of *regulating trade*—of making *treaties with foreign powers*—of establishing *post offices*—and in short of doing *every thing* which the *well-being* of the Commonwealth may require, and which is *not compatible* to any particular State, all of which require money, and cannot possibly be made effectual without it.

They must therefore of necessity be vested with a power of taxation. I know this is a most important and weighty trust, a dreadful engine of oppression, tyranny, and injury, when ill used; yet, from *the necessity of the case*, it must be admitted.

For to give a supreme authority a power of making *contracts*, without any power of *payment*—of appointing *officers* civil and military, without money to *pay* them—a power to *build ships*, without *any money* to do it with—a power of *emitting money*, without any power to *redeem* it—or of *borrowing* money, without any power to make *payment*, &c. &c. such solecisms in government, are so nugatory and absurd, that I really think to offer further arguments on the subject, would be to insult the understanding of my readers.

To make all these payments dependent on the votes of *thirteen popular assemblies*, who will undertake to judge of the propriety of every contract and every occasion of money, and *grant* or *withhold* supplies according to their opinion, whilst at the same time, the operations of the whole may be stopped by the vote of a single one of them, is absurd; for this renders all *supplies* so *precarious*, and the *public credit* so extremely *uncertain*, as must in its nature render all *efforts in war*, and all *regular administration in peace*,

utterly

utterly impracticable, as well as most pointedly ridiculous. Is there a man to be found, who would lend money, or render personal services, or make contracts on such precarious security? of this we have a proof of fact, the strongest of all proofs, a fatal experience, the surest tho' severest of all demonstrations, which renders all other proof or argument on this subject quite unnecessary.

The present *broken state of our finances*—public debts and bankruptcies—enormous and ridiculous depreciation of public securities—with the total annihilation of our public credit—prove beyond all contradiction the vanity of all recourse to the several Assemblies of the States. The recent instance of the duty of 5 per cent. on imported goods, struck dead, and the bankruptcies which ensued on the single vote of *Rhode-Island*, affords another proof, of what it is certain *may be done again* in like circumstances.

I have another reason why *a power of taxation or of raising money*, ought to be vested in the supreme authority of our commonwealth, viz. the monies necessary for the public ought to be raised, by a *duty imposed on imported goods*, not a bare 5 *per cent.* or *any other per cent.* on all imported goods indiscriminately, but a duty *much heavier* on all articles of *luxury or mere ornament*, and which are consumed principally by the *rich* or prodigal part of the community, such as *silks* of all sorts, *muslins*, *cambricks*, *lawns*, *superfine cloths*, *spirits*, *wines*, &c. &c.

Such an impost would ease the *husbandman*, the *mechanic*, and the *poor;* would have all the practical effects of a *sumptuary law;* would mend the economy, and increase the industry, of the community; would be collected without the shocking circumstances of *collectors and their warrants;* and make the *quantity of tax* paid, always depend on the *choice* of the person who pays it.

This tax can be laid by the supreme authority much more conveniently than by the particular Assemblies, and would in no case be subject to their *repeals* or *modifications;* and of course the public credit would never be dependent on, or liable to bankruptcy by the *humors* of any particular Assembly.—In an *Essay on Finance*, which I design soon to offer to the public, this subject will be treated more fully. *(See my Sixth Essay on Free Trade and Finance, p. 229.)*

The delegates which are to form that august body, which are to hold and exercise the supreme authority, ought to be *appointed by the States in any manner they please; in which they should not be limited by any restrictions;* their own *dignity* and the *weight* they will hold in the great public councils, will always depend on the *abilities* of the persons they appoint to represent them there; and if they are wise enough to choose men of *sufficient abilities,* and respectable characters, men of sound sense, extensive knowledge, gravity, and integrity, they will reap the *honor* and *advantage* of such wisdom.

But if they are *fools enough* to appoint men of *trifling or vile characters,* of *mean abilities, faulty morals,* or *despicable ignorance,* they must reap the *fruits* of such folly, and content themselves to have *no weight, dignity,* or *esteem* in the public councils; and what is more to be lamented by the Commonwealth, to do *no good there.*

I have no objection to the States electing and recalling their delegates as often as they please, but think it hard and very injurious both to them and the Commonwealth, that they should be *obliged to discontinue them after three years' service,* if they find them on that trial to be men of sufficient integrity and abilities; a man of that experience is certainly much more qualified to serve in the place, than a new member of equal good character can be; experience makes perfect in every kind of business—*old, experienced statesmen,* of tried and approved integrity and abilities, are a great *blessing to a State*—they acquire great authority and esteem as well as wisdom, and very much contribute to keep the system of government in good and salutary order; and this furnishes the strongest reason why they should be continued in the service, on *Plato*'s great maxim, that " the man *best qualified* to serve, ought to be *appointed*".

I am sorry to see a contrary maxim adopted in our *American* counsels; to make the *highest reason* that can be given for *continuing a man in* the public administration, assigned as a *constitutional* and *absolute reason for turning him out,*

seems

seems to me to be a solecism of a piece with *many other reforms*, by which we set out to surprise the world with our wisdom.

If we should adopt this maxim in the common affairs of life, it would be found inconvenient, *e. g.* if we should make it a part of our constitution, that a man who has served a three years' apprenticeship to the trade of a *tailor* or *shoemaker*, should be obliged to discontinue that business for *the three successive years*, I am of opinion the country would soon be cleared of good shoemakers and tailors.— Men are no more born statesmen than shoemakers or tailors—Experience is equally necessary to perfection in both.

It seems to me that a man's *inducements to qualify himself for a public employment*, and make himself master of it, must be much discouraged by this consideration, that let him take whatever pains to qualify himself in the best manner, he must be shortly *turned out*, and of course it would be of more consequence to him, to turn his attention to some other business, which he might adopt when his present appointment should expire; and by this means the Commonwealth is in danger of losing the zeal, industry, and shining abilities, as well as services, of their most accomplished and valuable men.

I hear that the state of *Georgia* has improved on this blessed principle, and limited the continuance of their governors to *one year;* the consequence is, they have already the *ghosts of departed governors stalking* about in every part of their State, and growing more plenty every year; and as the price of every thing is reduced by its plenty, I can suppose governors will soon be very low there.

This *doctrine of rotation* was first proposed by some sprightly geniuses of brilliant politics, with this cogent reason; that by introducing a rotation in the public offices, we should have a great number of men trained up to public service; but it appears to me that it will be more likely to produce many *jacks at all trades,* but *good at none*.

I think that frequent elections are a sufficient security against the continuance of men in public office whose conduct is not approved, and there can be no reason for excluding

cluding thofe whofe conduct is approved, and who are allowed to be better qualified than any men who can be found to fupply their places.

Another great object of government, is the *apportionment of burdens and benefits;* for if a *greater quota* of burden, or a *lefs quota* of benefit than is juft and right, be allotted to any State, this ill apportionment will be an everlafting fource of uneafinefs and difcontent. In the firft cafe, the over-burdened State will complain; in the laft cafe, all the States, whofe quota of benefit is under-rated, will be uneafy; and this is a cafe of fuch delicacy, that it cannot be fafely trufted to the arbitrary opinion or judgment of any body of men however auguft.

Some natural principle of confeffed equity, and which can be reduced to a certainty, ought, if poffible, to be found and adopted; for it is of the higheft moment to the Commonwealth, to obviate, and, if poffible, wholly to take away, fuch a fruitful and common fource of infinite difputes, as that of apportionment of quotas has ever proved in all States of the earth.

The *value of lands* may be a good rule; but the *afcertainment of that value* is impracticable; no affeffment can be made which will not be liable to exception and debate—to adopt a good rule in any thing which is impracticable, is abfurd; for it is phyfically impoffible that any thing fhould be good for *practice,* which cannot be *practifed* at all;—but if the value of lands was capable of certain affeffment, yet to adopt that value as a rule of apportionment of quotas, and at the fame time to *except from valuation* large tracts of fundry States of immenfe value, which have all been defended by the joint arms of the whole Empire, and for the defence of which no additional quota of fupply is to be demanded of thofe States, to whom fuch lands are fecured by fuch joint efforts of the States, is in its nature unreafonable, and will open a door for great complaint.

It is plain without argument, that fuch States ought either to *make grants* to the Commonwealth of fuch tracts of defended territory, or *fell as much* of them as will pay their proper quota of defence, and *pay fuch fums* into the public

lic treasury; and this ought to be done, let what rule of quota soever be adopted with respect to the cultivated part of the United States; for no proposition of natural right and justice can be plainer than this, that every part of valuable property which is *defended*, ought to contribute its quota of supply for that *defence*.

If then the value of cultivated lands is found to be an impracticable rule of apportionment of quotas, we have to seek for some other, equally just and less exceptionable.

It appears to me, that *the number of living souls* or *human persons* of whatever age, sex, or condition, will afford us a rule or measure of apportionment which will for ever *increase* and *decrease* with the *real wealth* of the States, and will of course be a *perpetual rule,* not capable of corruption by any circumstances of future time; which is of vast consideration in forming a constitution which is designed for *perpetual duration*, and which will in its nature be as just as to the inhabited parts of each State, as that of the value of lands, or any other that has or can be mentioned.

Land takes its value not merely from the goodness of its soil, but from innumerable other relative advantages, among which the population of the country may be considered as principal; as lands in a full-settled country will always *(cæteris paribus)* bring more than lands in thin settlements—On this principle, when the inhabitants of *Russia, Poland,* &c. sell real estates, they do not value them as we do, by the *number of acres*, but by the *number of people* who live on them.

Where any piece of land has many advantages, many people will crowd there to obtain them; which will create many competitors for the purchase of it; which will of course raise the price. Where there are fewer advantages, there will be fewer competitors, and of course a less price; and these two things will for ever be proportionate to each other, and of course the one will always be a sure index of the other.

The only considerable objection I have ever heard to this, is, that the quality of inhabitants differs in the different

ent States; and it is not reasonable that the *black slaves* in the *southern* States should be estimated on a par with the *white freemen* in the *northern* States. To discuss this question fairly, I think it will be just to estimate the *neat value* of the labor of both; and if it shall appear that the labor of the black person produces as much neat wealth to the southern State, as the labor of the white person does to the northern State, I think it will follow plainly, that they are equally useful inhabitants in point of wealth; and therefore in the case before us, should be estimated alike.

And if the amazing profits which the southern planters boast of receiving from the labor of their slaves on their plantations, are *real*, the southern people have greatly the advantage in this kind of estimation, and as this objection comes principally from the southward, I should suppose that the gentlemen from that part would blush to urge it any further.

That the supreme authority should be vested with powers to *terminate* and *finally decide controversies arising between different States*, I take it, will be universally admitted, but I humbly apprehend that an *appeal* from the first instance of trial ought to be admitted in causes of great moment, on the same reasons that such appeals are admitted in all the States of *Europe*. It is well known to all men versed in courts, that the first hearing of a cause, rather gives an opening to that evidence and reason which ought to decide it, than such a full examination and thorough discussion,—as should always precede a final judgment, in causes of national consequence.—A detail of reasons might be added, which I deem it unnecessary to enlarge on here.

The supreme authority ought to have a power of *peace and war*, and forming *treaties* and *alliances* with all foreign powers; which implies a necessity of their also having sufficient powers to *enforce the obedience* of all subjects of the United States to such treaties and alliances; with *full powers to unite the force* of the States; and direct its operations in war; and to punish all transgressors in all these respects; otherwise, by the imprudence *of a few*, the whole Commonwealth may be embroiled with foreign powers,

powers, and the operations of war may be rendered useless, or fail much of their due effect.

All these I conceive will be easily granted, especially the latter, as the power of Congress to appoint and direct the army and navy in war, with all departments thereto belonging, and punishing delinquents in them all, is already admitted into practice in the course of the present unhappy war, in which we have been long engaged.

II. But now the *great and most difficult* part of this weighty subject remains to be considered, viz. how *these supreme powers are to be constituted in such manner that they may be able to exercise with full force* and *effect*, the vast authorities committed to them, for the *good and well-being* of the United States, and yet be *so checked* and *restrained* from exercising them to the *injury and ruin* of the States, that we may *with safety* trust them with a commission of such vast magnitude;—and may *Almighty wisdom direct my pen* in this arduous discussion.

1. The men who compose this important council, must be *delegated from all the States*; and, of course, the *hope* of approbation and continuance of honors, will naturally stimulate them to act right, and to please; the *dread* of censure and disgrace will naturally operate as a check to restrain them from improper behaviour: but however natural and forcible these motives may be, we find by sad experience, they are not always *strong enough* to produce the effects we expect and wish from them.

It is to be wished that none might be appointed that were not *fit* and *adequate* to this weighty business; but a little knowledge of human nature, and a little acquaintance with the political history of mankind, will soon teach us that this is not to be expected.

The representatives appointed by popular elections are commonly not only the *legal*, but *real*, substantial representatives of their electors, *i. e.* there will commonly be about the *same proportion* of grave, *sound*, *well-qualified men*,—*trifling*, *desultory men*,—*wild* or *knavish schemers*,— and *dull*, *ignorant fools*, in the *delegated assembly*, as in the *body of electors*.

D d I know

I know of no way to help this; such delegates must be admitted, as the States are pleased to send; and all that can be done, is, when they get together, to make the best of them.

We will suppose then they are all met in Congress, clothed with that *vast authority* which it is necessary to the *well-being*, and even *existence, of the union*, that they should be vested with; how shall we empower them to do all necessary and effectual *good*, and restrain them from doing *hurt?* To do this properly, I think we must recur to those *natural motives* of action, those *feelings* and apprehensions, which usually occur to the mind at the *very time* of action; for *distant* consequences, however weighty, are often too much disregarded.

Truth loves light, and is vindicated by it. Wrong shrouds itself in darkness, and is supported by delusion. An honest, well-qualified man *loves light*, can bear *close examination* and *critical inquiry*, and is *best pleased* when he is most thoroughly *understood*: a man of *corrupt* design, or a *fool of no design*, hates close examination and critical inquiry; the knavery of the one, and the ignorance of the other, are discovered by it, and they both usually grow uneasy, before the investigation is half done. I do not believe there is a more natural truth in the world, than that divine one of our SAVIOUR, " *he that doth truth, cometh to the light.*" I would therefore recommend that mode of deliberation, which will naturally bring on the most thorough and critical *discussion of the subject*, previous to passing any act; and for that purpose humbly propose,

2. That the *Congress shall consist of two chambers*, an *upper* and *lower* house, or *senate* and *commons*, with the *concurrence of both necessary to every act;* and that every State send one or more delegates to each house: this will subject every act to *two* discussions before *two distinct* chambers of men equally *qualified* for the debate, equally *masters* of the subject, and of equal *authority* in the decision.

These two houses will be governed by the same natural motives and interests, viz. the good of the Commonwealth, and the approbation of the people. Whilst, at the same time,

time, *the emulation* naturally arising between them, will induce a very *critical and sharp-sighted inspection* into the motions of each other. Their different opinions will bring on conferences between the two houses, in which the *whole subject* will be *exhausted* in arguments pro and con, and *shame* will be the portion of obstinate, convicted *error*.

Under these circumstances, a man of ignorance or evil design will be afraid to impose on the credulity, inattention, or confidence of his house, by introducing any *corrupt* or *indigested proposition*, which he knows he must be called on to defend against the *severe scrutiny* and *poignant objections* of the other house. I do not believe the many hurtful and foolish legislative acts which first or last have injured all the States on earth, have originated so much in corruption as indolence, ignorance, and a want of a full comprehension of the subject, which a full, prying, and emulous discussion would tend in a great measure to remove: this naturally rouses the lazy and idle, who hate the pain of close thinking; animates the ambitious to excel in policy and argument; and excites the whole to support the dignity of their house, and vindicate their own propositions.

I am not of opinion that bodies of elective men, which usually compose *Parliaments, Diets, Assemblies, Congresses*, &c. are commonly *dishonest;* but I believe it rarely happens that there are not *designing men* among them; and I think it would be much more difficult for them to unite their partisans in two houses, and corrupt or deceive them both, than to carry on their designs where there is but *one unalarmed, unapprehensive* house to be managed; and as there is *no hope* of making these bad men good, the best policy is to *embarrass* them, and make their work as *difficult* as possible.

In these assemblies are frequently to be found sanguine men, upright enough indeed, but of strong, wild projection, whose brains are always teeming with *Utopian, chimerical plans*, and *political whims*, very destructive to society. I hardly know a greater evil than to have the *supreme counsels* of a Nation played off on *such men's wires;* such baseless visions at best end in darkness, and the *dance*, tho' easy and merry enough at first, rarely fails to plunge the credulous, simple followers into *sloughs* and *bogs* at last.

Nothing can tend more effectually to obviate these evils, and to mortify and cure such maggotty brains, than to see the absurdity of their projects exposed by the several *arguments* and *keen satire* which a full, emulous, and spirited discussion of the subject will naturally produce: we have had enough of these *geniuses* in the short course of our politics, both in our national and provincial councils, and have felt enough of their evil effects, to induce us to wish for any good method to keep ourselves clear of them in future.

The consultations and decisions of national councils are so very important, that the *fate of millions* depends on them; therefore no man ought to speak in such assemblies, without considering that the fate of millions *hangs on his tongue*,—and of course a man can have no right in such august councils to utter indigested sentiments, or indulge himself in sudden, unexamined flights of thought; his most tried and improved abilities are due to the State, who have trusted him with their most important interests.

A man must therefore be most inexcusable, who is either *absent* during such debates, or *sleeps*, or *whispers*, or *catches flies* during the argument, and just *rouses* when the vote is called, to give his *yea* or *nay*, to the *weal* or *woe* of a nation.—Therefore it is manifestly proper, that every natural motive that can operate on his understanding, or his passions, to engage his attention and utmost efforts, should be put in practice, and that his present feelings should be raised by every motive of honor and shame, to stimulate him to every practicable degree of diligence and exertion, to be as far as possible useful in the great discussion.

I appeal to the feelings of every reader, if he would not (were he in either house) be much more strongly and naturally induced to exert his utmost abilities and attention to any question which was to pass thro' the *ordeal of a spirited discussion* of another house, than he would do, if the *absolute decision* depended on *his own house*, without any further inquiry or challenge on the subject.   As

As Congress will ever be composed of men delegated by the several States, it may well be supposed that they have the *confidence* of their several States, and understand well the policy and present condition of them; it may also be supposed that they come with strong *local attachments,* and habits of thinking limited to the *interests* of their particular States: it may therefore be supposed they will need much information, in order to their gaining that *enlargement of ideas,* and great comprehension of thought, which will be necessary to enable them to think properly on that *large scale,* which takes into view the interests of all the States.

The greatest care and wisdom is therefore requisite to give them the best and surest information, and of that kind that may be the most safely relied on, to prevent their being deluded or prejudiced by partial representations, made by interested men who have particular views.

This *information* may perhaps be best made by *the great ministers of state,* who ought to be men of the *greatest abilities* and *integrity;* their business is confined to their several departments, and their attention engaged strongly and constantly to all the several parts of the same; the whole arrangement, method, and order of which, are formed, superintended, and managed in their offices, and all informations relative to their departments centre there.

These *ministers* will of course have the best information, and most perfect knowledge, of the state of the Nation, as far as it relates to their several departments, and will of course be able to give the *best information* to Congress, in what manner any bill proposed will affect the public interest in their several departments, which will nearly comprehend the whole.

The *Financier* manages the whole subject of *revenues* and *expenditures*—the *Secretary of State* takes knowledge of the general *policy* and *internal* government—the *minister of war* presides in the whole business of *war* and *defence*—and the *minister of foreign affairs* regards the whole state of the nation, as it stands related to, or connected with, all foreign powers.

I mention

I mention a *Secretary of State*, becaufe all other nations have one, and I fuppofe we fhall need one as much as they, and the multiplicity of affairs which naturally fall into his office will grow fo faft, that I imagine we fhall foon be under neceffity of appointing one.

To thefe I would add *Judges of law*, and *chancery*; but I fear they will not be very foon appointed—the one fuppofes the exiftence of *law*, and the other of *equity*—and when we fhall be altogether convinced of the abfolute neceffity of the real and effectual exiftence of both thefe, we fhall probably appoint proper heads to prefide in thofe departments.—I would therefore propofe,

3. That when *any bill fhall pafs the fecond reading* in the houfe in which it originates, and before it fhall be finally enacted, copies of it fhall be fent to *each of the faid minifters of ftate*, in being at the time, who fhall give faid houfe *in writing*, the fulleft information in their power, and their moft explicit fentiments of the operation of the faid bill on the public intereft, as far as relates to their *refpective departments*, which fhall be received and read in faid houfe, and *entered on their minutes*, before they finally pafs the bill; and when they fend the bill for concurrence to the *other houfe*, they fhall fend therewith the faid *informations of the faid minifters of ftate*, which fhall likewife be read in that houfe before their concurrence is finally paffed.

I do not mean to give thefe great minifters of ftate a *negative on Congrefs*, but I mean to oblige Congrefs to receive *their advices* before they pafs their bills, and that every *act* fhall be *void* that is not paffed with thefe forms; and I further propofe, that either houfe of Congrefs may, if they pleafe, admit the faid *minifters* to be *prefent* and *affift* in the debates of the houfe, but *without any right of vote* in the decifion.

It appears to me, that if every act fhall pafs fo many different corps of *difcuffion* before it is completed, where each of them ftake their characters on the advice or vote they give, there will be all the *light thrown on the cafe*, which the nature and circumftances of it can admit, and

any

any *corrupt* man will find it extremely difficult to foist in any erroneous clause whatever; and every *ignorant or lazy* man will find the strongest inducements to make himself master of the subject, that he may appear with some tolerable degree of character in it; and the whole will find themselves in a manner compelled, diligently and sincerely to seek for the *real state* of the facts, and the natural *fitness and truth* arising from them, *i. e.* the whole *natural principles* on which the subject depends, and which alone can endure every test, to the end that they may have not only the inward satisfaction of *acting properly* and usefully for the States, but also the *credit and character* which is or ought ever to be annexed to such a conduct.

This will give the great *laws* of Congress the highest *probability, presumption, and means of right, fitness, and truth,* that any laws whatever can have at their first enaction, and will of course afford the highest reason for the confidence and acquiescence of the States, and all their subjects, in them; and being grounded in *truth* and *natural fitness,* their operation will be *easy,* salutary, and satisfactory.

If experience shall discover *errors* in any law (for practice will certainly discover such errors, if there be any) the legislature will always be able to correct them, by such repeals, amendments, or new laws as shall be found necessary; but as it is much easier to *prevent* mischiefs than to *remedy* them, all possible caution, prudence, and attention should be used, to make the laws *right at first*.

4. There is *another body of men* among us, whose business of life, and whose full and extensive intelligence, foreign and domestic, naturally make them more perfectly acquainted with the sources of our wealth, and whose particular interests are more intimately and necessarily connected with the general prosperity of the country, than any other order of men in the States.—I mean the *Merchants;* and I could wish that Congress might have the benefit of that *extensive and important information,* which this body of men are very capable of laying before them.

Trade is of such essential importance to our interests, and so intimately connected with all our staples, great and
small,

small, that no sources of our wealth can flourish, and operate to the general benefit of the community, *without it*. Our *husbandry*, that grand staple of our country, can never exceed our home consumption *without this*—it is plain at first sight, that the *farmer* will not toil and sweat thro' the year to raise great plenty of the produce of the soil, if there is *no market* for his produce, when he has it ready for sale, *i. e.* if there are no merchants to buy it.

In like manner, the *manufacturer* will not lay out his business on any large scale, if there is no merchant to buy his fabrics when he has finished them; a *vent* is of the most essential importance to every manufacturing country—the merchants, therefore, become the natural negotiators of the wealth of the country, who take off the *abundance*, and supply the *wants*, of the inhabitants;—and as this negotiation is the business of their lives, and the source of their own wealth, they of course become better acquainted with both our abundance and wants, and are more interested in finding and improving the best *vent* for the one, and *supply* of the other, than any other men among us, and they have a natural interest in making both the purchase and supply as convenient to their customers as possible, that they may secure their custom, and thereby increase their own business.

It follows then, that the merchants are not only *qualified to give the fullest and most important information* to our supreme legislature, concerning the state of our trade—the abundance and wants,—the wealth and poverty, of our people, *i. e.* their most important interests, but are also the most likely to do it *fairly* and *truly*, and to forward with their influence, every measure which will operate to the convenience and benefit of our commerce, and oppose with their whole weight and superior knowledge of the subject, any *wild schemes*, which an ignorant or arbitrary legislature may attempt to introduce, to the hurt and embarrassment of our intercourse both with one another, and with foreigners.

The States of *Venice* and *Holland* have ever been governed by *merchants*, or at least their policy has ever been

under

under the great influence of that sort of men. No States have been better served, as appears by their great success, the ease and happiness of their citizens, as well as the strength and riches of their Commonwealths: the one is the *oldest*, and the other the *richest*, State in the world of equal number of people—the one has maintained sundry wars with the *Grand Turk*—and the other has withstood the power of *Spain* and *France*; and the *capitals* of both have long been the principal marts of the several parts of *Europe* in which they are situated; and the *banks* of both are the best supported, and in the best credit, of any *banks in Europe*, tho' their countries or territories are very small, and their inhabitants but a handful, when compared with the great States in their neighbourhood.

Merchants must, from the nature of their business, certainly understand the interests and resources of their country, the best of any men in it; and I know not of *any one reason* why they should be deemed *less upright or patriotic*, than any other rank of citizens whatever.

I therefore humbly propose, if the merchants in the several States are disposed to send delegates from their body, to meet and attend the sitting of Congress, that they shall be permitted to form a *chamber of commerce*, and *their advice* to Congress be *demanded and admitted* concerning all bills before Congress, as far as the same may affect the *trade of the States*.

I have no idea that the continent is made for Congress: I take them to be no more than the upper servants of the great political body, who are to find out things by *study and inquiry* as other people do; and therefore I think it necessary to place them under the best possible advantages for information, and to require them to improve all those advantages, to qualify themselves in the best manner possible, for the wise and useful discharge of the vast trust and mighty authority reposed in them; and as I conceive the advice of the merchants to be one of the greatest sources of mercantile information, which is any where placed within their reach, it ought by no means to be neglected, but so husbanded and improved, that the greatest possible advantages may be derived from it.

Besides this, I have another reason why the merchants ought to be consulted; I take it to be very plain that the husbandry and manufactures of the country must be ruined, if the present weight of taxes is continued on them much longer, and of course a very great part of our revenue must arise from *imposts on merchandise*, which will fall directly within the merchants' sphere of business, and of course their concurrence and advice will be of the utmost consequence, not only to direct the properest mode of levying those duties, but also to get them carried into quiet and peaceable execution.

No men are more conversant with the citizens, or more intimately connected with their interests, than the merchants; and therefore their weight and influence will have a mighty effect on the minds of the people. I do not recollect an instance, in which the Court of *London* ever rejected the remonstrances and advices of the merchants, and did not suffer severely for their pride. We have some striking instances of this in the disregarded advices and remonstrances of very many *English* merchants against the *American* war, and their fears and apprehensions we see verified, almost like prophecies, by the event.

I know not why I should continue this argument any longer, or indeed why I have urged it so long, in as much as I cannot conceive that Congress or any body else will deem it below the dignity of the supreme power to consult so important an order of men, in matters of the first consequence, which fall immediately under their notice, and in which their experience, and of course their knowledge and advice are preferable to those of any other order of men.

Besides the benefits which Congress may receive from this institution, *a chamber of commerce*, composed of members from *all trading towns* in the States, if properly instituted and conducted, will produce very many, I might almost say, innumerable advantages of singular utility to all the States—it will give dignity, uniformity, and safety to

our

our *trade*—establish the *credit of the bank*—secure the *confidence* of *foreign merchants*—prove in very many instances a fruitful source of improvement of our *staples and mutual intercourse*—correct many *abuses*—pacify *discontents*—*unite* us in our interests, and thereby *cement* the general union of the whole Commonwealth—will *relieve Congress* from the pain and trouble of deciding many *intricate questions* of trade which they *do not understand*, by referring them over to this chamber, where they will be discussed by an order of men, the *most competent* to the business of any that can be found, and *most likely* to give a decision that shall be *just*, *useful*, and *satisfactory*.

It may be objected to all this, that the *less complex* and the *more simple* every constitution is, the *nearer it comes to perfection*: this argument would be very good, and afford a very forcible conclusion, if the government of *men* was like that of the *Almighty*, always founded on wisdom, knowledge, and truth; but in the present imperfect state of human nature, where the best of men know but *in part*, and must recur to advice and information *for the rest*, it certainly becomes necessary to form a constitution on such principles, as will secure *that information* and *advice* in the best and surest manner possible.

It may be further objected that the forms herein proposed will *embarrass the business* of Congress, and make it at best *slow and dilatory*. As far as this form will prevent the hurrying a bill thro' the house without due examination, the *objection* itself becomes an *advantage*—at most these checks on the supreme authority can have no further effect than to *delay or destroy a good bill*, but cannot *pass a bad one;* and I think it much better in the main, to *lose a good bill* than to suffer a *bad one to pass* into a law.—Besides it is not to be supposed that clear, plain cases will meet with embarrassment, and it is most safe that untried, doubtful, difficult matters should pass thro' the gravest and fullest discussion, before the sanction of law is given to them.

But what is to be done if the *two houses grow jealous and ill-natured*, and after all their information and advice, grow out of humor and insincere, and *no concurrence can be obtained?*

tained?—I anſwer, *ſit ſtill and do nothing* till they get into better humor: I think this much better than to paſs laws in ſuch a temper and ſpirit, as the objection ſuppoſes.

It is however an ill compliment to ſo many grave perſonages, to ſuppoſe them capable of throwing aſide their reaſon, and giving themſelves up like children to the control of their paſſions; or, if this ſhould happen for a *moment*, that it ſhould continue any *length of time*, is hardly to be preſumed of a body of men placed in ſuch high ſtations of *dignity* and *importance*, with the *eyes of all the world* upon them—but if they ſhould, after all, be capable of this, I think it madneſs to ſet them to making laws, during ſuch fits—it is beſt, when they are in *no condition to do good*, to keep them *from doing hurt*,—and if they do not grow wiſer in reaſonable time, I know of nothing better, than to be aſhamed of our old appointments, and make new ones.

But what if the country is invaded, or ſome other exigency happens, ſo preſſing that the ſafety of the State requires an immediate reſolution?—I anſwer, what would you do if ſuch a caſe ſhould happen, where there was *but one houſe, unchecked*, but *equally divided*, ſo that a legal vote could *not be obtained*. The matter is certainly equally difficult and embarraſſed in both caſes: but in the caſe propoſed, I know of no better way than that which the *Romans* adopted on the like occaſion, viz. that both houſes meet in one chamber, and chooſe a *dictator*, who ſhould have and exerciſe the *whole power of both houſes*, till ſuch time as they ſhould be able to concur in diſplacing him, and that the whole power of the two houſes ſhould be ſuſpended in the mean time.

5. I further propoſe, that no grant of money whatever ſhall be made, without *an appropriation*, and that *rigid penalties* (no matter how great, in my opinion the halter would be mild enough) ſhall be inflicted on any perſon, however auguſt his ſtation, who ſhould *give order, or vote for* the payment, or actually pay one ſhilling of ſuch money to any *other purpoſe than that of its appropriation*, and that no order whatever of any ſuperior in office ſhall juſtify

ſuch

such payment, but every order shall express what funds it is drawn upon, and what appropriation it is to be charged to, or the order shall not be paid.

This kind of embezzlement is of so fatal a nature, that *no measures or bounds* are to be observed in curing it; when ministers will set forth the most *specious* and *necessary occasions* for money, and *induce* the people to pay it in full tale; and when they have gotten possession of it, to neglect the great objects for which it was given, and *pay it*, sometimes *squander it away*, for different purposes, oftentimes for *useless*, yea, *hurtful ones*, yea, often even to *bribe* and *corrupt* the very officers of government, to *betray* their trust, and *contaminate the State*, even in its *public offices*—to force people to *buy* their *own destruction*, and *pay for it with their hard labor*, the very sweat of their brow, is a *crime* of so high a nature, that I know not any *gibbet too cruel* for such offenders.

6. I would further propose, that the aforesaid *great ministers of state shall compose a Council of State, to whose number Congress may add three others*, viz. one from *New-England*, one from the *middle States*, and one from the *southern States*, one of which to be *appointed President by Congress*; to all of whom shall be committed the *supreme executive authority of the States* (all and singular of them ever accountable to Congress) who shall superintend all the executive departments, and appoint all executive officers, who shall ever be accountable to, and removable for just cause by, them or Congress, *i. e.* either of them.

7. I propose further, that the powers of Congress, and all the other departments acting under them, shall all be *restricted to such matters only of general necessity and utility* to all the States, as cannot come *within the jurisdiction* of any particular State, or to which the *authority* of any particular State is not *competent*: so that each particular State shall enjoy all sovereignty and supreme authority to all intents and purposes, excepting only those high authorities and powers by them delegated to Congress, for the purposes of the general union.

There

There remains one very important article still to be discussed, viz. what methods the constitution shall point out, to *enforce the acts* and *requisitions of Congress* thro' the several States; and how the States which *refuse or delay* obedience to such acts or requisitions, shall be treated: this, I know, is a particular of the greatest delicacy, as well as of the utmost importance; and therefore, I think, ought to be decidedly settled by the constitution, in our coolest hours, whilst no passions or prejudices exist, which may be excited by the great interests or strong circumstances of any particular case which may happen.

I know that supreme authorities are liable to err, as well as subordinate ones. I know that courts may be in the wrong, as well as the people; such is the imperfect state of human nature in all ranks and degrees of men; but we must take human nature as it is; it cannot be mended; and we are compelled both by wisdom and necessity, to adopt such methods as promise the greatest *attainable* good, tho' perhaps not the greatest *possible*, and such as are liable to the *fewest* inconveniences, tho' not altogether *free* of them.

This is a question of such magnitude, that I think it necessary to premise the great natural principles on which its decision ought to depend—In the present state of human nature, all human life is a life of chances; it is impossible to make any interest so certain, but there will be a chance against it; and we are in all cases obliged to adopt a chance against us, in order to bring ourselves within the benefit of a greater chance in our favor; and that calculation of chances which is grounded on the great natural principles of truth and fitness, is of all others the most likely to come out right.

1. *No laws of any State whatever, which do not carry in them a force which extends to their effectual and final execution, can afford a certain or sufficient security to the subject:* this is too plain to need any proof.

2. *Laws or ordinances of any kind (especially of august bodies of high dignity and consequence) which fail of execution,* are much *worse than none;* they weaken the government;

ment; expose it to contempt; destroy the confidence of all men, natives and foreigners, in it; and expose both aggregate bodies and individuals, who have placed confidence in it, to many ruinous disappointments, which they would have escaped, had no law or ordinance been made: therefore,

3. To appoint a Congress with powers to do *all acts necessary for the support and uses of the union;* and at the same time to leave all the States at liberty to *obey them or not with impunity,* is, in every view, the grossest *absurdity,* worse than a state of nature without any supreme authority at all, and at best a ridiculous effort of childish nonsense: and of course,

4. Every State in the Union is under the highest obligations *to obey the supreme authority of the whole,* and in the *highest degree amenable to it,* and subject to the *highest censure for disobedience*—Yet all this notwithstanding, I think the soul that sins should die, *i. e.* the censure of the great supreme power, ought to be so directed, if possible, as to light on those persons, who have betrayed their country, and exposed it to dissolution, by opposing and rejecting that supreme authority, which is the *band of our union,* and from whence proceeds the *principal strength and energy* of our government.

I therefore propose, that every *person* whatever, whether in *public* or *private character,* who shall, by *public vote* or other *overt act,* disobey the *supreme authority,* shall be *amenable to Congress,* shall be *summoned and compelled to appear* before Congress, and, on due conviction, *suffer such fine, imprisonment, or other punishment,* as the supreme authority shall judge requisite.

It may be objected here, that this will make a Member of Assembly accountable to Congress for his vote in Assembly; I answer, it does so *in this only case,* viz. when that vote *is to disobey the supreme authority:* no Member of Assembly can have right to give *such a vote,* and therefore ought to be punished for so doing—When the supreme authority is disobeyed, the government must lose its energy

and

and effect, and of course the Empire muſt be ſhaken to its very foundation.

A government which is but *half executed*, or *whoſe operations may all be ſtopped by a ſingle vote*, is the moſt dangerous of all inſtitutions.—See the preſent *Poland*, and ancient *Greece* buried in ruins, in conſequence of this fatal error in their policy. A government which has not energy and effect, can never afford protection or ſecurity to its ſubjects, *i. e.* muſt ever be ineffectual to its own ends.

I cannot therefore admit, that the great ends of our Union ſhould lie at the mercy of a ſingle State, or that the energy of our government ſhould be checked by a ſingle diſobedience, or that ſuch diſobedience ſhould ever be ſheltered from cenſure and puniſhment; the conſequence is too capital, too fatal to be admitted. Even tho' I know very well that a ſupreme authority, with all its dignity and importance, is ſubject to paſſions like other leſſer powers, that they may be and often are heated, violent, oppreſſive, and very tyrannical; yet I know alſo, that perfection is not to be hoped for in this life, and we muſt take all inſtitutions with their natural defects, or reject them altogether: I will guard againſt theſe abuſes of power as far as poſſible, but I cannot give up all government, or deſtroy its neceſſary energy, for fear of theſe abuſes.

But to fence them out as far as poſſible, and to give the States as great a check on the ſupreme authority, as can conſiſt with its neceſſary energy and effect;

I propoſe that any State may petition Congreſs to repeal any law or deciſion which they have made, and if *more than half the States* do this, the *law or deciſion ſhall be repealed*, let its nature or importance be however great, excepting only ſuch acts as *create funds for the public credit*, which ſhall never be repealed till their end is effected, or other funds equally effectual are ſubſtituted in their places; but Congreſs ſhall not be obliged to repeal any of theſe acts, ſo petitioned againſt, till they have time to lay the reaſons of ſuch acts before ſuch petitioning States, and to receive their anſwer; becauſe ſuch petitions may ariſe from ſudden heats, popular prejudices, or the publication

of

of matters false in fact, and may require time and means of cool reflection and the fullest information, before the final decision is made: but if after all, *more than half* the States persist in their demand of a repeal, it shall take place.

The reason is, the *uneasiness of a majority* of States affords a strong *presumption* that the act is *wrong*, for uneasiness arises much more frequently from *wrong* than *right*; but if the act was *good and right*, it would still be better to *repeal* and *lose* it, than to *force* the execution of it against the opinion of a *major part* of the States; and lastly, if every act of Congress is subject to this repeal, Congress itself will have *stronger inducement* not only to examine well the several acts under their consideration, but also to *communicate the reasons* of them to the States, than they would have, if their simple vote gave *the final stamp of irrevocable authority* to their acts.

Further I propose, that if the *execution of any act or order of the supreme authority shall be opposed by force in any of the States* (which God forbid!) it shall be lawful for Congress to send into such State *a sufficient force to suppress it.*

On the whole, I take it that the very *existence and use of our union* essentially depends on the *full energy and final effect* of the laws made to support it; and therefore I *sacrifice all other considerations to this energy and effect*, and if our UNION is not worth this purchase, we must give it up—the *nature of the thing* does not admit any other alternative.

I do contend that *our UNION is worth this purchase—with it*, every individual rests secure under its protection against foreign or domestic insult and oppression—*without it*, we can have no security against the oppression, insult, and invasion of foreign powers; for no single State is of importance enough to be an object of treaty with them, nor, if it was, could it bear the expense of such treaties, or support any character or respect in a dissevered state, but must lose all respectability among the nations abroad.

We have a very *extensive trade*, which cannot be carried on with security and advantage, *without treaties* of commerce and alliance with foreign nations.

We

We have an *extensive western territory* which cannot otherwise be defended against the invasion of foreign nations, bordering on our frontiers, who will cover it with their own inhabitants, and we shall lose it for ever, and our extent of empire be thereby restrained; and what is worse, their numerous posterity will in future time drive ours into the sea, as the *Goths* and *Vandals* formerly conquered the *Romans* in like circumstances, unless we have the force of the Union to repel such invasions. We have, without the union, no security against the *inroads and wars of one State upon another*, by which our *wealth and strength*, as well as *ease and comfort, will be devoured by enemies growing out of our own bowels.*

I conclude then, that our UNION is not only of the most essential consequence to the well-being of the States in general, but to that of every individual citizen of them, and of course ought to be supported, and made as useful and safe as possible, by a constitution which admits that *full energy* and *final effect of government which alone can secure its great ends and uses.*

In a dissertation of this sort, I would not wish to descend to *minutiæ*, yet there are some small matters which have important consequences, and therefore ought to be noticed. It is necessary that Congress should have all usual and necessary powers of *self-preservation and order*, e. g. to *imprison for contempt, insult, or interruption*, &c. and to *expel their own members* for due causes, among which I would rank that of *non-attendance* on the house, or *partial attendance* without such excuse as shall satisfy the house.

Where there is such a vast authority and trust devolved on Congress, and the grand and most important interests of the Empire rest on their decisions, it appears to me highly unreasonable that we should suffer their *august consultations to be suspended*, or their *dignity, authority*, and *influence lessened* by the *idleness, neglect*, and *non-attendance* of its members; for we know that the acts of a *thin house* do not usually carry with them the same degree of weight and respect as those of a *full* house.

Besides

Besides I think, when a man is deputed a delegate in Congress, and has undertaken the business, the *whole Empire* becomes of course possessed of a *right to his best and constant services*, which if any member refuses or neglects, the Empire is *injured* and ought to *resent the injury*, at least so far as to *expel* and *send him home*, that so his place may be *better* supplied.

I have one argument in favor of my whole plan, viz. it is so formed that no men of *dull* intellects, or *small knowledge*, or of *habits too idle* for constant attendance, or close and steady attention, can do the business with any tolerable degree of respectability, nor can they find either honor, profit, or satisfaction in being there, and of course, I could wish that the choice of the electors might never fall on *such a man*, or if it should, that he might have *sense enough* (of *pain* at least, if not of *shame*) to decline his acceptance.

For after all that can be done, I do not think that a good administration depends wholly on a good constitution and good laws, for insufficient or bad men will always make *bad work*, and *a bad administration*, let the *constitution and laws be ever so good;* the management of able, faithful, and upright men alone can cause an administration to *brighten*, and the *dignity* and *wisdom* of an Empire to *rise into respect;* make *truth* the line and measure of *public decision;* give *weight* and *authority* to the government, and *security* and *peace* to the subject.

We now hope that we are on the close of a war of mighty effort and great distress, against the greatest power on earth, whetted into the most keen resentment and savage fierceness, which can be excited by wounded pride, and which usually rises higher between brother and brother offended, than between strangers in contest. *Twelve* of the Thirteen United States have felt the actual and cruel invasions of the enemy, and *eleven of our capitals* have been under their power, first or last, during the dreadful conflict; but a good Providence, our own virtue and firmness, and the help of our friends, have enabled us to rise superior

to

[228]

to all the power of our adverfaries, and made them feek to be at peace with us.

During the extreme preffures of the war, indeed, many errors in our adminiftration have been committed, when we could not have experience and time for reflection, to make us wife; but thefe will eafily be *excufed, forgiven, and forgotten*, if we can now, while at leifure, *find virtue, wifdom*, and *forefight enough to correct them*, and form such eftablifhments, as fhall fecure the great ends of our union, and give dignity, force, utility, and permanency to our Empire.

It is a pity we fhould lofe the honor and bleflings which have coft us fo dear, for want of that wifdom and firmnefs in meafures, which are effential to our prefervation. It is now at our option, either to *fall back* into our original atoms, or *form fuch an union*, as fhall command the *refpect* of the world, and give *honor and fecurity* to all our people.

This vaft fubject lies with mighty weight on my mind, and I have beftowed on it my utmoft attention, and here offer the public the beft thoughts and fentiments I am mafter of.* I have confined myfelf in this differtation intirely

to

---

* At the time when this Differtation was written *(Feb.* 16, 1783) the defects and infufficiency of the Old Federal Conftitution were univerfally felt and acknowledged; it was manifeft, not only that the internal police, juftice, fecurity, and peace of the States could never be preferved under it, but the finances and public credit would neceffarily become fo embarraffed, precarious, and void of fupport, that no public movement, which depended on the revenue, could be managed with any effectual certainty: but tho' the public mind was under full conviction of all thefe mifchiefs, and was contemplating a remedy, yet the public ideas were not at all concentrated, much lefs arranged into any new fyftem or form of government, which would obviate thefe evils. Under thefe circumftances I offered this Differtation to the public: how far the principles of it were adopted or rejected in the New Conftitution, which was four years afterwards *(Sep.* 17, 1787) formed by the General Convention, and fince ratified by all the States, is obvious to every one.

I wifh here to remark the great particulars of my plan which were rejected by the Convention.

1. My plan was to keep the *legiflative* and *executive* departments entirely *diftinct*; the *one* to confift of the *two houfes of Congrefs*, the other to reft entirely in the *Grand Council of State*.

2. I propofed to introduce a *Chamber of Commerce*, to confift of *merchants*, who fhould be *confulted* by the legiflature in all matters of *trade* and *revenue*, and which fhould have the *conducting the revenue committed to them*.

The

to the nature, reason, and truth of my subject, without once adverting to the reception it might meet with from men of different prejudices or interests. To *find the truth,* not to *carry a point, has been my object.*

I have not the vanity to imagine that my sentiments may be adopted; I shall have all the reward I wish or expect, if my dissertation shall throw any light on the great subject, shall excite an emulation of inquiry, and animate some abler genius to form a plan of greater perfection, less objectionable, and more useful.

The first of these the Convention *qualified;* the second they *say nothing of, i. e.* take no notice of it.

3. I proposed that the *great officers of state* should have the *perusal of all bills,* before they were *enacted* into laws, and should be required to give their *opinion of them,* as far as they *affected the public interest in their several departments;* which *report* of them Congress should cause to be *read* in their respective houses, and *entered* on their minutes. This is *passed over* without notice.

4. I proposed that *all public officers* appointed by the *executive* authority, should be amenable *both to them* and to the *legislative power,* and *removable* for just cause by *either* of them. This is qualified by the Convention.

And in as much as my sentiments in these respects were either *qualified* or totally *neglected* by the Convention, I suppose they were *wrong;* however, the whole matter is submitted to the politicians of the *present age,* and to *our posterity* in future.

In sundry other things, the Convention have gone *into minutiæ, e. g.* respecting elections of *President, Senators,* and *Representatives* in Congress, &c. which I proposed to leave *at large* to the wisdom and discretion of *Congress,* and of the *several States.*

Great *reasons* may doubtless be assigned for their decision, and perhaps some *little ones* for mine. TIME, the great *arbiter of all human plans,* may, after a while, give *his decision;* but neither the Convention nor myself will probably live to feel either the exultation or mortification of *his* approbation or disapprobation of *either of our plans.*

But if any of these questions should in future time become objects of discussion, neither the *vast dignity of the Convention,* nor the *low, unnoticed state of myself,* will be at all considered in the debates; the *merits* of the matter, and *the interests connected with or arising out of it,* will alone dictate the decision.

A SIXTH

A SIXTH ESSAY ON FREE TRADE and FINANCE.

Particularly showing what Supplies of Public Revenue may be drawn from MERCHANDISE, *without injuring our Trade, or burdening our People.*

Humbly offered to the Public.

[*First published in Philadelphia, March* 24, 1783.]

HAVING lately published ' A Dissertation on that Political Union and Constitution, which is necessary for the Preservation and Happiness of the Thirteen United States of *North-America*,' I now go on to consider some of the great departments of business, which must fall under the management of the great Council of the Union, and their officers.

The first thing which naturally offers itself to consideration, is the expense of government; this is a *sine qua non* of the whole, and all its parts. No kind of administration can be carried on without expense, and the scale or degree of plan and execution must ever be limited by it. Two grand considerations offer themselves here. 1. *The estimate of the expenses which government requires*: and, 2. *Such*

ways

ways and means of raising sufficient money to defray them, at will be most easy, and least hurtful and oppressive, to the subject.

The first is not my *present principal object:* I shall therefore only observe upon it, that the *wants of government,* like the *wants of nature,* are *few* and *easily supplied;* it is *luxury* which incurs the most expense, and drinks up the largest fountains of supply, and what is most to be lamented, the same luxury which *drinks up* the greatest supplies, does at the same time *corrupt* the body, *enervate* its strength, and *waste those powers* which are designed for use, ornament, or delight. The *ways and means of supply* are the object of my principal attention at present. I will premise a few propositions which appear to me to deserve great consideration here.

I. When a sum of money is wanted, *one way of raising it may be much easier than another.* This is is equally true in States as in individuals. A man must always depend for supply on those articles which he can *best spare,* or which he can furnish with *least* inconvenience: he should first sell such articles as he has *purposely provided for market;* if these are not enough, then such articles of his estate as he can *best spare,* always sacrificing *luxuries first,* and necessaries *last* of all.

II. *Any interest or thing whatever, on which the burden of tax is laid, is diminished either in quantity or neat value,* e. g. if *money* is taxed, part of the sum goes to pay the tax; if *lands,* part of the produce or price goes to pay it; if *goods,* part of the price which the goods will sell for, goes to pay it, &c.

III. *The consumption of any thing, on which the burden of tax is laid, will always be thereby lessened,* because such tax will *raise* the price of the article taxed, and fewer people will be able or willing to pay *such advance* of price, than would purchase, if the price was *not raised:* and consequently,

IV. *The burden of tax ought to lie heaviest on such articles, the use and consumption of which are least necessary to the community; and lightest on those articles, the use and consumption*

sumption of which are most necessary to the community. I think this so plain, that it cannot need any thing said on it either by way of illustration or proof.

V. *The staples of any country are both the source and measure of its wealth,* and therefore ought to be *encouraged and increased* as far as possible. No country can enjoy or consume more than they can raise, make, or purchase. No country can purchase more than they can pay for; and no country can make payment beyond the amount of the *surplus* which remains of their staples, after their *consumption* is subtracted. If they go beyond this, they must run in debt, *i. e.* eat the calf in the cow's belly, or consume this year the proceeds of the next, which is a direct step to ruin, and must (if continued) end in destruction.

VI. *The great staples of the Thirteen United States, are our* HUSBANDRY, FISHERIES, AND MANUFACTURES. *Trade* comes in as the *hand-maid* of them all—the *servant* that tends upon them—the *nurse* that takes away their redundancies, and supplies their wants. *These* we may consider as the great *sources* of our wealth; and our *trade*, as the great *conduit* thro' which it flows. All these we ought in sound policy to guard, encourage, and increase *as far as possible,* and to load them with burdens and embarrassments *as little* as possible.

VII. When any country finds that any articles are growing into use, and their consumption increasing so far as to become hurtful to the prosperity of the people, or to corrupt their morals or economy, *it is the interest and good policy of such country to check and diminish the use and consumption of such articles,* down to such degree as shall consist with the greatest happiness and purity of their people.

VIII. This is done the most effectually and unexceptionably, by *taxing such articles, and thereby raising the price of them so high,* as shall be necessary to *reduce* their consumption, as far as is needful for the general good. The force of this observation has been felt by all nations; and *sumptuary laws* have been tried in all shapes, to *prevent or reduce* such hurtful consumptions; but none ever did or can do it so effectually as *raising the price of them :* this touches

the

feelings of every purchaser, and connects the use of such articles with the pain of the purchaser, who cannot afford them, so closely and constantly, as cannot fail to operate by way of *diminution* or *disuse* of such consumption; and as to such rich or prodigal people, as can or will go to the price of such articles, they are the very persons who, I think, are the most able and suitable to pay taxes to the State.

I think it would not be difficult to enumerate a great number of such articles of *luxury, pride, or mere ornament,* which are growing into such excessive use among us, as to become dangerous to the *wealth, economy, morals,* and *health* of our people, viz. *distilled spirits* of all sorts, especially whisky and country rum, all imported *wines, silks* of all sorts, *cambrics, lawns, laces,* &c. &c. *superfine cloths and velvets, jewels* of all kinds, &c. to which might be added a very large catalogue of articles, tho' not so *capitally* dangerous as these, yet such as would admit *a check* in their consumption, without any damage to the States, such as *sugar, tea, coffee, cocoa, fine linens,* all *cloths and stuffs* generally used by the *richer kind* of people, &c. all which may be judiciously taxed at *ten, twenty, fifty,* or *one hundred per cent.* on their first importation; and to these might be added, a small duty of perhaps *five per cent.* on all other imported goods whatever.

Two things are here to be considered and proved. 1. That *this mode* of taxation would be more *beneficial* to the community than any other: and, 2. that this mode is *practicable.* If these two things are fairly and clearly proved, I think there can be no room left for doubt, whether this kind of taxation ought to be immediately adopted, and put in practice.

I will offer my reasons in favor of these propositions as fully, clearly, and truly as I can, and hope they may be judged worthy of a candid attention. I will endeavour in the first place, to point out *the benefits arising from this mode of taxation.*

I. This mode of taxation may safely be raised to such a degree, as *to produce all the money we need for the public ser-*

vice, or sufficiently *near* it; perhaps a *small tax* in the ordinary way would be more beneficial to the States than *none,* because this tax keeps the customary avenues from the wealth of individuals to the public treasury always open, which may be used on emergencies, and the *habit and practice* being settled, would avoid the difficulties naturally arising from *novelty* or *innovations.*

But to return to my argument. It is greatly in favor of this kind of tax, that it will bring money *enough* for the public service; it is matter of great animation in the pursuit of any object, to know that, when accomplished, it will be *adequate to its purposes.* People all want to see the *end of things,* and to know when they are to *have done:* this will naturally produce much stronger efforts, vigor, and cheerfulness, than if the thing, when accomplished, would be but *half adequate* to its purposes.

II. This mode of taxation *applies for money where it is to be had in greatest plenty, and can be paid with most ease and least pain.* If we apply to the *farmer, tradesman,* or *laborer* for cash, they have mighty little of it, and it is hard for them to raise the necessary sum; but it is matter of *common course* with the merchant, *thro' whose hands the great current of circulating cash passes;* he will consider the tax as part of the *first cost* of his goods, and set his price and sell accordingly: it matters little to him, whether he *pays half* the cost of his goods *abroad,* and the *other half at home,* or whether he pays it all abroad; his object is to get the whole out of his sales, with as much profit to himself as he can.

III. This mode *lays the burden of tax on that kind of consumption which is excessive and hurtful, and lessens that consumption, and of course mends the economy, and increases the industry and health, of the people.* For it is plain, that *no more money* will be paid for the goods taxed, than would have been paid for the same kind of goods, had they *not* been taxed: the difference is, the same money paid for the taxed goods will not buy *so many* of them as before the tax, because the tax will *raise the price* of them.

And

And when the confumption or ufe of fuch goods is exceffive and hurtful, this *leffening* of it is a *benefit*, tho' the fame money is paid for them as before, for the fame reafon that it is better for a man that happens to be at a tavern with exceffive drinkers, to pay his *whole fhare of the reckoning*, but drink *lefs than his fhare* of the liquors, and *go home fober*, than to pay the *fame* reckoning, drink his *full fhare* of the liquors, and *go home drunk*. It is always better for a man to buy poifon and *not ufe* it, than to buy the fame poifon and *ufe* it; in the one cafe he lofes nothing but his *money*, in the other cafe he lofes his money and *health* too. For the fame reafon it is better for a reaper to drink *half a pint* of rum in a day, than to reap for the fame wages, and drink a *quart* of rum. This reafoning will hold in its proper degree, with refpect to every kind of confumption, which is exceffive and hurtful.

IV. This mode of taxation *faves the whole fum of the tax to the States*, while at the fame time *it mends the habits and health of the people*: for it is plain, that if the confumption of fuch imported goods is leffened by the tax, *a lefs quantity* will be *imported*, and of courfe a *lefs* fum of money need be *fent abroad* to pay the firft coft of thefe goods; and this excefs of money, which is thus faved from going abroad (from whence it *would never return*) is paid by the tax into the *public treafury*, from whence it iffues on the public fervice, and is directly thrown *into circulation again* thro' the States, and of courfe becomes a *clear faving*, or balance of increafe of the circulating medium, and confequently of *realized* wealth in the country; whilft at the fame time, the people are better ferved and accommodated by the *reduced* confumption, than they could have been by the *exceffive* one.

V. It appears from what has been juft now obferved, that *this mode of taxation naturally increafes the circulating cafh of the States*, and every one knows what *a fpring, what vigor* this gives to every kind of bufinefs in the country, whether of hufbandry, mechanic arts, or trade. There is no comparifon between the advantages of carrying on any fort of bufinefs in a country where *cafh circulates freely*, and in a country where cash is *scarce*. In the one case, every kind of business will *flourish*, and industry has every sort of *encouragement* and motive for exertion; in the other all business must be sadly *embarrassed*, and of course make but a feeble and slow progress.

We can scarce form a conception, what a *different face these two circumstances will give a country* in a short time; in the one case, *buildings* rise, *husbandry* improves, *arts* and *manufactures* flourish, the country is *alive*, and every part of it *abounding* with industry, profits, and delight; the other can produce little more than *languishment, decay, dullness,* and *fruitless anxiety, disappointment,* and *wretchedness*.

VI. The tax I propose, *will operate in a way of general equality, justice, and due proportion*. A tax on general consumptions cannot fail to bring the burden in *due* proportion on individuals, because every one will pay in proportion to his consumption; and the presumption is, that the man who spends *most*, is *best able* to spend.

If this proposition admits of exceptions, they are generally in favor of the *economist*, the careful, penurious man, and against the *prodigal* who dissipates his estate, and will operate as a check upon him, if he is not past all considerations of interest. If this is the case with him, the sooner his estate is run thro' the better it is, both for himself and the public, for when this happens, he must either *die* or *work* for his living, and of course do *some good* in the world, or at least *cease doing hurt;* he will then no longer be able to set an *example* of idleness, extravagance, and dissoluteness, and draw other *gay spirits* into his pernicious practices; and if his constitution shall happen to out-last his estate, he may by temperance enjoy some good degree of health, and his adversities may perhaps bring on serious reflections, sincere repentance, and amendment of life, and if his fortune is desperate in this world, he may at least find strong inducements to prepare for the next; so that he is in no sense injured by the tax, but may by prudence derive great benefits from it.

Besides,

Besides, I am of opinion that **government** ought to leave every man *master of his own estate*, and permit him to *judge* for himself *how fast* and *in what way* he will spend it; he knows well what **tax** he pays on every expenditure, and every part of it is subject to his own *free choice*, and if his career of *dissipation* cannot be *restrained*, it is as *well* for *him*, and much *better* for *the public*, that he should give part of his wealth to the public treasury, than waste the whole of it in his luxury and pleasures; so that I do not see that he has in this case the least ground of complaint of *injury* or *oppression*.

Besides, I think there is a kind of *justice* in framing the public institutions in such a manner, that a man cannot spend a dollar in *luxury* and *dissipation*, which is *hurtful* to the public, but he must at the same time *pay another dollar* into the public treasury, to make thereby some *compensation* for the injury which the public receives from his *luxury*.

And as to the *niggard, the penurious man,* who does not spend his money in proportion to his *wealth*, and of course does not pay *his share* of tax; it is observable that even his very *penury* inures to the *benefit* of the community, for what he does *not spend*, he *saves,* and thereby enriches himself, and of course adds to the *wealth* of the community, for the *wealth of the community* is always the *aggregate of the wealth* of every individual who composes it; this ought therefore to be a *favored case*, as the community eventually gains more by a shilling *saved*, than it could by a shilling consumed and *lost*, tho' the consumer should pay *six-pence* into the public treasury.

In fine, the *tax* on this principle *is carved out of the expenditures of the nation*, not indeed *all* expenditures indiscriminately, but is so calculated as to fall *heaviest* on those expenditures which are the most general *indices of wealth,* and are usually made by the *rich* who are the best able to bear them; and the few exceptions which may be supposed to take place, will generally operate *in favor of virtue* and *economy*, and against *vice* and *dissipation;* and where it falls heaviest, and becomes most burdensome, it is designed, and does actually tend, to *correct* that very *vicious taste* and corrupt

rupt *habit*, which is the *true cause* of the burden, and which it is always *in the power* of the sufferer to *ease* himself of, whenever he pleases.

Point out any other mode of taxing, if you can, that *finds its way* so surely to the *wealth* of individuals, and *apportions* itself thereto so *equitably*, that no subject can be burdened beyond his due proportion, without having *a full remedy always in his own power;* yea, a *sure, easy, and excellent remedy*, because a man may always avail himself of it, without the expense and trouble of a *law-suit*, or being subjected to *any body's decisions, opinions, or caprices,* but his own.

VII. This mode of taxing will make *the quantity and time of the tax depend on the free choice of the man who pays it.* If a man has a mind to drink a bowl of punch or bottle of wine with his friend, or buy a silk gown for his daughter, he knows very well how much *tax is incorporated* with the purchase, and adopts and pays it with cheerfulness and good-humor; a *humor* very different from the *irritated sensibility* of a man, who sees an *awful collector* enter upon him with his warrant of *plenary powers* to *distrain* his goods, or *arrest* his person, for a *tax* which perhaps he *abhors*, either from religious scruples, or an opinion that he is rated beyond his due proportion, or because he is not at that time *in condition* to pay it.

The good-humor of the subject is of great consequence in any government. When people have their *own way* and *choice* in a matter, they will bear *great* burdens with *little* complaint; but when matters are forced on them *contrary to their humor*, they will make *great* complaints on *small* occasions, and the public peace is often destroyed, much more by the *manner of doing*, than by *the thing done.*

VIII. This mode of taxing *will give our treasury some compensation for the monies which our people pay towards the tax of other countries which they travel thro', or reside in, when abroad.* An *American* cannot travel thro' any country of *Europe*, and drink a bowl of punch or eat a dinner, but he *contributes to the tax* of the country; and if our taxes, like theirs, were laid on such *luxurious consumptions* as

travellers

travellers usually indulge themselves in, *their* people who travel thro' *our* country, or reside in it, would contribute towards *our* taxes, in like manner as *our* people who travel or reside in *their* countries, contribute to *theirs*.

And as we expect that the intercourse between us and all the countries of *Europe* will be very great, it is highly reasonable that *our treasury* should receive the *same benefit* from *their* travellers among us, that *their* treasuries receive from *our* people who travel or reside among *them*, and a little attention to the subject will be sufficient to convince any man that this article *is more than a trifle*.

IX. This mode of taxing, which brings the burden of the tax principally on articles of luxury, or at most on articles of not the first necessity, *gives easement and relief to our husbandry and manufactures, which are in danger of ruin from the present weight of taxes which lies on them*. If we tax land, we *lessen its value*, and of course diminish the whole *farming interest*. If we tax *polls*, we in effect tax *labor*, which discourages it, and of consequence we cast a damp and deadening languor on the very *first springs*, the *original principle* and *source* of our national wealth, and *wound* the great staples of the country *in their embryo*.

Now I think that any mode of taxing, which gives *remedy and relief* against so great, so *fatal an evil*, would deserve consideration, even tho' it had not these advantages in its favor, which I have before enumerated. I have heard a stupid and cruel argument urged, that taxing labor has this advantage, that it promotes industry, because it increases necessity. This argument proves in a very cogent manner, that it is best to make every body poor, because it will make them work the harder.

But I should think it would be more humane and liberal in a government to manage the public administration so, that *industry* might have all possible *encouragement*, that it might be rather *animated* by an increase of happiness and hope of reward, than *goaded on* by dire necessity and the dreadful spurs of pinching want.

I freely give it as my clear and decided opinion, that it is the interest, duty, and best policy of every government,

to

to give all possible ease, exoneration, and encouragement to that industry, those occupations, and kinds of business, which most *enrich, strengthen,* and *happify* a nation, and to lay the *burdens* of government as far as possible on those *fashions, habits,* and *practices,* which tend to *weaken, impoverish,* and *corrupt* the people; and therefore that any mode of taxing which tends to encourage the *first* of these, and discourage the *last,* is worthy of the most serious attention.

But perhaps the advantage of this kind of taxation will appear in a more striking light, by considering its *practical* and *general effects* on a nation which adopts it; in which view of the matter I think it will be very manifest,

I. That any man of business, whether he be merchant, farmer, or tradesman, *may live easier and better,* i. e. *be happier thro' the year, and richer at the end of it, in a country where this tax is paid,* than he could live in the same country, *if the tax was not paid;* for as the tax is laid on *useless consumptions,* it would of course *diminish* those consumptions, and of course *save the first cost* of the part diminished, and all the *additional expense* which the use of that part would require.

If a man lives in a country abounding in luxury, he must go in some degree *into it,* or appear *singular* and *mean,* and that part which he would be in a manner compelled to adopt, would probably cost him *more* than his *tax.*

But it is here to be considered, that the *first cost* of an article of luxury is not near *all the cost of it.* One article often makes another necessary, and that a third, and so on almost *ad infinitum;* if you buy a silk cloak, there must also be *trimmings,* and that will not do without a *hat* or *bonnet,* and these require a *suitable accommodation* in every other part of the dress, in order to keep up any sort of *decency and uniformity* of appearance; and there also must be spent a great deal of time to put these *fine things on,* and to *wear* them, to *show* them, to *receive* and *pay* visits in them, &c.

And when this kind of luxury prevails in a country beyond the degree which its *wealth can bear,* the consequence is *pride, poverty, debt, duns, law-suits,* &c. &c. The farmer finds the proceeds of the year *vanished into trifles;* the merchant and tradesman may sell their goods indeed, but cannot *get payment* for them. Every family finds its expense greatly *increased,* and the *time* of the family much *consumed* in attending to that *very expense.* Many families soon become embarrassed, and put to very mortifying shifts to keep up that appearance, which such a corrupt taste almost *compels* them to support.

But were these families with the same income, to live in a country of *more economy* and *less luxury,* they would easily pay the taxes on the luxuries they did use, keep on a *good footing* with their neighbours, appear with as *much distinction,* live *happy* and *unembarrassed thro'* the year, and have money in their pockets at the *end* of it. In such a country, payments would be punctual, and industry steady, and of course all business both of merchandise, husbandry, and mechanic arts, might be carried on with ease and success.

These are no high colorings, but *an appeal to plain facts,* and to the *sense* of every prudent man on these facts; and I here with confidence ask every *wise man,* if he would not choose to live in a country where articles of *hurtful luxury* and *needless consumption* were, by taxes or any other cause, raised so high in their price, as to prevent the *excessive use* of them, rather than in a country where such articles were of *easy acquirement,* and the use of them so *excessive* among the inhabitants, as to *consume* their *wealth, destroy* their *industry,* and corrupt the *morals* and *health* of the people.

II. I think it is very plain, that articles of *hurtful,* or at best of *needless, consumption* are making such *rapid progress* among us, and growing into such *excessive use,* as to throw the *economy, industry, simplicity,* and *even health* of our people into danger; and of consequence, *raising the price of such articles so high as will be necessary to produce a proper check to the excessive use of them, will require a tax so great, as, when added to a small and very moderate impost on articles of general and necessary consumption, will bring money enough into the public treasury, for all the purposes of the public service.* We will

will suppose then that all this is done, and when this is done, we will stop a moment, and look round us, and view the *advantages* resulting from this measure, over and above the capital one of checking and restraining that excessive luxury that threatens, if not an *absolute destruction*, yet at least a *tarnishment of every principle* out of which our prosperity, wealth, and happiness must necessarily and for ever flow. I say, we will stop a minute and view the advantageous effects of this measure.

The first grand effect which presents itself to my view is, that *our army will be paid;* and that our brethren, our fellow-citizens, who, by their *valor*, their *patience*, their *perseverance* in the field, have secured to us our *vast, extensive country*, and all its blessings, will be enabled to *return* to their friends and connexions, not only *crowned* with the *laurels* of the field, but *rewarded* by the *justice* and *gratitude* of their country, and be thereby enabled to support their *dignity of character*, or at least be put on *a footing with their fellow-citizens* (whom they have saved) in the procurement of the means of living.

The next advantage of this measure which occurs to me is, *the easement and exoneration of the laborers of the community, the husbandman and tradesman*, out of *whose labor* all our *wealth* and *supplies* are derived; by them we are *fed*, by them we are *clothed*, by the various modifications of *their labor* our *staples* are produced, our *commerce* receives its principle, and our utmost *abundance* is supplied; we are therefore bound by every principle of *justice, gratitude*, and *good policy*, to give them encouragement and uninterrupted security in their peaceful occupations, and not, by an *unnatural* and *ill-fated* arrangement of our finances, compel them to *leave* their *labors*, which are the grand object of *their* attention and *our* supplies, *to go and hunt up money* to satisfy a collector of taxes.

But *justice* and *gratitude* operate only on *minds* which these virtues can *reach*. There may be some few among us, of no little weight, who are content, if they can obtain the *services*, to let the *servant shift for himself*; and who, when they are *sure* of the *benefit*, remember *no longer*
the

the *benefactor*, and, as in this great argument of univerfal concern, I wish to find the way to *every man's sense*, and address myself not only to those who *have virtue*, but even to those who *have none*, I will therefore mention another advantage of this measure, which I think will *(virtue or no virtue)* reach the feelings of every man who retains the least sense of interest, viz.

That in this way *all our public creditors would be paid and satisfied*, either by a total discharge of their *principal*, or an undoubted, *well-funded security* of it, with a *sure and punctual payment* of their *interest*, which would be the best of the two; because a total discharge of the principal at once, if sufficient money could be obtained, would make such a *sudden, so vast an addition* to our circulating cash, as would depreciate it, and reduce the value of the debt paid, much below its worth at the time of contract, and introduce a *fluctuation* of our markets, and other *fatal evils* of a depreciated currency, which have been known by experience and severely felt, enough to make them dreaded.

It would therefore be much better for the creditor to receive a certain, *well-funded security* of his debt than *full payment*: for in that case, if he needed the cash for his debt, he might sell his security *at little* or *no discount*, which is the constant practice of the public creditors in *England*, where every kind of *public security* has *its rate of exchange* settled every day, and may be negotiated in a very short time. Supposing this should be the case, stop and see what an *amazing effect* this would have on *every kind* of business in the country.

The public bankruptcies have been so amazingly great, that vast numbers of our people have been reduced by them to the condition of men *who have sold their effects to broken merchants, who cannot pay them, their business is lessened, or perhaps reduced to nothing for want of their stock so detained from them.* Supposing then that their stock was restored to them all, they would instantly all *push into business*, and the proceeds of their business *would flow thro' the country in every direction of industry, and every species of supply.*

In

In fine, the whole country would be alive, and as *it is* obvious to every one, that it is much better living in a country of *brisk* business than in one of *stagnated* business, every individual would reap benefits from this general animation of industry, beyond account *more than enough* to compensate the tax which he has paid to produce it.

All these advantages hitherto enumerated will put the labor and industry of our people of all occupations on such a footing of *profit and security*, as would soon give a *new face* to the country, and open such extensive prospects of *plenty, peace, and establishment*, throw into action so many *sources* of wealth, give such *stability* to *public credit*, and make the *burdens* of government so *easy* and almost imperceptible to the people, as would make *our country* not only a most *advantageous* place to live in, but even make it abound with the *richest enjoyments* and *heart-felt delights*.

These are objects of great *magnitude* and *desirableness:* they *animate* and *dilate* the heart of every *American*. What can do *the heart more good* than to see our country a *scene of justice, plenty*, and *happiness?* Are these rich blessings within our reach? Can we believe they are so absolutely within our power, that they require no more than very practicable efforts to bring us into the full possession of them? *These blessings are doubtless attainable, if we will go to the price of them;* and that you may judge whether they are worth the purchase, whether they are too dear or not, I will give you the *price-current* of them all, the price which, if *honestly paid*, will certainly purchase them.

In order to have them, then, we must pay about a *dollar and a half* a gallon for *rum, brandy*, and other distilled *spirits;* a *dollar* a gallon above the ordinary price for *wines;* a *dollar* for *bohea tea*, and about that sum above the ordinary price for *hyson tea;* a *double price* on *silks* of all sorts, *laces* of all sorts, *thin linens* and *cottons* of all sorts, such as *muslins, lawns*, and *cambrics*, and on *jewellery* of all sorts, &c. about a *dollar and a third* a yard above the ordinary price for *superfine cloths* of all sorts, &c. &c. a *third of a dollar* a bushel for *salt* (for I do not mean to lay *quite all* the tax on the *rich*, and *wholly* excuse the *poor*) about a

dollar

dollar a hundred for *sugar*, one *tenth of a dollar* a pound on *coffee*, and the same on *cocoa*, above the ordinary prices, &c. &c. with an addition of *five per cent.* on all articles of *importation* not enumerated, except *cotton, dying woods*, and other *raw materials* for our own manufactures; for whilst *importations* are *discouraged*, our *own manufactures* will naturally be increased, and ought to be *encouraged*, or at least to be *disburdened*.

On this state of the matter I beg leave to observe, that the war itself for seven years past has laid a tax on us nearly *equal to the highest of these*, and on some articles of necessary consumption, from *two hundred* to a *thousand* per cent. higher, such as *salt, pepper, allspice, allum, powder, lead*, &c. &c. and yet I never heard any body complain of being ruined by the war, because *rum* was *twenty shillings* per gallon, *tea* twelve shillings per pound, or *mantuas* three dollars a yard, or *pepper* ten shillings a pound, or *superfine cloths* eight dollars a yard, &c. Nor does it appear to me, that the country has paid *a shilling more* for rum, *silks, superfine cloths*, &c. for the *last seven years*, than was paid for the same articles the seven *preceding years*, i. e. the whole tax was paid by *lessening the consumption* of these articles.

Nor do I think that the health, habits, or happiness of the country have suffered in the least on the whole, from its being obliged to use *less of these articles* than was before usual; but be this as it may, it is very certain that the country has suffered but little from the increased price of these articles which I propose to tax, except at some particular times when those prices were raised much higher than the point to which I propose to raise them, i. e. at particular times *rum* has been as high as *three dollars* a gallon; *tea, three dollars* a pound; *sugars, three shillings and six-pence*, and *coffee, three shillings and six-pence* a pound; *mantuas* four dollars a yard, &c.

But it is observable, that the principal increased prices which have really hurt and distressed the country during the war, have been of *other articles* which I propose to tax very lightly, or not at all; such as *salt*, which has at times

been

been six dollars a bushel, and perhaps three or four dollars on an average, *coarse cloths* and *coarse linens*, *osnabrigs*, *cutlery*, and *crockery wares*, &c. which have often rose to *five or six* prices, and stood for years together at *three or four*, and yet the burden of these excessive prices of even necessary articles of unavoidable consumption, has not been so great, if you *except the article of salt*, as to be so much *as mentioned* very often among the *ruinous effects* and *distresses* of the war.

The use I mean to make of these observations is, to prove from plain, acknowledged fact, that the *increased price* of the articles which I wish to tax, up to the utmost point to which I propose to raise them, will be but a *light inconvenience* (if any at all) on the people, and the *diminished* consumption of those articles, and the *increase* of *circulating cash* (both which will naturally and unavoidably result from the tax) will be *benefits* which will at least compensate for the *burden* of the tax, and I think it is very plain, will leave a *balance of advantage* in favor of the tax.

But if you should think I conclude too strongly, and you should not be able to go quite my lengths in this argument, so much, I think, does at least appear incontestably plain, that if there is a *real disadvantage* arising from my mode of taxing, it is *so small*, that it holds *no comparison* with the burden of tax *hitherto in use* on polls and estates, which *discourages industry*, *oppresses* the *laborer*, *lessens* the value of our *lands*, ruins our *husbandry* and *manufactures*, and with all these dreary evils, cannot possibly be collected to *half the amount* which *the public service requires*.

But to save further argument on this head, I will with great assurance appeal to the sense, the feelings of our *farmers*, who make the great bulk of our inhabitants, if they would not *prefer living* in a *country* where they must pay the afore-mentioned *increased prices* on the goods I propose to tax, rather than *where* they must part with the same number of *cows*, *oxen*, *sheep*, *bushels of wheat*, or *pounds of pork* or *beef*, &c. which are now, in the present mode of taxing, annually demanded of them to satisfy the tax.

I dare

"I dare make the same appeal to all our *tradesmen*, and even to our *merchants*, who, in my opinion, would have clear and decided advantages from my mode of taxing, as well as the farmers. I do not see how the merchant or any body else can be hurt by the tax; but will all be clearly benefited by it, if the following particulars are observed:

I. That *the tax be laid with such judgment and prudence, and different weight on different articles, that the consumption of no article shall be diminished by it, beyond what the good and true interest of the nation requires;* for it is certainly *better for the merchant* to deal with his customers in such articles as are *useful* to them, and in such way that they shall derive *real benefit from their trade with him*, than to supply them with articles that are *useless* or *hurtful* to them, and which of course impoverish them.

In the first case, he will make his customers *rich* and *able to continue* trading with him, and to make him good and punctual *payments*: in the other case, he makes his customers *poor*, and of course subjects himself to the danger of *dilatory payments*, or perhaps of a *final loss* of his debts.

II. That *the tax be universal and alike on every part of the country*, for if one State is taxed, and its neighbour is not, the State taxed will lose its trade. This proves in the most intuitive manner, that every tax of impost on imported goods must be laid by the *general government*, and not by any *particular State*, whose laws cannot be extended beyond its own jurisdiction. And,

III. *That the tax be universally collected.* Smuggling hurts the *fair trader;* favor and connivance of collectors to particular importers, thro' *bribery, friendship,* or *indolence,* has the same effect; the person who *avoids* the tax can *undersell* him who *pays* it; therefore it is the *great interest of the merchant,* when the duty is laid, to make it a *decided point,* that *every* importer shall *pay the duty.*

And I am of opinion, that when the *body of merchants* make it a *decided* matter to carry any point of this nature, they are very *able* to accomplish it; they certainly *know better* than all the custom-house officers and tide-waiters on earth. How to *prevent or detect* smuggling, and to *discover and punish* the indulgence or connivance of collectors, who may be induced to *favor* particular importers, and they have the *highest interest* in doing this, of any set of people in the nation; and therefore I think it *good policy* to trust this matter to their *prudence*, with proper powers to execute it in the most effectual way.

From a pretty extensive acquaintance, I am convinced there is a *professional honor in merchants* which may be *safely* trusted; and I apprehend it is a policy both *needless and cruel*, to subject the persons and fortunes of merchants, the great negotiators of the nation's wealth, and a body of men at least as respectable as any among us, to the *insults* of custom-house officers and tide-waiters, the rabble of whom, in *Europe* (I hope ours may be better) are generally allowed to be as corrupt, unprincipled, intolerable, and low-lived a set of villains as can be scraped out of the dregs of any nation; and to set such fellows to watch and guard the *integrity and honesty* of a most respectable order of men, and subject *honorable and useful citizens* to such mortifying inspection, appears to me to be such an *insult* on *common sense*,—such an *outrage* on every natural principle of *humanity* and *decency*,—such a gross corruption of every degree of *polished manners*, that I should imagine it must require ages to give it that degree of practice and establishment which has long taken place in Great-Britain.

The quickest way to *make men knaves*, is to *treat them as such*. It is a common observation, when a woman's *character* is gone, her *chastity* soon follows. Few men think themselves much obliged to exhibit instances of *integrity* to men, who will return them neither *credit* nor *confidence* for their uprightness. Let every man have the credit of his own virtues, and be *presumed to be virtuous* till the *contrary appears*. Honesty is as essential and delicate a part of a *merchant's character*, as *piety* is of a clergyman's, or *chastity*, of a woman's, and you wound them all alike sensibly, when you show, by your conduct towards them, that

that you even suspect that *they are wanting* in these characteristic virtues.

I conceive nothing more is necessary to make the collection of this tax easy, than to convince the *merchants*, and indeed the whole *community*, that the tax is *necessary for the public service*,—for the essential *purposes* of government; and that every one who pays it, receives a full compensation in the *benefits* he derives from the union; and that the *management of the affair* be committed to the *merchants*, to which, from the nature of their profession and business, they are *more adequate and qualified*, than any *other* men; and as it falls directly within the sphere of their business, it seems to be an *honor*, a *mark of confidence*, to which they are entitled.

Indeed, let the community at large be *convinced* that the money proceeding from this tax, is *necessary for the public service*, and that it can be assessed with *less burden* on the people *in this way*, than in the *mode hitherto practised*, and the collection will be *easy and natural*.

The tax will cease to be considered, like the taxes formerly imposed on us by the *British Parliament*, *unconstitutional* in their *assessment*, and *useless* in their *expenditure*, for they plagued us with taxes only to satisfy their harpies (little or none of the money ever reached the *British treasury*) but *this tax* is imposed by our own people,—by our own representatives, and for our own benefit.

It must be imposed by Congress indeed, as the authority of any particular Assembly cannot be adequate to it; for it must operate alike in all the States, be alike universal in its effects, and uniform in its mode of assessment and collection; and must therefore proceed from the *general* authority which presides over the whole Union, *i. e.* from the Congress; but it is a Congress of our *own appointment*: for the members of Congress are as much *our representatives*, and chosen by *our people*, as the members of the several *State-Assemblies;* and the end and use of the tax is *our own public service*, to secure the benefits of *our* union, without which it is impossible we should obtain *respectability abroad*, an *uniform administration* of civil police

lice at *home*, an eftablifhed public *credit*, or full *protection* againft *domeftic or foreign* infult.

I never knew any meafure of government oppofed in its execution by the people, when a general conviction took place that the meafure was properly planned, and was neceffary to the public good. We have had full proof thro' the war, what *great burdens* our people will, very cheerfully and even without complaint, bear, when they are *convinced* that the *exigencies* of the State, and the *public fafety*, made *them neceffary*.

This exhibits *the tax in an advantageous light*, rather *eligible* than *fhocking*, connects the ideas of *burden* and *benefit* together, and naturally brings the *evils* removed by the tax, and the *advantages* refulting from it, into one view, and may ftrike the minds of the people fo ftrongly, as to make the *burden* of it appear light, when compared with its *benefits*.

This brings me to the confideration of the *practicability of my mode of taxation* which I propofed, and which I do conceive is a matter of capital weight in this difcuffion, for which I do rely on thefe two grand propofitions:

1. *That whatever is the real, great intereft of the people, they may, by proper meafures, be made to believe and adopt:* and,

2. *That whatever is admitted to be a matter of common and important intereft, in the general opinion of the people, may be eafily put in practice by wifdom, prudence, and due management of the affair.*

I do contend, that when this tax is fairly propofed to the public, with a proper elucidation of the *evils* it avoids, and the *advantages* which refult from it, it will not be looked on as a *burden of oppreffion*, an *impofition of power*, but as the *purchafe* of our moft *precious bleffings*, as a meafure abfolutely *neceffary* to our moft effential and important *interefts*.

Therefore any attempt to *avoid* this tax, by *fmuggling* or any *other way*, will be deemed by general confent an act of *meannefs*; an *avoidance* of a *due* fhare of the public burden; fruftrating the *neceffary plans* of public fafety, and rendering

ing ineffectual the *public measures* adopted by general consent, for the public security, tranquillity, and happiness.

Such an action implies in it great *meanness* of character in the agent, and a *high crime* against the State, and the detection of it will be considered as a very material *service* to the Commonwealth. Where any actions are deemed *crimes, scandals,* and *nuisances* by the general voice of the people, *detections and informations* against them are reputable; they cease to be *infamous—the infamy of an informer* does not take place in such instances.

The reasons of governmental measures ought always to attend their publication, so far as to afford good means of conviction to the people at large, that their *object and tendency* is the *public good*. This greatly facilitates their execution and success. It is hard governing people *against their interests*, their *persuasions*, and even against their *prejudices*. It is better to court their *understandings* first with reason, candor, and sincerity, and we may be almost sure all their *passions* will follow soon.

I abhor a *mysterious government*. I think an administration, like a private man, which affects to have a great *many secrets* that must not be explained, has generally a great many *faults* which will not bear *telling*, or a great deal of *corruption* which will not bear *examining*. Government, like private persons, may indeed have *secrets*, which ought to be kept so; but in that case, caution should be used against any intimations or hints getting abroad, even *that there are such secrets*, or any secrets: for this would produce an anxious inquiry and solicitous inspection, which might make the *keeping* the secret more *difficult*, and besides bring on many other inconveniencies arising from numberless apprehensions, which such a circumstance would give birth to.

An *ostentatious giving out* that there are *mighty secrets* in the cabinet, or many *mysteries* in the State, that must not be *pried* too closely *into*, is the very contrary of all this, and generally is a sign of a *weak administration*, and not seldom of a *corrupt* one; but of all public measures which require explanations to the people, *that of taxes*, which touches their

their money (which is always a very fenfible part) may ftand *as chief;* and to make thefe go down any thing well, it is always neceffary to fpread an univerfal conviction,

1. *That the money required in taxes is neceffary for the public good:* and,

2. *That it will certainly be actually expended only on the objects for which it is afked and given.*

And if thefe two things are *really true,* there will rarely be much difficulty in making them to be *believed* thro' the moft fenfible part of the Commonwealth; but if thefe two things either are not *really true* or not *really and generally believed,* I do not know that a *ftanding army* would be fufficient to collect the taxes.

I am of opinion their force, authority, and influence, like the conquefts of the *Britifh* army, would laft no longer in any place than they ftaid to fupport it. Whenever they fhall go away, I imagine they will find that they have left behind them infinitely more *abhorrence* than *obedience* among the people.

Tho' I am clearly of opinion that there muft exift *an ultimate force* or *power of compulfion* in every effective and good government, yet it is plain to me, that fuch force is never to be put in action *againft the general conviction* or *opinion* of the people; nor indeed do I believe it ever *can* be fo exercifed with fuccefs and final effect, for every attempt of this kind tends to *convulfions and death.*

Such an ultimate force indeed ought to fall upon and correct thofe who fin againft the peace, intereft, and fecurity of the public. But this can be done with fafety and advantage only in cafes where the *crime punifhed* is againft the *opinions,* the *fentiments,* and *moral* or *political principles,* which generally prevail in the people; for if the moft violent declaimer and mover of fedition in a government, fhould happen to be received by the people *as a patriot,* and his harangues fhould be eagerly adopted as the *doctrines of their liberties and rights,* any attempt to *punifh* him would be vain or ufelefs.

For either the people would *interpofe* and *refcue* him, or, if he was punifhed, they would confider him as the *martyr of their cause,* and thereby the public uneasiness, tumult, and uproar would be augmented: but when single persons or parties counteract the laws, and disturb that peace and order of government which is established by general consent, and in which there is a general persuasion that the security of every individual is concerned, there will be no difficulty in making such examples of punishment, as shall be sufficient to curb those *turbulent and factious spirits,* more or less of which may be found in every community, and which would become intolerable, if not kept under a *rigorous restraint.*

In all cases of this sort, the *righteous severities* of government will be *approved, supported,* and even *applauded* by the general voice.

Yea, if we were to suppose that the general opinion was wrong in any particular matter of importance, yet it is plain, that vicious opinion could not be *controlled by force:* it must continue till the ill effects of it shall produce a *general conviction* of its error, or till the people can be convinced by reason and argument of the danger of such opinion, before the ill consequences of it are *actually* felt; in both which cases the people will *turn about fast enough of their own accord,* and the *error* will be *corrected* most effectually, and with ease, and without any danger of disturbing the public tranquillity.

Opinions indeed of a dangerous, hurtful nature may spread among the people, and, when they become general, are to be considered as great public calamities, which admit of no remedy but that which they carry with them, and which will prove effectual in the end, viz. their *own evil tendency,* and therefore must be *let alone,* like inundations, which, however calamitous, whatever waste and destruction they make, cannot be controlled; any attempt to *stop* their force, *increases* their violence and mischief; they do *least hurt* when they are *unmolested,* and are suffered to drain themselves off in their own natural channels.

In short, there is no forcing every body, and therefore I reject with abhorrence every idea of *governing a country by a standing army,* or any other engines of force. I confider

sider every plan of this kind as a departure from the true principles of government, as destructive in its consequences, as absurd and ineffectual to its own ends; for such a government, whenever it has been tried, instead of promoting the *peace, security,* and *happiness* of the State, has generally been found to have operated by way of *tyranny and oppression.*

It appears from all this, that the true art of government lies in *good and full information of the facts* to which its ordinances are to be accommodated, and *in wisdom in adopting such institutions, laws, and plans of operation,* as shall best suit the state and true interests of the people; and *acting openly, fairly, and candidly with them.* You may as well attempt, by finesses, to cheat people into *holiness* and *heaven,* as into their *real political interests.*

There are people scattered over the whole nation, who understand the great interests of the community and the wisdom of public measures, and are as firmly attached to them as those who sit in the seat of government, and who are always dissatisfied, and their confidence in the public counsels is lessened, when they observe public measures are adopted, which they do not see the *use of,* and the *ends* for which they are calculated; and of course *little mystery* and *few secrets* are necessary in government. Let the administration be such as will *bear examining,* and the more it is *examined, the better it will appear.*

In such a mode of administration as this, if burdens that are *really heavy* are *necessary* for the public safety, they will be *cheerfully* taken up, and *patiently borne,* by the people without endangering the public tranquillity.

Another objection against my mode of taxing (which, in my opinion, is the greatest by far that can be fairly urged) remains yet to be considered. I once almost concluded not to mention it here, because its hurtful operation is *distant,* we are in no *present* danger of its effects, and its *evils may be prevented* or *remedied* in future time by necessary measures, without requiring our present attention. But I will subjoin it, because I think it best to communicate every quality, effect, and tendency of this subject, which my

utmost

utmost investigation of it has been able to discover, that the public may take it up or reject it on the fullest reason that I can lay before them. The objection is,

That this tax is insensible, and will produce more money than the people are apprized of, and in future time, when our trade and consumptions shall increase, may produce more than the public service will require, and of course *will tend to public dissipation and corruption.* For *frugality* in a *court* ever springs from *necessity,* and a *rich treasury naturally makes a prodigal administration,* and too often a *corrupt one.*

It may be answered, that it will always be easy to *lessen or take the tax off,* whenever it shall become *too productive.* This may be *easy,* but will always be *dangerous.* The imposing it at the close of the war will prevent the *fall of the goods taxed,* and keep them *up partly to the war price,* and of course *save the merchants* who have goods by them, from *very great loss,* and is a good reason for imposing it now; but when it shall be taken off, it will *reduce* the price of the goods taxed, in so *sudden a manner,* as will be very *hurtful* to those who have stock on hand, and may ruin very many families.

There is another, and perhaps better, way of guarding against the evils of the objection. It will be easy to transmit to each State an account of the annual proceeds of the tax, and when the *amount* shall exceed the *annual expenditures,* an *account of the surplus,* together with an estimate of the proportion of each State (according to the established quota of burdens and benefits) may be returned with it, and the said *proportion of the surplus* may be made *subject to the orders of each State respectively;* and if they judge that they can *more safely trust their own economy,* than that of the *supreme administration,* each State may draw its quota out of the *general treasury* into *its own,* and there keep it as a deposited fund of public wealth, or dispose of it as they please. Perhaps *a fund to defray the internal expenses of each State* might be as easily raised in this way as any other; but I leave a further discussion of the objection and its remedies to the wisdom of future times.

But

But if this my mode of taxing, or any other that may be adopted, should not be sufficient for the public service, I could wish the deficiency might somehow be made up *at home*, without recurring to the ruinous mode of supplies by *public loans abroad*. I think that *every light* in which this subject can be viewed, will afford *an argument* against it. I have known this cogent argument used in favor of foreign loans, viz. we give but *five per cent.* interest *abroad*, and our people can make *ten per cent. advantage* of the money *at home*, therefore they gain five per cent. by the loan.

This stupid argument, if it proves any thing, just proves that it is every man's interest to borrow money, for it is certainly profitable to buy any thing for five pounds which will bring ten; but the natural fact is the very reverse of this, for if you bring money into a kingdom or family, which is not the *proceeds of industry*, it will naturally *lessen the industry* and *increase the expenses of it*. It has been often observed, that when a person gains any *sudden acquisition of wealth* by treasure-trove, captures at sea, drawing a high prize in a lottery, or any other way *not connected with industry*, he is rarely known to *keep it long*, but soon *dissipates it*. The *sensible value* of money is lost, when the idea of it becomes *disconnected* with the *labor and pain of earning it*, and expenses will naturally *increase* where there is *plenty of wealth* to support them. The effect is the same on a nation.

Is *Spain* a whit richer for all the mines of *South-America?* The industry of *Holland* has proved a much surer source of durable wealth. We already find a dangerous *excess of luxury* growing out of our *borrowed money*, and our *industry* (especially in procuring supplies of our own) wants *great animation*.

Besides, the aforesaid argument is not grounded on fact; it is true, I suppose, that we pay but five per cent. interest on our foreign loans, but they cost us from fifteen to twenty per cent. more to get them home, for that is at least the discount which has been made on the sale of our bills for several years past, and if we bring it over in cash,

there

there is freight and insurance to be paid, which increases the loss.

From this it appears, that for every eighty pounds of supply which we obtain in this way, we must pay at least an hundred pounds, even if we were to pay the principal at the end of the year, and the consuming worm of five per cent. interest every year after, if the payment is delayed: to all this loss is to be added, all the expense of *negotiating* the loans abroad, *brokerage* on sale of the bills, &c. &c.

To escape the ruinous effects of this mode of supply, I think *every exertion* should be made to obtain our supplies *at home*; it is certainly very plain our country is *not exhausted*, it is *full* of every kind of *supply* which we need, and nothing further can be necessary, than to find *those avenues from the sources of wealth* in the hands of individuals, which *lead into the public treasury*, those *ways* and *proportions* that are most *just*, most *equal*, and most *easy* to the people. This is the *first great art* of finance; that of *economy* in expenditures is the next.

Any body may receive money and pay it out; borrow money and draw bills; but to *raise and manage the internal revenue*, so as to make the *wealth* of the country *balance* the *public expenditures*, is not so easy a task, but yet I think not so hard as to be impracticable; unless this can be done, the *greatest conceivable abilities* must *labor in vain*; for it is naturally impossible that any estate, which cannot pay its expenditures, should continue long without embarrassment and diminution; the load of debt must continually increase, and the interest will make a continual addition to that debt, and render the estate more and more unable every year to clear itself; but if the estate *can pay its expenditures*, it is the height of madness *not to do it*.

If revenues can be spared sufficient to discharge the interest of the debt, so as to stop its increase, the estate may be saved, and a future increase of revenue may in time wipe off the principal; but no hope is left, if *interest upon interest* must continue to *accumulate*.

K k   And

; And as the *interest of every individual is inseparably connected with the public credit* or state of the finances, it follows that this affair becomes a matter of the utmost concern and very important moment to *every person* in the community, and therefore ought to be attended to as a matter of the highest national concern; and *no burden* ought to be accounted *too heavy*, which is sufficient to remedy so great a mischief.

It may be objected to all this, that the duties I propose are so extremely high, that, 1. *they will hurt our trade:* and, 2. *can have no chance of obtaining a general consent.*

To the first I answer—as far as this tax tends to lessen the importation of hurtful luxuries and useless consumptions, it is *the very object I have in view;* and it is so very *light* on all other articles, that the *burden* will be almost *insensible.*

But as to the second objection—it is in vain to *trifle with* a matter of such weight and importance, or weary our people with *small plans* and *remedies*, utterly inadequate to the purpose. In weighty matters, *weak, half-assured attempts* will appear to every one to be *labor lost*, and a *ridiculous disproportion* of the means to the end: it is better in itself, as well as more likely to succeed with the people, to take strong hold, and, with a bold, firm assurance, propose something, which, when done, will be *an adequate and effectual remedy.*

Our national debt, including the supplies for the present year, I am told, by the Financier's estimate delivered to Congress, amounts to about 35,000,000 *of dollars*, the annual interest of which will be somewhat above 2,000,000 of dollars, which, I think, may be raised by the tax I propose (tho' it is impossible to tell with much precision, what the proceeds of a tax will be, which has not been tried:) it is very plain that the proceeds will be large, and so calculated as to be almost wholly a clear saving, not to say a benefit, to the country; and if there should be deficiencies, a small additional tax may be laid in the usual way to supply them.

Our

Our annual expenditures, on the peace establishment, may, I think, be reduced to a quarter or third of a million of dollars, and perhaps, if our national debt *was liquidated as it ought to be*, a great saving might be made both of *principal and interest;* but the detail of these matters is in every one's power, who has leisure and proper documents to make the calculations.

Without descending to *minutiæ*, I only mean to examine the *great principles* of resource and *mode* of supply which are within our power, and give my reasons as clear as I can for adopting a *practical trial*. Such a practice would doubtless *discover* many things which no *foresight* can reach, and *experience only* can elucidate; it is an *untrodden path* which I recommend, and tho' it cannot be perfectly known, yet it seems to me to have such an *appearance of advantage* as deserves a trial.

The *expense* and *difficulty* of collection will be *no greater* on the *high tax* I propose, than it would be on a *trifling one*, which would produce less than a *tenth part* of the supply which this would furnish.

Therefore, if it should be judged prudent to make the trial, I think it most advisable to take it up on *such a large scale*, as will make it *sufficiently productive* to become an object worthy of *strong effort* and *persevering diligence*, in order to give it *a full effect*.

In fine, we have not children or dunces to deal with, but a people who have as quick a sight of their interest, and as much courage, readiness, and cheerfulness to support it as any people on earth. We can have, therefore, nothing more to do, than to make such propositions to them as are *really* for their interest, to convince their minds that the thing proposed is *necessary and beneficial;* and this is to be done, not by *refinement of argument*, but by devising and explaining *such measures* as will, from their *nature and operation*, produce *beneficial effects*.

We must, with candor and fairness, in a manner open and undisguised, *tell them* what we want money *for*, and *how much*, and by a *wise and upright management* of their interests deserve and gain *their confidence*, that their money,

when

when obtained, shall, to the *last shilling*, be paid for such *necessary purposes;* the tax will then cease to be *odious*. It will become an object of *acknowledged interest*, and every person who *smuggles* or otherwise *avoids* the tax, will be considered as *shrinking from a burden* which the public good makes necessary.

Every attempt of this sort will become *disreputable* and *infamous*, and when you can connect the *tax* and *character* together, there will be *little difficulty* in collecting it.

This will effectually obviate the great objection, viz. that it will be *impracticable* to collect a heavy tax on goods of *great* value, but *little* bulk, such as *silks*, *laces*, and the like, because they may be *easily* smuggled, &c. Whenever they are to be sold, they must be exposed to view, and let the *burden of proof* ever lie on the *possessor*, *that the tax has been bona fide paid*.

I should think it advisable to commit the management of this matter to the merchants; they are *most hurt* by *smuggling*, and of course have the *highest interest* in preventing it. It will be *ten times more difficult* to cheat and impose on them, than any others, because the matter falls wholly within their *own sphere of business*. *Two of a trade cannot cheat one another as easy as either* of them might cheat *a stranger*. If the merchants would take the matter up, and make it a kind of *professional honor* to prevent smuggling, and see that the duty is *effectually paid*, there is little doubt but *they* could effect it.

All this reasoning depends on this one principle, viz. that our *public measures* must carry in them *wisdom*, *natural fitness*, *justice*, and *propriety;* then they will gain character, reputation, and confidence among the people at large, and mutual interest will soon make the government easy and effective; every individual will soon find his *interest* connected with *that of the public*, and he will have every inducement both of *honor and profit* to stand well with the government, and effectually support it.

And in this way, even the great doctrine of taxation itself, that *common and almost universal source of complaint*, may become an object of *acknowledged necessity*, of *confessed right*,

right, and the payment made like that of any other debt, with *conviction of right and full satisfaction.*

I will conclude this Essay with one argument more in favor of my principle of taxation, which appears to me of such mighty weight and vast importance, as must reach the feelings, and govern the heart, of every upright *American*, viz. *that our public union, with all its blessings, depends on it, and is supported by it,* and must, without it, dissolve and waste away into its original atoms.

To refuse any plan its *necessary support*, and to *murder and destroy* it, is the *same thing;* the union cannot be supported without so much money as is necessary to that support, and that money *may be raised in the way* I propose, and *cannot in any other.* We have a most plain and undeniable proof of fact, that the usual mode of taxation of polls and estates, is in its principle *unjust* and *unequal*, because it does not operate on our people in any *due proportion to their wealth:* this mischief was less felt, when our taxes were *very small*, and therefore, tho' *unjust*, were not *ruinous;* but the case is greatly altered, now the taxes are *grown up into the burden* which the present exigencies of the nation require.

The said tax hitherto in use is further ruinous, because it carves what money it does produce, out of the very *first resources*, the *original principle of our national wealth*, which, like *tender cions*, should be *nursed and guarded* with all care, till they arrive to strength and maturity;—then we may *pluck the fruit* without *hurting the tree:*—to cramp and diminish any of these, is like making bread of our *seed wheat*, or feeding our *mowing grounds*, every *quantity* we take *lessens the next crop ten;* but what gives decision to the point is, that we have the clear proof of experience, that the utmost efforts in this way have not been sufficient to produce *one quarter* of the sum necessary for the public service; nor is there any probability of an *increased* production.

The mode of supply by *foreign loans* need not be further reprobated; it is plain to every body, that if they can be continued (which is doubtful) they will soon involve us in *a foreign debt*, vastly beyond all *possibility of payment:* our

bankruptcy

bankruptcy muſt enſue; and with our bankruptcy will go all our *national character* of *wiſdom, integrity, energy* of government, and every kind of *reſpectability*. We ſhall become *objects of obloquy, butts of inſult*, and *by-words of diſgrace abroad;* an *American* in *Europe* will be aſhamed to tell *where he came from*. Every ſtranger takes ſome ſhare in the *character*, in the *honors* or *diſgrace*, not only of the *family*, but *nation* to which he belongs.

The ſcheme of iſſuing any more Continental money, I take for granted, nobody will think of; and therefore I conclude, that all the ways and means which *have hitherto been tried*, have proved utterly inſufficient for the purpoſe: and I further conceive, that it will be allowed, that the *mode I propoſe*, if put into practice, would *be ſufficient*. I further contend, that *no other mode* within our reach is or can be *equally eaſy* to the people, and *equally productive* of ſufficient money for the various purpoſes of our union; this is then the *only practicable way* our union can be ſupported, and of courſe *the union depends* on it, and, without it, muſt inevitably fall to pieces.

To ſay all this, may be thought very *great preſumption* in an individual; be it ſo; ſtill I am ſafe, for no man can contradict me, who is not able to find and explain ſome *other way of ſupply, equally eaſy* to the people, and *equally productive* of all the money which the ſupport of the union requires: but in as much as the eagerneſs of inquiry for ſeveral years paſt has not been able to diſcover any *ſuch other mode*, I conclude there is *no ſuch*, and of courſe, the one I have propoſed is the only one that can be adopted, to ſave our union from diſſolution.

And under the impreſſion of this full perſuaſion, may I be permitted to addreſs our public adminiſtration, not only in Congreſs, but in all the States, in the ſtrong language of Lord *Chatham—Set me down as an idiot, if you do not adopt it, or rue your neglect;* and it is not certain that *our poſterity* in the next age, and *all our neighbours* in the preſent, will not ſet *you down for idiots*, if you do not adopt it ſoon, before the miſchiefs it is deſigned to obviate, ſhall grow up to ſuch degree of magnitude and ſtrength, as to

become

become incapable of remedy; for what can they think, when they shall see that you suffer our union, which is committed *to your care, to fall to pieces under your hands*, because you will not attempt to give it *that support*, which, to say the least of it, is in its nature *practicable*, and the *due practice* of which would produce the *great remedy* required.

But you will say perhaps, we admit your principle to be just and good, but we cannot raise our ideas up to *your height of scale or degree of impost; your tax is too high; it grasps too much, and is thereby in danger of losing all; it will scare our people out of their wits*. I do not think much of this; if the *wits* which the people now have, *are not sufficient* for their salvation, it matters little how soon they are *scared out of them;* but it is not certain that their wits are so volatile; there is at least a possibility, a chance, that they may have *wit enough to adopt the remedy* that will prevent those calamities, which (if not prevented) will soon drive them out of their *security*—their *property*—their *national honor*—their *country* and *wits too;* at least I think it needless for *you* to lose *your wits*, for fear the *people* will lose *theirs*.

But I would ask you seriously, do you think that a less scale of tax than that which I propose, would be sufficiently productive for the public service, or the support of the Union? I think you must probably say no, on the bare presumption (for the produce of an untried tax cannot be reduced to a certainty:) to what purpose then, I further ask, would it be to set on foot so expensive and troublesome an operation, which, when completed, would be *utterly inadequate* to its purposes? or what funds have you, out of which you expect to draw the deficiency?

If there is any wisdom or effort in our counsels and plans, they must *reach thro';* they must *connect the means with the end*, and make the *one adequate* to the *other*. Would you not laugh at a sailor, who should moor a ship with an inch rope, and so lose the ship, for fear his owners should find fault with him for wetting a cable? Where *means are inadequate* to their *end*, they become *ridiculous*, especially

ally when adopted in matters of confequence; people lofe all *confidence* in their effects, and therefore lofe *all courage and inducement* to ufe ftrong efforts to make them operate.

I am clearly of opinion, if our people have loft their confidence in our public counfels, and are backward in pufhing them into practice, the reafon is, not becaufe they *ftupid* and *blind* to their interefts, or *wanting in zeal* to promote them, but becaufe their *courage* is all *worn out*, and their *patience exhaufted*, by a feven years' courfe of *vifionary, ineffectual, ill-contrived*, and *half-digefted* plans, which promifed little in *theory*, but conftantly in *practice*, proved the bafelefs fabrics of a vifion, and vanifhed at laft, not only *without ufe*, but with confequences very *detrimental* to our national character of integrity and wifdom, as well as to the interefts and morals of our people; not the leaft difcouraging of all which was this conftant effect which they all had, viz. that thofe States or individuals, which *promoted them with moft zeal, ardor, and effort, always loft moft by them*.

I am of opinion it is quite time to quit this *childifh miniature* of counfels, and adopt fomething *up to the full life*, and propofe fome fyftem to our people, that will, when executed, be *effective and fufficient* for its purpofe. I imagine fuch a propofal would find our people full enough of fenfe to difcufs it, candor to approve of it, and zeal to promote it.

But if you will continue to believe that my *high fcale* of tax will ftupify our people with terror on firft fight of the dreadful, dreary object, I will ferioufly afk you if you are acquainted with one individual, who, you think, would be likely to hang himfelf, or run diftracted, or give up the *American* Union or Independence, on being told, that he muft, for the reft of his life, pay a *dollar* a gallon tax on diftilled *fpirits* and *wine*; a duty equal to the *firft coft* on *filks, cambrics, lawns, muflins, laces, jewellery*, and fo on thro' all the grades of the tax I propofe.

Or how does the dreadful fpectre affect your own conftitution? Does it make your own blood run cold and ftiffen in your veins? As you are moftly men of fafhion and

and fortune, I conceive you will be as deeply interested in the tax as the most of your constituents, and you may pretty well judge of *their* feelings by *your own*. I do not apprehend that your anxiety is excited at all for yourselves, but for your people; but cannot you suppose that your constituents have sense to discern the necessity and utility of a public measure, judgment and patriotism to approve it, and firmness to bear the burden of it, as well as you?

Some objects, when seen thro' a mist, or at a distance, appear frightful and clothed with terrors, which all vanish on a *nearer* view, and more *close* inspection. Some disagreeable things, when they *come home* to our feelings, are found to have *less pain* than *distant* expectation painted out.

Let us suppose and realize to ourselves then, that my scale of tax was adopted and become habitual to the people; can you imagine that the country would be thereby rendered a whit the worse, or more inconvenient to live in, than if the tax was not paid? or if you cannot come quite up to this, do you conceive the inconvenience of the tax paid in this way, by any comparison *so heavy and burdensome*, as the present tax on *polls and estates*, or any other of equal product, that has *ever been practised* or *proposed*, would be to the people at large.

I do not know how far our people at large are impressed with a sense of the *importance of our union*; it is, in my opinion, an object of the utmost weight; I conceive that the very existence of our *respectability abroad*, the interest which we are to derive from our *connexions with foreign nations*, and our *security* against foreign and domestic insults and invasions, *all depend on it*, and even our *independence* itself cannot be supported *without it*; and as I know well that the attachment of our people to their independence is almost universal, I should suppose that our union, which is so closely and inseparably connected with it, would likewise be an equal object of their attachment and concern.

If this is the case, I cannot be persuaded that our people will revolt against any reasonable and necessary means of supporting both the one and the other, and as the tax I propose appears to me the *only possible* and *practicable*

means,

means, any how within our power, which can be *adequate* to this great purpose, I cannot say that I shudder to propose such a tax; but I think we may safely presume on the *good sense of our people*, their *patience*, and *discernment* of their interests, enough to expect their concurrence in the measure, and even cheerfulness and zeal in supporting it.

But if this cannot be obtained, I can add no more; I have no conception that the *Americans* either *can* or *ought* to be governed *against* their consent, or that the collection of taxes, of any kind, or in any mode, can be made with success, whilst an opinion becomes general among the people, that the *taxes* are *unnecessary, unjust*, or *improperly applied*.

I think it would not be very difficult to make out *the detail of particulars* necessary to form the plan or system, both of the tax and its collection, on the principles herein urged; but the whole is humbly submitted to the consideration of the public, who, I hope, are enough impressed with the importance of the subject, and the necessity of adopting some decisions relating to it, without delay, to induce every one to give it that attention that its *nature and weight* requires, and which our present critical circumstances make indispensable to our political salvation.*

I do

---

* It may be of use to the reader, to advert to some particulars of the state and condition of the country and its revenues, at the time when this Essay was first published.

1. The *Continental money* had been entirely *out of circulation* near two years, and all kinds of *estimates, payments*, and *accounts* were made in *hard money*.

2. That the *Bank of North-America* was instituted by Congress, and pretty well established at *Philadelphia*: the charter of it bears date *Dec.* 31, 1781.

3. Very strong exertions had been made to *obtain money from the States*, by a tax levied on polls and estates in the old and usual way, and such conviction of the necessity of public supplies generally took place thro' the States, that considerable sums were obtained in this way, and remitted in bank bills to the Financier General, mr. *Morris*.

But these taxes were levied by the States neither in any *due proportion* of quotas, nor with any *equality of* either *quantity* or *punctuality* in the payments, and *power of compulsion was vested in Congress* at that time, the supp of the public exigencies; large loans indeed were negotiated at and many wild and vain schemes for raising money were proposed at home; but all was languor and deficiency.

4. A strong

I do not set myself up to propose systems of *political union* and *plans of revenue* because I think myself the fittest and

4. A strong and laborious effort was made by Congress for *an impost of only five per cent. on imported goods*, which, with great difficulty and delay, *was at last ratified* by all the States *except Rhode-Island*, which, by its *final negative*, frustrated the plan, rendered it wholly void, and it died without any effect.

5. A very considerable *foreign debt* was contracted, and every department at home was *deeply involved*, and *no payments could be made* either at home or abroad; it was with the *utmost difficulty* that money could be procured for *daily supplies*, which were absolutely indispensable.

6. *Very great arrears were due to the army*, and had there not been *more patriotic virtue* in the *army*, and *greater abilities* in their *General* and *other officers*, than scarce ever existed before, it would have been impossible to have *kept them together*, or to have *governed* them with any proper *discipline*.

7. We were just upon the close of the war; the peace was expected soon; the preliminary articles of it were indeed settled and signed, *Jan.* 20, 1783, but the advice of them had not reached *America* at that time: but,

8. *Peace*, tho' the most *desirable* of all things at that time, yet was clothed *with terrors*, and the near approach of it excited the most *anxious apprehensions*.

The *murmurs* of the army *for their pay* ran high; there was no money to *pay* them, yet they were to be *disbanded*; and *whether they would suffer themselves to be dismissed, and sent to their several homes, without their pay*, was a question of great importance.

These difficulties were afterwards obviated by the prudence of General *Washington*, but in a way that harrowed up all his feelings; he ordered small divisions of the army to be marched off to diverse distant places, and then directed them to be *dismissed, without any pay* indeed, but *with a profusion of promises* and *assurances* that speedy provision should be made for the settlement and payment of their accounts.

Commissioners were indeed appointed to settle all unliquidated public accounts, both of the army and other creditors, but *no payments* were made but *in certificates* of the debts due, with promise to pay them with interest to the creditor or *bearer*.

These were *worth about 2s. 6d. in the pound*, and the circulation of them soon became very great *at that exchange:* but to return to the time of writing this Essay—

9. Tho' the *public treasury was so very poor and distressed*, yet the States were *really overrun with an abundance of cash:* the *French* and *English* armies, our *foreign loans*, *Havanna trade*, &c. had filled the country with *money*, and *bills on Europe* were currently sold at 20 to 40 per cent. *below par*.

10. This induced the merchants to buy these bills, and remit them to *Europe*, and in return to import great quantities of *European* goods, which arrived under the great expense of a *war freight* and *insurance;* yet their *scarcity*, the great *plenty of cash*, and the *luxury and pride* of the people were such, that they sold *rapidly* and to *great profit;* all which made the *tax of impost* I proposed, very peculiarly *necessary* at that time for many reasons; not only,

1. To supply the treasury; but,

2. To restrain and check the *luxurious consumptions* which were growing fast into fashion.

3. To keep up the price of goods, and thereby save the merchants from ruin, or at least, from very great loss, by the reduction of the price of their goods on hand, which would be the natural consequence of the peace.

4. To

and most capable man to do it; but because I am convinced that every system of this sort must be the work of *one mind*, carefully and deeply comprehending the whole subject, and *fitting all the parts to each other*, so that every part may form a coincidence with the rest. It is scarcely possible for *twenty or thirty men* of the best abilities collected in a room together, to do this; either of them might do it *alone*, but all of them *together* cannot.

The twenty together may examine the system or plan, when made and proposed, and note its faults, but even then they cannot mend them, without danger of destroying its uniformity; they must do as you do with your clothes which do not fit, send for the tailor who made them, point out the faults, and direct him to take them home, and make the alterations.

Any man of a clear head may comprehend his own thoughts, but cannot so well enter into those of another. You might as well set twenty watchmakers to make a watch, and assign to each his wheel; tho' each wheel should be exquisitely finished, it would be next to a miracle if the teeth and diameters fitted each other, so as to move with proper uniformity together; if this great work is done, *somebody must do it, somebody must begin*. A moderate genius may hit on, and propose, a thought, which a richer mind may improve to the greatest advantage. If I can attain this honor I shall have my reward, and please myself with the hope, that I may be in some degree useful to the country I love, which gave me birth, and in which I expect to leave my posterity.

4. To prevent a *deluge of imported goods* flowing in upon us, which soon drained the country of its cash, and filled the States with luxury; but the tax would have either *prevented* the evil, or would have brought an *immense sum into the public treasury*, which would have eased our public embarrassments.

Perhaps both might have been produced by the tax to such a degree, as would have afforded *very great and desirable advantages;* but the measure was not adopted, tho' I believe every one regrets at this day that it was not then pursued.

The principles of it have since been adopted by the *new Congress*, and tho' on a much *less scale* than I proposed, yet we find the tax richly productive, and very little burdensome to our people.

A SEVENTH

A SEVENTH ESSAY

ON

FREE TRADE and FINANCE;

In which the Expediency of Funding the Public Securities, Striking further Sums of Paper Money, and other important Matters, are considered.*

[First published in Philadelphia, Jan. 10, 1785.]

PUBLIC *securities are notes or promises of payment, made in writing, to the public creditors, who had demands on the public for monies lent, supplies furnished, services rendered,* &c. &c. Of these there are a great variety, and distinguished by divers appellations, such as *loan-office certificates, depreciation certificates, final settlements,* &c. &c. As

---

* The funding act of *Pennsylvania* was printed for public consideration some months before it was enacted into a law *(March* 16, 1785) during which time *this Essay was published:* the said act directed, among other things,

1. That *one year's interest* should be paid by this State on all Continental certificates, which originally issued to *any citizen or citizens* of this State, &c. *with a proviso,* that that species of certificates, commonly called *final settlements,* which should be intitled to interest, should not have been *alienated or transferred,* but shall *remain the property* of the *original holder,* his heirs, &c. (which proviso, in my opinion, ought to have extended to *all the other kinds of certificates,* as well as to the *final settlements:*) by this proviso, *every possessor* of a final settlement, except he was the *original holder of it,* was *excluded* from receiving interest.

But

As the public was in no condition to pay these securities when they became due, they suffered *a great depreciation:* the owners sold them for what they could get, and they have long been *an article of traffic* in the hands of the *brokers* and *speculators;* and the price-current, or estimated value

But I take it, that the *true spirit, design, and reason* of this proviso was, in a considerable degree, *eluded* in the subsequent practice; for the statute, among other *proofs* that the man who claimed interest, was *really the original holder,* prescribed this one, viz. that such claimant should make *oath* before a prothonotary, that he was *truly the original holder* of the certificate, and had *not alienated* it; and this certificate of the prothonotary of such oath being made, being annexed to the certificate on which *interest was demanded,* by *construction of the statute,* entitled the *possessor* of it to draw *interest,* tho' he was *not* the *original holder;* by which means very many certificates were sold with such affidavits annexed, and the possessor, tho' an *alienee,* drew the interest on them as well as if he had been the *original holder.*

2. A tax was instituted for raising an annual sum of 76,945*l*. 17*s*. 6*d*. and,

3. An emission of 150,000*l*. in paper money, 50,000*l*. of which was reserved for a *loan-office,* and the other 100,000*l*. together with the aforesaid tax of 76,945*l*. 17*s*. 6*d*. were appropriated to the *payment of said year's interest,* and other public purposes. The year's interest at 6 per cent. paid under this act, amounted to 267,694 dollars, the capital of which, of course, was 4,461,570 dollars, nearly.

This high tax proved a *heavy burden* upon such of our people as happened to have *no certificates* on which they could receive *interest,* and *little benefit* even to the most of those *who had them;* for the certificates were monopolized in to few hands, and not many of our people drew more interest than would pay their taxes.

And as these heavy sums were mostly paid to *such holders* of certificates, as had never *rendered any services* to the State, or *contributed any supplies,* or had any kind of *merit* or *earnings,* on which they could, with any pretence, found their claim to so *great a contribution* from the public, *much uneasiness* was generated, and our people found that their *labor was vain,* in as much as the *profits* of it were drained from them, for purposes of *no use* or *advantage* to them.

For it is to be noted here, that altho' interest was granted by this act for *but one year,* yet it was expected to be *continued,* and *really was so,* for several years afterwards, by a *subsequent act (March* 1, 1786) tho' under a somewhat *different form,* yet with the *same burden* as before.

The paper bills emitted by this act never passed as a *general currency,* but were *negotiated* in market, like other *commodities,* at *the exchange* which they happened to gain, but always in a *depreciated state, i. e.* at a *discount from* 10 *to* 30 *per cent.*

In fine, this *unhappy measure* has cost this State *already more than* 500,000*l*. and *still we are not clear* of it.

And, I believe, no man can count up 500*l*. *benefit* which the State ever received from it.

I clearly foresaw the mischiefs of this fatal measure, and to *obviate* and *prevent* them was the *design of this Essay,* and tho' I did *not succeed,* yet I have *real satisfaction* in reflecting that I exerted my *utmost abilities,* and *faithfully performed my duty* in the attempt, tho' it proved not successful, to *avert the calamities* of the State of which I am a citizen.

value of them, as they pass from hand to hand, is become as much *fixed* and as *well known* in the brokers' offices, as that of any *other goods* or merchandises.

And this *price-current*, made in market by the general consent of buyers and sellers, *determines the value* of all articles of traffic, whether *goods, bills of exchange, public securities, stocks* of every kind, or even *money itself:* and this rule of estimation is so *fixed* and natural, that no external force or height of authority can *alter* it, as has been clearly proved by experiment (the strongest proof in nature) in the instances of *tender-laws and regulation of prices*, which have often been attempted *in vain*, tho' pushed as far *as law, authority, violence,* and *force* could go.

Therefore it follows, that the public securities, when they become articles of exchange or traffic, are really *worth* what they will *bring* in market, and no more; *i. e. let their nominal value be what it will, their real value is so much as, and no more than, they will bring in market:* this is plain, natural law, which it is in vain for the greatest force or highest authority to oppose; it will prove too strong for the most mighty opposition; it is therefore most wise to submit to it, and obey its sovereign dictates, without reluctance.

The price-current of public securities has been different at different times, and the different kinds of them are estimated at different prices; very many have been purchased at 2*s*. 6*d*. in the pound, or 8 for 1; others at 6*s*. or 7*s*. in the pound, or about 3 for 1. A few instances may be produced of sales at higher and lower prices; but in general, I believe, the above prices may be estimated as the extremes: very great numbers of *final settlements* have been bought at 2*s*. 6*d*. in the pound, or 8 for 1.

It is very certain, and undoubtedly confessed on all sides, that our *soldiers*, when their *services were over*, and their accounts were fairly adjusted, were entitled to the liquidated balances in their favor, *in genuine money;* this was in *justice* due to them for their services, and if they were paid, *no more than justice* was done them; but if, instead of this, they were paid nominally *twenty shillings* in a certificate, note of public promise, or any other article of negotiation

or

or traffic, which was worth, by general consent of buyer and seller, in the public exchange, *no more than* 2s. 6d. and would bring no more, it is plain they were paid but 2s. 6d. in the pound, and the *remaining* 17s. 6d. *is still due to them.*

We will suppose, that instead of a certificate of 20s. which would bring but 2s. 6d. they had been paid in *brass*, at 20s. *per lb.* which was worth in market, and would bring *no more than,* 2s. 6d. *per lb.* it is plain their condition would have been exactly the same, *i. e.* the soldier that received the *pound of brass,* which he could sell for 2s. 6d. and no more, would be just as well off, and as well paid, as the soldier who received the *certificate of* 20s. which he could sell for 2s. 6d. and no more; it is a very plain case that neither of them are paid more than 2s. 6d. in the pound, and that the remaining 17s. 6d. remains unpaid, and consequently due to them.

And if any *justice or honor to the public faith* is designed or attempted, it must be effected by *paying* to them what still *remains due* to them. But can the human mind conceive, that any sort of justice or honor to the public faith would be done, not by *pitying* the poor soldiers, and *paying* the balance due to them, but instead of this, by raising a large sum of money, by taxing the community, to buy in *all the brass,* and giving 20s. per lb. for it to the speculators who had bought it of the soldiers for 2s. 6d. per lb. (even whilst the current market price was but 2s. 6d.) and giving interest till the cash was paid? which would be giving those speculators *eight times* as much money as the *capital* they advanced, and 48 *per cent. per ann. interest* for it, till the cash was paid.

The brokers' interest of 4 per cent. per month, is a fool to this; for this not only recovers 4 *per cent. per month interest*, but secures the payment of *eight-fold the capital*, when the interest ceases. Besides, the brokers run some risk of *opprobrium and loss* of their debt; but this plan gives *honor and security* to the whole transaction, by giving it the sacred sanction of the supreme power of the State.

It

It makes no difference to the argument, whether the article of traffic paid to the foldiers, and purchafed in again by the State, be *brafs* or *certificates;* becaufe both, by the fuppofition, are of *equal price* in the market, and make a payment of *equal value* to the foldiers.

The whole argument holds good and in equal force, with regard to all *original holders* of public fecurities, as to the *foldiers,* all of whom are fuppofed to have furnifhed to the public, *cafh, goods,* or *fervices,* to the amount of the certificates they received.

The argument alfo has the fame force, with refpect to fpeculators, who have purchafed public fecurities at a *higher exchange* than 8 for 1: with refpect to thefe, the conclufion is the fame in *nature,* but differs only in *degree.*

This plan of paying the vaft fums of public monies to fpeculators, which were originally due to the foldiers and other original holders of the public fecurities, and the payment being *withheld* from them to whom it ought to have been made, *ftill remains due:* I fay, the plan of paying thefe monies to the fpeculators, who at prefent hold the fecurities, *i. e.* paying to thefe fpeculators *eight times* the capital they advanced for the purchafe of them, *with* 48 *per cent. per ann. intereft,* till actual payment is made to them, and taxing the State to raife thefe monies, and of courfe *taxing the poor foldiers* (who, in their penury and diftrefs, fold their certificates at 2*s.* 6*d.*) in the pound, for the *money* neceffary *to pay them at* 20*s.* in the pound, with intereft, to the fpeculators who purchafed them: I fay, this plan is adopted by fome folks with great ferioufnefs and gravity; and their ideas are fupported with very fpecious arguments, the detail of which I wave confidering juft now, that I may mention one propofition, which I think neceffary to introduce here, viz.

No ingenuity of argument can ever fupport *an abfurd conclufion;* the abfurdity of the conclufion for ever deftroys the argument, however fpecious and ingenious the premifes may be found: this is called by logicians *reductio ad abfurdum,* has been taught in the fchools a thoufand years, and has always been allowed to be good reafoning.

All the arguments that can be adduced, can never convince any body that this plan is right; there is not a *boy* in a compting-houſe, or *maid* in a kitchen, who would not exclaim againſt the injuſtice of it, the moment they heard and underſtood it; the *common ſenſe* which reſides in every human breaſt, *revolts* againſt it; for this I appeal to the ſentiments and feelings of every body who has any.

Do not you think, my fellow-citizens, that a ſpeculator in public ſecurities muſt be pretty well brazed, yea, braſſed over, who can *expreſs his joy* without bluſhing, in the face of the world, and tell us that he is *enlivened* with hopes of obtaining a public act, entitling him to *eight times the capital* of his ſpeculations, with 48 *per cent. per ann. intereſt*, till he receives the principal in *good, ſolid, hard caſh;* all which he knows to be the *earnings* of the poor, diſtreſſed ſoldier, who, with his family, languiſhes for want of the payment, which is withheld from him by means of the *failure of the public faith?*

This plan, however cruel, ſhocking, and execrable it may appear, is defended by ſome folks by this argument, viz. the *public ſecurities, like bonds, bills of exchange, promiſſory notes,* &c. are aſſignable or transferable over, by which the aſſignee becomes poſſeſſed of *all the right and intereſt,* which the *original holder* had therein; that the whole property paſſes by the aſſignment, and the ſum paid by the aſſignee to the original holder, whether *little or much,* is of no conſideration in the caſe.

I ſuppoſe this holds true *generally* with reſpect to bonds, bills of exchange, promiſſory notes, &c. but I do not think it holds true *univerſally:* the rule has its exceptions, and I think the *caſe in point* is manifeſtly one of the *ſtrongeſt inſtances* of them. The *Continental money* is a moſt notorious one; the *public faith* was plighted for the redemption of *that money,* as ſacredly as *force* of words, *height* of authority, and *appeals to Heaven* could do it. Yet every man acknowledges, that if that money, tho' all made *payable to the bearer,* was to be redeemed at a *hard dollar* for every *Continental one,* the moſt abſurd *injuſtice* would be done.

The *old State money* of this State affords another instance of the same kind. The *loan-office certificates* afford a third instance, the value of which is estimated by Congress, by a public *scale of depreciation*, grounded on the *real value of the certificates*, at the several *dates* at which they were issued. Nobody pretends to object to this measure, or the principle on which it was founded.

Another instance may be adduced from a clear, decided rule of the law of the land, viz. if an executor buys up the bonds of his testator at a discount, *i. e.* by paying less than the nominal value for them, when he comes to make up the accounts of his executorship, he shall not be allowed the *nominal value* of those bonds, but so much only as he *actually paid* for them.

To all this I will venture to add here a proposed case, with my opinion on it, viz. suppose a merchant stops payment, who has thousands of bonds, notes, &c. against him, and upon the best survey of his affairs, it becomes the general opinion that he will pay 2*s.* 6*d.* in the pound, and his *bonds and notes* are generally passed from hand to to hand, *at that exchange*. Every broker and banker has them, and passes them for years together at that rate; but, after a series of time, the debtor becomes able and willing to pay his whole debt, and is cited into a most sovereign court of chancery, where *mere right and justice* is the rule of the court; where it is confessed that the 2*s.* 6*d.* is either paid or now due to the assignee of the note for 20*s.* and the sole question before the court is, *who shall have the other* 17*s.* 6*d.* whether the *original creditor*, to whom the debt was due, for full consideration paid, or to the assignee who had never paid *any thing* for it?

We will suppose the court is under no bias, but *honestly* mean to make such a decree as will be *most just*, do the *most honor* to their court, and be *best approved in Heaven.* I make no difficulty in giving my opinion, that the court will award in favor of the original creditor, who has paid the *full consideration* of the debt, in preference to the assignee, who has *never paid any thing* for it.

Find

Find fault with and difprove this opinion, whoever of you can; I expofe it with confidence, to the cenfure of you all. Where two perfons are in equal poffeffion of an eftate, *it fhall be given to him that hath right.* *Original right* is fuch a *facred thing*, that it can and will go great lengths in favor of its proprietor, is ever *reverenced by the law*, and ever claims the principal *attention of the court.*

I take it, that the facts out of which *the reafons grow*, that govern affignments of bonds, bills of exchange, and negotiable notes, are fo *toto cælo* different from thofe in the cafe now under difcuffion, that it is impoffible to argue from the one to the other without the moft manifeft abfurdity.

One inftance of this difference, of full notoriety, and ftriking enough, is this, viz. that in the cafe of transfer of bills of exchange, negotiable notes, &c. a *valuable confideration* is always prefumed to be given; but in the cafe in point *no fuch thing*, but the *very contrary*, *appears* in full blaze of evidence; 2*s.* 6*d.* in the pound has not the *leaft pretenfion* of being a valuable confideration for *eight times* the principal advanced, and 48 *per cent. intereft* for the fame, till the whole fhall be paid, together with 48 per cent. for feveral years' intereft due on the certificate, *before the purchafer ever faw it,* or even *paid his* 2*s.* 6*d. for it.*

This fact ftands glaring in the *face of the world,* and ftrikes conviction of its own injuftice and abfurdity into every beholder; it gives concern to the moft avaricious fpeculator, and brings a *blufh* even into the *anvil countenances* of the fanguine promoters of the bleffed fcheme of making provifion for the enormous payment.

They endeavour to *palliate* it, or *fhuffle it out of fight*, by fuggefting that the inftances of this fort are but *few* and inconfiderable, and fo blended with the right and juftice due to the diftreffed widows, orphans, foldiers, and other worthy citizens, who are public creditors, that they cannot be feparated, and are therefore not worthy to be noticed; but here again the fact is notorioufly againft them. I fhould think a man had need of a *front as hard as an andiron,*

andiron, to affirm, in the face of the public, that *these in-stances are but few and inconsiderable*.

It is a matter of public notoriety and general belief, that almost the *whole* of the *widows, orphans, soldiers,* and other *distressed public creditors*, have sold their certificates, which are now in the hands of the speculators, who are known to be very numerous, and many of whom have a vast amount of them.

But let these instances be few or many, it is a vain pretence to say they are *so blended with the other public creditors, that they cannot be separated*. A method of *justice* and *due discrimination* is *easily investigated;* the public creditors are *easily found;* their *names* are all on the *public books*, with the *balances which were due to them* when their accounts were settled.

I propose then, that *they shall be debited with the certificates they received, at the price, exchange, or value at which they passed or could be sold, when they received them, and have the residue of their balance paid to them honestly, with interest.*

It will take *no more money* to pay *them* than to pay the *speculators;* and as to the certificates, except such as are in the hands of the *original holders*, let them be paid *to whoever brings them in*, at a scale of value founded on their original value when they were issued, or the mean exchange at which they have passed for two or three years back.

This will repay to the speculators all the cash they have advanced, which, I think, is all the justice or tenderness to which they are entitled from the public; for, to say the best of them, I esteem them a sort of men *barely tolerable*, but by no means worthy of *encouragement*.

Some people say they have merit, and support the public faith, by giving *something* for certificates, when others would *not buy them at all;* but I think we are not much beholden to them, for vilifying and decrying the public faith, till they have persuaded the poor soldiers to sell their certificates for 2*s.* 6*d.* in the pound, rather than trust the public any longer.

As my proposal leaves no ground of complaint on the part of the speculators, so I think it will do manifest justice

to

to' the *widows, orphans, foldiers,* and other diftreffed *public creditors,* who, in my opinion, moft juftly deferve all the *groans of compaffion* which are fo liberally beftowed on them by our honorable Affembly, and the *committee of public creditors.*

I fhould be forry to fee the *zeal* of thefe patriots for the public faith *abate,* and their *concern* for the diftreffed creditors *cool away,* if the fpeculators fhould happen to *lofe their point,* and, of courfe, fhould lower *their* cry for juftice and compaffion, when they find they are not like to *finger the money.*—Hinc *ifta lacryma.*

What now remains for me is, to fhow that the cafe above propofed is *(mutatis mutandis)* in fact the cafe in point. The *public* is the *merchant* who ftopped payment (no body will difpute this) the thoufands of *bonds and notes* againft him, are the public *fecurities* or *certificates* of all kinds; the *general confent* which determined that he would pay 2*s.* 6*d.* in the pound, is the *exchange* fettled by general confent, at which the public fecurities, efpecially the *final fettlements,* have been bought and fold for a long fucceffion of time.

And the *high court* of chancery, with fovereign power, totally unbiaffed by any confiderations but thofe 'of *mere right* and *juftice,* and who mean to make fuch decifions as fhall do the *higheft honor* to the State, deferve the higheft *efteem* and *approbation* of their fellow-citizens and the world, and merit the *beft approbation* of Heaven; I fay, this high court of chancery is our General Affembly.

And the parties who appear before this auguft court of chancery, *i. e.* our General Affembly, are the *foldiers,* who ferved us with *fatigue and blood* thro' a feven years' war, and other *virtuous citizens,* who *furnifhed the public,* in the greateft public exigence and diftrefs, with *cafh and other fupplies,* and who altogether faved the liberties of the country, and procured for our Affembly itfelf, the very privilege of fitting, uninterrupted, within the walls which they now occupy, and of debating whether they will pay them or not; I fay, thefe *foldiers* and *other creditors* are the original creditors, and the *affignees* are the *ftock-jobbers*

and

and *speculators* in the public funds and securities, who have in their hands the certificates, which, during the reputed bankruptcy of the State, they purchased at 2*s*. 6*d*. in the pound, or 8 for 1, without any allowance for interest at all.

I say, these two parties are the original creditors and the assignees of the bonds who appear before this court, and the grand question now before the court is, whether they will pay these public monies to the *soldiers* and *other* virtuous *citizens*, who are the *original creditors*; or whether they will pay these same monies to a *parcel of stock-jobbers and speculators* in the public funds and securities, at the rate of 8 for 1 of the principal they have advanced, and 48 per cent. per ann. interest, till the principal is paid, together with 48 per cent. interest from the date of the certificate, to the time of the purchase of it by the speculator, which, in some cases, is several years, and raises the interest due on the certificates at the time of purchase, to a *much greater sum* than was paid for the *whole certificate?*

We will then, if you please, suppose our venerable high court of chancery, viz. our Assembly, to be sitting, with the public monies all on the table before them; and the two parties appear and make their claim to the money; it is confessed that the public have had a valuable consideration for it, and therefore justly owe it to somebody, and the only question before the court is, *who shall have it?*

The speculators bring in their certificates signed over to them, and claim to be admitted *in the place of the original creditors*, and *paid* as such, on the *equity* and common *reason of assignments*.

The *widows, orphans, soldiers*, and other original *creditors*, come in and say,—we claim this money, because we have *earned it*, and have *paid* the full, valuable *consideration* for it. We have *not yet been paid*. We received these certificates when they were not so good as money, and have sold them mostly at 2*s*. 6*d*. in the pound, which was *all that they were worth*, and would bring in market, *when we received* them, and which we are willing to allow should be *debited* to us. So far we have been paid, but no further

the

the *remainder* of the debt due from the public to us at the time of settlement, is *still due* to us and *unpaid*, and we now *claim it*. The speculators have no such plea of a valuable *consideration given*; they have purchased at such vast discount, that they have no pretensions to a valuable consideration given; what they have paid we are content they should *receive back* with interest; the *rest* is our *dear earnings*, which the public have had the *full benefit* of, and which we now claim as *our due*, and *demand payment*.

This is stating the matter, I conceive, clearly and fairly, and I beg leave to give my opinion decidedly in favor of the original creditors. It does appear to me, that the *quid pro quo, or valuable consideration, goes so into the nature, and makes such a part of, the very essence of commutative justice, that it is impossible that an equitable debt should be generated without it, by any contract whatever.*

It is a matter of the most public notoriety, that the *quid pro quo*, or valuable consideration paid by the speculators, is *no more than the exchange* at which they purchased the certificates, which is such a *mere trifle*, that it affronts the common feelings of the human mind, to pretend that such a trifle (say, one sixth or eighth part) is a valuable consideration for *the whole;* it is a valuable consideration for *no more than was paid*, and of consequence can generate a debt of *no more;* the *rest* still stands connected with the original consideration paid, *i. e. sticks* to the original creditor, and there will adhere, till it is discharged by an adequate payment.

For no man is born with, or *can acquire*, a right to the *earnings* or *fortune* of another, without giving a *valuable consideration* for it, and that consideration must be of *adequate value;* for a *penny* can no more be a valuable consideration for a *pound*, than *nothing* at all can be for a *penny;* for it strikes the human understanding as plainly, and with as much force, that a *pound* is worth more than a *penny*, as that a *penny* is worth more than *nothing at all*.

Therefore I do conclude, and contend strongly for the conclusion, that the speculators are entitled to no more than they have paid a valuable consideration for, and *the rest*

rest remains due to the original creditors, as their *dear earnings* for which they have *not yet been paid*.

I know very well that the speculators have many ingenious arguments, spun as fine as silk, to prove their right to the whole debt specified in their certificates; but the soldier has a much better one, strong as iron, yea, made of iron, I mean his *earnings with sword and musket*, thro' a seven years' war, which yet remain *unsatisfied*. Do you think that the finest silken arguments of the speculator can stand any the least chance with this iron one of the soldier?

There is something in *original right*, which strikes the human mind with irresistible force: this *original right* will for ever attach itself to *original earnings;* there it will *stick*, and cannot be *torn* away by any force, nor be *decoyed* by any fraud, till it is *satisfied* by adequate payment. A *just debt* will for ever *remain a debt due, till it is paid*.

It therefore follows, that if we pay the speculators the immense sums which they demand, the public debt of the whole sum will *still remain due to the original creditors*, who have, by their *cash*, *supplies*, and *earnings*, advanced the full, valuable consideration, out of which the debt first grew, and who have *never been paid*.

Public justice and the honor of the *public faith* require, not only that we pay as *much money* as we owe, *but that we pay it to the persons to whom it is due;* for paying it to any *body else* can be no satisfaction of that justice and faith which we owe to our *real creditors*, but is an additional injury to them.

The human mind can no otherwise know *right and wrong*, than by the *force and manner* in which they strike the mind, and raise an *approbation or disapprobation* in it; and I appeal to the *feelings* of all my readers, whether my propositions do not *strike* their minds strongly, and *force their approbation* of my conclusion. I challenge the hardiest speculator to believe it *right*, if he can, or rather not to believe it *wrong*, to lay the burden of a tax on the community, and among the rest on the *public creditors themselves*, to raise money to pay the public debt, and when it is collected, to pay it away, not to the *real creditors*, who, by their earnings and advances, have paid the full consideration for the debts due to them, but to *others who never earned* any thing for us, nor paid any valuable consideration to us, and, of consequence, can have nothing due to them from us.

There is another very serious consequence, which I apprehend from our paying such an enormous sum to the speculators, as they demand, if we now had the whole money in the treasury, viz. it would be such a drain of our public money, as would put it wholly *out of our power to pay our real creditors* in any tolerable season, and would, in a great measure, *reduce them to despair*, of ever receiving their debts due, and of course would greatly lessen all *confidence in the public faith*.

But if the money is not in the public treasury (which I take to be the fact) our issuing another deluge of *public promises*, by way of *funding* such an enormous sum, I fear would hurt the credit of the State still more; for *public promises*, like all other promises that are broken, become of *less and less value*, the oftener they are *repeated*, and the more they are *multiplied;* and tho' I profess to believe fully, that these new and multiplied public bills would be good enough to pay the speculators with, yet I should be sorry that our *real creditors* (who have paid a full consideration for their debts due from the public) should partake of the inconveniencies of them.

I therefore humbly propose, that the first thing we do, should be to set about *raising the money;* for *this* will be more acceptable when it comes, whoever is to have it, than *any promises* we can make.

And in the next place I would propose, that the *real creditors* should be *paid first*, and the speculators *last of all*, if it is judged necessary that they should ever be paid. I have several very urgent reasons for this proposition, both moral and political.

1. The real creditors have lain out of their money *longer* than the speculators, and it seems to me very reasonable and just, that the *oldest* debts should be *first* paid.

2. The

2. The speculators who expect *eight-fold their principal*, and 48 *per cent. interest*, can *better afford* to lie awhile out of their money, than the *real creditors*, who have no pretensions to *any more than barely their principal*, and 6 per cent. interest.

3. The general esteem of the people, and public conviction of the justice of the demand, is much greater with respect to the real creditors, than to the speculators; and therefore, when the citizens of the State are told, when the money is to be collected, that it is designed *for the payment of the real creditors*, the tax will probably be paid *more cheerfully*, and with *less uneasiness and disturbance*, than may be expected if it was publicly known that it was *to go to the speculators*.

4. The real creditors are poor, and would be greatly relieved by the payment made to them, and be enabled *to go into business* for their *own* and the *public* advantage. But when the speculators are paid, they will all at once become so *amazingly rich*, that they will probably set up their carriages, and run into other courses of *idleness and pleasures, luxury and dissipation*, which are ever hurtful to the public; and I think it good policy to pay that money *first* which is like to do the *most* good, and to pay that which is like to do the *most hurt*, *last of all*, if it must be paid at all; for I shall ever think it sound wisdom, if *evils and mischiefs* cannot be *wholly avoided*, to keep them at *as great a distance* as possible.

On the whole, whether any or all my propositions can be admitted or not, it does at least appear that the real, original *creditors*, and *speculators*, are characters of such *different* predicament and merit, and their demands on the public, founded on such *different original considerations, reasons*, and *real earnings*, that the least consequence that can be drawn from the whole matter, is a most manifest necessity that there should be a *discrimination between them*; that they can, with no propriety, or appearance of justice, be considered on an *equal footing* with each other, or in any manner entitled to the *same consideration* and *treatment* from the public.

But

But I must stop here a moment, to consider a capital argument advanced very seriously, *" that if all the certificates are not indiscriminately paid up to the holders of them, the public credit will receive such a wound that we shall never be able to persuade any body in future to loan money, or furnish supplies or services on the public faith, let our necessities be ever so great."* I believe it will be readily admitted, that I have stated this argument in the *same light* in which it is *urged* by those who make use of it; but I think there is a *delusion* in this statement of the argument, which I will endeavour to *correct* in the following manner, viz.

If, by any *mismanagement or neglect*, if, by any *deficiency or misapplication* of the public monies, it shall so fall out, that the *real, worthy, public creditors* cannot be paid; if matters are *worked about* by any *shifts, arts, combinations, contrivances,* or *deceits,* so that the man who has *loaned money, furnished supplies,* or *rendered services* to the public in its necessities, *cannot be paid;* no *pretty, plausible excuse,* no *fine-spun arguments,* no *force* of words, which really mean *nothing,* no pathetic *addresses* upon perverted facts, can help us out; but the public credit must suffer; and if the very men who make these mistakes, or even some wiser men, were to rule the roast in any future time of public distress, there is the highest probability that they would find people *backward to lend their money,* furnish *supplies,* or render *services,* on the credit of the public.

On the other hand, if we consent to pay the speculators the *bare principal,* which they have paid, with the interest of it, but shall refuse to secure by the public sanction, the *profits of* 8 *or* 900 per cent. which they demand, the amount of which, in moderate computation, cannot be less than 2 or 3,000,000 *of dollars,* which they never *earned or paid* for, nor we ever received any *benefit* or valuable consideration for; I say, if we refuse to pay to the speculators these *enormous profits,* it will so *discourage* them, that it may make them *backward* in venturing again, and so we may be obliged to do *without them* in future times, let us *want them ever so much.*

Both these alternatives are doubtless very *dreadful,* and

I think

I think there can be no doubt, but we are under an unavoidable neceſſity of incurring *one of them;* but I am in no condition to give my opinion, which would be the moſt *terrible* of the two. So having clearly and fairly ſtated the facts, I leave the reſt to the reader.

But it may be further objected,—if all this is to be admitted, will it not put it out of the power of the holder of any public ſecurity, *to ſell it?* Experience will perhaps furniſh the beſt anſwer to this queſtion. The *depreciation* of Continental money never *ſtopped* the circulation of it. As long as it retained any value at all, it paſſed quick enough; and would purchaſe hard money or any thing elſe, as readily as ever, when the exchange was 200 for 1, and when every *hope*, or even *idea*, of its being *redeemed* at nominal value, had *entirely vaniſhed.*

I am told, the price of *ſtocks* or *public ſecurities* in *England* is now at 55 per cent. *i. e.* reduced by depreciation to near half their nominal value; and not a man in *England* has the moſt diſtant idea that they will *ever be redeemed* at their nominal value, yet *they paſs* quick enough *at their exchange,* and any perſon who is diſpoſed *to ſell out,* has no difficulty in finding a *purchaſer.*

It may be further objected, that if the ſpeculators could have known before-hand, that they ſhould *come off ſo,* they would not have been concerned in ſuch ſpeculations at all; but would have laid out their money in *trade, huſbandry, manufactures,* or ſome *other way.* However *lamentable* this may be, I muſt leave it unanſwered.

It may be further objected, that this doctrine will overſet and throw into confuſion the common *rules and laws,* which regulate aſſignments of *bonds, bills of exchange, negotiable notes,* &c. which have had the ſanction of long uſage and practice, and have ever been found by experience to be both juſt and neceſſary.

I anſwer, it will not, for this plain reaſon, which would demonſtrably govern the caſe, if nothing elſe could be ſaid upon it, viz. every *law or rule of right,* whether commercial, political, moral, or divine, holds *right and juſt, only in its mean;* the moment it is puſhed *out of its mean,* into

its

its *extremes*, it loses the *reasons* on which it is founded, and becomes *wrong* and *unjust*.

We have a law which forbids to make *graven images*; but this prohibits not *statues* in gardens or *heads* on ships. We have another forbidding to do any *work on the Sabbath*; but this does not make it unlawful to *put out the fire* of a house that is burning, or laboring hard to *save a drowning man*, or to pull *an ox out of the mire*. We have a law that says, " thou *shalt not kill*;" but this prohibits not the *execution* of a malefactor, or *fighting a battle*. We have another that says, " thou shalt not *steal*;" yet a man may *lawfully steal* to *satisfy his hunger*.

The only question, I conceive, which the subject admits in this place is, whether the demand of the speculator is an *extreme case*, which comes not *within the reasons*, and of course cannot be justified or supported by the *rule, of common assignments?* I contend for the affirmative of this question, and for reason say the demand is *morally wrong*, because it would take an immense sum of money from the community, which must be a large proportion of their earnings, and give the same to the speculators, *without any adequate valuable consideration*, either paid by the speculators, or received from them by the citizens, contrary to the most fundamental law of *commutative justice*, which requires that a *quid pro quo*, or a valuable *consideration*, shall always be given *in lieu* of the property transferred. This is the most *essential part of the moral law*, which regards property.

Further, this is not only *morally* wrong, but *politically* so too.

1. Because it takes an immense property from those who had *earned* it, and would, of course, probably make the *best use* of it, and places it in the hands of people who have *not earned* it, and who would, of course, probably make the *worst use* of it. And it is certainly high policy to keep the wealth of the State as far as possible in the hands of those people who will make the *best use* of it.

2. Because this would *impoverish the great body of the people*, who are ever the strength of every nation, in order to

throw

throw immense wealth into the hands of individuals, which would not only *weaken* the State, but destroy that *equality of the citizens* which is necessary to the continuance of our republican form of government.

3. Because this plan will *retard the increase* of our *trade* and our *population*, and lessen the *value* of our lands. We all know that burdens on trade lessen it; heavy taxes on the country will discourage people from coming to settle on our lands, and, of course, the increase of our population will be retarded, which will reduce the number of purchasers of lands, and, of course, lessen their value.

Our neighbours, especially *New-York*, have a vast extent of unsettled lands; they court settlers with this powerful motive, that they have means to pay their debts without any burdensome recourse to *taxes* on their *lands, labor,* or *cattle*.

The funding plan in question, I am told, will require about 300,000 dollars per ann. to defray the interest only; besides which, we have sundry immense demands against the State. The principal debt, the funding of which is now under consideration, is *about 5,000,000 of dollars,* near half of which I take to be designed for *clear profit* to the speculators; to be due to them, or from us, it cannot be said, for they never paid us any thing for it; it must then be *excessive generosity* to them.

It may do for people to be *generous*, when their *incomes* are *affluent*, and *cash*, *plenty*; but when they are oppressed with *debt* to such an amount as to bring their *credit*, and even their *capital*, into danger, in this critical circumstance, the strictest *economy*, yea, even *close parsimony*, become very important duties. But in such a crisis of distress and danger, to assume an immense, needless, additional debt, even if a due consideration was paid for it, would be extreme ill policy; but to do it without *any consideration* at all, would be the height of *absurdity and madness*.

At all times we ought to be *just*, before we are *generous*. But at such a crisis, a lavishment that will put it *out of our power to be just*, must be reprobated as downright wickedness. And as the *criminality* of all crimes is estimated

mated by the *damage* they do, that *conduct in a ruler*, which deftroys the *credit* of a State, and even puts it out of the power of it to be *juft*, and of courfe deftroys the *rights* of thoufands of its moft meritorious citizens, ought to be branded, as the moft cenfurable of *any crime* which can affect human *property, character, and honor*.

4. This plan is impolitic, becaufe it will convey the money collected from the people to *a great diftance* from the places where it was collected, and of courfe the people who paid it, will have *little or no benefit* from its future circulation. If the fame monies were to be paid (as they ought to be) to the *real creditors, i. e.* the foldiers and others, who furnifhed monies, fupplies, &c. who are fcattered over the whole State, and are to be found in every part of it; I fay, if the monies collected from the people were to be paid to thofe, it would be *diffufed over the whole State*, and every perfon who paid the tax to raife thefe monies, would have a chance of *taking benefit of its circulation*.

But the cafe will be widely different, when it fhall be paid to the fpeculators; moft of them live in the city, and the few who refide in the country, when they come to receive their immenfe fortunes, will immediately come to the city, with all their money; the country will be no proper place to parade in; they will find nobody there fit to rank with; and that is not all; but when they clatter along in their carriages, they may chance to hear fomebody fay, " there goes a fpeculator or ftock-jobber, who revels in " the fpoils of his country."

In fhort, this will not do at all; they muft move into the city, where they can find people of their own clafs to affociate with.

And this is not the worft of it; the fpeculators, I fuppofe, muft *nominally belong to this State*, but doubt not but they are in company, and fhare profits with many who *live out of it*, and confequently convey their wealth out of the State.

And this is not the worft of it, but I conceive that many of them, tho' they refide in this State, are not natives

tives of it; the *domus animæ, domus optima, i. e.* home is home, tho' never so homely, is a strong affection in most men; and on the inducements of it, foreigners, when they travel abroad and *acquire fortunes*, have an inclination to return to their native country, to *spend and enjoy* them; and I think our speculators of foreign birth will have a motive additional to this natural one, to set off to their native country, viz. the powerful one of getting out of hearing of the curses of the people among whom they live.

It is here to be noted in a manner which I think deserves great attention, that however *dirty, ragged, poor,* and *despicable* an *injured people* may appear, they always have one *species of revenge* left to them, which they rarely fail to make the most of, viz. the *power and privilege of cursing* their oppressors; they curse them in the *streets*, they propagate their curses by their fire-sides to their *children*, who are not commonly apt to have much defect of memory, and they *mix* their execrations with their *prayers to Heaven*.

It is said that the *curse causeless will not come*; but I believe few States or individuals have reason to make themselves very easy under *those curses which are not causeless*. There is most certainly a *Providence* which governs the world, which pays the utmost attention to *right* and *wrong*, without the least respect imaginable to the *lace* or *rags* of the suitors.

Many more arguments might be adduced, but I deem the above fully sufficient, to prove that the plan in question is in its nature *immoral* and *dishonest;* and, in a *political* view, extremely *injurious* to the State, and I might almost add, *fatally ruinous;* and therefore is demonstrated to be *an extreme case*, not at all *within the reasons* of, and of course *not justifiable* by, the common *law or rule of assignments*, which, by long use, has been found to be both *morally* and *politically good* and useful.

The *Committee of Public Creditors*, in their last petition to the Assembly, have introduced one proposition, which pleases me very much, viz. " *Nothing that is morally* " WRONG *can ever be politically* RIGHT." I could wish this

this was written in *letters of gold* in the frontifpiece of all our *chambers of public council;* and, what is more, might be engraved on the *hearts* of all our public men, as a practical principle *too facred* to yield to any *views of intereſt*, however *gaudily dreffed*, or *finely colored:* and, by way of giving it my little mite of improvement and fupport, I beg leave to add, that nothing which is both *morally* and *politically wrong*, can ever be *right* in any fenfe whatfoever.

I have one argument againſt fatisfying the demands of the fpeculators, which I have not marked under either moral or political arguments, becaufe it appears to me ſtrongly to partake of both, and therefore ought to be mentioned by itfelf. It is this, viz. *it gives public fanction*, fupport, and even a kind of *dignity*, to a fort of fpeculation, which, if not wicked in itfelf, is of a nature very ruinous to the public, as it affords *enormous profits without any earnings*, viz. eight-fold the principal, and 48 per cent. intereſt, which (were they to be freed from *difgrace and danger*, and to be made *reputable* and fafe by the *fanction and fupport* of the Legiflature) would be enough to induce *bad men* of all profeffions to *withdraw their ſtock in bufinefs*, from their ufual occupations, and *veſt it* in fuch fpeculations of high *profit and honor*.

In my opinion, nothing fcarcely can be worfe than *public laws or inſtitutions*, which tend to draw people from the *honeſt and painful* method of *earning* fortunes, and to encourage them to purfue *chimerical ways* and *means* of obtaining *wealth* by *ſleight of hand*, without any earnings at all.

But were thefe fpeculators to gamble on *each other's purfes* only, I fhould think lefs of it; but it becomes publicly ruinous, when the *public* are to pay the *lofings*.

The fatal experience of *Europe* might, methinks, be a warning to us. Ever fince the bleffed fcheme of *funding* was firſt invented there, every nation has had a *race of ſtock-jobbers* and *fpeculators* in the public fecurities, who never fail to appear in plenty whenever a State gets *into diſtrefs*, and the public faith *faulters* a little: they appear, to be fure, with a mighty pretty grace, in aid of the *public credit*,

credit, not indeed to keep it *found and whole*, but to evince that it is not *quite dead;* and for a practical proof of this, they will offer to give at least *something* for it.

In the last days of *Lewis XIV.* (that noted *æra of distress, in France*) this sort of people had the modesty to accept public securities of 32,000,000, for the loan of 8,000,000, which is 4 for 1. But our speculators go far beyond this; they give 2*s.* 6*d.* in the pound, which is 8 for 1. But it is no wonder that our speculators should exceed those of the most ingenious nation in *Europe*, since the *American genius* sets up to *outdo all the world* in every thing.

A crisis of *public distress* is the proper time for this kind of vermin to swarm, like *flies* about a *sore*, or *crows* round a *carcass*, not with any design to *heal the sore*, or *restore life*, but to *feed themselves*. This I admit to be a principle natural enough; but however excusable it may be in itself for these, like all other noxious animals, to pursue the means of their own preservation, yet I cannot think they are entitled to the *gratitude*, or *support*, or *rewards*, of the public.

I beg the reader to note here very particularly, that I do not mean by any thing I write, to oppose any practicable and wise plan of funding or paying the *real public debts;* all I object to is, *funding or paying the profits of the speculators*.

But however our public counsels may settle this question, and whatever is to be done with our public monies, when we get them, I here beg my readers' attention a little, to the *ways and means* of raising them.

1. In the first place, *I do object as strongly as I am able, to laying any considerable tax on polls and estates.* This is taxing the labor, cattle, and lands of our people, which are the *embryo*, the *first principles*, the very *seed*, the *raw materials* of our wealth; and of course ought to be most carefully and tenderly *nursed, cultivated*, and *encouraged;* but by no means to be *burdened* and *discouraged*.

We have *imported luxuries* enough, which are hurtful to the public; the necessary restraints of which require a tax sufficiently large for the public use. It would be better for

our

our people to pay a tax of a dollar per gallon on rum and wines, 50 per cent. on filks, &c. &c. than to fuffer their *labor* and *lands* to be taxed. But if this, with our ufual taxes on trade, &c. is not fufficient, I would rather tax our *exported goods* than our *labor* and *lands;* becaufe I think it manifeftly better to tax our *finifhed goods*, than our *raw materials*.

Befides, our paft experience has fufficiently taught us, that the collection of any confiderable tax on polls and eftates is impracticable; the vaft arrears of moft of our counties are a full proof of this; and to make our *treafury* depend on revenues of *uncertain product*, is a fure way to fubject our finance to *conftant difappointment*, and of courfe to keep our *public credit* in a perpetual ftate of *depreffion*, and fcandalous, as well as ruinous, *deficiency*. But I will not dwell longer here on this fubject, having treated it more largely in my Sixth Effay on Free Trade and Finance, to which I refer the reader, if he defires to hear any more about it. [*See p.* 230.]

2. *I object moft ferioufly to iffuing paper money, in our prefent circumftances*, for the following reafons:

1. *We have already a full fufficiency of circulating cafh.* The labor of our people, and all the great ftaple commodities of our country, produced by it, will and do bring not only immediate *cafh*, but a *high price;* and it is not poffible that money fhould be *too fcarce* in any country, where the *labor* and *produce* of it have *quick fale, good price,* and command immediate *cafh;* whilft this is the cafe, every natural and neceffary *end* and *ufe* of cafh is fully anfwered and fatisfied; and, of courfe, if any body in fuch cafe wants money, the want muft arife, not from any *fcarcity of cafh*, but from a want of fomething that will *purchafe it, i. e.* from poverty; which the introduction of an additional quantity of circulating cafh will by no means remove, but muft increafe, becaufe it will directly tend to leffen induftry, and introduce luxury.

It is no objection to this, that *European* and *Weft-India* goods will not bring ready cafh; it is well known that the market is greatly glutted with thofe articles; and when a

market

market is *overstocked with any articles*, they will not bring *quick sale* and *ready cash*, let money be ever so plenty.

2. Our cash for a year past has been not only fully sufficient for the purposes of our trade, *but has been in a very settled, steady state, with very little fluctuation or variation in its value.* This appears from the *settled prices* which our staple commodities have born thro' the last year. The same thing appears from the *negotiations of the Bank*; from which it is manifest, that the state and quantity of hard cash is nearly the same with us now as it was a year ago; this proves that the quantity of circulating cash is sufficient; for were it not so, it would undulate and vary; for cash, like water, will always flow from the *higher* to the *lower* surface, and will never become *fixed and steady* till the true *equilibrium* is obtained.

3. *It is admitted by every body, that cash was plenty enough before the war; but it is plain we have now much more of it than we had then;* because the price of labor and the produce of the country are much higher now than they were then. On an average, about 40 or 50 per cent. more can now be obtained for labor and country produce, than their current price was in 1774.

It is no objection to this, that it is more difficult to *borrow money on interest now* than it was *then;* it is a want of public and private *faith*, and *distrust* of all security, and not a *scarcity* of cash, which makes the difficulty. Besides this, another cause may be assigned, viz. our monied men who used to dispose of their money in that way, have, at least many of them, *lost their money*, loaned on either public or private securities, by the *defect of those securities*, and of course the lenders of money are in this way reduced to a *fewer* number, whilst at the same time, the same cause *adds to the number* of those who have occasion to *borrow;* each of which naturally increases the difficulty of borrowing.

Striking paper money will *lessen* none of these difficulties, but will *increase* them all; as it is evident that it will much lessen all *confidence in any securities* of long continuance,

ance, and, in every view, *diminish* the number of lenders of money.

4. *Making large and sudden additions (of either paper or hard money) to our circulating cash, will not increase our wealth;* its effect will be an *increase of the price* of all articles of traffic, *i. e.* it will destroy the *steady value* of our money, by lessening its worth in an *inverse ratio* of the increase of its quantity, and so, without any benefit, will introduce the ruinous mischiefs of a fluctuating currency, *from which, good Lord, deliver us!*

5. *I do not apprehend that we have the least chance of supporting the credit of paper money, if it should be issued;* and, to expose our public credit to further *disgrace* and *insult*, and to waste the public wealth in further *stupid, absurd*, and *iniquitous appreciations* of depreciated paper, appears to me the height of political frenzy. The pressure of a vast public debt, the low state of the public credit, the universal diffidence in that sort of money which prevails among the people of all ranks, and the dreadful apprehensions of its consequences, which are expressed *by the Bank*, and by all *our merchants* (who are certainly the best judges of the matter) I say, all these put together appear to me to destroy every degree of probability of supporting the credit of any additional paper currency.

And I cannot suppose any body distracted enough to think it *proper to issue it*, if every idea of the probability of *supporting its credit* must be given up. But I am apt to conjecture, that if our speculators fail in their scheme of getting their *immense profits funded*, the demand for *that money* will be greatly lessened, and so, perhaps, the *zeal* for striking paper may *cool away*, and, of course, any further arguments against it, may not be necessary. But if nothing can hinder the attempt, I am of opinion it must die in the birth.—For,

6. *I do not believe it possible to usher paper money into general currency, either with or without a tender-act.* Making it *a tender* is indeed too shocking to be admitted by any sober man that I have heard of; and *without it*, it must, I think, have

have the same effect, and share the same fate, as the other paper which has recently gone before it.

But after all, if it should gain a *general currency*, and a *credit* but *little inferior* to hard money, the effect, I think, must plainly and evidently be, *that it will soon drive all the hard money out of the country, or at least out of circulation*, as it will certainly be either hoarded or purchased up for exportation; and then we shall have nothing before us, but to increase the *quantity* of our paper, and supply the *deficiency* of its *value* by *additions* to its *quantity*, and make the most of it, Continental like, as long as we can make it pass at all.

7. With respect to the plan of opening a *Loan-Office*, and striking a sum of paper money to put into it, *to be loaned out on private security* to such persons as may want to borrow, I have to observe,

1. *That all the objections which lie against striking paper money at all, lie with equal weight against striking any for this particular purpose.*

2. *This will bring the borrowers into difficulty, instead of helping them;* for if they give a *good security* for the money, and find, when they have got it, that it is not *equal to good money*, but must be passed at a *discount* or *depreciated* value, their purposes will not be answered, nor their *necessities be relieved* by it. And,

3. *This inconvenience will fall heaviest on the most distressed part of the community*, for no others will give *good security* for *bad money*. And,

4. *If the money should, by any strange turn, prove equal to hard money, the sum proposed, viz.* 50,000*l. is by no means equal to this demand*, and, of course, will be immediately snapped up by *favorites*, or such who happen to stand *nearest*, and of course it will by no means operate by way of *public* benefit, or *general relief* of the distress of our people, but will be engrossed by a *few sharp-sighted* folks, with, perhaps, not the best title to public favors, or most likely to make the best use of them. I think that any scheme of this sort had better be put off, till we are *in a condition to make*

make it operate in a way of *effectual, impartial,* and *general* utility.

Upon the whole matter, the great principle I go upon with respect to public securities, is this, viz. *that all bills issued on the public credit, of every sort, under whatever denomination they may appear, whether of certificates, paper money, annuities, &c. &c. take their value, not from the sums specified in the face of them, but from the price or exchange at which they generally pass in market, and, of course, when they are redeemed by the public, it ought to be either at their original value, or at that price or exchange at which they generally pass at the time of redemption,* EXCEPTING ONLY *such securities as are in the hands of the original holder, and have never been alienated.* Such securities are *evidences of* full confideration *paid, and, of course, of a* full debt *due to such holder: but securities in the hands of a purchaser cannot be* such evidence.

When public securities gain a currency, or become objects of traffic, and depreciate in the hands of the possessor, *he doubtless sustains loss,* and is really *injured;* and when the depreciation is great, say 8 for 1, or 200 for 1 (both which we have seen) the mischief becomes *very heavy,* and in its nature lies in the *loss which the possessor of the securities sustained, by their depreciation whilst they were in his hands:*

Hence it appears clearly enough *where the mischief* lies, and, of course, it is easy to see what must be the *nature* of the remedy it requires, viz. *such a remedy as will make up the losses which every one has sustained by the depreciation of the public securities whilst in their hands.* This is manifestly impracticable, and perhaps the utmost power of human invention cannot hit on any plan which will do this; what then ought the public to do? I answer, the same which any private man must do, who knows that he has had a *valuable confideration* for money, and *honestly owes* it, but *knows not to whom* it is due, or cannot *find his creditor.*

From this view of the matter it appears very plain, that *appreciating* the securities, and redeeming them at *full value,* gives not the *least remedy* to the *sufferers by the depreciation,*

tion, but is an *additional injury* to them; becaufe the fecurities, *at the time of redemption, will not be in the* fame *hands in which they depreciated*, and, of courfe, the fufferers will find *themfelves taxed* to make up the money, which *they loft* by the depreciation, that it may be paid to the prefent holders of the fecurities, who *never loft* any thing. But if any one wifhes to fee this fubject further difcuffed, I refer him to my *Fifth Effay on Free Trade and Finance*, where this matter is fully confidered, with refpect to Continental money. [*See p.* 97.]

I will conclude here by obferving, that not one argument can be adduced for redeeming the public fecurities at full value, which will not apply to the *Continental* and *old State money*, and prove that both ought to be redeemed at *full nominal value*.

I take it that the public accounts are nearly all adjufted, and the public creditors have received certificates or public fecurities for their refpective balances. But as thofe fecurities are moftly Continental, it will lie with *Congrefs*, and not with any *particular State*, to prefcribe the time, mode, and value of their redemption.

In the mean time, I think we may do much for the prefent relief of our own diftreffed citizens, who fuffer greatly by the *delays* of Continental payment; and I efteem the attempts of *our Affembly* very *laudable* in their *principle*. What I complain of is an *error* in the *application*. It is certainly very good in them to ftrain every nerve to raife money for the *relief of our widows, orphans, foldiers*, and *other worthy and diftreffed public creditors;* but I think it *a miftake* to plan the matter fo, that when the money is raifed, it *fhall not be applied* to the relief of thofe *worthy, diftreffed citizens*, but fhall go, at leaft a very confiderable part of it, to a *parcel of fpeculators*, who neither ever *earned* it, nor are in any *diftrefs* for want of it; for they are generally rich, and can command plenty of cafh.

With the good leave of the public, I will fum up the matter, and humbly offer fome propofitions, which appear to me worthy of confideration.

I. *I propofe to fet about raifing all the money we can, not by a* tax on polls and eftates, *which will be very burdenfome* to our people, *hurtful to the capital interest of the State, and of very* uncertain product; *but by continuing our present* duties on trade, *with such further* additional duties on LUXU-RIES, *as will be necessary to* restrain the excessive *use of them:* and this, I conceive, will require duties *so high*, as will be sufficient for the *exigencies* of the State, and will be of *certain product.*

II. *I propose to pay all the interest which is now due to the inhabitants of this State, on all such public securities as are in the hands of the* original holders, *and have* not been alienated (to be ascertained by *affidavit* or any *other* sufficient proof) and also to *stop payment* of all interest on any certificates which are *not in the hands of the original holders;* for I do not know that among citizens of equal merit, we can with justice make fish of one, and flesh of another.

III. *I propose that commissioners be appointed to* purchase up *such public securities as were originally given to the citizens of this State, but have* been alienated *by the original holders, and are now in currency as objects of traffic or exchange; to purchase such securities, I say, at the* current exchange, *or as low as they can be bought.* It is certainly as right for *the State* to buy up these securities, which are become a common object of traffic, as it is for *any individual.* Two great advantages will result from this:

1. *The present holders will have the value of them paid in money:* and,

2. *The State will have them to produce to Congress, whenever our quota shall be demanded for the redemption of them;* for the securities themselves will doubtless be accepted as good payment of our quota, both of principal and interest; and it will then be indifferent to us *at what exchange*, or in *what manner* or *time,* Congress may direct their redemption.

IV. *I propose that all those original holders of public securities, who have alienated them, shall be debited on the public books, with the certificates they received, at the* value *(and no more) at which they could be* sold at the time they received them, or the time of their date, *and that the residue of their balance may be paid, together with the principal of the certificates,*

cates, which are now in the hands of the original holders, and have not been alienated. I say, that both these *be paid as soon as money sufficient can be raised by the State.*

It will require, I know, a heavy sum of money to do this, but we shall have this satisfaction to animate our exertions, that we are doing *an act of justice in favor of those to whom the money is justly due*, and shall have the advantage of paying it to people who are scattered thro' the State, and will immediately circulate the money among our citizens, in every part of the State, which, if the justice was equal, will be much *preferable to paying the same money* to people who would carry it all *away to distant parts*, from whence it would have little chance of returning into circulation, to the places where it was collected.

V. As the pressures of the State are very heavy, I think we ought to make all the savings we can; I therefore propose *to lessen the House of Assembly, by taking away two-thirds of the members, and limiting the sessions of the Council* to the Assembly's sessions, unless the President should, on emergent occasions, summon them. I think *one-third* of our Assembly would do the business much *better* than all of them; and the President, with a good Secretary, would be sufficient for the common and usual business of the Council. I know of no advantage arising from *over-numerous Legislatures*, or *Councils* that sit too long. The extremes of democratical government tend to anarchy, or despotism, or ruin.

An idle, useless, or corrupt member is less noticed and easier lost in the crowd, in a *large* Assembly, than in a *small* one. *Virtue and merit* are, for the same reason, *less* conspicuous in a large than small Assembly; *cabals, party-schemes*, and *interested plans*, are easier formed in a *large* than in a *small* house, and the *guilt* or *folly* of an individual is more easily sheltered or concealed in *great* than in *small* numbers.

For when Assemblies are large, the business is most commonly done by a few, under the umbrage of the whole; the major part are not commonly *in the secret*. The *American Congress* rarely consists of more than thirty members present,

present, yet no complaint has been made that their number is too small. The *British House of Commons* consists of more than five hundred members, not very famous for gravity, wisdom, or order. Their proceedings are commonly directed by the *Premier*, and a few *leading members;* yet if you ask Lord *North*, why he pushed the *American* war, he will tell you with great composure, that it was not *his war, but the war of the Parliament.*

When *more people* are employed about any business than are necessary to do it, the consequence has ever been found to be, that the business is not *done so well,* is clogged with *more delays,* is less *consistent* in its several parts, and not so *well methodized.* The people who are interested in the business, and have occasion to attend upon it, are not so *well served,* and a *greater expense* is incurred, than would happen, if people *just enough* for the business, and *no more,* had been employed.

This, one would think, was grounded on natural fitness; for we find it holds true in all human affairs, from a house too full of *servants,* a field with too many *reapers,* a town-meeting of too many *people,* a kitchen with too many *cooks,* a committee of too many *members,* a church with too many *deacons* or too large a vestry, a court with too many *judges,* and so on, up to an assembly of the first dignity, with too many *representatives.*

Now to admit any principle or circumstance into our gravest and most important councils, which has ever been found hurtful in all cases where it has been adopted, is highly imprudent and dangerous, and tends to ruin. The fatal experience of many great nations proves this in a manner very forcible and convincing.

Rome and *Greece* lost their liberties by over-numerous Senates, &c. and *Poland* is now in desolation from the same cause; their *Pospolite,* which was instituted for the great defence of their nation, and their *liberum veto,* which they hugged with enthusiasm, as the *standard* of their liberty, together with their *over-numerous Diets,* have completely ruined them. But whether these observations are proper or not, we shall, by this propofition, at leaft fave a *vaft expenfe*, at a time when the utmoft economy is neceffary.

VI. At all times, but efpecially in times of public prefſure, the *peace and quiet* of the State fhould be confulted, and the general *confidence* of the people in the government fhould be as far as poffible *fecured*, in order to its firm eftablifhment, and the great *principles* of our civil policy fhould be *ſtrictly regarded*. I therefore humbly propofe *the repeal of the teſt-act;* for we can no how expect the internal peace and quiet of our people, and their confidence in our government, fo long as we exclude *one-third* our citizens from any fhare in it.

Nor can we any how call our civil policy a government *of the people*, or reap the advantage of fuch a government, as long as fo *large a proportion* of our citizens (if reckoned by numbers, influence, wifdom, or eftate) are *ſhut out* and *disfranchifed*. We need the *counfels* as well as the *wealth* of *all* our people, and our conftitution gives *equal right*, as well as prefcribes *equal duty*, to them all.

That the major muſt rule the minor, is undoubtedly a maxim effential to a democratical or republican government; but it is equally manifeft, that the *extremes* of this maxim will deftroy the very *nature*, as well as *ufes*, of fuch governments. For if *two-thirds* can disfranchife the *minor* third, a *majority* of the remaining two-thirds may disfranchife the *minority* of them, and fo on *toties quoties*, till there will be but *two* left undisfranchifed, to govern the whole; which, I fuppofe, every body will allow to be fomewhat *worfe* than to have *but one* fovereign defpot; for the two might quarrel, and each form his party, and fo the State might be involved in a civil war, which could not happen, if there was but *one* defpot, and nobody elfe left capable of forming a party.

It is doubtlefs neceffary to adopt good maxims of government, but it is equally neceffary to exercife fome *prudence and difcretion* in the ufe of them; for we may be ruined by the *extremes* of thofe very maxims, which, in their *mean*, are very falutary and ufeful.

It has been suggested by some ill-minded people (but for the honor of *Pennsylvania*, I must think, without the least reason) that some Members of our General Assembly are *deeply interested* in *stock-jobbing and speculations* in certificates, and are possessed of, or concerned in, *public securities* to a large amount, which they are not the original holders of, but obtained by purchase at 6 or 8 for 1, and are now using all their endeavours, power, and influence, in the Assembly, under the sanction of their *sacred public character*, to procure a vote of the Assembly, for funding their certificates, and, of course, to vote the money of their constituents by thousands into their *own pockets*.

I think it necessary that the honorable Assembly should take proper measures to vindicate themselves from such scandalous aspersions; and if there are any such members, to take the necessary care that one *scabby sheep* shall not spoil the *whole flock*. There can certainly be no more reason or fitness, that a Member of Assembly, under the sacred sanction of his public character, should vote the money of the State into his *own pocket*, than that a *judge* or *juryman* should sit in judgment in a cause, in the event of which he is *personally interested*.

We are told by some folks of delicate feelings, that "*the public credit or honor is like the chastity of a woman;*" and we all know that the wife of *Cæsar* ought not to be suspected; it will therefore follow, by consent of every body, that every cause of suspicion of the integrity and disinterestedness of our honorable Assembly should be removed as far as possible; and this is the more necessary, as our Assembly is a *single Legislature*, whose acts are not subject to a *revision*, or require the concurrence of *another* house; and of course, if *they err*, the subject is *without remedy*.

On these considerations there can be no doubt but our Assembly, and every body else, will be thoroughly penetrated with the necessity of having every member of that august body most effectually acquitted from all *suspicion of interestedness*, when they come to decide a question, which demands 3 or 4,000,000 of dollars from the State.

I therefore

I therefore propose, with all modesty, that when the great question shall be put finally in that supreme house, ' Whether the public securities shall be funded,' that there shall be some sort of *voyer dire* oath or test imposed on every member, to this purpose, viz. that he is not directly or indirectly *possessed*, *interested*, or *concerned*, otherwise than as an original holder, in any *public securities*, proposed to be funded, by the vote of Assembly now depending.

The *principle* of this proposition will doubtless be admitted by every body; and I conceive the Assembly will have no objection to the mode, as they are in their sentiments very favorable to *test-acts*. This method, I conceive, would set the character of the Assembly in the most unexceptionable point of light, and would give great dignity and weight to their decisions; and tho' they might happen by this method to lose a vote or two, yet there is no doubt but they would have *upright souls* enough left, to make an ample majority in *favor of any vote*, which the *real interest* or *honor* of the State might make necessary.

It has ever been my fortune to write in the *muns of popular prejudices;* and in justice to my subject, and to my own judgment, I have often been obliged to mix some kind of *censure* on public measures, which were adopted by the leaders of the times, when I thought they were founded on *principles of mistake and error*, and tended to the *ruin* of the cause they were designed to *support*, and would, in their nature, operate in a manner very *hurtful* to my country. I accordingly met with *little thanks*; *my rewards* were such as any body may expect, who opposes the *current tide* of popular opinion, and the favorite plans of *warm, zealous* men.

I have sometimes met with that *warmth* and *malignancy* of censure, which can hardly be supposed to arise from an opposition to error of *mere judgment*, without some degree of *corruption* of heart. Yet *time* has evinced my most *censured propositions* to be necessary, and they have been *adopted* by our gravest and most dignified councils, and are now become very *orthodox*, and are justified by the sanction of *general opinion*. I therefore think I have some right to

claim

claim the attention of my fellow-citizens, at least I flatter myself I am intitled to their candor, while they read my propositions.

Nothing but my opinion of the vast importance of the subject of this Essay, could have induced me to write it. I had long determined to write no more on political matters; but when I came to see the State in danger of having *some millions of the public money* (in this our pressure of public debt) diverted from the *objects* who have every *claim* of justice to it, and lavished on people *who never earned* it;*

and

---

* I am told, that in the public debates on this subject which have since taken place, *my plan of paying the original creditors* in preference to *the speculators*, was admitted to be *just and desirable*, but it was *objected to* and *rejected* because it was thought *impracticable to make the discrimination;* and this supposed *impracticability* was strongly urged and greatly insisted on: on which I beg leave to observe,

1. That the *names* of the original creditors are *on the public books*, with the *balances* due to them, and are *easily found;* to which a reference must be made *equally on both plans;* for if a certificate is offered for payment, which is *not entered there*, it will be *rejected* as counterfeit.

2. *The proof will lie on the man who demands payment, that he is an original creditor:* if he cannot make this appear, he will *fail* of payment, as *all persons must*, who *bring suits* which they cannot support with proof.

3. If there are *some*, or even *many*, original creditors who *cannot prove* their demand, and so *must lose* it, it does not follow that such as *can prove their claim*, should be *rejected:* this would be a mad conclusion.

4. If the original, rightful creditor cannot *be found*, he cannot *be paid;* but it does not follow, that the money *due to him* must be paid to *any body else*, who has no claim of either original or derivative right; it is certainly very plain, that, in such case, the money ought not to be *paid at all to any body*, as must be the case with every *private* man who *owes money*, but cannot *find his creditor;* or with the *public*, to whom all estates or property escheat, if the owners *cannot be found*, as in case of *treasure-trove, wreck of sea, lands*, when the owner dies without *will or heirs*, &c.

5. The whole objection, tho' true, when urged *against* paying the original creditors, and *in favor* of paying the *speculators*, is *nugatory and trifling;* for such original creditors as *cannot be found*, or cannot *prove* their demands, are *left equally without remedy* under *both* plans; for payment to the speculators makes *no more provision* for such cases, than payment to the original creditors.

6. If such cases exist (as probably many of them may) no one pretends that they bear *any proportion* to the vast number (that can be found) of creditors possessed of full proof; and it is very plain, that the *defect of proof* in the one cannot *injure* or *diminish* the right of the other, whose claim is *capable of full proof*.

Indeed I think that nothing can be plainer than this, viz. that we ought to pay all the real creditors, whose *wealth or services* we have had the *benefit* of, and who are possessed of *full proof* of the *debts due to them therefor*, but by no means to pay the whole money to *speculators*, who *have certainly no right*

and also to see a deluge of *paper money* rolling in upon the State, when I had not the least reason to suppose either that our public *credit*, in its present state of pressure and weakness, could *support* it, or that the *quantity* of our circulating cash (which is demonstrably quite sufficient) could *bear* such *vast* and *sudden* additions, without the most ruinous consequences. I say, when I viewed those matters, I really thought it a duty I owed to the State in which I live, to explain my sentiments, and, as far as in me lay, endeavour to avert these mischiefs.

I doubt not but the public will judge favorably of my intentions, and allow my arguments their due weight. The *facts* alleged are all of *public notoriety;* the *reasonings* are *open* to every man; and I have only to wish, that the reader may peruse this Essay with the same *love of justice* and *truth*, and the same *zeal* for the *good, honor,* and *prosperity* of this State, as occupied my whole breast when I wrote it.

---

right at all, because some may probably have *right* which they cannot make *appear*.

The State of *Pennsylvania*, in their funding act (1785) made the discrimination I propose, with respect to one species of certificates (final settlements) but I never heard any difficulty was found in the practice or execution of the statute, on that account.

Some people are wild enough to propose to pay the public money to the *speculators*, for fear the *real, original creditors* should *perjure* themselves in *proving their accounts.* This is too foolish to require an answer: for,

1. If we are to reject *oaths in proof of accounts*, for fear of perjuries, the rule ought doubtless to be made *general* and extend to *all accounts* of all descriptions of persons; for certainly one man has as good a right to take benefit of his *own perjuries*, as another. But,

2. If such perjuries should happen, it surely cannot follow from thence, that the speculators ought to have all the money paid to them, which is due to the real, original creditors.

In fine, I think it really disgraceful to human nature, to suppose such arguments and such objections require answers, and I have to beg my reader's pardon for offering them.

A PLEA

FOR THE

Poor Soldiers:

OR, AN

ESSAY

To demonstrate that the SOLDIERS *and other* PUBLIC CREDITORS, *who* really *and* actually *supported the Burden of the late War,* HAVE NOT BEEN PAID, OUGHT TO BE PAID, CAN BE PAID, *and* MUST BE PAID.

[*First published in Philadelphia, Jan.* 2, 1790.]

WHEN the funding bill of *Pennsylvania* was published for confideration, five years ago, I wrote my *Seventh Essay on Free Trade and Finance,* in which I advanced fundry principles and arguments, which, perhaps, may apply as well to the finance of the Union in general, as to that of *Pennsylvania* in particular; and, of course, it may be neceffary here, to repeat and revife many of the principles and arguments therein advanced and fully difcuffed; but a reference to that Effay will make a full enlargement on them unneceffary in this place.

In an Effay of this fort, it will probably be expected, I. *That the monies neceffary for the public exigence, fhould be ftated:* II. *The refources out of which thefe monies are to be raifed, fhould be confidered:* and, III, *The mode of affeffments and collections fhould be attended to.*

I am

I am informed, that these will be the first great objects of attention in Congress, on the opening of the ensuing session.

My present design is, to state and advocate the *rights* and *claims* of a great and very respectable class of our citizens, whose *distinguished merit* entitles them to the *justice*, and, indeed, to the *gratitude* also, *of their country*, but who are, I fear, at least many of them, in danger of being *neglected* and *losing the reward* due to them, for the supplies and services which they rendered their country in the greatest public distress.

And the very money which is *granted and paid* by the country, for the *just recompense* of these *worthy and deserving patriots*, is, by a strange *fatality* of events, *absurdity* of reasoning, and *perversion* of counsel and right, I say, this money is proposed by some to be diverted from, and *never paid to*, them; but to be given to another class of *citizens and foreigners*, who do not pretend *to any merit of their own*, or to have *earned any of the money*, but whose claim and demand is founded wholly on the *merit and earnings* of these worthy citizens, who are, by the very plan, *to lose it all, and get none of it*.

The *worthy patriots I allude to*, are *those who*, *during the war*, when our country was overwhelmed with infinite distress and danger, *rendered their services, supplies, and money in its defence*, but who, on the adjustment of their accounts, *could not be paid*, by reason of the deficiency of the public finances of the States, and, therefore, were *obliged to accept* certificates of the balances *due* to them, with promises of interest and payment in future time.

These certificates were made *payable to the bearer*, and of course were negotiable, and were worth about 2*s*. or 2*s*. 6*d*. in the pound, their value being estimated by the current or *common price*, at which they were generally *bought* and *sold* in the public market; for the value of certificates, as well as of every thing else that becomes an object of general exchange or transfer, *must, and ever will, be estimated by the current or common price it will bring in market*.

That

That the common price at which such certificates were generally bought and sold at the close of the war, was *in fact about 2s. or 2s. 6d.* may easily be made appear in a most incontrovertible manner, by the testimony of thousands and thousands, who bought and sold them the first year or two after the close of the war, when the great bulk of them were issued, and when the greatest sales of them were made by the original holders.

Since this period they have been hawked and jockied about by the speculators and brokers, like an *ignis fatuus*, at a great variety of desultory risings and fallings of price, according to the opinion, or whim, or caprice, or deception which happened to prevail in the minds of men at the time; the tracing or even considering of which, I conceive of no manner of consequence at present.

It follows from the foregoing observations, that the value of the public certificates, at the time of their being issued, *may be easily ascertained; and so much* the public creditors who received them, *were paid, and no more*, say 2s. 6d. in the pound; and the remainder, say 17s. 6d. in the pound, and the interest of it from that time, *is still due to them*.

That this remainder or *balance ought to be paid to them*, with the money which is, or may be, granted and paid by the public, for the *express purpose* of satisfying and rewarding these worthy citizens, for their *dear and painful earnings* in their country's cause, and that the said money ought not to be *diverted* from this most just and valuable purpose, on any reason or pretence whatever; I say, that the *balance* which they have *not received*, and which, of course, *is still due*, ought to be paid to them, is a most, *capital object to be proved, urged, and enforced in the present Essay*.

I shall attempt, and cannot doubt I shall be able, to prove to the satisfaction of every judicious reader,

That *they are not yet paid;*
That *they ought to be paid;*
That *they can be paid;*

And, to satisfy the grateful wishes of all our citizens, and to establish our national character of honor and humanity,

manity, both at home and abroad, That *they must be paid.*

For this purpose, I beg the candid attention of my reader to the following propositions:

I. *No public creditor who receives a certificate, is thereby paid any more than the value of the certificate at the time of delivery,* i. e. it is not the *nominal value* but the *real value* only, *i. e.* the current price of it, which is to be regarded in estimating the quantity of payment made by it.

When any body proposes to pay a debt in bills of exchange, bills of paper money, certificates, or any bills of public or private credit (if the creditor agrees to accept such payment) the first question that invariably occurs is, *what is the exchange?* i. e. *no regard* at all is paid to the *nominal* value, but reference is constantly had to *the exchange* or *current price* in market, in order to determine what amount of such bills shall be given to satisfy the debt. This practice is so *universal* among all men, and grounded on such *manifest principles of right*, that I cannot conceive that any man can be found, who will dispute either the reality or propriety of it.

The practice of Congress, the supreme council of the Union, *affords a precedent of this same principle*, adopted by them, respecting their *loan-office certificates.*

They published by their authority a *scale of depreciation*, by which the value of those certificates was estimated at the *real exchange* they had at the *time of their dates*, and the rate of their *final redemption* was fixed on the same principle.

All the States adopted the same principle, either by making use of the scale of Congress, or establishing scales of their own, by which the value of Continental money was estimated thro' all the stages of its depreciation.

This practice of Congress and of all the States was founded not only on absolute necessity, but on the plainest principles of right; and if they made any deviation from justice, in the adjustment of any of their scales, this was no error in the principle, but merely a fault in the practice or use of it. And surely there can be *no reason why* the

same

same rule (if a good one) of estimating the real value of certificates issued in 1777 and the subsequent years, should not be applied to the certificates which were issued at the close of the war.

But there is certainly *great reason why* our most virtuous citizens, who, by their patriotic efforts, services, and supplies, *supported the war*, and *saved our country*, should not be subjected to the loss of *seven-eighths* of their just dues, for want of such a rule, or some other means of saving them from such ruinous and *shameful injustice*.

Farther, let us appeal to *plain, common sense* on this subject. When the public accounts were settled at the close of the war, the public creditors were entitled to their several balances due to them from the States, *in good hard money*. Now can any possible reason be given, why a certificate worth but 2s. 6d. should be good payment to them, of 20s. *at that time*, any more than *now at this time?* I believe it will be readily admitted, that if any body (personal or aggregate) should, at this time, seriously propose *to pay a debt of* 20s. with a certificate or any thing else, which *was worth but* 2s. 6d. the offer would be rejected with every degree of *contempt*, as a most *villainous* and *rascally insult*.

Is there one Member of Congress, who would not think himself abused by the offer of a certificate worth 3-5ths *of a dollar*, in full satisfaction of *six dollars*, which he expects for one day's attendance in the house? but how aggravated and keen, would be his feelings and chagrin, if he should neglect his family and private concerns, and attend Congress seven years, and, at the end of the term, should be paid off in *certificates of the same depreciated value!*

Or, do you think his vexation would be *softened* any, by being told, that tho' his certificates were really worth at present *but* 2s. 6d. *in the pound*, yet the sum *expressed on the face* of them was 20s. in the pound, and therefore he must be satisfied with them as good and *full payment*, and if he would have patience to keep them *long enough*, they might perhaps bring him the full, real value expressed in them?

I believe

I believe every Member of Congress will readily allow, that I have hit on what would be the *true feelings* of any of his brethren, and even of himself, in such a supposed case. If so, gentlemen, please to *do as you would be done by;* this *rule of conduct* is enjoined upon you by an authority much superior, and far paramount, to any you can lay the least claim to, in your utmost dignity, and fullest possession of sovereign power.

From all this it appears evident, that the public creditors, who have received certificates in payment, were paid *no more than the current value or exchange* of the certificates, at the time they received them. *So much is paid and no more,* and so much and no more they ought to be *debited,* and the *residue of the debt,* not having been paid, is still *due to them.*

It farther appears, that the certificates which were delivered to the *soldiers* and *other public creditors,* on the final settlement of their accounts, after the close of the war, were worth *not more than* 2s. 6d. in the pound, which ought to be *debited* to them, and the *remaining* 17s. 6d. *in the pound,* being unpaid, still *remains due* to them.

II. *These balances which remain unpaid to the public creditors, ought to be paid as soon as possible.* The sums due to them are their *dear, their painful earnings;* these claimants are the *soldiers who fought,* and the *citizens who supplied* them, when the *salvation of our country* was the great *prize contended for;* it is owing to their virtuous and strong exertions, that we have *any thing left,* either for our *own enjoyment,* or the *payment of them.*

We have no instance in history, of an army who discovered and practised more spirit, firmness, patience, discipline, fortitude, and zeal, either under the instant pressure of the greatest *hardships and sufferings,* or in the solemn and awful *march to the most dangerous enterprises,* or in the arduous *moments of battle,* than were found in our troops.

Nor did they hesitate or faulter in the least, till they had *completed their great work,* raised their *own,* their *general's,* and their *country's* honor and character to the utmost height, and reached the arduous goal which they had constantly

stantly in view, thro' every stage of their fatigue and danger; this *glorious goal* was the *complete liberation of one of the greatest empires* of the earth, which *empire we are*, who sit clothed in all the majesty of empire, wealth, and power, solemnly deliberating, *whether we shall pay these our deliverers, or not.*

That " the *laborer* is worthy of his *hire*," is the great doctrine of COMMUTATIVE JUSTICE, that *divine law* of nature, and *nature's God*, which, in the utmost *majesty* of command, connects the *quid pro quo*, that august principle on which alone all *thrones* and *governments* can acquire and fix a *permanent establishment;* this sacred principle, I say, requires that these worthy claimants should be paid the money due to them, because they have *dearly, nobly, and faithfully earned* it.

There is in every human heart, a *principle of right*, a principle planted by the *great Creator*, ever approving the things which are most excellent; how far soever this sacred principle may become *generally practical, emanate* and spread in society, and *govern and direct the general mind;* yet the *dispensation* of public justice and right, lies *in the power*, and becomes the *peculiar duty, of a few men*, the chosen and dignified *few*, to whom the administration of the great affairs and interests of the nation are committed.

These dignified personages are sometimes called *gods:* they certainly sit in the place of God, and whether given to the people in *wrath* or *mercy*, are certainly appointed by him, and the sacred *charge and duty* of imitating his government lies on them; *judgment and justice* are the habitation of his throne; and these sacred virtues ought always to be found in our supreme council, not as *transient persons* who may be called in on favorite occasions, where their presence may be pretty well admitted, and their inspection may be tolerable, but as *constant residents*, who take up their dwelling there, as the place of their *uniform habitation.*

With a heart melted in sympathy with the *sufferings* of my country's *deliverers*, with a sublimated sense of the
importance,

importance, as well as *sacred nature*, of the *justice* and *judgment* of our nation, I most devoutly implore (and doubt not the concurrence of every honest *American*) that these *sovereign and sacred virtues* may *dwell*, not only in our supreme *councils*, but in the heart of every *member who shall give his vote* in the decision of this most capital and interesting cause which I am pleading.

Another thing which ought to induce us to pay these worthy citizens is, *their brilliant success, and the most important benefits we derive from their exertions.* I do not say that *success* simply is a *virtue*, but it is a very great *proof* of it, in as much as success generally follows *prudent, spirited,* and *persevering* conduct; nor do I say that *rewards* ought to be proportioned to the *benefits* received; for by this rule we can never *pay enough* to our deliverers; but where the benefits accruing from virtuous exertions are very great, they at least become entitled to a *full compensation*, and perhaps liberal minds will think *a generous one* might with great propriety be allowed.

We call general *Washington*, the *father* and *saviour* of his country, and with great propriety; the virtues *of a father* he might have possessed *alone*, but *the saviour* of his country he *could not have been without his army*. He indeed designed with *discernment*, commanded with *prudence*, and led on his troops with *fortitude*; but altho' these virtues were carried by him beyond the power of imitation, the success must have failed, had not his *army co-operated* with his designs effectually, *obeyed* his orders cheerfully, and *followed* him with firmness; without these, neither his laurels could have been obtained, nor our deliverance have been completed.

They were his faithful companions in *distresses*, in *dangers*, in *battles*, in *victories;* they shared his *fortunes*, they shared his *merits*, and they persevered with him, till they also shared his *final successes*, which put a period to *their* long and patient *labors*, and our *country's calamities*.

How would all the fine feelings of the human mind have *glowed in the breast* of that exalted general, if, in that period of *triumphant and final success*, he could have

called

called thefe his *dear* and *worthy fellow-laborers* and *fellow-sufferers* together, met their brightened countenances with the warmeft *mutual congratulations, thanked* them for their fervices, and *difmiffed* them with *fuch rewards*, as would have enabled them to return to their families with fome degree of *advantage*, as w.. ! as *honor*.

But I will draw a veil over the reft, and only fay, the *hard neceffity* of the times prevented this; the general knew it, the foldiers knew it, and fubmitted with *patience* to accept their difcharge, and find their way home as they could, with *empty hands* and dry lips.

Is it poffible that the *great councils of America fhall fuffer fuch perfevering fortitude, difcipline, and patience to go without their reward?* Generous allowances are not demanded; *liberal appointments* are not folicited; no more is required than the *fimple pay* which was *promifed* them by Congrefs; all they afk for, is the fulfilment of that *facred contract*, which is grounded on the *public faith and honor of an empire*.

Indeed, I think that the *patient and quiet behaviour* of the *real* public creditors, both at the clofe of the war and fince, entitles them to the *higheft efteem* and refpect of all our citizens, and fhould excite a very ftrong zeal, to make the moft powerful efforts *to do them right*; it is certainly *mean, bafe,* and *fhameful*, it is *below* the *dignity* of a nation, to *deny* or *delay that juftice* to virtuous, *quiet*, and *well-behaved citizens*, which would be granted to *tumult, uproar,* and *infurrection*.

Will any man prefume to fay they are *quiet*, becaufe it is not in their power to make *difturbance?* This is very ill-natured; but were it really the cafe, it would bring them into the rank of *helplefs perfons*, like the widows and fatherlefs, who have *rights which they are not able to affert* and fupport; thefe are entitled to the moft *peculiar* and *tender protections* of the government; the *wrongs* and *oppreffions* of fuch as thefe, are always ranked among the *moft horrid* and *cruel acts* of injuftice.

But I do not conceive this to be the *real fact*; all States have found that there may be as great force and ftrength
in

in the *still, small voice*, as in the *explosions* that break the cedars of *Lebanon;* it is not commonly *a fretfulness of temper* in the people, but the *cause of complaint*, which breeds disturbances in a State; it is rare that people can be worked up into general insurrection, without some *great and general cause*.

Wrongs and *oppressions* diffused over a State will always *sow the seeds* of discontent; these sit *easy on nobody;* but always operate by way of fret and resentment, and are generally the *causes of serious insurrections*, and sometimes of most *capital* revolutions, in government; I know of *but one sure way* to keep the people quiet and easy in any government, and that is, to cause ' *justice* and *judgment* to run down its streets, and *righteousness* to cover it.'

But it ought to be noted here, that tho' the proper way to keep the subjects of any State in *quietness*, is to do them *justice*, yet it does not follow, that no men will be *quiet* under wrongs; many virtuous and good citizens will put up with injuries, and bear them with patience, rather than engage in pursuits for redress, which may make the *remedy worse than the disease;* few men would be willing to foment public disturbances, and make the land of their nativity a *scene of desolation* and horror, to gain *redress* of personal wrongs, or to gratify a *spirit of revenge*.

Many good men would patiently suffer injuries, rather than even give *uneasiness* to their oppressors, especially where the wrong happens to proceed from some *near connection*, a *brother*, a *father*, or perhaps the *fathers* of their country; but this virtuous patience under injury I deem highly *meritorious*, and deserving the utmost *attention* to their *rights*, and the *redress* of their *wrongs*.

But when the very people from whom redress is expected, begin to take advantage of the peaceable disposition of such a citizen, to think him *void of spirit*, and proceed to *insult* his wrongs, *trifle* with his demands, *ridicule* his pretensions, and plead *absurd arguments* in avoidance of his claims, *arguments* which are a *burlesque of common sense*, and which cannot meet the approbation of that *discerning power*, which the all-wise Creator has *planted* in every human

man mind, as the great *index of right and wrong;* I say, when insults of this sort are added to injuries, there is a *point, a bound, beyond which* human patience will not endure, and, of course, such injuries never will be *offered* to any person who is supposed to be in condition to *assert and vindicate his own rights,* or to *resent properly the insults offered to him.*

For example, let us suppose that the *Continental army,* officers and men, with *those who, by their contributions, fed and clothed them,* were all *met together,* with their august general at the head of them,* and, in this *respectable* state, should present their humble petition to Congress *for their pay;* do you think, gentlemen, that there *is a man in all the States,* either in or out of Congress, who would venture to tell them *they were paid already, and had no right to expect any thing farther from their country?*

If a speech of this sort is supposable, it may be proper to consider it a little more particularly. I conceive that any speech directed to an army, the great subject of which is, to persuade them, after seven years' hard service, *to go off quietly without their pay,* must necessarily carry in it *materials somewhat rough, harsh,* and not much suited to the *taste of the hearers;* it will therefore, doubtless, be necessary to *soften and sweeten* it as much as may be, in order to insure its *proper effect.*

I will go on then to suppose, if you please, that some grave person of known wisdom, candor, and polished manners, should rise up to make an address to this *great* and *respectable body* of citizens, which, I think we may presume,

---

* When I wrote this I had no doubt but that, if such an assembly of *fellow-laborers* and *fellow-sufferers* had appeared, their *general* would have cheerfully put himself at their *head,* and have *supported their suit* with all his power and influence.

It is also very manifest, that both *they* and their *rights* are all, at this time, in *real existence and full life,* tho' not all *met together* in condition to *assert and demand* the justice which is due to them.

It is further certain, that the *known rights* of an *absent man* ought not to be neglected, because he is *not present* to assert them, or in condition to vindicate his demand; *infants,* and all other *helpless* persons, have rights which are ever *recognised* by the *law of right,* and ought ever to be *supported* by the *government,* to which the administration of that *law of right* is committed.

fume, might be pretty nearly in the following manner, viz.

"Gentlemen—I addrefs you as moſt reſpectable citizens; your *conduct* has been *noble;* your *merits* are known to all *the world,* and acknowledged by *all the States.* Your arduous, perſevering efforts have *ſaved your country.* What a pity is it then, that after ſo much worthy action, and ſo much triumphant virtue, you ſhould be *inadvertently betrayed* into ſuch an improper conduct, as to petition for your pay; *inadvertently betrayed,* I ſay, for I do not attribute your preſent application to any *evil deſign;* but to your having *ſomehow* imbibed very *improper ſentiments.* I muſt be ſo free, gentlemen, as to tell you, you *have been paid, fully paid* already."

Here the ſoldiers interrupt the orator.—"*Paid already! fully paid!* with *certificates worth but* 2*s.* 6*d.* in *the pound,* and *hard work to get ſo much.*"

The orator reſumes—"Have patience, my friends; do not interrupt me; I am delivering the *ſenſe of your country.*"

SOLDIERS. *Is it the ſenſe of our country, that a debt of* 20*s. can be paid, fully paid, with a certificate, or any thing elſe, which is worth, and will ſell for, but* 2*s.* 6*d.?*

ORATOR. "I again beg your patience a little, my dear friends; it is true, your certificates, when you received them, were indeed ſomewhat *dull and low;* they would not fetch *more than* 2*s.* 6*d. in the pound,* and hardly that; 2*s.* 6*d.* was the *extent* of the general current *price* of them; but ſurely you ought to conſider this was *no fault of the certificates;* they were wrote on as *good paper,* and with as *good ink,* as need be, and 20*s. was wrote* on them as plain as could be wiſhed; and not only ſo, but the *public faith* of the States, the *ſacred honor* of your country, was *annexed to that* 20*s.* and *ſolemnly pledged* to make it good, and what could you wiſh more? Certainly, gentlemen, you cannot have the aſſurance to *ſuggeſt,* or even to *think,* that the *public faith,* the *ſacred honor* of your country, was worth but 2*s.* 6*d.* in the
"pound!

" pound! that their *State-bills of* 20*s.* were worth but *half*
" *a crown.*"

SOLDIERS. We do not wish to enter into any conversation about *public faith* and *honor*; it seems to us, that this subject is not very proper to talk much of, at this time; for the *least said is soonest forgot*: but one thing we *know* and *feel*, that we could get *no more* than 2*s.* 6*d.* in the pound for our certificates; and our *necessities obliged* us to part with them for what we *could get*.

You will please to consider, sir, it is no small thing for people in our condition, to be deprived of seven years' hard earnings, carved out of *the prime of life*, and to be left with nothing to *begin the world* with, or even to keep ourselves and families *from starving*.

ORATOR. " I do not blame you in this distress for
" selling your certificates; but you ought to have consider-
" ed, that, when you sold them, you *made over* and *transferred* all your *right to payment*, for all your *services* and
" *advances* to your country, and, therefore, ought not to
" have sold them *so cheap*; you really *hurt* yourselves, and
" *debased* the honor and credit of the States, by that im-
" prudent step; had you been *wise enough* to have sold
" them at 20*s.* in the pound, *your necessities* had been bet-
" ter relieved, and all *this trouble* and *perplexity* which you
" give yourselves and *us*, would have been prevented."

SOLDIERS. You might as well blame us for not turning our certificates into *joes* and *guineas*; you know as well as we, that it was *absolutely impossible* to get *more* for them, or do *better* with them, than we did; we received the certificates made *payable to the bearer*, and of course, *negotiable*, and *calculated* to be *bought* and *sold*, *i. e.* to circulate like cash thro' *any and every hand*; but we had no idea when we sold them, that we *sold any more* than we *received*; or that our selling them *destroyed* our demand on the States, for *that part* of our earnings which we had *not received*, and which was *not paid* to us; nor can we conceive, how our sale of *negotiable* certificates can operate on our *real earnings* like an *enchanter's wand*, so as to *annihilate* them, or turn them into a *mist*.

ORATOR.

ORATOR. "I observe, gentlemen, you grow somewhat warm; I wish to avoid all ill-humor and hard language; you have *deserved nobly*; you have gained *great honor*; you have *saved your country*; and I hope, after all this merit, you will neither *tarnish* your own *honors*, nor *disturb* your country's *peace*, by your uneasiness and *discontent*.

"What is done is passed and cannot be recalled; I earnestly recommend to you, my dear and honored fellow-citizens, to *return home peaceably and quietly* like virtuous and good christians, and *go to work double tides*, to raise money to pay the *present holders* of your certificates; for however foolishly you parted with them *under value*, yet the *public faith* is annexed to them, and must be supported."

I appeal to every man in the Union, whether this address, or rather dialogue, does not state *every fact* and *every argument*, *truly* and *fairly*; and whether such a statement of facts and arguments would be likely to *send the bearers home* contented and quiet, without their pay; I trow not. If the above statement is *not right*, I challenge *any body that can*, *to mend it*; for my part, I freely own my opinion, that the whole harangue, tho' ever so *well-dressed and polished*, is, and must be, from the *nature of the facts*, an *insult* not only on these worthy *citizens*, who rendered their supplies and services to their country during the war, but on *common sense itself*, and must *wound* the *natural feelings* of the humane mind, and which no man of honesty and candor could ever make in the *absence* of the parties, and which no man, who had any regard to *personal safety*, would dare to make in the *presence* of them.

The Orator's plan is, to consider the certificates delivered to the public creditors, on the settlement of their demands, for supplies and services rendered during the war, to consider these certificates, I say, as *full payment of the sum due to them*, and to *redeem* the certificates at full *nominal* value, by *payments* made to the *bearers* of them.

It is farther a most plain fact, that the certificates were not worth *more than 2s. 6d. in the pound*, at the time they were

were *delivered to the real public creditors*, on the final settlement of their accounts, after the close of the war.

And it is a farther plain fact, that by far the *greatest part* of these certificates have been sold by the original holders, in their necessities and distresses, to persons who are *now possessed* of them, *at* 2*s.* 6*d. in the pound*, or at most for some *trifle* which bears but small proportion to the *nominal value*.

Now this plan, *dress* it, and *cook* it, and *season* it, and *color* it in *any* and *every* way you possibly can, if carried into execution, will most *necessarily* and *unavoidably* draw after it these two consequences:

1. That a sum of *many millions* of money must be levied and collected from the *labor* and *painful earnings* of the citizens of the States, *not to be paid* to the *worthy citizens*, who, by their *supplies* and *services*, during their country's *distress*, have *merited* and *earned* it, but to be paid to numbers of rich *speculators*, who have *no pretence* of having *merited* or *earned* any of it, and who will, upon the *earnings of those others*, make a *profit immense*, not less in thousands of instances than 1000 *per cent*. Whilst,

2. The great bulk of the worthy citizens, who, by their supplies and services, *really* and *dearly merited* and *earned* the money, but who *have sold* their certificates (which is the case of by far the greatest part of them) must and will *absolutely and finally lose* 7-8*ths*, and very many *even eleven parts out of twelve*, of their *real merits* and *painful earnings*, from which *shameful* injustice, *Good Lord, deliver us.*

I beg leave here to ask the gentlemen who compose our supreme administration, legislative, executive, and official,

1. Whether they can possibly reconcile their own minds *to any plan* which involves such *gross injustice*?

2. Whether any of them could be prevailed on, at any time of their lives, on any consideration, to pay *a private debt of their own of* 20*s.* with a *certificate*, or any other *depreciated paper, worth but* 2*s.* 6*d.*?

3. Whether in heaven or earth (and farther we need not go) I say, whether in heaven or earth, there can be
found

found a *reason* which can *justify* a *minister of State*, or any *public man*, employed in the difpenfation of the *juftice and judgment* of a nation, in *devifing or doing* any thing, which, in his *perfonal* capacity, would *wound his honor* and *confcience*, and *damn* him to *eternal infamy and contempt*.

It is known to every body, that at the clofe of the war, our nation was *bankrupt;* at leaft they *ftopped payment*, could not, and did not, *do juftice* to thofe to whom they were *juftly indebted;* and if we could not pay them *when we ought,* the only way to heal and remedy the matter, is *to pay them when we can;* and it is mighty plain, if we *honeftly mean* to pay our debts, we muft not only pay the *whole money we owe,* but muft pay it to thofe *to whom we owe it;* for paying it to any *body elfe* can be no fatisfaction of the debt.

Nothing can be more abfurd than to apply the *common rule of affignments* of negotiable notes, bills of exchange, &c. to the public certificates; the exchange of the one rarely rifes or falls more than 4 *or* 5 *per cent.;* the depreciation of the other is 15 *or* 20 *times as much,* and is fo enormous, that the *principal value* is abforbed by it, and not more than 1-8*th or* 1-10*th part of the nominal value in reality remains;* here is an *extreme cafe* indeed, and it is well known that every *law, right,* or *rule of morality* is *limited to its mean or reafonable application;* the moment it diverges therefrom, and flies into *its extreme*, it lofes its *rectitude* and *equity*, and becomes *injurious and wrong;* and the fure and infallible *criterion* of fuch extreme, is when fuch application operates by way of *injuftice* and *deftruction of right*.

And in the cafe in point before us, the application of the common rule of affignments, to the certificates, has a neceffary operation, moft *cruel, injurious*, and *hurtful* in two refpects:

1. It takes an immenfe *fum* of money from *virtuous citizens*, *who dearly merited* and *earned it*, and fubjects them to a *total* and *ruinous* lofs; whilft,

2. It conveys the fame *immenfe fum* to *other men, who never merited or earned it all,* and gives them an *enormous profit*

profit of 1000 per cent. on the *merits and earnings* of the losers.

This whole doctrine is so perfectly known and familiar to all doctors in *law* and *morality*, that they have adopted it for a proverb or maxim, *summum jus, summa injuria*, i. e. *right in extreme* becomes *extreme wrong;* and nobody ever pretended to dispute this maxim, who was not either most poignantly pressed with argument (in which case the schoolmen will make any shifts) or hurried and impelled *by some favorite scheme or interest*, out of all their *philosophy, decency, and common sense*.

There is another plan or method of doing this business, which appears to me much more *just and equitable*, and quite *as easy* as the one I have been exploding, viz. Let *every certificate be estimated by a scale of value*, grounded on *the current price or exchange of it at its date, and at this value let it be debited to every public creditor who received it, and at the same value,** *or at the current value (as the case may require)*

---

* I apprehend that certificates should never be redeemed at a higher rate than their value or current exchange was at the time of issuing them; for the public never received a valuable consideration for any more than was paid; and to demand their redemption at a higher value would be charging the public with *usurious interest*, which would be as wrong between *public*, as between *private, contractors*.

It may be objected, perhaps, that the public do not *literally receive* 2s. 6d. and give their bond or certificate for 20s.: but I answer, they *really* do this; for it is very plain, that the certificate, when issued, was worth no more than its current exchange at that time, say 2s. 6d.: the public creditor received *no more*, and ought to be *debited with no more*; but the certificate is made payable to the *bearer, who is a stranger*, at 20s.

Now if I pay 2s. 6d. and, in consideration thereof, take a bond to a third *person, who is a stranger*, for 20s. it is plain that the *bond is usurious and void*, and if it *passes by assignment* thro' a thousand hands, the *usury* will always *stick* to it, and, of course, it will ever carry with it its *legal defect*, or *principle of avoidance*.

For it is plain, that if a private man should receive 2s. 6d. and give his bond for 20s. the bond would be usurious, and of course void.

My proposition is plainly just, and acknowledged by Congress and every body else, and has the sanction of general practice with respect to *loan-office certificates, Continental money*, &c. and I challenge any man to give a shadow of reason, why all *subsequent certificates*, or *paper of public credit*, should not be estimated, and in every respect be governed, by the same rule.

But if the certificate depreciates *below its original value*, the aggregate public *sustains the loss*. This is manifestly the case with respect to all paper money;

require) let it be redeemed, with interest from its date to the time of its redemption, and let *the remainder of the balances due to the public creditors, who have received certificates, be paid them in money with interest*, as soon as that can be done.

I know no reason why the real or current value of the certificates in question should not be fixed by a scale, as well as the loan-office certificates, and other depreciated public paper, during the war; this principle, as I before observed, was adopted not only by Congress, but by all the States, as a matter of both justice and necessity, and the tender-acts and other infringements of this plan, were found totally wrongful, and, of course, were repealed.

No human plan of dispensing commutative justice to a nation, can ever be perfect and wholly free from error; all that human wisdom and human virtue can do, is to adopt that plan, which, in its operation, shall produce *the most justice and right*, and the *least injury and wrong*, of any that can be devised, and carry the plan into effect by the most equitable *administration* which can be practised.

If this then is a good rule or criterion of a good plan (which certainly no man can seriously deny) let us try the two plans by this infallible touchstone, viz. which of them, in its operation, will produce the *most justice and utility*, and avoid the *greatest injury and wrong*.

1. The justice and utility of the one is reduced by its operation *to almost nothing*, whilst the *injuries* and *wrongs* it produces

money, certificates, and other public securities of every kind, which gain a general currency, or become objects of common exchange and negotiation thro' the community, and happen to depreciate during such currency.

The loss by depreciation becomes divided into *innumerable parts*, every *single one* of which consists of the *loss* each individual severally *sustained* by the depreciation of the paper, whilst *it was in his hands*, and the aggregate sum of all *these parts* or losses, makes up the *whole sum* of the depreciation, or the *difference* between the *current value* of the paper at the time, and the *original value* of it when it first issued.

By this it appears, that the aggregate public has sustained the whole loss, not in a way of perfect equality indeed (and perhaps no public assessment ever did or can do this) but by way of general tax, of which innumerable individuals (tho' not strictly every one) has sustained or paid his share, and, of course, it would be very unjust to tax the same public over again for such sum, not to pay it to the *persons who have suffered* by the depreciation, but to *other* people, who have *lost nothing*, nor have any *claim of merit* to it.

produces are *enormous, deteſtable,* and *almoſt infinite;* no leſs than depriving numberleſs citizens of 9-10*ths* of the reward due to their great *merits* and *ſervices,* and ſubjecting them to a *final* and *total loſs* of the ſame, whilſt it heaps the *immenſe wealth* (which is *their due,* and *which they lóſe*) on *another claſs* of men, who have *no pretence to any merit* at all.

2. The other plan gives to thoſe *meritorious citizens all the rewards* to which they are entitled, and if any injuſtice has been done them by the long delay, it is in ſome meaſure made up to them by the intereſt it propoſes to give them, whilſt it gives to the *purchaſers* of alienated certificates, the *ſame price* for them which they were *worth when firſt iſſued,* with *intereſt* from *that* time till their *redemption;* and I think this is all they have a right to expect, and we may very well ſay to each of them, *Take what is thine own with uſury, and more we will not give thee.*

If this claſs of men ſuſtain any loſs, it muſt ariſe from their having purchaſed certificates at a *higher exchange* or *price* than they bore when they were *firſt iſſued,* and this is a loſs to which ſpeculations of that ſort are *always expoſed;* if any of our rich and enterpriſing citizens are diſpoſed to *deal in ſtocks, gamble in the funds,* or to be concerned in any *negotiations of hazard* whatever, they all expect to be liable to a *run of ill luck,* as well as to *good fortune;* and I do not know that the public have much occaſion to trouble themſelves about either their profit or loſs.

But if the loſſes of theſe men ſhould be thought pitiable, they certainly, in either *magnitude* or *diſtreſs,* bear not the leaſt proportion to the *heavy, ruinous loſſes,* which our moſt *virtuous* and *meritorious citizens* muſt ſuſtain on *the other plan;* much leſs can they juſtify the adoption of a plan in their favor, which will *deprive* our moſt reſpectable citizens of the *immenſe ſums* due to their painful *merit* and *ſervices,* in order to *laviſh* the ſame away on theſe adventurous *ſpeculators,* and thereby accumulate the *fortunes of the one,* and the *diſtreſſes of the other,* to a degree almoſt infinite.

But

But after all, if the losses of these speculating gentry must be thought to require compensation, I beg it may be made by *the public*, but by no means let it be *carved out of the dear merits and earnings* of the *noblest patriots* of our country.

But the sacred duty of paying these worthy citizens, who have *done and suffered* so much for our country, and from whose *noble exertions* we actually derive and enjoy most *inestimable benefits*, is not only enforced on us by every *principle of justice, honor,* and *gratitude;* but it is farther recommended by many *advantages* and great *inducements of interest*, which are either involved in it, connected with it, or consequential from it. It may be proper here to mention some of these.

The *reverence and respect which we owe to general* Washington, *ought to induce us to pay with punctilious honor and justice, these his faithful followers and fellow-laborers;* it is known only to God, and the humane heart of that august commander, what *anguish of mind*, what *poignant sensibility of regret* and *compassion* occupied his breast, at the close of the war, when the exhausted finances of the country reduced him to the *dreadful necessity* of dismissing his faithful followers *without their pay*, and leaving them to find their way home as they could, without a shilling, either to *relieve the distresses of their families* on their return, or even to buy a cup of good liquor *to recruit their exhausted spirits*, or make their *meeting cheerful.*

It is known only to *God*, and to the *humane heart* of that august commander, how animated, how alive would be every *fine sensibility* of that great man, how dilated his *whole heart*, could he be informed that the *justice and gratitude* of his country would furnish the *reward* due to the virtues and merits of these *his worthy followers and supporters*.

With what a *suffusion of pleasure* would he *hasten* to find out these *noble spirits* in their retreats of *obscurity and distress*, extend to them the *welcome relief*, and sympathize in their *joy and gladness;* is it possible we should hesitate to indulge *a man we reverence and esteem* so highly, with this

gratification,

gratification, in which every *good heart* in our nation would sympathize, and which every *feeling of honor and compassion* strongly requires of us?

On the other hand, do you think he could bear a *disappointment in this*, with his usual equanimity? He can bear *hardships and dangers*, he can bear a *retreat* before his enemies, he can bear the *horrors of war*, and the *dreadful collisions of a battle*, he can bear the *joys and triumphs of victory*, he can bear *final and decided successes*, and he can bear the universal *applause, gratitude, and melting hearts* of his fellow-citizens; I say, he can bear all these with that *heroic strength of mind*, which, indeed, feels *every incident*, but can control *every passion into calmness and decency*.

But were he to see the *immense sum* of money due to his *companions and supporters, twice earned*, first by *their* toils and supplies, and then again by the *citizens at large*, out of whose *labor* the money was *carved and collected*, were he to see, I say, this *immense sum* all *swept away* into the coffers of those who never *earned any of it*, whilst his dear *companions* were left to lament, in *remediless despair*, the savage *injuries* of their country, the *disappointment of all their last expectations*, and the *hopeless ruin* of their *fortunes and families*; this, I think, would be too much for his *mighty fortitude* to sustain, would shake that FIRMNESS OF MIND, that great POWER OF SELF-COMMAND, which perhaps forms the most *inimitable part of his character*; and *what has he done*, that you should subject him to this *insupportable mortification*, this *agony* of sympathizing wo?*

I do

---

* When this Essay was written, I had not the least idea that any possible consideration could have induced general *Washington* to sign any act, which, in its operation, would cut his soldiers out of their pay, and leave those without compensation, who, by their advance of money and supplies, had fed and furnished his army; nor do I apprehend, that when he signed the funding bill, he conceived these effects would follow its operation: but I see two ways only, in which these effects can be avoided:

One is by *paying both* original creditors and speculators; which, I suppose, will be considered either extremely difficult or desperate, for want of cash.

The other is by a *repeal* of the funding act, or, which amounts to the same thing, by an *explanatory declaration* that by *public creditors*, in the act, is meant the *real, original creditors*, and not the *speculators*.

But

I do not mean by all this, to suggest that the *simple humor or caprice* of any individual, however dignified, ought to be the basis of any *public measure*, in which *national interests* are concerned; but where any man exists in a nation, whose long practice and example have demonstrated that all his *powers* are directed by *wisdom*, all his *passions* are controlled and governed by *discretion*, and every *action* excited and animated by *virtue and patriotism*, I say, to form public acts *agreeable to the wishes* of such a citizen, is paying court *to virtue itself*.

Whilst, at the same time, the government makes a very *high compliment* to the great body of the people, in supposing that *their minds* are all under the influence of a *similar virtue and patriotism*, and, of course, that it is highly proper to propose such an act to their *approbation, on full presumption* that a *public act*, dictated by the *wishes of such an illustrious citizen*, would certainly meet with a *co-incidence of sentiment in the people at large*, and, of course, must be equally *grateful to their wishes also*.

I do not offer this as *an airy compliment* to the citizens of the States; but I do *most seriously believe*, that the wishes of our august *general*, in the case before us, and those of *the great body* of our people, are the *same*, or at least, *similar:* the operations of the war being under the *direction* of the general, and the more important parts, both of *action and events*, happening under the *inspection of his own eye*, will doubtless excite in his mind more *lively sentiments* of *many things and circumstances*, than the people at large can have; yet I think the conduct of those worthy patriots who supported the war by their supplies and services, *meets the approbation of the people* in so universal a manner, that very few can be found, who would not sincerely join *their august general*, in wishes that they may be paid. This leads me to observe,

III. That *the patriots who supported the war* by their supplies and services, not only *ought to be*, but in fact *can be, paid*.

But be this as it will, I conceived it impossible for the general to sign such an act, and, of course, thought it would be great cruelty, and even insult, to offer such an one to him.

paid. Let their *merits* be ever so great, and our *obligations* to do them justice be ever so sacred, yet if our case was such that we *could not* pay them, no more need be said on the subject; but if we *can* pay them, and *do not*, one would think that *heaven and earth* would rise in their favor, and *revenge their wrongs*.

To prove that they can be paid, the following facts may, and doubtless will, be admitted to be *true and convincing evidence*.

1. That the *country is rich enough* to pay them: 2. That the *people are generally convinced*, that *the debt* demanded is *justly due to their merits and earnings*: 3. That they are *willing* to pay them: and, 4. That our *government, or supreme council, is also willing to pay them*, and *vigorously* to set on foot and pursue the *ways and means proper to effect it*.

1. That the country is *rich enough* to pay their deliverers, is too manifest to admit a doubt, or need any proof. It is easily demonstrated, that an additional impost on *imported luxuries* (such as spirits, wines, silks, jewellery, &c. &c.) but *barely high enough to reduce the consumption down to that moderate degree*, which is really necessary to the *health, wealth, and morality* of the inhabitants, would make our finances amply *sufficient* to pay every shilling we owe *to these worthy citizens*, and not this only, but also *to discharge every other debt which either honor, justice, or gratitude demands of us*.

2. That our people are generally *convinced* that the money demanded by these worthy citizens is *justly due to them*, is abundantly manifest from many considerations: 1st. They have *discernment enough to know* that a *debt justly due* will always be due *until it is paid*. That *long delay of payment* is no *extinguishment of a debt*. 2d. I believe their *genius* rises high enough to comprehend, that a *debt of* 20*s.* cannot *be paid and satisfied by a payment of* 2*s.* 6*d.* or, which amounts to the same thing, that *the whole is greater than a part*, or that 20 of any thing cannot be balanced or equalized by *an eighth part* of the same thing.

3. That

3. That our people at large are *universally willing* to pay these worthy citizens, is also very manifest.

1st. *The habits of morality are strongly impressed on our people in general.* The country is not old enough to establish *vice, oppression, and injury,* or to obliterate the natural *index of right and wrong,* in the human mind: in the old countries, the *luxury* of an *individual* may consume the *labor* of *thousands;* a *nation* may be taxed and oppressed to support the *lust, pride, and haughty grandeur of a few;* a court of inquisition may be instituted to *force the mind,* and *infringe the rights of conscience,* and *the people will bear it;* but with us *it is otherwise.*

In *America, oppressors* have not lost their *shame,* nor the *oppressed* their *resentment,* nor *the people* their natural *sense of good and evil;* when these worthy citizens exhibit their *merits and services,* show their *wounds,* and plead their *constitutions and fortunes broken in the cause of their country,* and *cry for their pay,* the general mind is instantly affected, a *sense* of both justice and compassion is strongly *excited,* and the universal *wish and murmur is,* ' *let right be done,*' and, ' why has it been so long *neglected and delayed?*'

2d. For the truth of the fact, I appeal to every man in the States, whether, within the circle of his acquaintance, there does not prevail a *general pity* for the soldiers and other liberal supporters of the war; *a decided opinion and high sense* that they have been *injured and ill used;* and a strong and sincere *wish* that they may be *paid:* as far as my acquaintance with my countrymen extends, this wish is almost universal, and if any exception can be found, I conceive it must be among *two classes* of people. 1. The *present holders of alienated certificates,* some of whom, I suppose, wish to *grab and secure* to themselves, the *rewards* due to the *merits and services* of these worthy patriots. 2. The other class are those who always *abhorred* both the *war* and *Revolution,* and are therefore well enough pleased to see all those who were concerned in *promoting both the one and the other,* most effectually *mortified and disappointed.* This leads us to consider,

T t   4. The

4. The *happy facility and ease with which our supreme council can adopt the measure of paying these worthy, injured citizens,* and put into most effectual operation the *ways and means* necessary to accomplish it; nobody doubts that this is the ardent *wish of their hearts,* or that they will *speedily adopt* the favorite measure, and vigorously support and push it to its *final effect,* and thereby demonstrate to the world, how strongly they are *animated and gratified with the pleasing task* of repairing the *wrongs of our injured citizens,* and restoring the *justice, honor, and dignity of our country.*

By large and repeated trials of the temper of our people, we find that they will *bear great pressures and burdens,* and will freely devote their *services and fortunes* for what they deem to be the *good* of their country, for *objects* which fall in with their *wishes,* and meet their *approbation;* this temper will enable government to institute any *proper modus of supply,* for the payment of our worthy patriots, when that very payment is the *favorite wish* of the people who are to pay the tax which is collected for that purpose.

Two different bodies of claimants now present their demands on government; these *worthy patriots* are one of them; and the *present holders* of alienated certificates are the other; it will require *equal sums* of money to pay either of them; the only question is, *which of them shall have it?* but I conceive, that the *difficulty* of raising the money for the payment of each of these, will not be by any means *equal,* but *extremely different.*

This brings into view another consideration, which, in the present state of our finances, appears to me of great moment; our revenue system is *young and tender,* and it is of great importance to introduce the *practice* of it, and get it formed into a sort of *habit* in the States as soon as possible; and this may require *delicate management;* if taxes are called for in *ways,* and for *purposes,* which are generally *approved,* the collection may be made with *little difficulty and few murmurs;* but if *immense sums* of money are demanded in ways that are *disgusting,* and for *purposes not generally approved,* and perhaps *abhorred,* the difficulties of
collection

collection will be *great*, and the *murmurs, infinite;* this may bring *embarrassments* on the revenue, which we may *long* feel very sad effects of. To apply this to the case before us—

A large impost laid purposely for the payment of the *real supporters of the war*, will meet the *approbation*, and coincide with the *wishes*, of the *great body* of our people, and, of course, the *collection* will be made with *ease and good humor;* but let our people be told that this *immense sum*, which is levied for that favorite purpose, when *carried* into the treasury, is not to be *given to those favorite patriots*, but is to be *grabbed* up by another class of men who have no pretence to either *service or merit*, but claim only what is due to the *merits and the services of the others*, I conceive, in this case, that all *good humor* will take its flight in an instant, and *murmurs plenty and sour* enough will ensue.

What effect such general murmurs, complaints, and discontents may have on the *revenue*, may be easily foreseen, and I should be glad to know, that these mischiefs would *end* with the revenue, without *extending* farther to disturb and derange the *general police* of the nation; the least mischief which can be expected from this general dissatisfaction may be, that it will furnish a plausible *excuse or plea for smugglers and those who wish* to *defraud* the revenue, viz. that there cannot be much harm in *eluding a tax* which is levied for the very purpose of *satisfying claims*, which are, in their nature, *wrongful*, and not grounded on any such *valuable considerations*, as the *laws of commutative justice* make essentially necessary to the existence of any *rightful transfer of property*.

I imagine it would be pretty much in vain for government to attempt to compose all this confusion, and pacify the general ill humor, by holding out an *old law of trade*, *or mercantile rule* (good enough, indeed, within its proper limits) but which is *racked and tortured* far beyond the *reach* and *influence* of that *reason*, on which alone all its *fitness and propriety* ever *did*, and ever *must*, *depend;* and which is *stretched* to such a degree of extravagance, as no

nation

nation under heaven ever thought of *adopting into practice*, and which no man of common sense can ever *reconcile* to that *natural sense of right*, which exists in his own mind; I mean the old law or usage of assignments.

I do not recollect more than two instances which ever happened in *Europe*, of stock, bills, or certificates (for they are all different names for the same thing) of such magnitude as to *affect national credit*, the variations of exchange of which ever were so great as from par to 8 for 1; these two instances were, the *Mississippi scheme in France*, in 1719; and the *South-Sea scheme in England*, in 1721.*

These

---

* In the original publication of this Essay, the following short account of the *South-Sea scheme* in *England* was inserted by way of preface, viz.

"The *South-Sea scheme* in *England* affords us the only instance I ever heard of in that country, of any national stocks or funds, whose fluctuation or exchange ever varied, *i. e.* rose or fell, so much as from par to 8 for 1, or, vice versa, from 8 for 1 to par.

"National stocks or funds I call them, not because those stocks were properly *public money*, but because they were of such *magnitude and extent* as to affect the *trade and credit* of the nation, and were managed under the *sanction and protection of national authority*, and controlled by the inspection *of Parliament*.

"The *South-Sea Company* was *incorporated* by act of Parliament, *in 1711*, *i. e.* a great number of proprietors of *navy bills, debentures, and other public securities*, were incorporated into a Company, to which was given a great variety of *duties on wines*, tobacco, India *goods, &c.* to pay the annual *interest* due to them, amounting to above *half a million* sterling; and also, with this grant was joined a grant of a monopoly of the trade to *Spanish South-America*, grounded on the *Assiento* treaty, *&c.*

"This Company soon grew amazingly rich, had the King and most other capital personages for stock-holders, and, in 1718, *his Majesty himself* was chosen their *Governor*; at which time, the Company was become the great favorite of the court and nation, and, in 1720, were in such good condition, that 100*l.* share *of their stock* was worth 130*l. i. e.* 30 per cent. above par.

"At this time, *i. e.* in 1720, the scheme of reducing all the *public funds into one*, for discharging the national debt (which, by the by, at that time was alarming enough) *was set* on foot.

"The *South-Sea Company* and *Bank of England* were competitors, and bid on one another for the privilege of taking in the *national debts*, and thereby increasing their *capital stock* and *yearly fund*. The offer of the Company to Parliament for this privilege, was above 7,000,000*l.* sterling, &c. which was more than the Bank would give, and, of course, was accepted and ratified by an act of Parliament.

"Having thus carried their point, the next thing was *to go to work*, and make the most of their privilege, which was generally thought *so great*, that their stocks rose from 130 to 330*l.* for a share of 100*l.* by the time their contract with Parliament was completed.

The

These were both established and authenticated by *acts of the supreme legislature;* acted under the *inspection and control*

"The first thing they had to do, was to purchase in *the public securities*, which they were able to do on pretty favorable terms; for the *Revolution*, and the *wars* of King *William* and Queen *Anne*, had raised the national debt to about 40,000,000*l.* sterling (if I remember right) which was in those days thought a very alarming sum (tho' the nation have learned better since) of course, the credit of the public debts was somewhat *doubtful;* and as the stock of the *South-Sea Bank* or *Company* was *in the first credit*, the proprietors of the public securities thought themselves *happy to carry in and sell* their public securities, on such terms as they and the Company could agree on. Above 26,000,000*l.* sterling was subscribed into the *South-Sea* stock, in this manner.

"In short, the Company opened their books and sold out stock to an immense amount, and to a profit from 300 to 1000 per cent. Their first subscription was for 1,000,000 at 300*l.* *April* 12, 1720; and the stock rose so fast, that on the 24th of *August* following, the books were opened for a subscription of 1,000,000 capital stock, at 1000*l.* for every 100*l.* capital stock, which was filled in *three hours;* such was *the rage* for that sort of speculating, at that time. And, what is *more amazing*, after the books were closed, in the afternoon of the same day, this *same subscription* was sold in *Change-Alley* at 30 or 40 *per cent. advance.*

"The cash and credits of the Company were vastly accumulated by this time; and as they lent millions on interest, and sold most of their stocks for about 1-5th cash in hand, the rest on credit at several future payments, the debts due to them were immense.

"When the bubble burst, as it did in less than six months after, and the stock the subscribers had purchased at 1000 per cent. was reduced down to about 150, and, of course, the loss of every such subscriber was 850*l.* out of every 1000*l.* subscribed; I say, when this happened, legal suits (of which very many were commenced) for these debts due to the Company, would have reduced most of the monied men in the kingdom to a state of remediless bankruptcy, and the Company must have lost most of their money in the bargain. The public creditors had lost most of their public securities, which they had subscribed into that fund. And infinite other mischiefs of a like nature must have accrued, of a kind most ruinous and wrong, and of an amount so great as to affect national interest, honor, and credit, and of such an extreme and extraordinary nature, that no ordinary rules of law could be applied in any such manner as to afford the least remedy, but would rather increase the evil, and give the wrong a kind of sanction of law.

"In *this extreme case*, the Parliament found themselves under an absolute necessity of assuming the powers of *sovereign equity*, and, as *supreme chancellors* of the kingdom, to *supersede* the ordinary *rules of the law*, control its *force*, soften its *rigor*, and adopt such *equitable principles*, as would afford *some remedy of an evil, an injury, a wrong,* of such magnitude, as brought the *justice, credit,* and *safety* of the nation into danger.

"On this principle they *suspended law-suits;* annulled *special bails;* discharged numberless *debtors who owed for stock*, on paying 10 *per cent. of their debts;* compelled *compensations* in favor of the sufferers; forced *dividends and appropriations* of the stock of the Company; and even *punished* many for mismanagement, who seemed to have conformed themselves to the letter of the law, &c. &c.

"Vide *Tindal*'s Continuation of *Rapin*, in the pages referred to in the index, under the words, *South-Sea Trade and Company.*"

[334]

trol of it; were the *channels* thro' which the *public monies* were circulated; and the *final accounts of both* were settled and adjusted under the *direction and authority* of the same *supreme power* of the respective nations. These schemes were so extensive as to affect national interests; most of the monied men in both nations were deeply concerned in them, and when the *enormous and ruinous effects* of that great *variation of exchange,* which these stocks suffered, came to be *be generally felt,* applications without number were made to government for relief.

Very strong remonstrances were made against the interference of the legislature, and that the matter should be left to the course of common law, *i. e.* to be decided according to the common rule of assignments of all negotiable notes, bonds, &c. But on a close inspection of the matter, it was soon clearly seen, that the variation of exchange of these stocks (or their depreciation, as we call it) was so *enormous and extreme,* that any application of the *ordinary rules of law and practice* to them, would produce the most *ruinous injustice and wrongs,* and, of course, every idea of *that mode of settlement and adjustment* was instantly given up.

Their great principle was, that justice and right was the *grand end* of law, and paramount to any *particular rules or established practice,* and, of course, ought to *control them* in all cases of so *extreme* and *extraordinary a kind,* as could not fall within *the reason on which those rules were founded,* but so circumstanced, as that an application of these *common rules* would *unavoidably* produce such *injury and wrong,* as was totally *destructive of all that right* which was the essential *principle and end* of all law.

Upon full consideration of all this, by an act of *sovereignty* they adopted the most *equitable principles,* which they could devise in those great confusions, which would apply to the *particular cases* that lay before them, and which would, in their operation, produce the *most right and avoid all wrong,* in the best manner they could think of.

The *English* House of Commons went so far as to *suspend all judgments and executions* recovered upon any contract,

tract, for *sale or purchase of any stock* or subscription, and also ordered that all persons, who had become *indebted* to the Company for South-Sea *stock, &c.* should, on *payment of* 10 *per cent.* be *discharged* from any farther demands. They made many other resolutions (which were afterwards made acts of parliament) totally *repugnant* to the *common rules of law and practice*, but absolutely *necessary* to be adopted in those *extreme cases*, to which these common *rules* could not be *applied* without the most manifest and ruinous *wrongs* and *injustice;* wrongs of such magnitude as to affect the *trade* and *credit of the nation*, as well as to bring remediless *ruin on* thousands of *individuals*, and, at the same time, heap *immense fortunes* on others who had never *deserved them.*

I know very well that great pains were taken in *France*, to throw much *odium and blame on* mr. Law, and to make him chargeable with the great and ruinous mischiefs of the *Mississippi scheme;* and the same industry was used in *England*, to cast *blame on the directors of the South-Sea Company*, and to father the pernicious consequences of that scheme on their corruption and mismanagement.

But tho' it may be probable enough, that in schemes of that vast magnitude and national interest, *faults in the management* might be found, which are always made to rest on the *prime movers and directors* of them, yet the *most capital and destructive mischiefs sprung from the nature of the schemes themselves*, and would necessarily happen (tho', perhaps, not in every possible excess and aggravation) if the *same plans were to be set on foot a thousand times* over.

But as these schemes were established under the *sanction of the Legislature*, in the fullest manner that could be devised, it was not *quite decent to admit* in the national assemblies, that their *mischiefs flowed from their nature*, but the blame must be thrown on somebody, as some *stupid committees,* in the late times, attributed the *depreciation* of the Continental money *to the merchants.*

This, to be sure, in *England*, was natural enough, where they adopt this principle, that when popular discontents rise very high, *one man must die for the people, i. e.* one or

more

'more victims must be sacrificed, like scape-goats, to appease the people, and thereby *parry the resentment* due to the *minister*, or *prince*, or *Parliament*, or *other principal*, from whose *folly* or *misconduct* the mischief originally proceeded; witness, admiral *Byng*, and many others.

But let the mischief originate wherever it might, the grand object of attention was *a remedy*, and this, doubtless, engrossed and occupied the whole wisdom of the legislatures and the respective nations, at the time; for whilst their great interests, both *national* and *individual*, were rapidly melting down under the fatal influence of these *destructive schemes*, even *supreme councils* were willing to *hearken to advice*; and, therefore, we may well presume that we have an *example of the most consummate national wisdom* that could be collected, in the *modes of remedy* which they adopted.

Nor does any body suppose that one man in *England* expects that *their national debt* will ever be paid *at par*, tho' the present discount or depreciation is but *about* 25 *per cent.*; or that *more interest* will be paid than the *real value* of these stocks or certificates require; the *present interest* paid on them being 3 or 3½ *per cent.* whilst the *common interest* of that country is 5 per cent.

I do not pretend to refer to any thing, which might be done in the old days of barbarity and ignorance; but I do not recollect having ever heard of one modern prince or State in *Europe*, who ever attempted to pay *his soldiers or other public creditors*, in *certificates*, or stocks, or negotiable securities of any sort; except when such payment made *a part of the original contract*, as the contracts for navy supplies are payable in navy bills, &c. All that I know, which is at all like it, is paying armies, &c. with *base coin*, which some princes have done; but this was a *State-cheat* universally detested; nor could all the authority of such prince ever give such base coin a currency beyond its *real value*; nor did I ever hear of much it being called in and redeemed at *full nominal value*.

This I take to be the practice of the nations of *Europe*, in cases similar to the one I am pleading; and, I think, a very little discretion on our part might induce us to imitate
their

their prudence and virtue, profit by their example, and avoid their errors.

But it may, perhaps, be more important to our internal quiet, to advert to what has been the practice of our own States in similar cases; for *any innovations*, or *departure from known usages and customs among ourselves*, may give more dissatisfaction to our people, than any deviation from *European* practices, which, tho' perhaps *equally wise*, yet are *less known* and considered among us, than our own.

The *loan-office certificates* issued by our own supreme council during the war, are all *estimated by a scale*, the principle of which is the value of them at the time of their dates; the *value of our Continental and State money* has been estimated by either the general *scale of Congress*, or that of *particular States;* this method was indeed neglected too long, but was at last fully adopted, upon the plainest reason and most urgent necessity; and when our *Continental* and *State* money depreciated down to nothing, *it all died where it was;* nobody ever thought of *appreciating it* again, by a redemption at its *original value*.

The *Old Tenor and other bills* which had a currency in many of the States long before the Revolution, were redeemed at their *current exchange*, without the least regard to their *nominal value*.

And can any possible reason be given, why we should adopt *an innovation* (proposed and urged by many) respecting *the certificates in question*, which is a *total departure* from the constant practice of all the States *before, at, and since the Revolution*, in all cases of *similar reason;* an *innovation*, which, by its natural and necessary operation, must and will not only produce *immense and ruinous wrong* to numberless individuals of most *deserving citizens*, but will also disgrace and disparage our *public credit*, honor, and dignity, and discourage the *confidence* of our *own citizens and foreigners* in our *national justice and morality?*

Indeed, the *ordinary rules* of law would do infinite *mischief and injustice*, were not the *rigor* of them to be *softened and corrected by chancery;* the powers of chancery ought always to *control the common law*, whenever, in any case,

U u

the application of the ordinary rules of law will manifestly destroy *right and justice*, or work *a wrong;* for law is certainly *perverted and needs correction*, whenever it destroys *right*, or does *wrong*.

The supreme power of every State is the *supreme chancery* of it, and always hath, and must have, *sovereign authority* to *repeal*, to *limit*, or *control* every rule of law; and *may, and ought* to, do it, whenever that rule operates by way of *destruction* or *defalcation of right*, or producing of *wrong*, for *justice and security of right* can never be *perfect*, or even *tolerable*, in any State, without the *existence* of this power, and the *prudent exercise* of it.

When all the foregoing *reasons*, the *practice* of all our own *particular States*, and also, that of our own *supreme council*, as well as that of all the *States of Europe*, in similar cases, as far as their practice is known to us; I say, when all these things are duly considered, I think my great conclusion will be admitted very readily, viz.

That our most deserving and patriotic citizens (whose cause I have been advocating) *must be paid;* that the *wishes* of our own citizens require it; that our *character* of honor and justice, both at home and abroad, requires it; and that we shall be deemed by the nations of *Europe*, the veriest *novices* in policy and finance, as well as *knaves* in practice, if we do not do it.

I will subjoin one short observation here, because I think it of great importance, viz. it is the great interest, duty, and honor of every government, not only *to pay their contracts* honestly and in good season, but also to grant *proper compensations* to all their citizens, who, by *patriotic exertions*, deserve the *notice* and *rewards* of their country; this will enable government at all times to command every *possible exertion* of their people, either in the way of *services or supplies*, and will induce them to hasten with cheerfulness and pride, to *offer to government any thing they have or can produce*, which the public service stands in need of.

Whereas, if these noble spirits find themselves *neglected and forgotten*, and that in their country's service they have

labored

labored in vain, and *spent their strength for nought*, their zeal for the public service will become *very languid*, and not only so, but the *example of their disappointment* will operate by way of *great discouragement* of their neighbours. *Nothing animates and keeps up the spirit and good-humor* of a nation so effectually, as a *full confidence* in the *justice and gratitude* of its government; and this is the *deepest and firmest* foundation on which the *wealth*, the *peace*, the *honor*, and the *establishment* of a nation can be built.

For this great purpose, *excessive and extravagant allowances* are by no means necessary, but are *even criminal*, when the finances are *low* and *straitened*, for we ought, at least, to be *just* before we are *generous*; the *honor* of the service and the *acceptance* of government, are the grand *inducements to noble, patriotic actions; and moderate compensations*, adequate to the services and merits, will be perfectly satisfactory; *more than enough* need not be given to any one, for that will make it necessary to give *less than enough* to some other.

On the whole, raising the great sums of money necessary to satisfy all the *real public creditors*, will, under proper *management*, be no *great burden* to the States; the levying them as fast as the honor and justice of the States require, will *not impoverish* them. Large sums *collected* from the body of the nation, if they are *paid out* again and *distributed* over the same nation, especially if the collection is principally made from the *richer sort*, and the payments made to the *poorer sort* (which will be the case, on the plan I propose) this tax, I say, will rather prove a *benefit* than a *burden*.

It will increase the *circulation* of cash; it will stimulate *industry*; it will enable thousands *to pay their debts*, who otherwise could not do it; and, of course, it will enable thousands *to receive the debts due to them*, who must otherwise lose them; it will enable very many *poor* to support themselves, who otherwise would be a *burden on the public or private charity*; it would tend to *equalize* the wealth of the community, by giving every one his due portion of it; and

and thereby prevent the riches of the country from *accumulating in few hands*, &c. &c.*

These are no small advantages resulting from taxation; and, I think, *their effects* on the nation at large will compensate *the burden* of it, and probably yield a *balance of advantage*; especially if the tax should be levied by an *impost on imported luxuries*, and thereby *lessen the consumption* of useless and hurtful articles; which would operate to the *benefit* of the community, even if the *money* produced by the tax was all *thrown into the sea*.

This mode of taxation may easily be made adequate to all the exigencies of the State, and leave no occasion of reverting to either an *excise* or *direct taxation*, both of which will be much more *difficult* in their assessment, more *expensive* in the collection, more *disgusting* in the mode of demand, more *burdensome* to the subject, less *equable* in pressure, and much more *uncertain* in the product.

I now, with the utmost confidence, submit it to the *heart*, to the *feelings*, and to the *conscience*, of every citizen of the States, that I have exhibited proofs, not barely sufficient

---

* It is here very worthy of notice, that these salutary effects will *naturally and surely* flow from *my plan* of paying the public monies to the *real, original creditors*, who are scattered over all the States; and payment to *them* will, of course, not only afford such relief as will be highly convenient to them and their neighbours, but will also produce such a brisk circulation of the money so paid, as will be greatly beneficial to the whole nation.

Not so, but in a manner *widely different*, will be the operation of the *scheme* of paying these monies to the *speculators*; about one-third of whom, I am told, are *foreigners*, who will carry their share of the money *out of the country, never to return again*; and the other two-thirds, if paid to the speculators here, will not probably produce any general increase of *circulation* of money, or *other benefit* to the public.

For money obtained by *sudden acquirement*, without *industry, merit, or earnings*, seldom proves any *benefit* either to the *possessors* or to the *public*, but generally produces *luxury, vanity, pride*, and hurtful example of *prodigality and waste*, till the whole is *expended*, and then the poor *objects* and *their families* are left much *more forlorn and distressed* than they would probably have been, had the money never have come into their hands.

I think any body may observe the very *different effects and operations* of these two plans, and it appears to me, that *little penetration* will be necessary to discern that the *gain* lies on the side of *godliness*; and, of course, if we *reject the right*, with so *many benefits* annexed, and *adopt the wrong*, with such a train of *mischiefs* at the heels of it, however our *integrity* may be unimpeached, our *wisdom* will be *doubted*, and will appear to many people altogether *inadequate* to the management of the finances of a nation.

sufficient for full conviction, but so plain, that any person must put violence on himself, who will not be convinced,

I. That the real public creditors, whose cause I am pleading, *have not yet been paid;* this is as plain as that 20*s.* is more than 2*s.* 6*d.*

II. That *they ought to be paid,* with the first monies we can get; this is as plain as that " the laborer is worthy of his hire," or, that contracts made on valuable consideration given, ought to be fulfilled.

III. That I have exhibited such a statement of our finances or resources of supply, as demonstrates that *they can be paid;* that the payment of them would not be *a burden or distress* on the country, but rather a *benefit,* a manifest *advantage,* to our people at large: and,

IV. That from most essential considerations of public justice and honor, of national character, both abroad and at home, and of the internal peace and establishment of our nation, it follows most clearly, that *they must be paid.*

I do not know any thing farther necessary or that can be done, but to give this Essay some inscription, which may direct it to some *particular attention;* for that which is offered to the *public at large,* is generally considered as *every body's business,* and so is apt to be in fact *nobody's,* and, of course, becomes *neglected.*

As I mean, in this Essay, to plead the cause of national justice, I wish to address it to Congress, and beg the patronage of that august body;

Not merely because they are the *fountain of national justice,* and their decisions alone can administer *the remedy* which I solicit; but also,

Because many very respectable personages, who now compose that supreme council, were, during the war, either concerned in the *most capital public transactions* in the cabinet, or were *officers of most distinguished rank in the army;* and therefore, by near inspection, were enabled to *judge in the best manner,* not only of the *importance* of the *merits and services* herein urged; but also of the *spirit, fidelity, and patriotism,* with which they were rendered to the public; and also,

Because

Becaufe I wifh to fet up the *claim* of thefe *worthy, deferving patriots*, along fide of *that* of the prefent *holders of certificates*, who (I am told) have prefented their *petition to Congrefs*, in which they count very largely on the *merits, fervices, and fufferings* of thefe worthy citizens, of which they exhibit *pathetic and very moving defcriptions*, but after all, very *modeftly* requeft, that *the money due* to thefe very meritorious *citizens*, may be paid *to themfelves*.

I think, I can introduce my friends at leaft under the advantage of *old acquaintances;* whereas the others, I conceive, are moftly *new faces*.

I have great confidence, that my plea for citizens of fuch merit and refpectability, will meet at leaft the *attention*, if not the *approbation and patronage*, of Congrefs.

But after all, if it fhould be the final determination (which I cannot fuppofe) that the certificates fhall be confidered *as full payment* to thofe who received them, and that nothing is now due *to any* but to the *poffeffors of thofe certificates*, I have one more motion to make, viz. that the *original holders* of thefe certificates fhould be *preferred and firft paid*, as claiming payment of debts of an *higher nature*, and grounded on *greater merit*, than the others can pretend to.*

I know

---

* Congrefs, in their laft feffion, after long debate, *rejected the whole plan of difcrimination* between the *original creditors* or holders of certificates, and the *fpeculators* or the holders of *alienated certificates*, and, without *any diftinction*, admitted alike the claims of all the prefent poffeffors, and, by their funding act of *Auguft* 4, 1790, funded all the certificates at full value, or 20*s.* in the pound, with intereft payable quarterly on two-thirds of their amount, from the firft day of *January*, 1791; and the other third, with intereft to commence the firft of the year 1801, or ten years from faid *January* 1.

The certificates for intereft, called *indents*, are excepted out of this provifion, and are funded at an intereft of 3 per cent. only.

By this act, an *enormous fum of the public money* is appropriated for the payment of fpeculators, who never *earned it*, nor pretend to hold out any fort of *right* to it, which is founded on *their merits*, or *earnings*, or *valuable confideration paid*, but claim it entirely in *right of others*, to whofe *merits* and *earnings* the money was righteoufly due, and which they make title to merely by force of the *common rule of affignments*, which, it appears to me, cannot admit any *reafonable application* to this cafe.

Whether it is the defign of Congrefs, by this ftatute, to *cut the real, original creditors off* from their pay of *that part* of the balances which they have
never

I know that Congress, like all other similar bodies of supreme authority, must necessarily have a great variety of important, different, and sometimes, contending interests, referred to their decision; and, of course, the several parties will use all possible *arts, address, and influence* in their power, to *bend* the mind of that august body to their several wishes.

It is very difficult for any body of men, thus beset and surrounded (if they have any passions or prejudices at all) to pursue a course *perfectly direct*, and *free from error;* yet so very important and consequential is *every decision* they make, and every *measure* they adopt, that the *fate of millions* hangs on their lips, and the *fortune of millions* is balanced by the *motion of their hands*.

Therefore, under a due impression and sense of both the *difficulty* and *importance* of their *stations, councils,* and *actions,* all good men ought to be *candid in their opinions, moderate* in their *censures,* and very *zealous* and *sincere* in their *prayers* that Almighty God would, in all their difficult consultations, give them that *wisdom* which may *direct and lead* them to such decisions as may be conformable to natural *right* and *justice,* conduce to his *glory,* and establish the *peace, happiness, security,* and *best good* of our country.

---

never yet received (and which, I suppose, is yet *justly due* to them) I know not; but I take it, that this is the light in which it is *generally understood*.

If this is really the case (which I cannot yet believe) I have only to lament that all the *arguments* I have published, which appear to me to be very *strong, clear, and conclusive,* and all the *concern* I have felt for this great subject, are vain and fruitless, and I suppose I ought to set myself down as *an idiot,* stupid as a post, because I cannot perceive an iota of *reason or justice* in a measure, which appeared to Congress so *clear* and *just,* as to induce them to adopt it in a *solemn, public act:* or may I rather be indulged in the thought that a *Prince,* a *Diet,* a *Parliament,* a *Congress,* an *Assembly,* however *high in dignity,* and however *important* to mankind their *decisions* are, may err, and, what is more, may, on revision, be convinced of their error, and—correct it?

———*Facilis descensus Averni:*
Noctes atque dies patet atri janua Ditis;
Sed revocare gradum, superasque evadere ad auras,
Hoc opus! hic labor est!——— VIRGIL.

A REVIEW

A REVIEW

OF THE

PRINCIPLES AND ARGUMENTS

Of the two foregoing ESSAYS, viz.

The Seventh Essay on Finance, and *The Plea for the Poor Soldiers;*

WITH SOME

OBSERVATIONS

ON THE

FINANCES of the UNION.

I. THE *finances* or *management of the stock or revenue* of every State or individual, from the *greatest Empire* down to the *least Republic*, from the highest *company* to the lowest *partnership*, from the richest *landholder* or *merchant* to the poorest *peasant* or *pedlar*, determines their *fortune or fate*, is the *great principle* out of which their *peace* and *plenty*, or their *embarrassment* and *straits*, must grow, and from which must proceed their *final honors* and *success*, or their *disgrace* and *ruin*.

This subject, of course, becomes an object of most *capital concern*, and ought to be an object of *first consideration*, both of every community and also of every individual.

Therefore,

Therefore, when any plan, either of political manœuvre in a nation, or bufinefs in leffer communities or individuals, is in contemplation, *to count the coft* becomes an indifpenfable part of the deliberations.

And when the coft is properly computed or counted, the next thing is, to look out for and find *revenues or incomes fufficient to pay it.*

An *error* in either of thefe, *i. e.* a *wild calculation of the expenfe* of any propofed plan, or a wild and deficient *eftimate* of the income or revenue fufficient to pay it, is the common and ufual *caufe of bankruptcy, breach of faith,* and *lofs of credit,* in both the one and the other, and of all the difgraces, embarraffments, and other ruinous confequences which muft flow therefrom.

II. The *capital ftock* of a nation or individual *is the wealth each poffeffes,* and the *refources* which are with certainty *within their power;* but the more proper and fafe way of computing the ftock is rather by the *yearly income or revenue,* than by the *capital;* becaufe if the annual expenditures exceed the annual incomes, the *capital ftock* muft be *left in debt* at the end of the year, which, if continued, muft foon produce *embarraffments* and *ftraits,* and even *bankruptcy* in the end.

It often happens that much valuable property is fo conditioned, that it will not produce any *yearly income,* or, at moft, not any that is adequate to the intereft of its value; therefore, it would be very imprudent for a nation or individual to make calculations of *yearly expenditures,* grounded on *fuch eftates,* for they will fail of fupply otherwife than *by way of mortgage,* which ought to be avoided as a *laft,* becaufe it is a *fatal, refort.*

III. But let the ftock or finance of a nation or individual be ever fo good and affluent, yet *every advantage* of it muft and ever will *arife* from, and be *limited* by, the *juftice, honefty,* and *truth, with which it is negotiated or adminiftered. Honeft payment* of *juft debts,* and *fulfilment of contracts,* are moft effentially neceffary to give either a nation or individual the *command and control of all the fupplies and services,*

services, which can be furnished within the circle of their influence.

For all persons will *hasten with eagerness* to render all supplies and services in their power to an *honest, grateful paymaster*, and will *avoid, with a proportionate reluctance,* furnishing either the one or the other to a *dishonest, dilatory, or trickish* paymaster.

And, of course, all supplies and services, in the *one case*, will be obtained in the *easiest, quickest* manner, and will be executed and rendered in the *highest perfection* (as there will be *choice* of materials, stores, and workmen) and in the *cheapest way*, and at the *lowest rates*.

But, in the *other case*, both the supplies and services will be *embarrassed* in their *acquirement*, will be executed and rendered in *deficient manner*, and at very *high prices*; for every one is loth to deal with a *bad paymaster*, nor will suffer himself to be *engaged* or *employed* by him, unless he is impelled by *some urgent necessity*, or *induced* by the *offer of very high price*, or *great emoluments*.

IV. *Economy and prudence in expenditures* is absolutely necessary to the obtainment of the great *advantages and benefits* of the *revenue or national stock*; without this, that *justice and honesty* in the management of the revenue can never be practised, which is essentially necessary to its ends and uses: for if the revenue or stock is *wasted* by *needless expenses*, those which are *necessary* must be *unprovided* for; if large, *fictitious*, and *groundless demands* are *accepted* and paid, debts which are by *honor, contract*, and *real merits, justly due*, must lie *unpaid*.

This operates not only to the *great injury* of the *real creditors*, but also to the *embarrassment* of the *whole community*; for *every branch* of business in the nation *stands connected* with the *public finance*, as the *public debts* are great and extensive objects of *dependence* and *exchange*, and, of course, any *disappointment* in these will generate *innumerable disappointments* in the course of currency thro' which they ought to pass; and, of course, will either *directly or remotely affect* every branch of business.

We have had late and large proof of this kind of vexation, in the numberless instances of persons who could not carry on their business, or pay their debts, because they were disappointed of receiving monies due to them by the public: such a mode of financiering as this will ruin any nation in the world.

The foregoing propositions and remarks I consider as *maxims* or *first principles*, which force the assent of the mind *at first sight*, by a kind of *intuitive proof* or *instant perception*, and which nobody will ever think of *disputing*, much less of *denying;* I therefore premise them like *axioms*, on which I may safely proceed to build *any doctrines or plans* which really rest on these foundations, or come within their essential principles and reasons.—I go on now with my Review of the Principles and Arguments of the two foregoing Essays.

The great principles of the two foregoing Essays are comprised in the following propositions:

I. *That all certificates delivered to the public creditors, ought to be placed to the debit of their account,* at the *value or exchange of them at the time they received them,* and the *remainder or residue of the debt due to them, ought to be paid to them with interest;* and that *all certificates,* when brought into the treasury, *ought to be paid to the bearer,* whether an *original holder or alienee,* at the *value or exchange, which each of them bore at the time of its date,* or at the *current exchange at the time of redemption,* as the case may require. If this cannot be admitted, my second proposition is,

II. To pay *all certificates brought in by the original holders,* at *full nominal value, with interest;* and to pay *all the alienated certificates* at the *value or exchange they bore at their dates,* or at the *time of redemption,* as the case may require. If this cannot be admitted, I propose,

III. That the *original holders be first paid,* and the *speculators, last of all,* if they must be paid at all.

The great principle or substance of my argument is, that *the public money ought to be paid to the real, original creditors,* who, by rendering *supplies and services* to the country, have *really, meritoriously, and painfully earned it:* for,

1. Their

1. Their demand is founded on the *most solemn contract of Congress*, who had *good right to make such contract*, which *binds the honor, the morality, and justice of the country*, and nothing but *payment* can discharge the country from the *guilt of injustice*, and *violation of faith* and *truth* most *solemnly* plighted to them.

2. They *fulfilled* the whole of said solemn contract virtuously, honestly, and very painfully *on their parts*, and therefore, on every principle of *merit* and *earning, are entitled* to their pay.

3. The *infinite benefits* we derive from that *contract* and their faithful *fulfilment* of it, afford *another argument* why we should pay them: we cannot *honestly* enjoy the *benefit* of any *man's labor*, without paying him his *hire;* it is to the supplies and services of these men, that we are indebted for *our country, our lives, our estates, our liberty*, and *our independence*, and all the blessings of a *free government*, uncontrolled and unbiassed by any *foreign* power or influence; and it ought not to be thought *possible*, that such an *American government*, which derives its *existence* from the *exertions*, the *travails*, and *persevering virtue* of these *patriots*, should, by a public act, *deny* them their *pay*, their *hire*, their *reward*, for merits which have been so *beneficial* to us, and *painful* to them; or should suffer *any how* the *public money*, carved out of the wealth and earnings of our citizens for the *very purpose* of paying these worthy patriots, to be *diverted* from this desirable object, or to be *applied* to any *other* purpose whatever.

4. The heart-moving and unparallelled distresses of very many *thousands* of these worthy patriots for *want of their pay*, is another cogent reason why they should *be paid:* I do not say, that the *benefits* we receive from their merits, or the *distresses* they suffer from our breach of faith and promise in denying them their pay, *increase* or *alter* the *stipulations of their contract;* but both have a *strong effect* on the *gratitude,* the *benevolence,* and *compassion* of the human mind, which are virtues of such *precious* and *primary* consideration in society, that, I think, no government ought to be *callous* to their *influence*, or *hardened* into an *insensibility*

lity of their force. We all think it worse to refuse a laborer his hire, when he and his family must *starve and perish* for want of it, than to deny payment of an equal sum to a rich man, who had an *equally just demand*, but whose fortune would enable him to bear the loss *without pain.*

5. These original creditors have *not yet been paid*, but in *small* part, and therefore the *remaining balance* is still due to them, and *ought* to be paid. Nobody pretends they have ever received *any payment* but *negotiable certificates* made payable to the *bearer*, and worth on average, when they received them, about 2*s.* 6*d. in the pound;* these certificates, I say, ought to be debited to them at *their value or current exchange* when they *received* them; *so much* they have received, and *no more;* and the residue of balance due to them ought to be paid to them.

I have attended to all the debates on this great subject, both public and private, which have fell in my way, but I do not recollect one person who ever seriously insisted, that the certificates delivered to the public creditors were *full payment of the debt due to them;* but this notwithstanding, I have heard *many objections*, silly and nugatory enough, strongly urged against making any further payment to those who had sold their certificates.

1. One was, that if they had not sold their *debt*, they had sold the *evidence of it*, and so could have *no further demand:* this is *not true;* the *evidence* of the debt is *the public books*, where their accounts are *adjusted*, and the *balance* due to them is *entered;* and nothing can justly be objected to this but some evidence that the debt *has been paid;* which evidence, the *certificate*, if produced, could not supply. Further, the *certificate*, if produced, could not be so *good* evidence as the *public books;* for the one might be *counterfeit*, the other *could not be:* suppose a man brings suit on a *record*, of which he has some time or other taken a copy, and produces the *record* in court; can it be objected to his recovery, that he has *not produced the copy?* Or, if a man brings suit on a contract, and has *three* witnesses to it, *two* of which he produces, who fully verify the fact; shall he
lose

lose his cause, because he did not call in the *third witness?*

The public creditor who demands his pay, must doubtless bring *evidence sufficient* to support his suit, *i. e.* the *proof will lie upon him,* and if he can, in any way, *verify the facts,* and *support his right,* he doubtless *ought to be paid.*

2. Another objection has been made, viz. that *all* the original creditors who sold their certificates, were not *driven by necessity* to do this; and what if they were not? can there be any *crime* or *disqualification* in selling a negotiable certificate, made payable to the *bearer,* and purposely *calculated,* like bills of money, for *negotiation* and *currency* thro' *any* and *every* hand?

3. It has been objected, that *some* original creditors sold their certificates thro' *diffidence of the public faith.* And what if they did? Do you think they were *singular* in their diffidence? Suppose any man wants confidence in his debtor, and *fears or doubts* that he shall lose his debt; Can that affect the *justice* of his demand, or his *right to payment?*

4. Another objects to *any further payment,* because *some* of the creditors who sold their certificates for 2*s.* 6*d.* in the pound, had *managed their* 2*s.* 6*d. so well* by a seven years' negotiation, as *to make* 20*s. out of it.*

5. Another objects, that *many* of the public creditors were of such a *dissipating turn,* that if they were paid the whole 20*s.* due to them, they would soon *spend* it, and, of course, would be *no better* but rather *worse* off, than if they had never been paid.

Now, gentlemen-readers, suppose any private debtor should be summoned into court, at the suit of his creditor, for a debt of 20*s.* and he should shew that he had, seven years ago, paid his creditor 2*s.* 6*d.* of the debt of 20*s.* and plead *any or all the foregoing objections* against any further payment of the 17*s.* 6*d.* which remained due; can you imagine that the court would allow such plea to be good in *law or equity,* and *sufficient to discharge* the debtor from any further payment? And if these *pleas* and *objections* should

appear

appear trifling and ridiculous in a *private concern*, can you bring yourselves to believe they would receive any additional weight or dignity from being introduced by any most dignified perfonage, and urged in the moft auguft affembly on earth, againft paying *public creditors* circumftanced in the fame manner.

But the *great objection* ftill remains, the *clincher* that is to fupport the whole plan, and fo connect the parts together, as to make the whole confiftent with *law*, *reafon*, *right*, and *juftice*; for certainly no plan can be juftified, which has not all thefe qualities. This capital objection to paying the original creditors, who have fold their certificates, the balance of the debt, which has never been paid to them, is this, viz.

They have *fold their certificates*, and thereby *conveyed to the purchafer all their right* to their demand or debt due to them. As much ftrefs is laid on this objection, it requires a particular confideration.

1. If the public promife or faith is *fuppofed to be given* in the certificate, it was *broken the inftant it was made*; it was *violated in the very birth of it*; it was *verbal* only, not *real*; the *words* expreffed the *nominal* value, but the *reality* or *meaning* funk down inftantly to the *current value*, by the very *conftruction* which Congrefs itfelf fixed, by their fcale, on like words in the loan-office certificates, and under this conftruction they paffed, by univerfal confent of buyer and feller, from hand to hand.

The *wrong* was *inftantly* done to the original creditor, and he inftantly fuftained the *injury* and *damage*, and, confequently, if any thing is to be done in future time to compenfate or repair that damage, it ought *fo to be done*, that he who *fuffered* the *injury* and *damage*, may receive the *benefit* of it; making this compenfation to a *ftranger*, who fuffered nothing, is no *repair of the wrong done*, is no fort of *reftoration* of injured right, and is, of courfe, nugatory and ridiculous.

2. But, in real truth, if the public faith was defigned to be really plighted at all, it was annexed to the *debt*, not to the *certificate*; the debt was founded on the *merits or*

valuable

valuable confiderations out of which it grew, and to thefe it adheres, and carries with it the promife or public faith which is annexed to it.

The *certificates* and thefe *merits* are very widely different things; the one *depreciated* to 2s. 6d. in the pound; the other *kept their value* without the leaft diminution; the one *was transferred;* the other *was not.* The fpeculators can produce the *certificates,* but they cannot produce the *merits,* of the original creditors: thefe they never bought or paid for, and, therefore, can have no right or claim to them, or the rewards of them, *i. e.* to the debt annexed to them; for it is impoffible that one man fhould have a *right* to the *labor* or *hire* of another, without paying a *valuable confideration* for it; if it was even *agreed to be transferred without this,* the transfer would be *void* as a *nudum pactum,* not only by the *laws of the land,* but by the immutable *laws of commutative juftice.*

3. The certificate was never either delivered to, or received by, the original creditor, as *full payment of the debt* due to him, and therefore never *comprifed or carried in it that debt;* nor is it pretended or pleaded by any body as any thing more than the *evidence* of that debt; and, of courfe, if the debt can be fufficiently *proved by the public books,* or any other evidence, the want or abfence of the certificate can be no objection to the claim of the original creditor.

4. The certificate, when firft delivered to the public creditor, being made payable to the bearer, and exprefsly fitted and calculated for circulation or exchange, like other bills of public credit, comprifed and carried in it *fome value* as long as it could be fold, but, like all other articles of negotiation or exchange, that value was *liable to variation* according to the *rife* or *fall* of the market.

From the two laft propofitions it clearly follows, that when the certificate was fold, all the *value* which it comprifed or carried in it was fold and transferred with it, and *no more;* and of courfe, the purchafer, by the fale, became entitled to that *value,* and *no more:* the reft of the debt ftaid behind, and ftuck faft to the original merits out of which it originally grew, and in the place where it always

ways belonged, *i. e.* the original creditor, by the sale of his certificate, sold and granted all that he received, and no more; and that part which he had not received, he retained, and has a right to call for and receive, whenever he pleases.

5. A reference to the *real design of Congress* in issuing the certificates, especially at the close of the war, may cast some light on this affair. We are not to suppose that Congress issued negotiable certificates *for* 40,000,000 *of dollars*, worth but 2*s.* 6*d.* or some such trifle, in the pound, with *real, serious design* to load the nation with the immense burden of redeeming them at 20*s. in the pound*, wholly for the benefit of the *bearers*; by far the greatest part of whom, they had every reason to suppose, would be *strangers* not only to the *merits*, out of which the debt certified originally grew, but to *any such services*, or even *kind wishes*, for our country, as could deserve the public notice; and many of them *strangers* to the country itself.

We never ought to impute bad intentions, especially to public bodies of dignity, where their actions will equally well bear a favorable construction. I think, we are rather bound in charity to suppose, that, as Congress found the public treasury so exhausted that it was impracticable to make even a small, partial payment to the public creditors, they might think that negotiable certificates would sell for *something*, which, tho' little, might be better than *nothing*, and afford *some relief*, till the country could recover a little from the ruins of the war, and arrange the finances into some productive state, which would supply funds sufficient for full payment; and that, in the mean time, they might safely trust to the wisdom of a future Congress, to adopt modes of redemption of such certificates, either similar to their own scales then in established practice, or some other which might do *justice to all*, or at least something near it, and bring *ruin on nobody*, nor even disappoinment; for such a limited redemption was expected by every body at that time.

They had been long accustomed to issue public paper with the public faith plighted in *words expressive and solemn enough*, which yet, by their own scales and by general acceptation, were reduced, *in construction* or *meaning*, down to the *current value* or *exchange* which their paper obtained; and when they iſſued the certificates in queſtion, I have no doubt but they conſidered themſelves merely *purſuing their long uſage or practice*, and conceived that the *public paper they then iſſued*, with all the *reſt* that preceded it, would, in time, find and meet ſome reaſonable mode of liquidation and final redemption, *tolerable to all*, and *ruinous to none*.

In this view of the matter, tho' the means they adopted may not be deemed *altogether proper* (and perhaps, under the public preſſures and neceſſities which then exiſted, no means could be hit on *wholly free* from exception) yet their *intentions* may be admitted to be *juſt, ſalutary, and benevolent*, and agreeable to the *general expectation*.

Whereas, on the other hand, to ſuppoſe them *deliberately* loading the States with a debt of 40,000,000 of dollars, for only 5,000,000 which they received and had the benefit of, is *monſtrous*, which becomes ſtill more *hideous*, if this horrible plan was *deſignedly* ſo formed that, by its natural operation, it would, in the end, cut all ſuch of the original creditors who took benefit of it, off from 7-8*ths* of their *pay or the debt certified* to be due to them. But,

6. To ſuppoſe that the whole debt due to the original creditors is compriſed in their certificates, and transferred by the ſale of them to the purchaſers, by the common rule of aſſignments, I ſay, this ſuppoſition will demonſtrably prove either that the common rule of aſſignments is *wrong* and *bad* in itſelf, or *wrongly applied* to this caſe: but *wrong in itſelf* it is not; for it is plainly enough very good and uſeful *in its place*, *i. e.* within its due *mean* and *reaſon*; therefore, in the caſe in queſtion, the application is *wrongful*, *i. e.* the rule will not admit a reaſonable *application to the facts*, on which its operation is demanded.

For *every law divine and human*, every practicable *rule of morality or ſound policy*, is and muſt moſt neceſſarily be *founded on juſtice and right*, and, in its application, muſt *produce juſtice and right*, and *avoid injury and wrong*; therefore, whenever any law or rule, however *ſacred in itſelf*, is applied *to any facts or caſe* to which it ſo *ill ſuits*, that its neceſſary and unavoidable operation will be to *deſtroy right*

right and *justice*, and to produce *wrong and injury*, the application is certainly wrongful: in such case, the true use and meaning of the rule is *mistaken* or *perverted*.

All laws of every country are so capable of application to cases which are out of their reason, that a Court of Chancery makes a part of every judiciary system; the authority and duty of which is to *control and soften* the *extreme rigor* of the law; and when any statute or other rule is of so high authority that the powers of the court, do not extend far enough to give relief, application is and ought always to be made to the *supreme authority, which is ever the supreme chancery of the State*, to *repeal* such law, or *explain* and *limit* its true meaning, and *correct* the errors and wrongs of it.

Now to apply the foregoing position (which certainly no man will controvert) to the case before us—The opinion in dispute, ‘that the sale of a certificate transfers the whole debt certified, to the purchaser, by the *common rule of assignments*,’ cannot be true, because this would necessarily involve and imply *great wrong* and *injustice*, viz. it would take away the *rewards due to the merits* and *earnings* of our most meritorious citizens, and give the monies *due to them* to *another class* of people, who are not entitled to any of it *by any kind of valuable considerations, merits*, or *earnings* whatever, i. e. it would cut the original public creditors, who, by their merits and services, *supported the war and saved their country*, off from the *rewards*, the *pay*, the *hire* due to them, and *give the same to the speculators*, who never *served* or *saved* the country, and to whom *we owe* nothing.

This takes the *public money to an immense amount*, from a vast number of most deserving citizens, scattered thro' every part of the Empire, who have *dearly and most virtuously earned* it, and have *never been paid*, and many of whom, with their families, for want of their pay, are now suffering the *pangs of ruin and extreme distress*, and *all* suffer *great* inconvenience and disappointment; I say, from these worthy, unhappy objects it takes the *public money due to their earnings*, and gives it to *speculators*, who have never earned any of it.

These

These effects are unavoidable. Turn, and twist, and cook the matter into all shapes possible, and these effects will be found. They must and will exist, if that plan is carried into effect; the great injustice of which strikes every one with a force which the mind cannot resist. No man ever adopted that plan, but he found the *gross, but unavoidable, final injustice* of it a great difficulty, *hard to be got over;* and this final injustice proves as plainly that the plan which involves it, is *wrong*, as that any effect indicates the nature of its cause, or that that which *does or works wrong,* is *wrong:* of course, there is an *error in the matter* so very gross and important as to be *fatal in society*. Society cannot exist, if the laws of it will not secure *to the laborer his hire*, or to the *virtuous the rewards of his virtue*, or to the *industrious the fruits of his industry*.

In fine, the facts under that plan stand glaring thus: the original creditors claim their pay by *solemn, public contract*, by *dear earnings*, and *most virtuous merits;* they have *not been paid;* the *money due* to them is carved out of the *labors of the nation*, in order to *pay them;* they can get *none of it*, are finally *cut off from it*, and the *speculators* are to *get it all*, without the least *claim* of *merit, services*, or *valuable consideration paid* for it.

These facts must be either *disproved* or *avoided* (which cannot be; they are of the most public *notoriety*,) or the *absurdities* and *injuries* resulting from them must be *swallowed* and *digested* (Good Heaven! what throats and stomachs men must have to do this!) or the *plan* must be *given up*.

Many people puzzle themselves to find where the error or wrong lies: some say, *in the breach of the public faith;* some say, *in the original issuing the negotiable certificates;* others say, *in the folly of the seller, &c. &c.* but I should think it very easy to see that the error lies in supposing that *property can be transferred by implication*, without any *intention* of the seller, and without any *valuable consideration* paid for it.

But it matters little *where* the error or wrong lies; it is quite enough to know that *it really exists*, and will *produce*

its

its baneful effects, and is of such *magnitude* as to affect the *essential interests of the nation*, and will do so for *ages to come;* and, therefore, as soon as the error is discovered, it ought immediately to be *corrected or remedied:* the *national safety, peace*, and *prosperity* require this.

If we *sow* all over the nation *errors and wrongs*, they may be *unnoticed* at first, but will soon *spring up* and *grow* into a *forest of chagrin* and *discontent*, of *wretchedness* and *ruin*. Nothing can give peace and establishment to a nation, equal to ' *judgment* and *justice* running down its streets, and *righteousness* overflowing it.'

It is not uncommon for men of *lively genius* and *eager reasonings*, and perhaps *honesty* too, to pursue their *fine-spun arguments* into conclusions that meet *obstinate facts*, which, like an impregnable *wall*, must and will stop their progress; but if *their obstinacy* happens to be equal to that of the *wall*, they will not be willing to turn about, or even stop, but will go on and beat and bruse their heads till their skulls are broken, and some *crevice* is opened, thro' which their *chimerical ideas can fly out;* then, indeed, they will soften into *calmness* and *moderation*, and grow willing to hearken to some plan that is *admissible by the hard facts which stand round them*.

I heard once of a doctor who was called to a sick patient; he felt his pulse, soon thought he found his disorder, and prescribed a dose *which killed him*. When the doctor was told his patient was *dead*, he answered with some emotion, that he had *no business to die;* for he could demonstrate by *the most approved rules of physic and medicine*, that he ought not only to have *lived*, but to have *got well* by this time.

Now, if you please, we will seriously compare *this plan* in question with *mine*, which is comprised in my first proposition, viz. *to debit the original creditors with the certificates they received*, at the *value* or *exchange* they bore at the *time of their dates*, and to pay the *residue* of the balance due to them with interest, and to pay the certificates at the same value or their current exchange (as the case may require) to the *bearers of them*, whether *original holders* or
alienees;

alienees; and let us judge of the two plans by this most *sure* and *unexceptionable criterion,* viz. *which of them* will naturally operate by way of *most justice* and *right,* and *least injury* and *wrong?* for no practicable plan that can be adopted, every one will allow, will operate by way of *perfect right* and *no wrong at all;* no public plan that ever was adopted ever came or can come up to *this degree of perfection,* and all that *is* or *can be in the power* of human wisdom and weakness is to adopt that plan, which, in its operation, naturally produces *most right* and *least wrong.* By this *criterion* then we will judge of the two plans before us, which *criterion* is (all *subtilties* of reasoning aside) the only *safe one* which is *practicable* within the extent of human power.

1. The plan I *oppose* pays the immense sum of public money given by the nation purposely to *reward the saviours* of their country, pays this money, I say, to the *speculators,* who never *earned any of it,* who do not pretend to found their claim to it on any *merits,* or *services,* or *valuable consideration,* which they ever rendered to the *nation* or *any body else,* but demand the compensations and rewards *due to the original creditors,* without *pretending to* have paid any *valuable consideration* therefor to them; and at the same time, the plan denies those immense rewards to those *worthy citizens,* who found their claim thereto on *the most sacred contract of Congress* to them, under *sanction* of the *public faith,* which *binds the country* " *by the laws of* GOD *and man;*" on the most *punctual fulfilment* of said contract, on their part; and on *their great virtue and merit,* in *saving their country* in its most *dreadful danger* and *distress:* if any body thinks there is any *honor, justice,* or *right* in this plan, let him look for it, and I believe he will easily find all *that is there.*

2. The plan I *propose* is, to *debit the original creditors* with all the *certificates they received,* at *their current value* at the time of their *dates,* and pay the *remaining balance* due to them *with interest;* and to redeem the *certificates* by payment to the *bearer,* let him be either *original holder* or *alienee,*

at

at the *same rate*, or at their *current exchange* at the time of redemption, as the cafe may require.

This plan pays the immenfe public monies to the people who *earned* them, *i. e.* to thofe who, by folemn, *public contract*, and by their *real fupplies* and *fervices* rendered as the *conditions* of that contract on *their part*, are moft *juftly* and *fubftantially entitled* to them; and, at the fame time, pays to the *fpeculators* the *proper value* of the certificates which they have purchafed.

This plan, I think, will do the *moft general juftice* to the citizens at large, which can be done by imperfect human wifdom, in the prefent circumftances of the matter. This will *place* the public monies *where they belong*, will give every one *his due*, and *no more than his due*. This will bring, on one fide, *wrong and ruinous diftrefs on nobody;* nor will it, on the other, heap *unmerited, unearned fortunes on any body*. This will, *in the end, do manifeft juftice and right to every one*. This ought ever to be our goal, whatever *confufion, doubt,* and *darknefs* may arife from the chaos of *fubtile arguments, dexterity* of management, and *artful difguifing* and *twifting of facts,* thro' which we may be forced to make our way in our paffage on to this realm of *juftice, truth, and light:* for whatever dark and gloomy paffages we may have occafion to pafs thro', in the deliberation and adjuftment of human concerns and difputes, *final juftice* and *right* ought ever to be the ftar that *directs* our fteps, and which will certainly *guide* us to the *rightful iffue* at laft.

I cannot fee that this plan will bear hard on more than *two* forts or defcriptions of men, viz.

1. Such public creditors who have *real merits* and *juft right* to a claim, but, by fome means, may not be able to *prove* their right; and probably, among the infinite number of real public creditors, there may be *fome* of this fort, and perhaps *many,* who muft fuffer without remedy; for what *cannot be proved,* cannot be *admitted* in any court in the world; but then it is to be noted, that the *plan* I *oppofe* leaves thefe fufferers as *much unprovided for*, and as much *defperate and without remedy,* as the plan *I propofe,* and, of

courfe,

course, this objection lies with *equal weight* against *both* plans, if it is of any weight against either of them.

2. The second sort of men who may think my plan imposes hardship on them, are such speculators as have purchased their certificates at a *higher exchange* than that at which I propose to redeem them; but this loss or hardship (if it is any) is and always must be *incident* to such speculations, which, at best, are but *games at hazard*, altogether *useless*, barely *tolerable*, and often very *hurtful* to the public: I do not, therefore, conceive their loss or gain deserves any consideration in the public deliberations or decisions of this great question, viz. *what rate or scale of redemption* of certificates, *Continental money, or any other public paper*, does the *general justice*, and *national honor*, and safety of our country, *require?* But if we were to allow that the losses and hardships of these men were *real* and *pitiful*, they bear not the *least proportion* to the infinite *hardship* and *ruinous distresses*, to which the plan I oppose subjects countless *thousands* of our most *deserving* citizens; even if the calculation is made on either the *numbers*, *amount of loss*, or the *merits*, of the sufferers.

If this alternative cannot be avoided, it can admit no doubt, but the *lesser* must yield to the *greater;* for it is certainly a less evil to incur the loss of a *penny* than a *pound*, or even to do *injustice* to *one* man than to a *thousand*, and of two evils we ought to choose the least.

But the morality of the two plans, *i. e.* the degree of *justice* and *right*, or of *injury* and *wrong*, which their operation will naturally produce, is not the only thing which ought to govern our choice of them; there is a most important *difference* both of *facility of collection* and *utility of payment*, under them. For,

I. Under the plan I propose, the public money paid will be *scattered* over the *whole nation*, thro' every part where the real public creditors will be found; and the money so paid will,

1. Do an act of *justice* long due to the receiver;

2. Will increase the *business* of the country; as most of the creditors will be thereby enabled to go into or increase their

their bufinefs, who are now *reſtrained* and *held back*, thro' want of their ſtock withheld from them by the public.

3. This money will immediately ſpread thro' every part of the nation, and cauſe a great increaſe of *circulation*, which will give *ſpirit* and *facility* to the general induſtry and wealth of our people at large; and as the taxes are all ultimately paid by the conſumers, who are ſpread over every part of the country,

4. The *facility of collection* of the ſecond tax will grow out of the *operation of the firſt*, as the payments will be made more *eaſy* and *ſatisfactory* thereby; for the people will naturally grow *contented* under a tax, when they perceive *advantages ariſing* out of the *increaſed circulation* of caſh produced by it, enough to compenſate the *burden* of the tax.

II. But under the plan I oppoſe, the caſe will be *greatly otherwiſe;* for,

1. One *third* of the ſpeculators are ſuppoſed to be *foreigners*, and, of courſe, their third of the money paid (ſay, 7 or 8,000,000 of dollars) will be *ſent* directly *out of the country, never to return* again; this *drain* of caſh by annual intereſt (for nobody thinks of paying the principal) when added to *that* of the foreign debt, is enough (if we had no other drains) to keep the country *poor, diſtreſſed*, and *behind hand* for ages to come.

2. The other two-thirds paid to the ſpeculators here, will not be ſcattered over the country, and increaſe the *general circulation*, but will be *accumulated in few hands*, moſt of which, according to the common courſe of human paſſions, will be applied to make and ſupport *nurſeries of vice, luxury, pride, vanity, diſſipation*, and *bad example:* for fortunes obtained by *ſudden* acquirement, without any *merits* or *earnings*, are uſually ſpent in this way; and if a few of them ſhould happen to employ their money prudently, it will *ſo far* contribute to *accumulating the national wealth into few hands*, which is one of the worſt things that can happen to a nation.

III. Another difference of the operation of the two plans will have great effect on the *revenue*. When the public

public money is paid for purposes of *acknowledged justice*, *utility*, and *general advantage*, the payment of taxes will be made without *murmur*, and the collection, of course, will be *easy* and *without disturbance*. Paying to the original creditors the *hire of their labors*, the *debt* due to them for exertions that *saved their country*, is a method of employing the public money of most *acknowledged propriety* thro' the nation; but the payment of speculators is not so popular; it is *hard* for people to see the fruits of their labor taken from them, and given to speculators who never earned any of it.

This will naturally make the taxes *odious*; and, of course, the *burden* of the *old* taxes, the *instituting of new ones*, and the *collection of both*, will soon become objects of general *uneasiness, murmur*, and *ill-humor*; which, when *general*, will be easily blowed up into *tumults, insurrections*, and a general *derangement* of the peace and political order of society; smuggling and other avoidances of the taxes may not be the most alarming of these national frets.

In a nation thus tempered, a few men of spirit and enterprise, who may happen to be *disgusted, soured with malevolence*, and *fired with thirst of revenge*, may do infinite mischief.

Without the aid of any such incendiaries, I am persuaded beyond a doubt, that any tax to *pay the speculators* will fit *very uneasy* on the most *quiet* and *peaceable* citizens that can be found among us.

I was lately in conversation with a gentleman of *great fortune*, and noted for a very *generous* and *peaceful temper*, who told me he had just been paying an impost of about 30 dollars for wines he imported for his own use, and added, " had it been to pay *our soldiers* and *other supporters* " of the *war*, I should not have begrudged it, had it been " *three times* as much; but the thought that it must go to " the idle *speculators*, makes my *blood boil* in my veins:"— and I conceive, every honest *American* that earns his own money, feels just so.

Taxes are ever ranked among the most *techy articles of civil police*, and require very *delicate* management; and our

revenue-

revenue-*syftem* is *very young, tender,* and not ripened enough into *firm, general habit;* and, tho' in its infancy, it is preffed with a much *heavier load* than the country ever felt before; I therefore conclude, that any plan that *tends to embroil the finances,* and furnifh *objections* and *murmurs* againft the *revenue,* ought to be *reprobated* as the moft *dangerous* and *fatal* meafure that can be devifed.

IV. There is another objection to the plan I *oppofe,* which I confider very great, and which, I think, is obviated by the one I *propofe,* viz. it encourages and fupports *idle and hurtful arts and contrivances* to procure *fortunes* by *dexterity* and *fleight of hand,* rather than by the *old, painful methods of induftry, economy,* and *care.* Thefe fpeculators all have for their *object,* the *acquirement* of wealth without *earning* it, *i. e.* of getting the *hire* and *rewards* due to the *labor* and *merits of another,* into their own *poffeffion* and *enjoyment, without any retribution :* this therefore is, in its nature and principle, wrongful; and people of this caft commonly fpend their *ftock and time* in thefe purfuits, which, otherwife, they would employ in *ufeful occupations* of hufbandry, manufactures, or trade; and, of courfe, fo much good *ftock and time is loft* to the public.

I think, this fort of fpeculations ought not to be confidered as *merely ufelefs,* but *hurtful alfo,* and, therefore, ought by no means to be *encouraged and fupported* by any meafures of government; efpecially when their *excefs* has been carried to fuch an *enormous pitch,* as to draw after it the *ruinous confequences* defcribed above, and obvious to every difcerning eye.

V. My next objection to the plan I oppofe, arifes from *the general ftate of the finances of the nation,* which I beg leave to introduce, with fome previous obfervations by way of preface.

1. I am not *alarmed at a heavy national debt;* much lefs do I apprehend any *deftruction* or *ruin* from it, if not too enormous; nor,

2. Am I under *any doubt or diffidence* of either the *ftrength* or *patience* of our people to bear it, if the following *limitations* and *qualities* of it are attended to:

1ft. If

1st. If the *debt contracted,* or the public monies to be paid, are for *necessary public purposes, i. e.* to support and maintain the *real justice, honor, safety, convenience,* and *well-being* of the nation, *e. g.* to pay the civil list and *just* debts, for defence against enemies or pirates, for public roads, inland navigation, encouragement of genius, useful arts, &c. &c. &c.

2d. That the debt or annual demand for money does not *exceed* the *product of an impost on imported luxuries,* no higher than is necessary to *reduce useless, luxurious,* and *hurtful consumptions* down to that *moderation* that is necessary for the *health, morality,* and *wealth* of our people; and,

3d. That the money collected by the tax shall be so paid out, that it may revert, in its circulation to, and diffuse itself over, the *same States and places out of which the money so collected was originally drawn, i. e.* that the expenditures or payments of the money raised by the tax, shall be *so made,* that it shall revert to and circulate thro' the *same countries* and *places that paid it.*

Under these limitations and restrictions, *strictly* and *uniformly* adhered to, no national debt can *hurt,* much less *ruin,* a nation; it would, in my opinion, operate like a sumptuary law, and would be rather an *advantage* and *benefit* on the whole, than a *detriment.* But this notwithstanding, I should choose to have the calculations made so, that the *annual incomes* might a *little exceed* the *expenditures,* that there might be a *small surplus* left to support accidents, or contingencies, or, as the country proverb is, that something might be laid up for a rainy day; but I would not wish to have such surplus *very great,* for if it was so, I should expect that most administrations would find *plenty of contingencies,* enough to consume it all—I will now go on to consider the present state of the public debt, as it is exhibited in estimates calculated up to the last of the year 1790.

The *certificates* of all sorts, now in circulation and to be provided for, amount, by the public estimates, *principal,* to 27,000,000 *dollars; interest* due, last of the year 1790, to 13,000,000; whole amount, 40,000,000 *dollars.*

By

By a *moderate* estimate, and much *below* what is generally supposed to be the real fact, *three-fourths* of these, *i..e.* 30,000,000 *dollars*, are *in the hands of the speculators;* the original value of which, when issued by Congress, at an average of 2*s.* 6*d.* in the pound, amounts to 3,750,000 dollars; this sum, of course, was paid by the speculators to the real creditors, at the first purchase of them, and, therefore, ought to be placed to the debit of their account; the remainder of the 30,000,000 dollars, viz. 26,250,000 is the clear gain of the speculators, which they never *paid any thing for*, either to the nation, to the original creditors, or to any body else; therefore, that sum, having never been paid by any body, still remains due to the original creditors, and ought to be provided for, and, of course, ought to be added to the estimate of the national debt, viz. 26,250,000 dollars.

The national debt then, in round numbers (for my calculation does not require accuracy enough to make it necessary to insert the broken or fractional quantities) the national debt, I say, as calculated up to the end of the year 1790, will then stand, in round numbers, nearly as follows, viz.

Foreign debt, including interest, about
(somewhat less) - - 12,000,000 doll.
Domestic debt, funded, about (somewhat more) - - - 40,000,000 do.
Domestic debt, unfunded, computed at 2,000,000 do.
State debts to be assumed, computed at 25,000,000 do.
Balance due to the original creditors, as computed above - - 26,000,000 do.
Provision for particular applications, where the justice of the demand and hardship of the claimants require relief (incomputable) but say - 4,000,000 do.

Total of the national debt 109,000,000 do.
Annual interest of foreign debt by public estimate - - - - 542,600 doll.

Annual

Annual interest of domestic debt, viz.
97,000,000 dollars, at 6 per cent.   5,820,000 doll.
Civil list, computed at   -   -   600,000 do.

All these added together, make the a-
  mount of the yearly expenditure, computed for full payment   -   6,962,600 do.
The whole *annual revenue* now in existence is estimated at about   -   2,600,000 do.

Which subtracted from the annual expenditures, leaves a deficiency to be provided for, of   -   -   4,362,600 do.

From this statement it appears, that the whole *present revenue* is less than *two-fifths of the yearly expenditures;* a little more than *two-fifths* of it are absorbed by the civil list and interest of the *foreign debt,* and about *two-thirds of the remainder* are appropriated to pay the *clear profits or gains of the speculators,* and the debts due to the original creditors come in for the other third, but by such an *unequal* distribution, that far the *greatest* part of them *get nothing at all,* and those who do come in for *something,* get but *two-thirds* of the debt confessed by every body to be due to them.

For the truth of this statement I appeal to the *public books, estimates, calculations, and records,* except *my estimate* of the exchange or value of certificates, which is a matter of public *notoriety,* and I leave any body to *correct it, who can.*

Out of this statement, I think, arises a very strong objection against the *plan I oppose.* I think it is manifestly wrong, especially in the *distressing straits and deficiency* of the revenue, to bestow 26,600,000 of the living funds which the revenue can supply, *on the speculators,* who never paid any thing for it, either to the nation, or to the original creditors, whilst there remains due to said creditors a debt of *above* 50,000,000, which is not only *unpaid, but totally unprovided for;* and especially when it is considered, that this *neglected debt* is originally founded on the most *solemn, public contract,* and the most *faithful* and *painful fulfilment* of it on *the part* of the creditors.

I do

I do not at present advert to any but the following questions, that can arife on this ftatement of the public debt and the exifting revenue.

The firft queftion to be confidered is,—whether this ftatement is *wild* and *ideal* only, or *really true* and grounded on *fuch facts as will fupport it?* For my part, I have not any particular knowledge of the facts on which it is grounded, and, of courfe, do not object to any of it, except that part which *adopts the clear gains of the fpeculators* into the public debt, and *loads* the nation with the *burden of* 26,000,000 *dollars* to pay them, and *of* 800,000 *more*, to raife the old Continental money out of the *grave* where it has quietly *flept* more than feven years.

The fecond queftion which offers itfelf is,—whether any part of the public debt, included in the above ftatement, can be *reduced, docked off*, or *thrown out?* There are but two items which, I conceive, can admit a doubt in this queftion:

The firft is,—*the* 26,000,000 *dollars* appropriated to the payment of the *clear gains* of the fpeculators. This, I think, ought to be *rejected* for all the reafons affigned above.

The fecond is,—the balance of the fame fum due to the original creditors. I think (whatever may be decided as to *paying* or *rejecting* the clear gains of the fpeculators) this item of the ftatement ought *to be admitted and paid*, for all the reafons above urged, and this additional one, viz. the *character* of the *nation abroad* for *juftice* and *honor*, requires this.

For let us fuppofe that one of our embaffadors at a foreign court fhould, in fome grand circle, happen to harangue a little on the *juftice, honor*, political conftitution, ftrength, riches, and bleffings of his country, and fome grave man, with much meaning in his countenance, fhould reply to him—" Sir, all you fay of the *bleffings* of your
" country, may be true for any thing I know; but it feems
" to me, the *juftice and honor* of it are not quite fo clear;
" for I think I have heard that your Congrefs *refufed to pay*
" *to thofe noble and patriotic citizens*, who, with their *blood*
" and

"and *travail, purchased* for you *all these blessings* you boast "of, the *rewards*, the *simple hire* due to them by the most "*sacred, public contract* that could be made, and *faithfully* "*fulfilled on their part*, by exertions and services, the most "*noble, arduous, painful*, and *persevering*, of which we have "any example in history."

I suppose, in such a case, you would not wish to see our embassador *dashed out of countenance, pocket the affront*, and *slink into a corner;* but if you think some reply necessary to *bring him off*, and as he may not have one ready cut and dried at hand, I wish any of you who oppose this payment, would make a *suitable one for him*, that he may be properly armed at all points to defend the *honor* of his country, whenever it may be *insulted or attacked.*

Third question. As the present revenue amounts to less than two-fifths of the yearly expenditures, according to the above statement, the next question is,—can the *revenues be increased up to the amount of the necessary annual expenditures? i. e.* can the *duties* or *taxes* be *raised* up to *three-fifths higher* than they *now are?* I conceive this will be *difficult* in the *assessment*, and more so in the *collection;* indeed, it appears to me *totally impracticable*, as things stand at present; and the idea of *deferring* payment, and *loading* the nation with an instalment to be paid *ten years hence*, brings to my mind a young rake, who bought a horse, and agreed to pay for it " *at the next election*," but surreptitiously drew the note payable " *at the resurrection;*" the creditor applied for payment; the rake plead that the time was not come; on which the creditor applied to his *father*, who was a grave, serious man; he called his son, and asked why he did not pay the debt; the son replied, that it was not yet due, as he would see by the note; the father replied, " Ah! young " man, pay the debt instantly; I fear, at the rate you go " on, you will have enough to answer for *at the resurrec-* " *tion*, without this note against you."

Fourth question. If the revenue is not adequate to full payment, ought not the *actual payments* to be made by *dividends*, payable to every creditor in *equal proportions* of the debt due? In such case, to pay *part* of the creditors *half*

or

two-thirds of their demand, and *nothing* to the *rest*, is contrary to the most received *rule of distributive justice*, in all cases of private *bankruptcies* or *stoppages of payment*, and I can see no reason why the same rule should not extend to the *deficiencies* of the *public revenue*.

Fifth question. If the public revenues are deficient, ought *any creditor at all to be paid any thing*, till the whole debt is *liquidated* and reduced to a *certainty*, without which it is impossible to make the requisite dividends? A *negative* answer to this question seems to be so clearly just and proper, that I cannot conceive that it will be disputed.

But after all, if the first proposition of my plan above urged cannot be admitted, and the *final decision* must be, that the original creditors who have *sold* their certificates, have, by the sale, *extinguished their demand* for any *further* payment; that no evidence of the debt can be admitted, but certificates; and *no payment* of the debt certified in them, can be allowed and made to any body but the *holders* of them (all which appears to me to be strange doctrine) I beg leave, if this must be the case, to introduce my second proposition, viz.

That all *original holders* of certificates *be paid the full nominal value of their certificates, principal and interest;* and that all *alienated certificates* be paid to the *bearer* at the *rate, value, or current exchange they had at their dates*, or at the *time of redemption*, as the case may require, *i. e.* so that no certificate shall be redeemed at *a higher value or exchange than it bore at the time of its date*, or (if, after its date, it depreciated) at no *higher exchange* than shall be its *current value* at the *time* of redemption; for the public never received any *valuable consideration for it, more than its value* at the time of its *date*, and therefore never ought to pay *any more to redeem it;* but if it has *depreciated* thro' the course of its currency or circulation, the *public* has paid that *depreciation once already,* for it operates by way of *tax on the innumerable hands* in which it depreciated, *i. e.* on the *public*, thro' which it circulated; and there can be no reason why the *public* should pay the *same loss over again;* and if they should do this, it would be no *reparation* to the *suf-*

ferer; for, at the time of doing this, the certificate would not be in the *same hands which suffered by the depreciation :* but this argument is more fully discussed in the preceding Essays, where the doctrine of *appreciation* and *depreciation* is often called up and considered.

The certificates are *evidence* of the debt certified, in the hands of the *original holder*, and my proposition is, to pay it to him : but in the *hands of the alienee* it causes not any *such evidence*, for it is plain enough, both in *fact* and *reason*, that, by the sale of the certificate, nothing more was either *transferred by the seller*, or *expected* or *paid for by the purchaser*, than the *chance* or *right* of receiving such *sum* or *value* for it, as the Congress should *set* or *fix* as the *price* or *exchange* at which it should be *finally redeemed;* and this *rate* or *scale* of redemption ought to be set or estimated without the least regard to the *loss* or *gain* of the speculators; but on *principles of general justice* and *right only, i. e.* in such manner as will do *most right* and *least wrong, i. e.* in such manner, that *no description* of citizens should be *more benefited or hurt*, or made *richer* or *poorer*, by it, than *another*; for all national *distributions* of justice, all public *institutions* and *decisions* whatever, ought always to be so made, that both the *burdens* and *benefits* of them may fall *equally* on all, and not lie *more heavily* or *more beneficially* on *one* than *another, i. e.* so that every one shall participate his *clear* and *proportionable share* both of the *burden* and *benefit* of them.

The rate or scale of redemption, thus estimated and fixed, will manifestly pay to the speculator all that he has right to receive, *i. e.* all that he ever bought or paid for; and if the overplus may not be paid to the original creditor, let it be retained in the treasury, and be paid to nobody; for I cannot see the use of paying it at all, where it is not due.

This proposition (which I advanced five years ago in my *Seventh Essay on Finance)* gave rise to the great question of *discrimination* between *original holders* and *purchasers* of certificates, and has been so fully discussed, that little need be added in this Review of the Arguments.

Perhaps,

Perhaps it may be enough to observe, that most of the *opposers* of the proposition acknowledge the *justice* of it, but object to it as *impracticable*. But I can see very little weight in the objection; every one who claims as an *original* holder, must *discriminate himself*, i. e. the *proof will lie on him* that he is *such*. I should suppose, that his *name* inserted in the certificate, and his *affidavit* that he has never *alienated* it, would be sufficient. If the certificate was taken out for *his benefit* in the *name* of another (as perhaps has been often done) the *balance due on the public books*, and the certificate *debited* to him, with his own *affidavit*, would make the matter clear enough; besides, the *negotiator* of such a matter would be a good witness.

There is no more danger of *perjuries* in this case, than there is in oaths to original entries on *books of accounts*, to *signatures*, &c. &c. After all, there can be but very few cases, if any, where the plan I *oppose* can give any *more* or *better remedy* to creditors who have lost their proofs, than the one I *propose*, affords.

My last proposition is,—if neither of the above-mentioned two can be admitted, that the *original holder* shall be *first paid*, and the *speculator last of all*, if he must be *paid at all*. The reason is, because the debt of the *original* holder is founded on *greater merits* and *real earnings* than the other, and, therefore, ought to be considered as of a *higher* and *more worthy nature*, and, of course, ought to be *preferred* in payment.

Upon the whole matter, I have *no conception* that the present arrangement of the public finances, *i. e.* of receipts and payments, is by any means *adequate to the exigencies of the nation*. I cannot form any idea, that our revenue either *is or can be made sufficient* to support the *immense load* of debt which lies upon it: nor can I conceive how any nation can exist without the *utmost deficiencies, disgrace,* and *even bankruptcy*, where the drafts on the revenue so greatly exceed the annual incomes of it; can exist, I say, without running over head and ears into the horrible gulf, the unbounded chaos of derangement, which will draw into it every conceivable embarrassment, not only of the public revenue,

i. e.

i. e. of the juftice and honor of the nation, but which will alfo, by its neceffary confequence, involve every branch of bufinefs thro' the whole nation in difappointment and diftrefs.

Deferring payments to future time is but putting *far away the evil day*, and avoiding the pain of *prefent preffures*, at the expenfe of *future embarraffment*. The unavoidable confequence of an over-loaded revenue will be a *deficiency of the public payments, i. e.* a *failure* of the *public credit*, and of the juftice and honor of the nation.

But in our own cafe, this is not *all our calamity*; for, under all this preffure of taxes, we can derive little *improvement* of our country, or even *fafety* and *fecurity*, from them: this immenfe *gulf of debt* fwallows up all our *revenues*, and is by no means *fatisfied with them all*; it leaves us not a *fhilling* for *public roads, inland navigation, encouragement of agriculture, manufactures, or genius* of any fort, or even for *defence* againft *enemies* or *pirates*, in cafe of a war; all the navy of the nation is not fufficient to fupprefs a *pilot-boat*, if it fhould be armed and manned by *pirates* to *infult* and *infeft* our coafts.

But this is not all; our people have not the *benefit* of that *increafed circulation* of cafh, which would arife from the heavy taxes they do pay, if the payments were made to creditors *fcattered over* the nation, who would inftantly circulate the money they received, among the *fame people* from whom it had been *collected*; but our money goes to *ftrangers*, or to fuch *accumulations*, that it is carried off far beyond our reach for ever, after we have paid it in taxes.

In fine, it is not poffible that our nation fhould continue even *to exift* in *honor, eafe*, and *peace*, under *thefe burdens*; a *penny* can never pay a *fhilling*, and a fhilling due will ever be *a debt*, and a *fretting one* too, *till it is paid*. The nature of our calamity admits but two alternatives, viz. Either to *reduce the debt* by *docking off fome part* of it, or to *increafe the revenue* up to an amount fufficient to pay it: the *latter* I take to be utterly *impracticable* and *defperate*, as the matter now ftands; the *other*, I think, might be done. The *only part* of the eftimate of the national debt that is

not

not for the nation's *benefit*, is the 26,000,000 *dollars* appropriated to pay the *clear profits* of the speculators. This, I think, might be *spared out of the estimate*, but as it is funded, I think it cannot be well docked off without a REPEAL *of the funding act*, which I *humbly wish may take place*. I know there would be *great difficulties* in doing this, but I conceive there will be much greater difficulties in not doing it. I am confident, the act, when it begins to operate, will be found, in its nature, wrong and impracticable, and necessity will compel the rescinding it sooner or later, and it is much easier to correct a new error than an old one; it is more honorable to correct an error with readiness of mind on first conviction, than to wait for the severe compulsions of necessity.

But if the repeal of the act should be thought improper, perhaps a supplement fixing a reasonable rate or scale of exchange at which the certificates and Continental money shall be received into the new loan, might prove a very salutary amendment of it: and if I could believe that any thing less than the nation's *well-being* made this repeal or amendment necessary, I should be silent about it.

Any attempt to pay this vast sum twice over, would draw consequences the most destructive and ruinous that can be conceived; and if both cannot be paid, and we cannot avoid the alternative, I would prefer sacrificing a demand which never *originated in real merit or earnings*, but receives its *whole force* from an *extravagant implication* of a *meaning* in words, which, by construction of *speaker* or *hearer* at the time of utterance, was *never comprised* or *conveyed* in them; I say, I would prefer this to any *violation* of the *solemn contract*, the *sacred public vows, sealed* and *plighted* to the *original* creditors, in the time of our country's *utmost danger* and *deep distress*, and to whose *faithful* and *painful fulfilment* of that *contract on their parts*, we are *indebted* under GOD for *our deliverance*.

If the first part of this alternative can be adopted, our desperation may cease, the great difficulty will diminish, partly because a large and the most exceptionable part of the burden will be taken off, and partly because what is

left

left will be a debt of such acknowledged and uncontroverted right, justice, and honor, as will give courage and force to our councils to assess, and our people to bear, such burdens of tax as will be necessary to support it, and gradually to wipe it off.

It is human to err, but it is the decided mark of strong intellects and a generous temper, to acknowledge and correct an error on conviction; yet such is the common weakness of the human mind, that error is often connected with obstinacy; those who are weak enough to make mistakes, are rarely wise enough to correct them; and the hard necessity which compels an amendment of an error, will not always produce an acknowledgment of it. The stability of public measures and decisions ought to rest on their rectitude and natural fitness, not on an obstinacy that is blind to their faults. Every body acknowledges that it is honorable and noble to own and correct an error, and that it is mean and base to persist in one; yet most men feel a sort of degrading shame, when they are called upon to correct their own mistakes. I hope our public councils are not affected with any of these little feelings: but, be it so or not, it is commonly true, that errors adopted on long deliberation are not easily given up and corrected. I do not wish to insinuate here, that any attention will be wanting to my arguments, drawn from religion and the fear of God (for his name has been called in to give force to the vows of the nation to their real creditors) or to arguments drawn from morality, national justice and honor, from gratitude and compassion, &c. these are arguments to be answered to God, to the nation, and to conscience.—But to wave all these for this time, I beg to conclude with the following questions, directed to every body:

First question. Whether paying the clear profits of the speculators, viz. 26,250,000 dollars, will not load and exhaust the revenue so much, as to put it out of our power to pay our real debts of the first honor, justice, covenants, and truth of the nation?

Second

Second question. Whether this payment will not be matter of general disapprobation and disgust, especially when kept alive and fresh in memory, by the annual demand of above 1,000,000 dollars to pay the interest of it?

Third question. Whether denying payment to such of our citizens, who, by their virtue and efforts, saved our country, will not be matter of great dissatisfaction to our people, and discourage their future zeal and readiness to serve their country, when their services may be necessary?

It is the *right* as well as *duty* of every citizen, to use his best endeavours to avert his country's *dangers* and *impending distresses*, whenever they appear threatening. Our country has a *right* to the *wisdom* as well as to the *wealth* of all its inhabitants, when the public exigence makes *either or both necessary*, and the *right of the nation* implies the *duty of its citizens*.

In discharge of this *duty*, I here offer my *mite of wisdom*, such as it is, to my country. If any *one sentence* of these Dissertations does not carry conviction, let it be rejected; but if my *principles* and *arguments reach the heart*, and compel the mind of the reader to yield to their *rectitude* and *force*, they will produce the effects I wish.

But whether I am gratified or disappointed, whether my country be saved or not, I have that *consciousness of upright intentions* and *faithful endeavours* for the salvation of the Union, which inspires me with the most *satisfactory expectation*, that I shall be glorious in the eyes of the LORD and of *posterity*.

A CITIZEN OF PHILADELPHIA.

Philadelphia, Dec. 20, 1790.

AN ESSAY

ON THE SEAT OF THE

Federal Government,

AND THE

EXCLUSIVE JURISDICTION

OF CONGRESS OVER A

Ten Miles District;

WITH

OBSERVATIONS

On the Economy and delicate Morals necessary to be observed in infant States.

[*First published in Philadelphia, Sep.* 21, 1789.*]

AS the *fixing the Seat of the Federal Government* is a subject, which has of late engrossed the attention of many people both in and out of Congress, perhaps a few observations on the nature and consequences of that measure may be useful, and, of course, acceptable at this time. I offer my best thoughts with freedom, without meaning to offend.†

It

---

* The seat of Congress was at *New-York* at that time.
† Tho' the *United States* of *America* contain about 640,000,000 acres of land, which have every advantage of soil and situation that any country can

It appears to me, that deciding, or even pressing, the question of the *permanent residence* of Congress is very improper *at this time*, because,

I. Congress have it in their power, without moving this question, *to obtain every accommodation for themselves which can be necessary* for years to come, and in a situation as nearly in the centre of the present population of the States, and as convenient for the whole Union, as any that can be obtained by any fixture of place that can be made, and all this without *any expense* of the States.

It is certain, that *Philadelphia* can and readily would furnish any and all public buildings, which Congress can need for their two Houses; and it is likewise certain, that all the public officers have such *liberal appointments*, that they can very well afford to pay any small rent which would be necessary for their offices.

It is farther certain, that *Philadelphia* is nearer to the centre and *general convenience* of the States, in their present state of population, than any spot either on the *Potowmac* or *Susquehannah*, or any *other place proposed* for the permanent residence of Congress, and will probably continue so for many years.

II. Fixing the seat of government will be altogether useless, *till a sum of money can be advanced, sufficient to purchase the soil, and erect the necessary buildings; which will require* (according to the estimate of the Lower House of Congress) 100,000 *dollars*. But it is certain, that, in the present state of our finances, and the numerous and pressing demands on the treasury, we are in no condition to *advance any such sum;* we have large debts called for in the most pressing manner, by creditors both foreign and domestic,

---

can boast, and tho' their territory is equal to *Great-Britain, Germany, France*, and *Spain*, taken together, yet their population and civil establishments are both young, and, as yet, in the tender state and small beginnings; and, of course, the greatest attention is necessary to that *police* and *economy*, which must strengthen, increase, and connect the whole. I therefore hope, that the humble attempts of the author to point out and patronize some leading principles of both these great objects, which are really of most essential consideration, will meet the candor and favorable attention of Congress and the Public.

whose demands we are bound to satisfy with the first monies we can raise, either from our own resources or our credit; these demands, I say, we are bound to satisfy, on every principle of *justice, public faith, national honor, and common honesty,* nay, by every inducement of *gratitude, and even compassion.*

It follows then, that *to delay these payments,* in order to squander away 100,000 dollars on buildings of no immediate use or necessity, is an act of very *high injustice,* and even *wickedness;* it is prostituting the *justice, honor,* and even *morality* of the nation, to very little more than *vain show* and *pageantry.*

It may, indeed, be doubtful what sort of justice or gratitude is due to the *purchasers of alienated certificates;* but there can certainly be no doubt of the *justice and gratitude too,* which is due to the *original holders* of certificates, who actually rendered their *services, supplies,* and *cash* to the States, in the time of their *highest dangers* and *distresses.*

These men did in fact pay the purchase of our independence; and can it be supposed, that *Americans* can enjoy all the rich blessings of their independence, and, at the same time, refuse payment to the *first purchasers* of it, who come like beggars to solicit payment, to relieve them from the penury and distress which they suffer for want of it?— Must all this scandal, meanness, and wrong be incurred, in order to lavish immense sums on a parcel of *large edifices,* to be reared up in the woods, and which are no more necessary to the present honor, safety, or even convenience of the States, than a fifth wheel to a coach? Common sense forbids it.

It is manifestly as wicked, shameful, inhuman, and ridiculous for a State to do this, as for an individual to purchase *a large estate,* enjoy the *rich produce* of it, and refuse to pay the *original purchase of it,* because the creditor happens to be a poor creature, who cannot *compel* him to payment. Can such a man, with any reason, expect either the *blessings of Heaven, esteem of mankind,* or any *kind of prosperity* in possession of such iniquitous affluence and inglorious grandeur? whilst the original purchase-money is
wrongfully

wrongfully withheld from the creditor; and the money due to him is laid out in fumptuous buildings and gaudy parade.

I fhould think, that gentlemen who can propofe fuch a plan, have forgot the great principles of *juftice, public faith,* and *economy,* on which alone the *honor, eftablifhment,* and *fafety* of a nation can be founded, and, inftead of thefe, have adopted the fentiments of young beaus and girls, who think the higheft diftinction confifts in the finery of their drefs, and fet that mifs down as undoubtedly the moft refpectable, whofe clothes and jewels are the richeft and moft brilliant.

When there is an eftate much involved, it commonly happens that fome debts, on account of *greater original merit, better earnings,* or other *caufes,* are deemed to be of a *higher nature* than others, and are therefore entitled to a *precedency* or *priority* of payment; the *original holders* of the public fecurities have undoubtedly this claim, and are therefore entitled to precedency of payment, and the States are undoubtedly furnifhed with fufficient refources to pay them, or, at leaft, their annual or half-yearly intereft; and thefe refources ought not to be diverted from fo neceffary and honorable an object, to the vain purpofes of ridiculous parade or extravagant appointments, or other *Utopian* expenfes.

But it may be objected to this by honeft men, who will fay, ' we approve the juftice and reafon of this propofition; it *coincides* with the *very fentiments of the heart,* and meets both the *honeft* and *grateful feelings* of our fouls; but, alas! it is *impracticable,* becaufe the original holders of the public fecurities cannot be *afcertained* and *difcriminated* from others who are not fuch; many who are really original holders, will not be able to prove that they are fuch.' In anfwer to this, I readily admit that any man who prefents himfelf as an original holder, and claims the benefit of precedence of payment, muft prove himfelf to be fuch, *i. e.* the proof will lie on him, and which almoft the whole of them will be able to produce with the utmoft certainty, becaufe their names are *recorded* in the *public offices,* in which their accounts were *fettled,* and out of which

their

their *certificates issued*, and tho' some few will not be able to make this proof, and so must lose the benefit, for want of proof, yet this affords no reason why those who *can make proof*, should lose the benefit of it; we might as well deny that *authenticated deeds* should be admitted as good evidence of titles of lands to the possessor, because many people have purchased estates, but have either neglected *to procure* the proper deeds, or, by some misfortune, *have lost* them, and, of course, must lose their estates, for want of the proper evidence of that *right* which is *really* in them.

III. In the late public debates of Congress on the subject of fixing the permanent seat of government, gentlemen differed so extremely *in their estimates of the distance of stations, convenience of passage both by land and water, salubrity or unhealthiness of places, state of population, and many other circumstances* necessary to be taken into account, that it appears very plain, that the internal geography and many other local qualities of the United States are not sufficiently defined and understood, to enable us to fix even the *centrality* of the States, and ascertain many other things absolutely necessary to be known and considered, in determining the permanent seat of government. Therefore, it is prudent to put off that determination, till the *data* on which it manifestly ought to depend, can be more fully known and ascertained.

IV. It is expected that *four or five States will soon be added to the present Union;** the accession of two of them we hope to be very near, and it is unreasonable to push the decision of a question (which is thought by many to be of the utmost consequence to the whole Union) *by only a part of the whole*, when, by a little delay, in no manner prejudicial to us, a decision may be obtained, in which *every part* may have its due weight and influence.

But there is another reason against an immediate decision of the question (and perhaps of more consequence

than

---

* *North-Carolina* and *Rhode-Island* had not, at the time this Essay was published, acceded to the Union under the New Constitution: the accession of some new States was expected, viz. *Vermont, Kentucky*, &c.

than this) which is drawn from the present state of Congress, viz.

V. In the late discussions of this subject in Congress, different gentlemen adopted *different spots or places for the seat of government*, and became divided into two parties nearly equal; each contending for his favorite spot with all force of argument and energy of zeal; and both parties adhered to their several favorite positions with such pointed and inflexible obstinacy, and worked themselves up to such an acrimony of debate, that it became impossible to force the decision, without giving a sort of triumph to one party, and subjecting the other to very sensible mortification; and as the majority must be very small, if the question is pushed on to a decision (for the parties are nearly equal) it is much to be feared that the affair will produce much dissatisfaction, and perhaps destroy mutual confidence and good-humor, which may in future *weaken our counsels*, and *lessen our unanimity* in matters that have *no connection with the seat of government*; for it is well known, that irritated parties rarely adopt much accommodating temper or benevolent condescension one towards another.

England and *France*, *Holland* and *Italy*, give us, in their histories, dreadful lessons of the tragical effects of state-parties, and I pray God, we may have prudence enough to put an early stop to them, if we find them in small beginnings growing amongst us.

For these reasons I wish the said decision may be postponed; I would wish this, if it was only to give gentlemen *time* to cool, and, *when cool*, to *revise* their *opinions* and *arguments*.—Time softens the acrimony of the mind, takes off the edge of the passions, makes room for charity and benevolence, and may perhaps produce such a spirit of accommodation, as, together with new information and new lights that may be thrown on the subject, may produce in a future time a decision which will strengthen our union, without any danger of weakening or destroying it.

Perhaps it may appear in future time, that neither of the spots contended for are on the whole eligible, and, of course, both parties may yield their favorite positions, without

out giving any cause of triumph to their opponents.—But there are still other reasons for a postponement of this decision not yet mentioned, viz.

VI. *Centrality will undoubtedly be (caeteris paribus) the principle on which the seat of government ought to be placed*, because every part of the Union has equal right to accommodation; but this must be a *centrality of population*, not of *territory;* it cannot matter much whether the seat of government is at little or great distance from those parts of the territory, which consist of uninhabited woods and lakes.

But this centre is, in its nature, a *moving point*, and must and will continue so, till the population of every part of the territory is complete, and becomes invariable, which, in the common course of human events, can never happen. And no kind of establishment which we can give to the seat of government, will keep it *fixed* and *unmoved*, when future reasons and future counsels shall operate against it.

Therefore, it is altogether vain and highly imprudent to endeavour to fix our seat of government by laying out any more money than is of immediate use and absolute necessity, in furnishing the accommodations of it, and especially at a time when *our finances* are extremely *low, and deranged*, our people greatly *burdened*, and the *honor* and *justice* of the States every where suffering in a scandalous manner, by our *breaches of faith* and *failure of public credit*.

But tho' centrality is the principle *(caeteris paribus)* on which the seat of government ought to be placed, yet *(caeteris non paribus)* it may become otherwise; many other things may occur, to make a removal from centrality absolutely necessary.

VII. The seat of government ought to be in a place where the *court* and *officers* of government, and all the *vast numbers of people*, both citizens and foreigners, who have occasion to resort there, *may be accommodated in the best and most convenient manner;* but it is certain, that neither the one nor the other have any chance for such accommodations on the desert banks of the *Potowmac* or *Susquehannah*

for

for many, many years to come; therefore, I think it best to defer moving to either of the places for the present.

VIII. The seat of government ought to be in a place of *the greatest attainable intelligence*; that the rulers may take benefit of the most extensive *correspondences* of men of all professions, of foreigners resorting from every part of the earth, of the most complete *libraries, maps, &c. &c.*

Congress may have concerns with all the world. Not a citizen in the States can have a connexion in any part of the earth, but, on some occasion or other, Congress may *have the matter before them*. They must preside over all improvements of the country, in which the experience and information of foreigners may be of essential use. We may be interested in the customs of foreign nations, which nobody can explain so well as their own people residing among us, &c. &c. &c.

It is not suppofable that the Members of Congress will come *from home*, furnished with competent knowledge of all the subjects they will have occasion to consider and decide; and if they have *not this knowledge*, they must obtain it *by information*, as other folks do, and, of course, must be furnished with *the means of information*; but I think we might as well immure them in the *bottom of a well*, or shut them up in a *cave*, where they would be effectually cut off from all intelligence of the world, as place them within the desert, dreary *fogs*, and disheartening *agues* of either the Potowmac or Susquehannah, where there is nothing *grand* and *majestic* to be seen, but the *ice* and *floods*, and nothing *lively* to be heard or felt, but *musketoes*. I am of opinion, the defects of nature must be corrected by art, before either of these places can become the best centre of intelligence in *America*; and therefore, I think Congress need not be in much hurry to move to either of them.

IX. It is necessary the seat of government should be placed where *the manufactures, agriculture, trade, and wealth of the country can receive the best protection and encouragement, and be most easily and properly directed and regulated by the government*. The great first principles of our wealth are our great staples of manufactures and agriculture; these

both

both receive their invigorating principle from our trade, for nobody would labor much to raise the produce of the earth, or make fabrics, if there was no trade to make a vent for them, or no market where they could be sold.

This, of course, brings the whole into action on the *various seats of navigation*, and, of course, it is absolutely necessary that the seat of government should be near such seat of navigation, that government may have the best opportunities to cherish and protect these most important interests, which not only comprise the grand *wealth* and *resources* of the subject, but out of which must be derived the great and most *capital supplies* of the government.

Farther, if it is necessary that the seat of government should be near *any* of these seats of navigation and trade, it is evidently most necessary, that it should be placed near to *the greatest seat and centre* of them.

But neither the banks of *Potowmac* nor *Susquehannah* are near any such centre, nor have either of them any chance of ever possessing such advantage; therefore, I think it best to put off at least for the present an emigration to either of them.

X. It is necessary that the seat of government should be placed in that position, which is most convenient for the *defence and protection of the Union*. Our State is yet young; we are yet ignorant how far, and in what light, we may be considered in the political systems of the *European* or *African nations*, or what designs they are or may be meditating concerning us; I suppose, our derangements and pressures since the peace have set us in a somewhat disadvantageous light among them; but *nature* will soon give us *consequence*, as, in the ordinary course of events, another century will make us as *numerous*, and perhaps as *powerful* and *rich*, as the *greatest* of them, and, of course, we shall be as *respectable*, if we have *wisdom* enough to improve our advantages.

The *two colonies* of the *European* powers, to which we are contiguous, are so thinly inhabited and weak, that I conceive we are in little danger from them; the *Indians* we can easily manage; our connexions with all the other nations

nations of the world muſt depend *on navigation,* for we can neither paſs to them, nor they to us, otherwiſe than acroſs the ſea.

I ſuppoſe nobody does now, or perhaps ever will, wiſh for any other than *commercial connections* with any of them; but even our commerce may require *protection,* and as the caprices of mankind are ſometimes very vicious, and may lead to actions very provoking, it is not impoſſible we may be inſulted *on our own coaſts,* or even in our harbours, if we are wholly *void of force* to protect them.

All this brings into view the very *great importance of our navigation,* which is the great means of our commerce, and, of courſe, of our wealth, which will doubtleſs require very extenſive and numerous ſhipping; and theſe will make a *naval force,* greater or leſs, at leaſt in ſome degree, neceſſary; and as this is an object on which not only the *wealth,* but even the *character* and *ſafety,* of the States will *capitally depend,* it inſtantly riſes into view as an intereſt, an accommodation, of ſuch vaſt magnitude, as to require a ſort of precedence of conſideration, of moſt capital and decided attention; and, of courſe, will at leaſt require the *ſeat of government* to be ſo near to the *ſeat of it,* as may be neceſſary to give it all the inſpection, ſupport, and protection, that a matter of ſuch capital conſequence muſt require from government.

The banks of *Potowmac* and *Suſquehannah* are too remote from any practicable *ſeat of a navy,* to admit any probability that it will ever be properly attended to by a court at ſuch diſtance. We have no inſtance of any nation, which pays a proper attention to their navigation, whoſe *ſeat of government* is at a *great diſtance* from their *principal harbours.*

France and *Spain* have good harbours, and every inducement and advantage for building and furniſhing a complete navy, but their capitals are far removed from the ſight of ſhips, and, of courſe, they are neglected.

On the contrary, the courts of *England, Holland, Venice,* and *Genoa,* have their harbours near them, and their ſhipping is rarely neglected or out of order.

C c c   In

In as much, then, as capital confiderations ought ever to control capital decifions, I have no doubt but a feat of the federal government will be looked for and found, not on the banks of *Potowmac* or *Sufquehannah*, but near to fome *navigable water*, proper for the *copital ftation of a navy;* and to recede from this principle will indicate not *error of judgment*, not *corruption of heart alone*, but *abfolute, total madnefs;* and for the juftice of this remark, I appeal to the fentiments of all the citizens of *America*, and of all their friends in the world.

Time has fully juftified *Peter* the Great, Czar of *Mufcovy;* who, on the force of this very principle, removed the feat of his Empire from its ancient pofition, near 500 miles farther from the centre of his dominions, and into a climate and foil much lefs defirable, merely to gain a fituation *contiguous to a harbour for his fhips;* in confequence of which his Empire is amazingly enriched by trade, and become very refpectable for its *naval force*.

But I fuppofe it will be ftrongly objected to any delay of fixing the feat of government, that, till that is done, Congrefs cannot come into poffeffion of their *exclufive jurifdiction over ten miles fquare of territory*, which is to furround their feat when fixed, and not before; and, of courfe, till then they cannot enjoy the advantages of it.

This is a meafure that has been adopted and approved by fo many votes of Convention, Congrefs, and particular States, that I fuppofe myfelf very ftupid, whilft I cannot fee any kind of fitnefs or propriety in the meafure, or any advantages that will naturally refult from it. But as *ftupidity is no crime*, and nobody can be rightfully *blamed for not underftanding* what is *totally out of the reach of his mental powers*, or for *not feeing* what does not appear *vifible* to him, I will venture to give my thoughts on this fubject, in full expectation, not of *blame* and *cenfure*, but of being deemed moft uncommonly *ftupid* and *dull*, in not being able to comprehend what is fo *very clear* and *plain* to other folks.

I. In the firft place, I can eafily conceive that Congrefs ought to have and enjoy all *powers, authorities*, and *jurifdictions*,

dictions, that are or can be *necessary to preserve their own dignity, respectability,* and *state;* sufficient fully to secure them, to all intents and purposes, against all contempts, violences, intrusions, or embarrassments, and to regulate and adjust their own order, economy, and even ceremony, in the most proper and decent manner, which they can devise; and that they shall be fully empowered to *try and punish* all violations and trespasses in any of these respects, either by acts of their corporate or aggregate body, or by such judges or officers as they shall appoint; and that all these powers shall be superior to, and uncontrollable by, any other power or authority whatever.

All *these powers of self-preservation* ought undoubtedly to exist in the fullest manner in that august body, and their prudence in the exercise of them may safely, and must necessarily, be relied on by the citizens of the States, without instituting any superior authority to control them.— But, in the second place, it appears to me,

II. That these powers, authorities, and jurisdictions must not be *fastened or limited to any particular place;* but must be *inherent* in that august body, and must *go and come* with them when and wheresoever *they move.*

If, by the invasions of an enemy, a conflagration of their edifices, the infections of a plague, or any other cause, they should find it convenient to remove their court or the seat of their residence to some distant place, they must *carry all these jurisdictions* and *powers with them;* it will not do well to leave them behind; their use will be as great and necessary in the place to which they move, as it was in the place they have left, and it would be hard upon that august body, to add to their calamities of removal, the additional mortification of being lessened and deflowered by it.

III. I have no idea that the citizens of any one district should be any more *subject to the authority and control* of Congress, or should be *entitled to their benefits or notice* in any way whatever, *more than all the rest.* Every citizen has *equal right* to all the benefits of, and owes *equal duty* to, that supreme body. Any *distinctions* of this sort lay a

foundation

foundation for partialities, expectations, or at least jealousies, which are very pernicious in society; and altho' the citizens of the ten miles district may be few at first, yet we shall probably find (whatever objections Congress have to a residence in cities) that buildings and inhabitants will multiply round their court very soon into a large city; in which numerous occasions will probably arise to operate on the above-mentioned sources of discontent and chagrin.

IV. Congress will have to make a *whole code of laws* for the *ten miles district*, to *appoint* every judiciary and executive *officer*, and to superintend the *administration* of the whole; and if they are as slow about that, as they are in organizing the federal government (and the case is quite as novel, and the ground equally untrodden) this work may probably take up their time many months; and as the States pay them about 1000 dollars a day, during their session, the administration of the district will soon cost the States 100,000 *dollars*; which is much more than either we *can spare*, or the district *can be worth* to us.

V. The whole *police of the district* will be a *solecism* in the federal government; their laws will be made and imposed by people that are not *of their election*, but by strangers, not by even their own fellow-citizens. It is altogether at the option of Congress, whether they may *appoint* one officer of their police, either judiciary or executive; they have no voice in *taxation* or giving their own money; they do *not belong* to the Thirteen States, for they are *no part* of either of them, and, of course, *not parties* to the confederation, nor are they a State of themselves; the *process* of none of the confederated States *can run* there, so that, for any thing they can do, their district will be a *refuge* for debtors, thieves, and even murderers.

They must submit, right or wrong, to the decisions of their rulers, for they have *no appeal*, no refuge from *injury or tyranny*; and this is no very comfortable circumstance, if we consider a little how common it is for courts to *oppress* the cities in which they reside. And if, under these circumstances, the district should think themselves oppressed, preffed, and fhould happen to *rebel or raife an infurrection*, the *force of the Union* muft be called in to quell them; and this will occafion another *expenfe* to the States, both of *blood and treafure*, which I ftrongly object to.

VI. Befides all this, I know not what *they will do*, or what will *become of them*, if Congrefs fhould happen to *remove from them* finally, and *not return;* here muft be another *new road cut* to their final deftination, I know not how nor where.

After all this trouble and expenfe, I cannot fee *one fingle benefit* or *advantage* which can accrue to the *Congrefs*, or the *States*, or the *diftrict*, from the whole of it; the powers and jurifdictions above defcribed appear to me to contain every thing, every authority which Congrefs can poffibly need. I take it they are all *comprifed* in the *conftitution*, tho' not *particularly* enumerated there; but if it fhould be judged that thefe powers are not given *explicitly enough* in the conftitution, they can eafily be added by way of *amendment*, and I dare believe every State will readily *ratify* them.

But I am tired of gazing at this ten miles diftrict, this *unnatural object*, this *fport of police;* for I can really make *nothing* of it; and fo I quit it, being willing to refer it over to Congrefs to make *fomething* of it, if they can.

I now return from this long and wearifome difcuffion of this great objection againft any delay in fixing the feat of government, and return to my principal fubject, which I mean briefly to revife, and reduce the matter to very few words, as follows:

We have every neceffary building for the ufe of Congrefs ready made, and have no need of new ones; and if we did need them, we have no money to fpare to build them, fo long as our debts (of moft poignant preffure and diftrefs) are unpaid;—the geography and other circumftances of the States are not fufficiently known, to enable us to afcertain the moft central place for a feat of government;—the prefent violent heats in Congrefs about this fubject render a decifion of it dangerous at this time;—we expect an acceffion of new States, who ought to have their

weight

weight in the decifion, but they muft be excluded, if the decifion is pufhed before their acceffion;—that any attempt to eftablifh a permanent feat of government of long duration, is impracticable and vain, as the juft and central point for fuch a feat will, in its nature, be always moving, and future reafons and counfels will alter any eftablifhments we can now make;—that the feat of government ought doubtlefs to be fituated in the place of the greateft intelligence,—in the centre of commerce and navigation,—and as near as may be to the moft capital and convenient ftation or harbour of the navy,—and in that place which is moft convenient for the general protection and defence of all the States.

Upon the whole matter, the *great internal fources of our wealth*, which are derived from the labor of our people, either in the way of *hufbandry* or *manufactures*, all tend to *a centre* in the *line of navigation*, which runs near the feacoaft, from one end of the States to the other; the *external* wealth derived from our *trade* with foreign countries, tends to and centres in *the fame line;* here *both meet and receive their invigorating principle,* viz. their *market*.

The *market* or *fale* is the principle which gives *life* and *vigor* to *both* thefe: this principle is put in action on this *great line of navigation;* here the fales of *both* are made; the one is *purchafed* and *fhipped* for *exportation*, the other is *purchafed* and *fent off* for *confumption*, into the various parts of the country.

On this *line*, then, is the great *feat* and *centre of negotiation*, both of our *home* produce, and our *imported* wealth; here are to be found the *great exchanges* of the nation, and, of courfe, the *greateft plenty of cafh*, and here are found the *great banks*, the richeft *repofitories* of money; and the grand *conduits* of its circulation.

On this fame line runs the greateft courfe of *intelligence* and *advice* from one end of the States to the other; and next to this are the *communications* which are conveyed *by fea*, from the *remoteft countries* on one fide, and by the great roads leading from the extremities of the *interior country* on the other; but both centre and unite on this grand
line

line of communication: for the truth of this I appeal to every post-office in the Union, and to every man whose business has any connexion with the general communication of the country.

It is farther obvious, and so intuitively plain that it cannot need a proof, that a court, whose business lies *with all men and all places*, ought to be seated in the *greatest centre of that communication which connects them all*.

It follows then, by the most intuitive evidence, that the *seat* of the federal government ought to be placed on the *great line of navigation*, and as near the geographical *centre* of it, as the great centre of wealth and communication can be found, and as near as may be to the grand *station of the navigation*, both of *commerce* and *force*, which must insure the wealth, honor, and safety of the whole.

Another obvious and very interesting reason why the seat of government ought to be placed in the grand centre of trade and communication, is this, viz. very *many people* will have *business* of importance *with the federal court* or some of its *public offices*, which may be well enough done *without their personal attendance*, and they will have many more opportunities of *sending* their business by some person of confidence who is going to the court, than they could find, if the court was held in some out-of-the-way place, far from such centre of general resort.

It is easily observed, that a person in *Boston* has more opportunities to send to *New-York*, which lies on the *great road* of general communication, than to *Albany*, which lies across the country: a person at *Pittsburg* has more opportunities to send to *Philadelphia*, than to any place of *half the distance*, which lies either *north* or *south* of it; any person in the country may send to their *capital easier* than to a *neighbouring town*, which lies in any direction which crosses the road to their capital at right angles.

Besides, many people will frequently have business with the court, and private business of trade, at the same time; and it is a great advantage to be able to do both with but one expense of journey and time; to people who live at great distance, these advantages will be very considerable,

and

and the inftances very numerous, tho' perhaps the mentioning the matter here may feem trifling.

These ftatements of facts, obfervations, and reafonings appear to me proper, important, and convincing; and for the truth, juftice, and fitnefs of them, I appeal to the heart of every *American*, to that *approving power* which is to be found in every *human breaft*, and which no man can *control*, when the matter propofed ftrikes the mind with a *force* of evidence, which, however *difagreeable* the fubject, will *compel the affent*.

I farther make the fame appeal to the *confcience* of every man, who makes *truth the fole object of his purfuit*, and who has *honefty* and *firmnefs* enough to control the *little fordid paffions*, which *local attachments, finifter interefts*, or party zeal may call up and ftimulate to *corrupt his judgment*, or to *proftitute* it; but perhaps, in the prefent corrupt ftate of human nature, no degree of virtue or natural firmnefs will make a man at all times proof againft thefe little paffions.

It is lamentable, when we fee a man of dignity of conduct, noble fentiments, great comprehenfion of mind, extenfive erudition, and found judgment, forget the great principles of his fubject, lofe his balance, and fret himfelf out of temper, in patronizing any little local interefts and partial attachments.—Good Heaven! how he leffens! how he finks! how out of character he appears! like a clergyman of fanctity grown foolifh with drink; a grave judge lofing his law in a paffion; or a fenator, entrufted with the confidence and counfels of a nation, fribbling and acting like a fool to pleafe a courtezan.

If the above principles and reafonings are allowed to be juft and conclufive, our next bufinefs will be to look for a place for a feat of government, to which they will apply; I will venture to propofe PHILADELPHIA for the place.

I. It is as near the *geographical centre* as any place in any manner capable of accommodating Congrefs; its diftance from the fouth line of the States is about 700 *miles*; from the north-eaft extremity, *about the fame*; from *Miffiffippi*, on an eaft and weft line, perhaps *a little more*; the faid eaft and *weſt line* will divide the territory of the Union into *two parts*, of *nearly equal acres*.

The computation cannot be made with accuracy, because the northern boundary, as well as the northern part of the weſtern boundary, is little known, and, of courſe, the lines, having never been meaſured, cannot by computation be reduced to certainty; but as far as the *beſt maps* we have may be depended on, the difference is not very great, tho' the *ſouthern part* is the largeſt of the two, but is greatly covered and incumbered by many *huge mountains of immenſe length*, every where rendered *incapable of cultivation* by their *height, precipices*, and *rocks*, alſo by *vaſt barren plains of hot, coarſe ſand*, and by *dry knolls* of land full of *ſhrubs, hard ſoil*, and *ſtones;* all which can never be capable of but ſmall cultivation, if any at all. The *northern part is better land*, more capable of *extenſive* and *uniform cultivation*, has a *better air*, and *climates* much more *healthy*.

The preſent population of the *northern* part is the *moſt numerous*, if we may compute from the *number of Delegates in Congreſs*, which are ſent from the two parts, allowing ſeven of the *Pennſylvania* Delegates to the northern part, and one of them to the ſouthern; as the ſaid line leaves about *one-eighth part of Pennſylvania* on the *ſouthern* ſide; but the inhabitants of the *northern* part are much the *moſt robuſt and induſtrious*, and, of courſe, the moſt likely to increaſe the *wealth* and *ſtrength* of the Union.

The inexhauſtible *fiſheries* in which the *northern* people are concerned, will add greatly to their *population* and *wealth*, for the *wives of fiſhermen* are noted for bearing the *moſt numerous* and *ſtrongeſt children:* the ſimple herring-fiſhery is ſaid to be one of the greateſt ſources of wealth and population in *Holland;* if ſo, it is probable the immenſe fiſheries of our northern people will have a ſimilar effect, and of much greater extent.

Indeed, the chance of rapid population is generally much greater in the northern part than in the ſouthern, for their natural increaſe is much greater, and their people are not only more enterpriſing, but ſtronger and more induſtrious,

D d d and,

and, of courſe, more able and fit to endure the hardſhips of new beginnings. The natural increaſe of *New-England* is not leſs than 30,000 *ſouls yearly*, and their emigrations will be almoſt wholly to the *weſtward, not to the ſouthward*, for they are generally prejudiced againſt the ſouthern climates.

From all this it appears, that *Philadelphia is as near the centre of the Union, as any point which can be found in the great line of navigation*, and in all probability will continue to be ſo for at leaſt an age or two to come.

II. *Philadelphia* is, and undoubtedly will be acknowledged by every one, the *greateſt centre of wealth, trade, navigation*, and *intelligence*, both foreign and domeſtic, which is any where to be found in the United States: this needs no proof.

III. It is ſeated on the banks of the river *Delaware*, which is the *beſt ſtation or harbour for ſhipping* that can be any where found, or even deſired. It has the following qualities or accommodations: 1. It is capable of *eaſy* and moſt *impregnable fortification* and defence from the *chaps of Newcaſtle Bay*, 80 miles from the ſea, up to *the city*, which is about 50 miles above the ſaid chaps. So that, by its diſtance from the ſea and its defences, it is *perfectly ſecure*, or may be eaſily made ſo, againſt any *ſudden ſurpriſal*, or even *invaſions*, of an enemy. 2. It affords *ſufficient water* for any ſhip that ever was built, as far up as *Wilmington*, which is 15 miles above the ſaid chaps, and 24 *feet water* from *Wilmington up to the city*. 3. It affords the *beſt anchorage*, and is wholly ſecure againſt *all winds, tides*, and *ſtorms*, the whole length from the ſaid chaps up to the city. 4. The common tides riſe and fall about *6 feet*, which is a great advantage in many reſpects. 5. Its waters not only produce no incumbrance *to a ſhip's bottom*, but inſtantly kill *all worms, cockles*, and other *vermin* which may happen to infeſt a ſhip on her firſt arrival from ſea. 6. It is furniſhed with the *greateſt plenty of timber, iron*, and all other *materials* and *ſtores* for *building, rigging*, and *repairing ſhips*, and *proviſions* for victualling them. 7. It is furniſhed with all natural conveniencies for *dry docks*; which may be built in sufficient number and extent for every purpose of *cleaning ships*. 8. It is *spacious* enough to afford *anchorage* and every other *accommodation* of security for perhaps *all the ships in the world*. 9. The port of *Philadelphia*, being the *grand centre* of commercial navigation, will always furnish *plenty of seamen*, and render the *manning* of a navy always *easy*, or at least practicable. These are the rare, singular, and excellent advantages of this port and river.

I know of *but one* considerable *inconvenience* which can be objected to it, viz. *the ice usually stops navigation in the river* about *two months* in the year; but this is in the *middle of winter*, when we rarely wish to have ships at sea; and if they should happen to come on the coast in that season, they may easily make a harbour in *New-York* or *Chesapeak Bay*; ships that winter in the river are easily *secured against any damage from the ice*, as we never have any *floods* which rise more than a *foot or two* above common high-water.

IV. *Philadelphia* can furnish more *local accommodations* for Congress, and all the vast number of people who will resort to the seat of government, than any *other city* in *America*. When compared with any of them, it has more *houses*, more *inhabitants*, more *riches*, more *churches*, and more *play-houses*, and quite as *much virtue*, tho' perhaps somewhat *less sociability*, but *more punctuality* in payments, which is some indication of *more honesty*.

V. The *climate* is *temperate*, and the *air*, *good*; the spring and fall are delightful; the winters mostly moderate, with no more snow or frost than in necessary for the convenience of the inhabitants and the growth of vegetables, &c. the *heat* of summer is *rarely intense*; and if at any time it becomes violent, it seldom *lasts long*; it is very uncommon to have the Mercury at 90°.

But I suppose the greatest objection to it is its *numerous population*. I cannot conceive what objection Congress can have to residing in *a large city*; their *accommodations* are better and cheaper, their *intelligence* and *communication* more full and easy, their *means of information* from conversation, large libraries, maps, &c. are much greater, and their

dignity

dignity and *respectability* more conspicuous than they could possibly be *in lesser places*.

I never heard of the least inconvenience, which the *English Parliament* ever suffered from sitting in *Westminster*, which is the *most populous spot in Europe*. The city of *Rome*, which contained 6,000,000 of people, was the seat of the *Roman* government, and all the inconveniencies which were felt, arose not from the *continuance* of it there, but from the *removal of it to Constantinople*; this soon brought on a division of the Empire into Eastern and Western, or *Roman* and *Grecian*; which soon terminated in the total ruin, and even extinction, of the Western Empire; the courts of most of the States and kingdoms of *Europe* are held in the *most populous cities*, without any mischiefs arising from their population that I ever heard of.

But if there are mischiefs in this, they are unavoidable, for let them fix their seat where they please, a *populous city* will soon grow round them, which can never be avoided without *repeated removals*.

I never heard of but one inconvenience arising from the largeness of the city which is the seat of Congress, which is this, viz. *the various allurements and pleasures of the place are apt to divert some of their Members from their attention to the public business and their duty in the House;* but this, I conceive, is by no means to be remedied by *running away* from the mischief, but by *imposing severe laws on their own Members, and rigidly punishing, and even expelling*, SUCH of them as are guilty of any immoral and scandalous practices, *which reflect disgrace on their body, or corrupt their morals or counsels;* or SUCH *who, on any account, neglect their attendance and duty in the House.*

When persons appointed to such high and dignified stations, happen to be so *lost to all sense of duty, honor, and even shame, as to disgrace themselves and the august body to which they belong, by levities, debaucheries, negligence of their duty, and of the most important interests they are appointed to manage,* these men, I say, are the proper objects of punishment; and if they cannot be reformed, the honor and safety of the States require that they be expelled from the House.

House. And this, I conceive, is the only practicable method of curing the mischief; and this, if put into proper execution, will very effectually cure it.

It is very manifest that the dignity, the honor, the respectability, example, and even universal visible virtue of Congress are *in their own keeping*. No *other authority* can interpose to correct a failure in any of these, unless it is *the awful tribunal of the press*, which is a most *dreadful court*, that always multiplies and increases the mischief in order to remedy it; and I should suppose, a Congress of the least degree of prudence would take the matter under their *own direction*, in order to prevent *an appeal* to that most *sovereign*, indeed, but most *mortifying* and *disgraceful*, of all umpires.

The *virtues and example of Congress are of infinite importance* to the Union. Vices and corruptions *planted in a court* (where they make their first appearance with a sort of brilliance, derived from their connection, or at least close neighbourhood, with the first honors of the nation) have a very *high introduction*, and *spread fast* among the people. Nobody can watch and suppress the first budding of this fruitful source of evil, more fatal than the opening of *Pandora*'s box, but Congress itself.

There is no situation in either town or country, no grandeur of show or pompous parade, no virtues of a few, no combination of every excellency in the President, nor any strength, wealth, and majesty of the States they represent, which can give *dignity to Congress*, so long as the Members have not *virtue* and *discretion* to *give dignity to themselves*, and *fitness* to their resolutions. The *vices*, the *negligence*, and even the *levities*, of a *few*, will tarnish the *glory* and lessen the *dignity* of that *august body*, and diminish the *confidence* of the subject in them.

Some very extraordinary things which have lately passed, induce me to turn my attention to the great principles of economy and delicate morals, which are absolutely necessary to be practised in an infant State.

I. Any appearance of *pomp*, *grandeur*, and *magnificence* of *dress*, of *equipage*, of *buildings*, or of *entertainments* should be carefully avoided.   1. Be-

1. Because the *dignity*, the *establishment*, the *defence*, and *internal polite* of the States, do not at all consist in any of these; *Fabricius*, with his disinterestedness and poverty, exhibited in *Greece* a much more striking sample of the *dignity* and *excellence* of the *Roman* mind and police, than *Lucullus*, when he returned to *Rome* thro'. the same place, with all the *blaze* of *Eastern luxury* and *magnificence*.

2. Our people being generally of middle rank, have not been accustomed to these *grand appearances*, and are apt to think there is something *foppish* and *puerile* in them, something that indicates *weakness* and *vanity*, or, which is worse, may imagine they are designed to exhibit and keep up a sort of *hauteur*, *loftiness*, and pride *of station*, which is to cow down and dispirit the subject, and depress him with a sense of his own inferiority, when he comes near the court.

3. Luxuries and levities, magnificence and show, take up *much time, and are inconsistent with that gravity of counsel, fixed attention, and steady pursuit,* which the great affairs of the nation require of its ministers; it is well known that hard students, or men deeply engaged in pursuit of any kind of business, neglect all *pageantries*, and generally despise them.

4. All these appearances are attended *with expense* which is not only *needless*, but *hurtful*; as it must be a burden either to the *public treasury*, or to the *individual concerned*, and may probably become a very *bad example of luxury and little pride*, which a young State, like all new beginners, should ever avoid.

Besides all this, the great bulk of our citizens are made up of people who set out in the world with *small beginnings*, and, by unwearied *industry and thrift*, have by little and little accumulated the competency they now enjoy. Any *departure* from this line of conduct they have commonly seen followed by *poverty* and *wretchedness*: such people have a high sense of the *value of money*, because, by long labor and careful economy, they have *earned* and *preserved* it. To people of these fixed habits, any excess of *liberal grandeur* and *sumptuous parade* must appear very *dangerous*;

gerous; like a gulf which will foon fwallow up all the public money; this makes them averfe to the payment of taxes, or cafh, which is like to be confumed and loft in prodigal expenfes.

More than all this, very great numbers of our people are derived from anceftors, who left their native foil *on account of religion;* whofe *devotion and morals* were very fevere, and a religious *gravity and aufterity of manners* has marked the character of their defcendants ever fince; not fo much as a play-houfe could be admitted, till very lately, in the moft capital cities; and, of courfe, every excefs of *levity, gaiety, drefs, equipage, parties of pleafure, gallantries, amours, &c. &c.* appear to fuch people like *debauchery, diffipation,* and *corruption of morals,* and prudence directs that not only *evil,* but *all appearance of it,* is to be avoided.

Some refpect fhould certainly be paid to the ftrong *habits, cuftoms, tempers,* and *fentiments* of any people, by perfons who refide among them, efpecially by perfons who have the *management* and *direction* of their moft *precious and delicate interefts.* I am fure the gaieties, pleafures, and expenfes of *New-York,* fince the new Congrefs have refided there, are the common talk and lamentation of the people where I live; who are not the moft noted in the world for *rigid manners* or *parfimony* of living.

II. Another great article of economy, moft neceffary to be obferved by Congrefs and all the States, is the *appointments or emoluments* annexed to all *public offices.* Making money or accumulating fortunes ought not to be the *ruling object* either in thofe who *give,* or thofe who *take,* public offices; the greateft *integrity, learning,* and *official abilities* are commonly found among men whofe habits are formed under the practice of *moderate living and prudent economy;* who would very cheerfully accept a public office with *very moderate* emoluments, and execute it in the *beft manner.*

An *abundant fufficiency* of men of this caft may be found in the Union, whofe *mediocrity of defires* and *prudent economy* will enable them to afford very well to accept the place on moderate terms; and whofe habits of induftry, fteadinefs, ness, and integrity will almost insure a faithful and proper performance of the duties of it.

What madness is it then to *pass by* this sort of men, and *offer* the public offices to men of either such *great fortunes or great business*, that they cannot afford to attend to the duties of them, without very *great emoluments?* To hear men talk in Congress of the sacrifices of fortune which they make by accepting their places, raises my indignation; not against the *impatient sufferer* so much, indeed, as against the *fools* who appointed him, who, I conceive, made much greater sacrifices of *their common sense* in giving him the place, than he did of *his money* in accepting it.

Besides, where a man's *wants are supplied by his diligence*, he will naturally be very *industrious and persevering;* but it is commonly found that industry is very apt to abate, where the occasions of it are lessened or removed. I do not know a more effectual way to *spoil a public officer*, than making him *too rich;* such a man is apt to turn over the public concerns to *clerks* or *subalterns*, and to devote more of his time to *indolence* or *pleasures*, than to the *business* of his office.

Whether any of these observations will apply to the compensations which Congress have voted to themselves, the great officers of state, the collectors and officers of the revenue, the door-keepers, and sundry other public officers, I leave to be discussed another time; without going into any detail of that matter at present, I have only to say, that the compensations are generally deemed (by people I have conversed with) to be about *double* of what they ought to be, in order *to insure the business of the respective offices to be well done:* and as they are amazingly higher than the States of the Union in general allow to their officers of a similar nature, I suppose they will be thought excessive, and, of course, will be complained of, and probably viewed with uneasiness and dissatisfaction.

Certainly the extravagancies of the courts of *Europe* in this respect are no kind of *rule* for us, and I think any gentleman might be ashamed to quote their example (which is and ever has been universally exploded in *America*) as a

reason

reason why we should *imitate* it. But it may be noted, that no compensations allowed in *Europe* or *America* to the Members of any *Parliament, Diet, States General, Assembly*, or any *other body* similar to that of Congress, ever were *one-third* of what Congress have granted to *themselves;* at least this is true as far as I could ever gain information of the matter.

I suppose they give no credit for the *honor* of their stations, their *acquaintance* with all the capital characters in *America*, and all those of *Europe*, which repair to the federal court, their *information* of the state and principle of the manufactures, agriculture, commerce, and policies of all the States of the Union, the opportunities they acquire of serving their children and friends, and the *consequence* which their residence in Congress will ever after give to *them* and their *families* in their respective States, whenever they shall return home. I should suppose *all* these advantages, or even *any one* of them, would be compensation enough for a few months' residence in Congress, without *any money* at all; especially if their *simple and necessary* expenses were born by the public into the bargain.

III. *Economy* absolutely requires the *payment of the public debts*, at least the annual or half-yearly interest of them; the public would derive greater advantages from this, by the *general animation* of every sort of business it would produce, than would *compensate the burden* of raising the money to do it, even if we pay no regard to the *public justice, honor, credit, morality, gratitude,* and *even compassion*, which all conspire to enforce the same measure.

But if all this cannot be done at present, enough may doubtless be done to satisfy the *original holders* of the public securities, who are manifestly the most *meritorious*, as well as the *greatest, sufferers*, and the most *distressed* and *ruined* by the *public defaults of any among us;* but I touched on this before, and it is needless to add more on this dreary subject in this place.

IV. Economy requires that the public monies should be raised in that way that is *easiest to the people, and least troublesome, disgusting, and expensive in the collection;* an impost on *imported luxuries* and articles of *unneceſſary* conſumption, but juſt *high enough* to reduce the *exceſſive* uſe of them down to that degree, which is moſt conducive to the *health, morals,* and *wealth* of our people, together with the *ſmall impoſt* on other articles already aſſeſſed, will, I conceive, produce all the ſupplies which the public exigences require; the collection of all this will be *cheap and eaſy; a few officers in the places of navigation* will be ſufficient; and the importers who pay the duty, will be *few*, and will all be *reimburſed* in their ſales.

But *a general excise* (which, I hear, is in contemplation) will require an almoſt *infinite number of officers,* whoſe *pay* will amount to *vaſt ſums*, and whoſe *duty* will be of the *moſt diſguſting and mortifying kind* to the people; for my part, I had rather pay a *dollar a gallon*, impoſt duty, on all the ſpirits and wines I conſume, than ſuffer the *mortifying intruſions of an excise-officer,* to examine my *liquors,* tho' his demand was but *a ſhilling;* and after all, it will be totally *impoſſible to collect* this duty in the exterior parts of the States with any kind of general uniformity and equality, as all experience has ever made manifeſt. But I have treated this more fully *in my Fifth, Sixth, and Seventh Eſſays on Free Trade and Finance,* to which I refer any body who wiſhes to ſee my ſentiments on this ſubject more fully explained.

I write with the moſt *unlimited freedom,* and I expect the *candor* of my countrymen; if my ſentiments are *wrong, condemn them;* if *right, approve and adopt them;* it is not *an itch of writing* which impels me, but *a zeal for a good government and a wiſe adminiſtration* prompts me to write, and dictates every line. I lament that any one advantage of my country ſhould be *loſt* for want of *proper management,* or that we ſhould ever incur the old cenſure of *fools,* having a *price* put into their hands, but no *hearts* to improve it. May Heaven direct our public counſels, and give proſperity and eſtabliſhment to our union.

REMARKS

REMARKS

ON THE

Addreſs of Sixteen Members

OF THE

ASSEMBLY OF PENNSYLVANIA,

TO THEIR

CONSTITUENTS,

Dated September 29, 1787.

With ſome Strictures on their Objections to the CON-
STITUTION *recommended by the late Federal Convention.* *

[*Firſt publiſhed in Philadelphia, October* 12, 1787.]

———I AM now to conſider the objections of our ſixteen Members to the *New Conſtitution* itſelf, which is much the moſt important part that lies on me.

1. Their firſt objection is, that the government propoſed will be *too expenſive.* I anſwer, that if the appointments
of

---

* When the *New Conſtitution* was laid before the *Aſſembly of Pennſylva-
nia,* in *September,* 1787, a reſolution paſſed the Houſe (forty-three againſt nineteen) to call a *Convention* to conſider it, &c. Sixteen of the Diſſentients publiſhed an *Addreſs to their Conſtituents, dated September* 27, 1787, ſtating their conduct and aſſigning the reaſons of it: but as there was very little in all this affair that reflected *much honor* on the *diſſenting Members* or *on the State to which they belonged,* and *nothing* that could *affect* or *concern* any body out of that State, I have here omitted my remarks on all of it, but *their objections* to the *New Conſtitution itſelf,* which being of general conſequence to the States, in as much as that Conſtitution (with a few amendments ſince adopted) is the ſame which now exiſts in full eſtabliſhment thro' the Union, I therefore here inſert, I ſay, *their objections and my remarks on them,* and leave out all the reſt as matter of *local* concern at *that time,* but like to be little intereſting to the public in general at this or any future time.

of offices are not more, and the compenfations or emoluments of office not greater, than is neceffary, the expenfe will be by no means burdenfome, and this muft be left to the prudence of Congrefs; for I know of no way to control fupreme powers from extravagance in this refpect. Doubtlefs many inftances may be produced of many needlefs offices being created, and many inferior officers, who receive far greater emoluments of office than the firft Prefident of the State.

2. Their next objection is againft a *legiflature confifting of three branches*. This is fo far from an objection, that I confider it as an advantage. The moft weighty and important affairs of the Union muft be tranfacted in Congrefs; the moft effential counfels muft be there decided, which muft all go thro' three feveral difcuffions in three different chambers (all equally competent to the fubject and equally governed by the fame motives and interefts, viz. the good of the great Commonwealth, and the approbation of the people) before any decifion can be made; and when difputes are very high, different difcuffions are neceffary, becaufe they afford time for all parties to cool and reconfider.

This appears to me to be a very fafe way, and a very likely method to prevent any fudden and undigefted refolutions from paffing; and tho' it may delay, or even deftroy, a good bill, will hardly admit the paffing of a bad one, which is by far the worft evil of the two. But if all this cannot ftop the courfe of a bad bill, the negative of the Prefident will at leaft give it further embarraffment, will furnifh all the new light which a moft ferious difcuffion in a third Houfe can give, and will make a new difcuffion neceffary in each of the other two, where every member will have an opportunity to revife his opinion, to correct his arguments, and bring his judgment to the greateft maturity poffible: if all this can not keep the public decifion within the bounds of wifdom, natural fitnefs, right, and convenience, it will be hard to find any efforts of human wifdom that can do it.

I believe

I believe it would be difficult to find a man in the Union, who would not readily consent to have Congress vested with all the vast powers proposed by the New Constitution, if he could be sure that those powers would be exercised with wisdom, justice, and propriety, and not be abused; and I do not see that greater precautions and guards against abuses can well be devised, or more effectual methods used to throw every degree of light on every subject of debate, or more powerful motives to a reasonable and honest decision can be set before the minds of Congress, than are here proposed.

And if this is the best that can be obtained, it ought in all prudence to be adopted till better appears, rather than to be rejected merely because it is human, not perfect, and may be abused. At any rate I think it very plain that our chance of a right decision in a Congress of three branches, is much greater than in one of a single chamber: but however all this may be, I cannot see the least tendency in a Legislature of three branches to increase the burdens or taxes of the people. I think it very evident that any proposition of extravagant expense would be checked and embarrassed in such an Assembly, more than in a single House.

Further, the two Houses being by their election taken from the body of the States, and being themselves principal inhabitants, will naturally have the interest of the Commonwealth sincerely at heart, their principle must be the same, their differences must be (if any) in the mode of pursuing it, or arise from local attachments; I say, the great interest of their country, and the esteem, confidence, and approbation of their fellow-citizens, must be strong governing principles in both Houses, as well as in the President himself. *

3. Another objection is, that the Constitution proposed will *annihilate the State-governments, or reduce them to mere corporations.* I take it that this objection is thrown out

(merely

---

* Vide this subject fully discussed in my Dissertation on that Constitution which is necessary for the United States, page 198.

(merely *invidiæ causa*) without the least ground for it; for I do not find *one article* of the Constitution proposed, which vests *Congress*, or *any of their officers* or *courts*, with a power *to interfere in the least in the internal police or government of any one State*, when the interests of *some other State*, or *strangers*, or *the Union* in general, are *not concerned;* and in all such cases it is absolutely and manifestly necessary that Congress should have *a controlling power*, otherwise there would be *no end of controversies and injuries* between *different States*, nor any *safety* for *individuals*, nor any possibility *of supporting the Union* with any tolerable degree of honor, strength, or security.

4. Another objection is against the *power of taxation vested in Congress*. But I answer, this is absolutely necessary and unavoidable, from the necessity of the case; I know it is a *tender point*, a *vast power*, and a *terrible engine of oppression* and *tyranny*, when *wantonly, injudiciously*, or *wickedly used*, but *must be admitted;* for it is impossible to support the Union, or indeed any government, *without expense*—the Congress are the *proper judges* of that expense, the *amount* of it, and the best *means* of supplying it; the *safety* of the States *absolutely requires* that this power be lodged *somewhere*, and no *other body* can have the least pretensions to it; and *no part* of the resources of the States can, with any safety, be *exempt*, when the *exigencies* of the Union or government require their *utmost exertion*.

The *stronger we make our government*, the *greater protection it can afford us*, and the *greater* will our *safety be* under it.

It is easy enough here to harangue on the *arts of a court* to create occasions for money, or the unbounded *extravagance* with which they can spend it; but all this notwithstanding, we must take our courts as we do our *wives, for better or for worse*. We hope the best of an *American Congress*, but if they disappoint us, we cannot help it; it is in vain to try to form any plan of *avoiding the frailties* of human nature.—Would any man choose a *lame* horse lest a *sound* one should run away with him? or will any man prefer a *small tent* to live in, before a *large house*, which

may

may fall down and *crush him* in its ruins? No man has any right to find fault with this article, till he can substitute a better in its room.

The sixteen Members attempt to aggravate the horrors of this devouring power, by suggesting the rigid severity with which Congress, with their *faithful soldiers*, will *exact and collect* the taxes. This picture, stripped of its *black drapery*, amounts to just this, viz. that whatever taxes are laid will be collected, without exception, from every person charged with them, which must look disagreeable, I suppose, to people who, by one shift or another, have avoided paying taxes all their lives.

But it is a plain truth, and will be obvious to any body who duly considers it, that nothing can be more ruinous to a *State*, or oppressive to *individuals*, than a *partial and dilatory collection* of taxes, especially where the tax is an impost or excise, because the man who *avoids* the tax, can *undersell*, and consequently *ruin*, him who *pays* it, *i. e.* smuggling ruins the fair trader, and a *remedy* of this mischief, I cannot suppose, will be deemed by our people in general such a *very awful judgment*, as the sixteen Members would make us believe their constituents will consider it to be.

5. They object, that the *liberty of the press is not asserted* in the Constitution. I answer, neither are any of the *ten commandments*, but I do not think, that it follows that it was the design of the Convention to sacrifice either *the one* or *the other* to contempt, or to leave them void of protection and effectual support.

6. It is objected further, that the Constitution contains *no declaration of rights*. I answer, this is not true: the Constitution contains a declaration of many rights, and very important ones, *e. g.* that people shall be obliged to *fulfil their contracts*, and *not avoid* them by *tenders* of any thing less than the value stipulated; that no *ex post facto* laws shall be made, &c. but it was no part of the business of their appointment to make *a code of laws;* it was sufficient *to fix the Constitution right*, and that would pave the way for the most effectual security of the rights of the subject.

7. They

7. They further object, that no provision is made against a *standing army in time of peace.* I answer, that a standing army, *i. e.* regular troops, are often necessary in time of peace, to prevent a war, to guard against sudden invasions, for garrison-duty, to quell mobs and riots, as guards to Congress and perhaps other courts, &c. &c. as military schools to keep up the knowledge and habits of military discipline and exercise, &c. &c. and as the power of raising troops is rightfully and without objection vested in Congress, so they are the *properest and best judges* of the *number* requisite, and the *occasion, time,* and *manner* of employing them; if they are not wanted on military duty, they may be employed in making *public roads, fortifications,* or any other *public works:* they need not be an *useless burden* to the States: and for all this the prudence of Congress must be trusted, and nobody can have a right to object to this, till they can point out some way of doing better.

8. Another objection is, that the New Constitution *abolishes trial by jury in civil causes.* I answer, I do not see one word in the Constitution, which, by any candid construction, can support even the remotest suspicion that this ever entered in the heart of one Member of the Convention: I therefore set down the suggestion for sheer malice, and so dismiss it.

9. Another objection is, that the federal *judiciary is so constructed as to destroy the judiciaries of the several States,* and that the *appellate jurisdiction, with respect to law and fact, is unnecessary.* I answer, both the *original* and *appellate* jurisdiction of the federal judiciary are manifestly necessary, where the cause of action affects the citizens of *different* States, the *general interest* of the Union, or *strangers* (and to cases of *these descriptions only* does the *jurisdiction* of the federal judiciary *extend)* I say, these jurisdictions of the federal judiciary are manifestly necessary for the reasons just now given under the third objection.

I do not see how they can avoid trying any issues joined before them, whether the thing to be decided is *law* or *fact;*

fact; but I think no doubt can be made, that if the issue joined is on *fact*, it must be tried by a jury.

10. They object, that the *election of Delegates* for the House of Representatives *is for two years*, and of Senators, *for six years*. I think this a manifest *advantage*, rather than an *objection*. Very great inconveniences must necessarily arise from a too frequent change of the Members of large legislative or executive bodies, where the revision of every past transaction must be taken up, explained, and discussed anew for the information of the new Members; where the settled rules of the House are little understood by them, &c. &c. all which ought to be avoided, if it can be with safety.

Further, it is plain that any man who serves in such bodies, is better qualified the second year than he could be the first, because experience adds qualifications for every business, &c. the only objection is, that long continuance affords danger of corruption, but for this the Constitution provides a remedy by impeachment and expulsion, which will be a sufficient restraint, unless a majority of the House and Senate should become corrupt, which is not easily presumable: in fine, there is a *certain mean* between too *long* and too *short* continuances of Members in Congress, and I cannot see but it is judiciously fixed by the Convention.

Upon the whole matter, I think the sixteen Members have employed *an address-writer* of great dexterity, who has given us a strong sample of *ingenious malignity and ill-nature*—a masterpiece of *high coloring* in the *scare-crow way*; in his account of the conduct of the sixteen Members, by an unexpected openness and candor, he avows *facts* which he certainly cannot expect to justify, or even hope that their constituents will patronize or even approve; but he seems to lose all candor when he deals *in sentiments*; when he comes to point out the *nature* and *operation* of the *New Constitution*, he appears to mistake the *spirit* and *true principles* of it very much; or, which is worse, takes pleasure in showing it in the *worst light* he can paint it in.

I however agree with him in this, ' that this is *the time for consideration and minute examination*;' and, I think, the

F f f

great *subject*, when viewed seriously, without passion or prejudice, will *bear*, and *brighten under, the severest examination* of the rational inquirer. If the *provisions* of the law or Constitution do not exceed the *occasions*, if the *remedies* are not extended beyond the *mischiefs*, the government cannot be justly charged with *severity;* on the other hand, if the provisions are not *adequate* to the occasions, and the remedies *not equal to* the mischiefs, the government must be *too lax*, and not sufficiently operative to give the necessary *security* to the subject: to form a right judgment, we must compare these two things well together, and not suffer our minds to dwell on one of them alone, without considering it in *connexion* with the other; by this means we shall easily see that the one makes the other necessary.

Were we to view only the *gaols* and *dungeons*, the *gallows* and *pillories*, the *chains* and *wheel-barrows*, of any State, we might be induced to think the government *severe;* but when we turn our attention to the *murders* and *parricides*, the *robberies* and *burglaries*, the *piracies* and *thefts*, which merit these *punishments*, our idea of *cruelty* vanishes at once, and we admire the *justice*, and perhaps *clemency*, of that government, which before *shocked* us as too severe.

So when we fix our attention only on the *superlative authority* and *energetic force* vested in Congress, and our federal executive powers by the New Constitution, we may at first sight be induced to think that we yield more of the *sovereignty of the States* and of *personal liberty*, than is requisite to maintain the federal government; but when, on the other hand, we consider with full survey the *vast supports* which the union requires, and the *immense consequence of that* UNION to us all, we shall probably soon be convinced that the powers aforesaid, *extensive* as they are, are not *greater* than is necessary for our benefit: for,

1. *No laws of any State, which do not carry in them a force which extends to their effectual and final execution, can afford a certain and sufficient security to the subject;* for,

2. *Laws of any kind, which fail of execution, are worse than none,* because they *weaken* the government, expose it to *contempt,* destroy the *confidence* of all men, both subjects and

and ftrangers, in it, and *difappoint* all men who have *confided in it.*

In fine, *our union* can never be fupported without *definite* and *effectual* laws, which are co-extenfive with their occafions, and which are fupported by authorities and powers which can give them *execution with energy;* if admitting fuch powers into our Conftitution can be called a *facrifice*, it is a *facrifice to fafety,* and the only queftion is, whether our UNION or federal government is worth this facrifice.

Our UNION, I fay, *under the protection of which* every individual refts fecure againft *foreign* and *domeftic* infult and oppreffion; but *without it* we can have no fecurity againft invafions, infults, and oppreffions of *foreign powers,* or againft the inroads and wars of *one State on another,* or even againft *infurrections* and *rebellions* arifing within particular States, by which our wealth and ftrength, as well as eafe, comfort, and fafety, will be devoured and deftroyed by *enemies growing out of our own bowels.*

It is *our* UNION *alone* which can give us *refpectability abroad* in the eyes of foreign nations, and fecure to us all the advantages both of *trade* and *fafety,* which can be derived from *treaties with them.*

The Thirteen States all united and well cemented together, are a *ftrong, rich,* and *formidable* body, not of *ftationary,* maturated power, but *increafing* every day in riches, ftrength, and numbers.

Thus circumftanced, we can demand the attention and refpect of all foreign nations, but they will give us both in *exact proportion* to the *folidity of our union:* for if they obferve our *union* to be *lax,* from *infufficient* principles of cement in our *Conftitution,* or *mutinies* and *infurrections* of our own people (which are the direct confequence of an *infufficient cement of union)* I fay, when foreign nations fee either of thefe, they will immediately *abate* of their *attention* and *refpect* to us, and *confidence* in us.

And as it appears to me, that the New Conftitution does not veft Congrefs with *more* or *greater* powers than are neceffary to fupport this *important union,* I wifh it may be admitted

mitted in the most *cordial* and *unanimous* manner by all the States.

It is a *human* composition, and may have *errors* which future experience will enable us to discover and correct; but I think it is pretty plain, if it has faults, that the address-writer of the sixteen Members has not been able to find them; for he has all along either hunted down *phantoms of error*, that have no *real existence*, or, which is worse, *tarnished real excellencies* into *blemishes*.

I have dwelt the longer on these remarks of this writer, because I observe that all the scribblers in our papers against the New Constitution, have taken their cue principally from him; all their lucubrations contain little more than *his ideas* dressed out in a great variety of forms; one of which colors so high as to make the New Constitution strongly resemble the *Turkish government* (vide Gazetteer of the 10th instant) which, I think, comes about as near the truth as any of the rest, and brings to my mind a sentiment in polemical divinity, which I have somewhere read, that there were once great disputes and different opinions among divines about the *mark which was set on Cain*, when one of them very gravely thought it was a *horn fully grown out on his forehead*. It is probable he could not think of a *worse mark* than that.

On the whole matter, there is no end of the extravagancies of the human fancy, which are commonly dictated by *poignant feelings, disordered passions*, or *affecting interests*; but I could wish my fellow-citizens, in the matter of vast importance before us, would divest themselves of bias, passion, and *little personal* or *local interests*, and consider the great subject with that dignity of reason, and independence of sentiment, which national interests ever require.

I have here given my sentiments with the most unbiassed freedom, and hope they will be received with the most candid attention and unbiassed discussion by the State in which *I live*, and in which I expect *to leave my children*.

I will conclude with one observation, which I take to be very capital, viz. that the distresses and oppressions, both of nations and individuals, often arise from the *powers of government*

government being *too limited* in their *principle*, too *indeterminate* in their *definition*, or too *lax* in their *execution*, and, of course, the safety of the citizens depends much on *full* and *definite* powers of government, and an *effectual execution* of them.

The Weaknesses of Brutus exposed:

OR, SOME

REMARKS

In Vindication of the Constitution

PROPOSED BY THE LATE

FEDERAL CONVENTION,

AGAINST THE

OBJECTIONS and GLOOMY FEARS of that WRITER.

[*First published in Philadelphia, Nov. 4, 1787.*]

THE long piece signed BRUTUS (which was first published in a *New-York paper*, and was afterwards copied into the *Pennsylvania Packet* of Oct. 26, 1787) is wrote in a very good style; the language is easy, and the address is polite and insinuating; but the *sentiments*, I conceive, are not only *unsound*, but *wild and chimerical;* the dreary fears and apprehensions, altogether groundless; and the *whole tendency* of the piece, in this very important crisis of our politics, very *hurtful*. I have, therefore, thought it my duty to make some animadversions on it; which I here offer, with all due deference, to the author and to the public.

HIS

His first question is, *Whether a confederated government is best for the United States?*

I answer,—If *Brutus*, or any body else, cannot find any *benefit* resulting from the *union of the Thirteen States*; if they can do *without* as well as *with* the respectability, the protection, and the security, which the States may derive from that union, I have nothing further to say: but if *that union* is to be *supported* in any such manner as to afford respectability, protection, or security to the States, I say it must be done by an *adequate government*, and cannot be otherwise done.

This government must have a supreme power, *superior to and able to control* each and all of its parts. It is essential to all government, that *such a power be somewhere existing in it*; and, if *the place* where the proposed Constitution has fixed it, does not suit *Brutus* and his friends, I will give him leave to stow it away in any *other place that is better*: but I will not consent to have it *annihilated*; neither will I agree to have it *cramped and pinched* for room, so as to *lessen* its energy; for that will *destroy* both its nature and use.

The supreme power of government ought to be *full*, *definite*, *established*, and *acknowledged*. Powers of government *too limited*, or *uncertain* and *disputed*, have ever proved, like *Pandora*'s box, a most fruitful source of quarrels, animosities, wars, devastation, and ruin, in all shapes and degrees, in all communities, states, and kingdoms on earth.

Nothing tends more to the *honor*, *establishment*, and *peace* of society, than *public decisions*, grounded on principles of *right*, *natural fitness*, and *prudence*; but when the powers of government are *too limited*, such decisions cannot be *made and enforced*; so the mischief goes without a remedy: dreadful examples of which we have felt, in instances more than enough, for seven years past.

Further, where the powers of government are not *definite* but *disputed*, the administration *dare not* make decisions on the footing of *impartial justice and right*; but must *temporize* with the parties, lest they lose *friends* or make *enemies*: and, of course, the *righteous* go off injured and disgusted, and the *wicked* go off grumbling too; for it is rare that

that any sacrifices of a court can satisfy a prevailing party in the State.

It is necessary in States, as well as in private families, that controversies should have a just, *speedy*, and effectual decision, that right may be done before the contention has *time* to grow up into habits of malignity, resentment, ill-nature, and ill offices. If a controversy happens between *two States*, must it continue *undecided*, and *daily increase*, and be more and more *aggravated*, by the repeated insults and injuries of the contending parties, till they are ripe for the *decision of the sword?* or must the *weaker States* suffer, without remedy, the groundless demands and oppressions of their *stronger neighbours*, because they have no *avenger*, or *umpire* of their disputes?

Or shall we institute *a supreme power, with full and effectual authority to control the animosities and decide the disputes of these strong, contending bodies?* In the one proposed to us, we have perhaps every chance of a *righteous judgment*, that we have any reason to hope for; but I am clearly of opinion, that even a *wrongful decision* would, in most cases, be preferable to *the continuance* of such destructive controversies.

I suppose that neither *Brutus* nor any of his friends would wish to see our government *embroiled abroad*, and, therefore, will admit it necessary to institute some *federal authority*, sufficient to punish *any individual or State*, who shall violate our *treaties* with foreign nations, insult their *dignity*, or abuse their *citizens*, and compel due reparation in all such cases.

I further apprehend, that *Brutus* is willing to have the *general interest and welfare* of the States well provided for and supported, and, therefore, will consent that there shall exist in the States an authority to *do* all this *effectually;* but he seems grieved that Congress should be the *judges of this general welfare* of the States. If he will be kind enough to point out any *other more suitable and proper judges*, I will consent to have them admitted.

Indeed, I begin to have hopes of *Brutus*, and think he may come right at last; for I observe (after all his fear and trembling

trembling about the new government) the constitution he *defines and adopts,* is *the very same* as that which the *Federal Convention* have proposed to us, viz. " that the Thirteen States should continue thirteen confederated republics, under the *direction and control* of a supreme *federal head,* for certain *defined national purposes* only." Where we may observe,

1. That the New Constitution *leaves* all the Thirteen States, *complete republics,* as it *found* them, but all confederated under the direction and control of a *federal head,* for certain *defined national purposes only,* i. e. it leaves all the dignities, authorities, and internal police of each State in *free, full,* and *perfect condition;* unless when national purposes make the control of them by the federal head or authority, necessary to the *general benefit.*

2. These powers of control by the federal head or authority are defined in the New Constitution, as minutely as may be, *in their principle;* and *any detail* of them which may become necessary, is committed to the wisdom of Congress.

3. It extends the controlling power of the federal head to *no one case,* to which the jurisdiction or power of definitive decision of any one State *can be competent.* And,

4. In every such case, the *controlling power* of the federal head is absolutely necessary to the *support, dignity, and benefit* of the *national government,* and the *safety of individuals;* neither of which can, by any possibility, be secured without it.

All this falls in pretty well with *Brutus's* sentiments; for he does not think that the New Constitution in its *present state* so very bad, but fears that it will *not preserve* its purity of institution, but, if adopted, will immediately verge to, and terminate in, *a consolidation,* i. e. a destruction of the State-governments. For argument, he suggests the *avidity of power* natural to rulers, and the *eager grasp* with which they hold it when obtained, and their strong *propensity to abuse* their power, and *encroach* on the liberties of the people.

He

He dwells on the *vast powers* vested in Congress by the New Constitution, *i. e. of levying taxes, raising armies, appointing federal courts, &c.* takes it for granted that all these powers will be *abused* and carried to an *oppressive excess;* and then harangues on the dreadful case we shall be in, when our *wealth* is all devoured by taxes; our *liberty* destroyed by the power of the army; and our *civil rights* all sacrificed by the unbounded power of the federal courts, &c.

And when he has run himself out of breath with this dreary declamation, he comes to the conclusion he set out with, viz. that the Thirteen States are *too big* for a republican government, which requires *small territory*, and cannot be supported in *more extensive nations;* that in large States *liberty* will soon be swallowed up, and lost in the *magnitude of power* requisite in the government, &c.

If any conclusion at all can be drawn from this baseless assemblage of gloomy thoughts, I think it must be *against any union at all;* against *any kind of federal government.* For nothing can be plainer than this, viz. *that the union cannot by any possibility be supported with success, without adequate and effectual powers of government.*

We must have *money* to support the union, and, therefore, the *power of raising it* must be lodged *somewhere;* we must have *a military force,* and, of consequence, the power of *raising and directing it* must exist; *civil* and *criminal causes* of national concern will arise, therefore, there must be somewhere a power of appointing *courts* to hear and determine them.

These powers must be vested in Congress; for nobody pretends to wish to have them vested in any *other body* of men.

The Thirteen States have a territory very extensive, and inhabitants very numerous, and every day rapidly increasing; therefore, the powers of government necessary to support their union must be *great* in proportion. If the *ship* is large, the *mast* must be proportionably great, or it will be impossible to make her sail well. The federal powers must extend to *every part* of the federal territory, *i. e.* to the *utmost limits* of the United States, and to every part of them; and must carry with them sufficient *authority* to secure the *execution* of them; and these powers must be vested *in Congress*, and the execution of them must be under *their* direction and control.

These powers are *vast*, I know; and the trust is of the most *weighty kind* that can be committed to human direction; and the execution and administration of it will require the greatest *wisdom, knowledge, firmness*, and *integrity* in that august body; and I hope they will have all the *abilities and virtues* necessary to their important station, and will *perform their duty well;* but *if they fail*, the fault is in *them*, not in the *Constitution*. The *best* Constitution possible, even a divine one, *badly* administered, will make a *bad* government.

The Members of Congress will be the *best* we can get; they will all of them derive their appointment from the States, and if the States are not *wise enough* to send *good and suitable* men, great *blame*, great *sin* will lie at their door. But I suppose nobody would wish to mend this fault by taking away *the election of the people*, and directing the appointment of Congress to be made *in any other way*.

When we have gotten the *best* that can be obtained, we ought to be quiet and cease complaining. It is not in the power of human wisdom to do more; it is the fate of human nature to *be imperfect and to err;* and no doubt but Congress, with all their *dignity of station and character*, with all their *opportunities* to gain *wisdom and information*, with all their *inducements to virtue and integrity*, will *err*, and *abuse* or *misapply* their powers in more or less instances. I have no expectation that they will make *a court of angels*, or be any thing more than *men:* it is probable many of them will be *insufficient* men, and some of them may be *bad men*.

The greatest wisdom, care, and caution, has been used in the *mode* of their appointment; in the *restraints and checks* under which they must act; in the numerous *discussions and deliberations* which all their acts must pass thro', before they can receive the stamp of authority; in the terrors

rors of *punishment* if they misbehave. I say, in all *these ways* the greatest care has been used to procure and form a *good* Congress.

The *dignity and importance* of their station and character will afford all the inducements to virtue and effort, which can influence a mind *capable* of their force.

Their own *personal reputation*, with the eyes of all the world on them,—the *approbation of their fellow-citizens*, which every man in public station naturally wishes to enjoy, and the *dread of censure and shame*,—all contribute very forcible and strong inducements to noble, upright, and worthy behaviour.

The *particular interest* which every Member of Congress has in every public order and resolution, is *another strong motive* to right action. For every act to which any Member gives his sanction, if it be raising an *army*, levying a *tax*, instituting a *court*, or any other act to bind the *States*, such act will equally bind *himself, his nearest connexions, and his posterity*.

Another mighty influence to the noblest principle of action will be, *the fear of God before their eyes;* for while they sit in the place of God, to give law, justice, and right to the States, they must be *monsters indeed*, if they do not regard *his law*, and imitate *his character*.

If all this will not produce *a Congress fit to be trusted, and worthy of the public confidence*, I think we may give the matter up as impracticable. But still we must make ourselves as easy as we can, under a *mischief* which admits *no remedy*, and bear with patience an *evil* which cannot be *cured:* for *a government* we must have; there is no safety *without* it; tho' we know it will be imperfect, we still must prefer it to *anarchy or no government at all*. It is the height of folly and madness to reject a *necessary* convenience, because it is not a *perfect* good.

Upon this statement of facts and principles (for the truth and reality of which, I appeal to every candid man) I beg leave to remark,

1. That

1. That the Federal Convention, in the Conftitution propofed to us, have exerted their utmoft to produce *a Congrefs worthy of the public confidence*, who fhall have *abilities* adequate to their important duty, and fhall act under every poffible inducement to execute it *faithfully*.

2. That this affords *every chance* which the nature of the thing will admit, *of a wife and upright adminiftration*.

3. Yet all this notwithstanding, it is very poffible that Congrefs *may err, may abufe or mifapply* their powers, which no precaution of human wifdom can prevent.

4. It is *vain*, it is *childifh*, it is *contentious* to object to a Conftitution thus framed and guarded, on pretence that the Commonwealth may fuffer by a *bad adminiftration* of it; or to *withhold the neceffary powers* of government from the fupreme rulers of it, left they fhould *abufe or mifapply* thofe powers. This is an objection which will operate with equal force againft *every inftitution* that can be made in this world, whether of *policy, religion, commerce*, or *any other human concern*, which can require regulations: for it is not poffible to form any inftitution however neceffary, wife, and good, whofe ufes may not be leffened or deftroyed by bad management.

If *Brutus* or any body elfe can point out any *checks, cautions*, or *regulations*, which have been hitherto omitted, which will make Congrefs more *wife*, more *capable*, more *diligent*, or more *faithful*, I am willing to attend to them.

But to fet Congrefs at the *head* of the government, and object to their being vefted with *full* and *fufficient power* to manage all the great departments of it, appears to me *abfurd*, quite *wild*, and *chimerical*: it would produce a plan which would deftroy itfelf as it went along, would be a fort of counter-pofition of contrary parts, and render it impoffible for rulers to render thofe fervices, and fecure thofe benefits, to the States, which are the only great ends of their appointment.

The Conftitution, under *Brutus*'s corrections, would ftand thus, viz. Congrefs would have power to *raife money*, but muft not direct the *quantity*, or *mode of levying* it; they might raife *armies*, but muft not judge of the *number* of foldiers soldiers necessary, or *direct* their destination; they ought to provide for the *general welfare*, but must not be judges of what that welfare *consists in*, or in *what manner* it is to be provided for; they might *control* the several States for *defined national purposes*, but must not be judges of *what purposes* would come within that *definition*, &c.

Any body with half an eye may see what sort of administration the Constitution thus corrected would produce, *e. g.* it would require much greater trouble to leave the work *undone*, than would be necessary to get it *well done*, under a Constitution of sufficient powers. If any one wishes to view more minutely this blessed operation, he may see a *lively sample* of it in the *last seven years'* practice of our federal government.

5. *Brutus* all along founds his objections and fears on *extreme cases* of abuse or misapplication of supreme powers, which may *possibly* happen under the administration of a *wild, weak*, or *wicked* Congress; but it is easy to observe, that all institutions are liable to *extremes*, but ought not to *be judged by them*; they do not *often* appear, and perhaps *never* may; but if they should happen in the cases supposed (which God forbid) there is *a remedy pointed out in the Constitution itself.*

It is not supposable that such abuses could rise to any ruinous height, before they would affect the States so much, that at least *two-thirds* of them would unite in pursuing a remedy in the mode prescribed by the Constitution, which will always be liable *to amendment*, whenever any mischiefs or abuses appear in the government, which the Constitution, in its present state, cannot reach and correct.

6. *Brutus* thinks we can never be too much afraid of the *encroaching avidity of rulers;* but it is pretty plain, that however great the natural *lust of power in rulers* may be, the *jealousy of the people in giving it* is about equal; these two opposite passions will always operate in *opposite* directions to each other, and, like *action and reaction* in natural bodies, will ever tend to a *good balance.*

At any rate, the Congress can never *get* more power than the people will *give*, nor *hold* it any longer than they
will

will *permit*; for should they assume tyrannical powers, and make encroachments on liberty without the consent of the people, they would soon atone for their temerity with *shame* and *disgrace*, and probably with their *heads*.

But it is here to be noted, that all the danger does not arise from *the extreme* of power *in the rulers*; for when the balance verges to the *contrary extreme*, and the power of the rulers becomes too much *limited and cramped*, all the nerves of government are weakened, and the administration must unavoidably *sicken* and *lose that energy* which is absolutely necessary for the support of the *State*, and the security of the *people*. For it is a truth worthy of great attention, that laws are not made so much for the *righteous* as for the *wicked*; who never fail to shelter themselves from punishment whenever they can, under the *defects of the law*, and the *weakness of government*.

I now come to consider the grand proposition which *Brutus* sets out with, concludes with, and interlards all along, and which seems to be the great gift of his performance, viz. *that a confederation of the Thirteen States into one great republic is not best for them*: and goes on to prove by a variety of arguments, that *a republican form of government is not compatible, and cannot be convenient to so extensive a territory as the said States possess*. He begins by taking one assumption for granted (for I cannot see that his arguments prove it at all) viz. that the Constitution proposed will *melt down* and *destroy* the *jurisdiction* of the particular States, and *consolidate* them all into one *great republic*.

I cannot see the least reason for this sentiment, nor the least *tendency* in the New Constitution to produce *this effect*. For the Constitution does not suffer the *federal powers* to *control* in the least, or so much as to *interfere in*, the *internal policy*, *jurisdiction*, or *municipal rights* of any particular State; except where great and manifest *national purposes and interests* make that control necessary.

It appears very evident to me, that *the Constitution gives an establishment, support, and protection to the internal and separate police* of each State, under the superintendency of the federal powers, which it could not possibly enjoy in an
independent

independent state. Under the confederation each State, derives strength, firmness, and permanency from its compact with the other States. Like *a stave in a cask well bound with hoops*, it stands *firmer*, is not so easily *shaken, bent*, or *broken*, as it would be were it set up *by itself alone*, without any connexion with its neighbours.

There can be no doubt that each State will receive from the union great *support and protection* against the *invasions and inroads* of foreign enemies, as well as against *riots and insurrections* of their own citizens; and, of consequence, the course of their internal administration will be secured by this means against any *interruption or embarrassment* from either of these causes.

They will also derive their *share of benefit* from the *respectability* of the Union *abroad*, from the *treaties* and *alliances* which may be made with *foreign nations, &c.*

Another benefit they will receive from the control of the supreme power of the Union is this, viz. they will be restrained from making *angry, oppressive, and destructive laws*; from declaring *ruinous wars* with their neighbours; from fomenting *quarrels and controversies, &c.* all which ever *weaken* a State, tend to its fatal *disorder*, and often end in its dissolution. ' *Righteousness exalts* and strengthens *a nation; but sin is a reproach* and weakening of *any people.*'

They will, indeed, have the privilege of oppressing *their own citizens* by bad *laws* or bad *administration;* but the moment the mischief extends *beyond their own State*, and begins to affect the citizens of *other States, strangers*, or the *national welfare,*—the salutary *control* of the supreme power will *check the evil*, and restore *strength and security*, as well as *honesty and right*, to the offending State.

It appears then very plain, that the natural effect and tendency of the *supreme powers* of the Union is, to give *strength, establishment, and permanency* to the internal police and jurisdiction of *each of the particular States;* not to *melt down and destroy*, but to *support and confirm*, them all.

By what sort of assurance, then, can *Brutus* tell us, that the New Constitution, *if executed, must certainly and infallibly terminate in a consolidation of the whole into one great republic,*

republic, subverting all the State-authorities. His only argument is, that the federal powers *may be corrupted, abused, and misapplied,* till this effect shall be produced. It is true, that the Constitution, *like every other on earth committed to human management, may be corrupted by a bad administration,* and be made to operate to the *destruction* of the very capital benefits and uses, which were the *great end* of its institution.

The same argument will prove, with equal cogency, that the Constitution of each particular State may be corrupted in practice, become tyrannical and inimical to liberty. In short, the argument proves *too much*, and, therefore, proves *nothing*: it is empty, childish, and futile, and a serious proposal of it is, I conceive, an affront to the human understanding.

But, after all, supposing this event should take place, and, by some strange fatality, the several States should be *melted down* and *merged* in the great Commonwealth, in the form of *counties* or *districts*; I do not see why *a commonwealth mode of government would not be as suitable and convenient for the great State, as any other form whatever;* I cannot see any sufficient ground or reason for the position pretty often and boldly advanced, *that a republican form of government can never be suitable for any nation of extensive territory and numerous population.*

For if Congress can be chosen by the several States, tho' under the form and name of *counties or election-districts,* and be in every respect instituted as directed by the New Constitution, I do not see but we shall have as suitable a *national council,* as wise a *legislative,* and as strong and safe an *executive, power,* as can be obtained under any form of government whatever, let our territory be *ever so extensive or populous.*

The most *despotic monarch* that can exist, must have *his councils and officers* of state; and I cannot see any one circumstance of their being appointed under *a monarchy,* that can afford any chance of their being any *wiser* or *better* than *ours may be.* It is true, indeed, the despot may, if he pleases, act *without any advice* at all; but when he does
so,

so, I conceive it will be very rare that the nation will receive greater advantages from his *unadvised edicts*, than may be drawn from the *deliberate acts* and *orders* of our supreme powers. All that can be said in favor of *those* is, that they will have less chance of *delay*, and more of *secrecy*, than *these*; but I think it probable, that the latter will be grounded on *better information* and *greater wisdom*, will carry *more weight*, and be *better supported*.

The *Romans* rose from small beginnings to a very great extent of territory, population, and wisdom; I do not think their constitution of government was near so good as the one proposed to us, yet we find their power, strength, and establishment were raised to their utmost height under *a republican form of government*. Their State received very little acquisition of territory, strength, or wealth, *after their government became imperial;* but soon began to weaken and decay.

The *Carthaginians* acquired an amazing degree of strength, wealth, and extent of dominion, under *a republican form of government*. Neither *they* nor the *Romans* owed their dissolution to any causes arising from *that kind of government*: it was the *party rage, animosity*, and *violence* of their citizens, which destroyed them both; *i. e.* weakened them, till *the one* fell under the power of their *enemies*, and was thereby reduced to ruin; *the other* changed their form of government to a monarchy, which proved in the end equally fatal to them.

The *same causes*, if they cannot be restrained, will *weaken* or *destroy* any nation on earth, let their form of government be what it will; witness the *division and dissolution* of the *Roman* empire; the late *dismemberment* of *Poland;* the intestine divisions, rage, and wars of *Italy*, of *France*, of *Spain*, and of *England*.

No form of government can preserve a nation, which cannot *control the party rage of its own citizens;* when any *one citizen* can rise *above the control* of the laws, *ruin* draws near. It is not possible for any nation on earth to hold their strength and establishment, when the *dignity* of their government is *lost*, and *this dignity* will for ever depend on the *wisdom* and *firmness* of the officers of government, aided and supported by the *virtue* and *patriotism* of their citizens.

On the whole, I do not see but that any form of government may be safe and practicable, where the *controlling authority* of the supreme powers is *strong enough* to effect the ends of its appointment, and, at the same time, sufficiently *checked* to keep it within *due bounds*, and *limit it to the objects of its duty;* and, I think, it appears that the Constitution proposed to us has *all these qualities* in as great perfection as any form we can devise.

But after all, the *grand secret of forming a good government is, to put good men into the administration:* for *wild, vicious, or idle men*, will ever make a bad government, let its principles be ever so good; but *grave, wise, and faithful men*, acting under a good Constitution, will afford the best chance of security, peace, and prosperity to the citizens, which can be derived from civil police, under the present disorders, and uncertainty of all earthly things.

A N

AN ESSAY ON CREDIT:

IN WHICH

The Doctrine of BANKS is considered,

AND

Some REMARKS are made on the PRESENT STATE of the

BANK OF NORTH-AMERICA.

[*First published in Philadelphia, Feb. 10, 1786.*]

CREDIT *is the confidence which mankind place in the virtue and good character of its object:* so when we say of a man, 'he is a person of credit and reputation,' the meaning is, that he is a man in whose virtue and good character people in general place confidence.

Credit, in a commercial sense, *is the confidence which people place in a man's integrity and punctuality in fulfilling his contracts and performing his engagements.* When we speak of a merchant of credit, we mean a merchant in whose ability, integrity, and punctuality in fulfilling his contracts and engagements, people have confidence, *i. e.* a man of integrity and truth, who is fit to be believed and trusted; the contrary or reverse of this is a man of no integrity in his dealings, who will quibble and shuffle, evade his contracts, violate his word and truth, delay his payments, disappoint

disappoint his creditors, use deceit, chicanery, and falsehood, &c. *i. e.* is not fit *to be believed or trusted*.

From this view of the matter it appears, that credit is a most valuable thing in society, it gives hearts-ease, it gives wealth, it is *a nurse of every social virtue*, it makes a soil suitable for the growth of public spirit and every public virtue; the worth and value of this may, perhaps, be best illustrated by comparing it or viewing it in contrast with its contrary; how much better do we feel, how much richer do we grow, how much more easy, safe, and satisfied do we enjoy ourselves, when we live among citizens to whom we can give full credit, in whom we can have safe confidence, and whom we can trust, than when we find ourselves among people to whom we can give no credit, in whom we can have no confidence, and whom we cannot trust, and where every concern or contract we make with them is attended with *anxiety*, uneasiness, and fear, and commonly followed by *deceit*, *loss*, and *disappointment?* In this case, I desire, I can need, no better argument, no better proof, no better explanation of my subject, than an appeal to the *instant feelings* of my fellow-citizens.

But however valuable and excellent in society, however profitable and happyfying, however soothing to our warmest wishes, *credit public* or *private* may be, *it is in vain to hope for it, or even to imagine the possibility of its existence, without its proper object, which is honesty or integrity;* it can no more be forced by laws, it can no more be obtruded by authority, however high and puissant, than an article of faith can be forced on the understanding, without proper proof or evidence.

Credit and honesty are in their nature correlatives, and must and for ever will imply and support each other. Integrity will generate credit and confidence the moment it is known in any part of the world; and the moment that integrity or honesty is observed to cease, the credit or confidence which was generated by it, instantly ceases too; it dies, it can never be brought to draw another breath, after the

integrity

integrity which generated it and fupplied all its vital motions, is gone.

It is here to be noted, that however neceffary and even effential *integrity* is to *credit*, yet in a commercial fenfe, *i. e.* as far as it relates to trade, money, or wealth, it is not the *only* thing neceffary; *power or ability muft be added;* for however clear and plain it is, that an honeft man will never contract beyond his power of performance, yet it often happens that his power of performance may be much leffened between the time of *contract* and the time of *fulfilment*, by many incidents which may and often do take place, which at once leffen his credit, or the confidence of his neighbours in his engagements.

Thefe incidents often affect honeft merchants fo deeply, as to occafion *their failure or bankruptcy,* and *their* failure often produces *another* in their creditors, that a *third,* and that a *fourth, &c.* This *fucceffion* of *failures* often originates in a *fwindler* or *rafcal,* who knowingly contracts vaftly beyond his ability of performance, and, of courfe, ruins not only himfelf, but a numerous fucceffion of honeft men.

This affords us one inftance of the vaft mifchief which a community may and often does fuffer, from *one difhoneft man* refiding among them; very many others might be produced of like mifchief, effected in a great variety of ways, and to fuch a degree that a *national character* may be deeply ftained by the *iniquity and knavery of a few.*

This fhows that it is of moft ferious confequence to every State, to ufe every poffible means, not only to preferve the national credit and character of their State in *good purity and honor,* but alfo to introduce, as far as may be, *habits of integrity and honor* among their *citizens,* and extirpate, as far as can be done, all fuch villainous and fcandalous practices, as naturally tend to difgrace the *national character,* and ruin the fortunes of *private* citizens.

Thefe obfervations will appear with greater force and advantage, if we recur for a moment to what I juft now mentioned, viz. the great eafe, fatisfaction, and convenience of living in a State where the *public finance* is fo managed,

naged, that all private citizens can *safely rely on the justice and punctuality of the public engagements*, and where the habits of honesty and integrity are so general among the *private* citizens, that they may safely trust *one another*, so that credit and mutual confidence in each other may prevail thro' the community.

Thus circumstanced, every man may safely employ his stock in any business of advantage, either of merchandise, mechanism, or husbandry; whereas if he lived in a State, and among citizens, of contrary character, *he would be afraid to let his stock go out of his own keeping, lest it should fall into hands, either public or private, which would retain it from him, so that he could not recover it again, tho' the advantages of improvement, both to the public and himself, might be very great and inviting.*

In a State, and among citizens, so happily disposed, *any man*, with industry and economy, tho' his means were small, might *live very easy and comfortable,* and the *man of fortune* might *improve* his estate very safely and happily, to the great advantage both of the public and himself. Strangers would have every encouragement to flock in to such a State, and thereby increase the population, and, of course, the commerce, manufactures, and husbandry of it.

From this view of the subject it appears strikingly evident, that *credit, both public and private,* and the *mutual confidence* of citizens in the *public justice* and *in each other,* is of most momentous advantage, of most capital convenience, both to the public and to the individual members of it; it contributes most decidedly and essentially to the internal establishment, security, and safety of the government, and to the ease, wealth, and happiness of private citizens; therefore, it follows, that *it is the high interest and great duty of every State to adopt and pursue every practicable method of securing, enlarging, and extending to the utmost degree, all the advantages and blessings which can result from such public and private credit, and the mutual confidence of the subjects of the State in the public and in each other.*

The wisest and richest nations of *Europe,* long before we were born, have seen this subject and its most momentous importance

importance in a light so strong and glaring, as induced them to adopt every practicable method in their power, to secure to themselves such invaluable advantages. In their *practice* we have an *example*, and in their *success* we have *encouragement*, and very strong *inducement* to imitate it.

For this purpose, the richest trading cities of *Europe* long since adopted the plan of establishing *public* BANKS; this plan they formed upon the most deliberate consideration; they had the greatest opportunities of information, had the greatest experience in the subject; they knew the *importance, operation, and effects* of both *cash and credit*, the best of any men then in the world, as their trade and wealth were then the greatest of any in the world. It is not to be supposed that their first essays reached the perfection of the subject, but they found advantages enough in their first trial, to induce them to continue the practice ever since.

Genoa was the first State in *Europe* which established a public bank; their bank of *St. George* was established in 1407, by a public act of that republic. The plan was soon followed by *Venice*, whose bank, which continues to this day with the greatest advantage to the State, as well as to their private citizens, and has ever been in the highest reputation and credit both at home and thro' all *Europe*, was established by a public act of their State.

The city of *Amsterdam* long after followed their example, and their *present bank* received a public establishment by an act of their States-General in 1609. The cities of *Rotterdam* and *Hamburgh* adopted the same practice; and *England*, who is always phlegmatic and late in adopting the example of the other *European* States, instituted and established its *bank* in 1694; and *France*, whose attention in those days was little turned to improvements in trade, came later into it; their royal *bank* at *Paris* was established by public authority in 1718.

Besides these, very many other banks of less extent and consequence, both public and private, are now established in the greatest trading cities and *banks* are become the

great

great receptacles of the *cash of Europe*, and almost all mercantile receipts and payments are made thro' them.

The bank of *Genoa*, indeed, failed in 1746, after that republic had, for a great length of time, enjoyed most signal and capital benefits from it; but its ruin was not brought on by *any defect of its principle*, or *mismanagement* of its directors, but by the *madness of the rulers* of that State; they were not mad enough, indeed, to decry it as an useless or dangerous institution, but they adopted the contrary extreme, they magnified its strength and power too much, and compelled the directors to make *advances* to the State, beyond what their *funds* would bear.

The other *banks* have continued to this day, and with such incredible and most acknowledged benefit to the several States in which they are established, that their *credit or decline* has generally been considered as a sort of *sure criterion of the strength or weakness* of the State in which they are established. When nations are at war, they ever have thought it a sure way to bring fatal embarrassments on an enemy, if they can by any possible means *shake the credit of their bank;* and every State has always been ready to go great lengths to *support their bank*, if, by any turn of affairs, it has happened to be in distress.

It must, therefore, be very absurd to suppose that *such an institution can be hurtful or even useless, that has stood the test of such extensive and durable trial and practice, among so many nations of the greatest experience and most accurate knowledge of the subject;* an institution thro' which not only the cash of *private merchants*, but of the greatest and richest *trading companies*, and even the *treasure of nations*, has been so long negotiated, and which, thro' so great a length of time, up to this very hour, supports its credit and character of vast utility, by the universal suffrage of nations, thro' all ranks of people, from crowns and the most dignified assemblies of statesmen, and the most wealthy companies of merchants, down to the lowest dealer.

But all this notwithstanding, people may be found, little acquainted with the subject, and wholly unexperienced in it, who will give their opinion *that such an institution is*

injurious

injurious to a State, and incompatible with the safety of it. This may be considered as an instance and proof of that height of absurdity which people may arrive at, who grow *zealous and positive in things they do not understand.*

But however well the nature of *banks* may be understood in *Europe*, and however immense the advantages and profits which are derived from them may be, yet the thing is new in *America*, and by many people thought unfavorably of.

The BANK OF NORTH-AMERICA, tho' established by act of Congress *(December* 31, 1781) which is the highest authority of the Union, and recognised expresly by many of the States, and implicitly by them all, is nevertheless treated by many people here as a most dangerous and injurious thing, utterly incompatible with the safety of the State, and, of course, they think it ought to be demolished without ceremony, and that even the *common forms* of dissolution are unnecessary, as people are not *very nice* in the manner, or *delicate* in the choice of means, of hunting down a *beast of prey*, or destroying a *common enemy.*

But as I suppose my fellow-citizens will ever be willing to *hear* before they *condemn* a thing that has *once saved them*, and very often afforded many of them a *material convenience*, I apprehend a short dissertation, showing the nature of a bank, will not be unacceptable.

A BANK *is a large repository of cash, deposited under the direction of proper officers* (say, a president and directors) *for the purpose of establishing and supporting a great and extensive credit, to be made use of in every case where an established credit will answer in exchange or payment as well as cash, or better than cash, as in many circumstances will manifestly and undoubtedly be the case:* for instance, suppose this State should incorporate a *bank*, and order all the *revenues of the State* to be paid *into it*, and should direct that all the *debts of the State* should be paid in checks on the bank, or in bank-bills, payable to the bearer, which bearer should have liberty, whenever he pleases, to carry his bill to the bank, and receive cash for it, and should direct further, that if such bank-bills, in any circumstance, happen to suit any citizen

citizen *better than cash*, he should be at liberty to carry his *cash* to the bank, and take out *bank-bills* for it.

The effect or operation of such a bank, when its credit becomes established (*i. e.* when the people at large believed with full confidence that the fund or stock was sufficient, and the management fair and upright) I say, the operation or effect of such a bank would be, that very few of the people who should be possessed of such bank-bills, would carry them into the bank, and receive cash for them, because the bills would answer by far the greatest part of the purposes of cash as well as specie, *i. e.* they would purchase any kind of commodities, and pay any kind of debts, as well as cash, as we find is the case of the bank-bills of the *Bank of North-America*, at this time.

Further, such bills would not only be as good as specie for almost every purpose where cash is used or needed, but, on many accounts, they would be better than cash, as any sum of them is *easier* and more certainly *counted* than cash; the danger of *counterfeits* would be less; the *carriage* would be easier; they would be less exposed to *thefts* and *robberies* than cash (for a man can conceal from a thief 1000 dollars in bills, or run from a robber with them, easier than with 1000 dollars of silver); in case they are destroyed by *fire, water*, or *other accident*, they are not *lost*, but on proof made at the bank, they may be replaced, &c.

The advantage would be still greater, if, instead of bank-bills, the owner would take *a bank credit*, and *draw checks* on the bank whenever he needed his money; this would enable him to pay any sum *exactly*, without the trouble of *making change;* he would be able in any future time *to prove his payments*, if he preserved his checks which he received cancelled from the bank, as every man ought to do; this would at once free him from all danger of loss by *fire, robbers, mislaying, dropping them on the road,* &c. &c. This practice is found by experience to be so very convenient, that it is almost *universally adopted* by people who keep their cash in our present bank.

These and many other advantages which bank-bills or bank-credit have beyond what cash can have, would doubtless

less induce most people *to prefer bills* or *bank credit* to *cash*, and, of course, very few possessors of either would demand cash at the bank; the consequence of which would be, that at the end of the year much of the cash would remain in the bank, tho' the whole amount of the bank-stock should have been paid out in bills, and been constantly circulating among the people, with every advantage that *cash could have*, and many other very valuable advantages that *cash could not have*, as has been just now shown.

The benefits or uses of the bank, when thus established, are various: 1. *The bank gains all the lost paper*, i. e. *all such bank-bills as are lost (where the loss cannot be proved)* and, of course, can never be brought to the bank for redemption or payment.

2. The bank can, on any public emergency, *emit bank-bills beyond the amount of the cash or stock in the bank*, and, of course, can have the benefit of a considerable sum to circulate or use for the public benefit, without paying interest, or *having it known to an enemy that they are embarrassed or in debt*. Or,

3. If the exigencies of the State should not require this, *they may accommodate their citizens with discounts or loans on interest, to the great increase of the bank-stock or revenue*, as well as doing great favor to individuals, and increasing the trade, manufactures, and husbandry of the State; *this is the best and perhaps the only proper way of supporting a public loan-office in a State*. And,

4. If the revenues should increase beyond the expenditures of the State, *they will accumulate in the bank till the amount may be very great;* and a rich State, like a rich individual, derives many and great advantages from wealth, and even from the reputation of wealth.

These advantages have been found by experience to be much greater, vastly greater, than a sanguine speculator, upon a bare view of the nature of the subject, would imagine. *The force and energy of credit, perfectly well established and permanent, is vast almost beyond conception;* it is found by experience to supply the place of cash, and much better than cash, in almost all transactions, except in small expenses,

penses, where small change is necessary, such as travelling expenses, market-money, &c.

It is also found by experience, that any sum of money in the stock of a bank well regulated and managed, is sufficient to support the credit of *double or treble its amount in bank-bills*, whilst each of those bills is indisputably as good as cash, because *the possessor may at any time exchange them at the bank for solid hard money, whenever, either thro' distrust of the bank, or his own conveniency, he may choose to do it;* it follows then,

5. That a good bank may increase the circulating medium of a State to double or treble the quantity of real cash, without increasing the real money, or *incurring the least danger of a depreciation.* And,

6. *A good bank will receive no money but good coin of standard weight and fineness*, and this will naturally and unavoidably keep the current coin, cash, or medium *good*, or discover its *defects;* for if, by any means, a debased or light coin, or public bills of depreciated value, should gain a currency in any State (all which have often happened) the standard of the bank will discover their defects, *and an exchange or agio of such depreciated money and that of the bank, will at once determine the true or real value of such depreciated currency.*

7. Another capital use and advantage of a bank is, *that it makes one of the best repositories for money that is designed to lie for any great length of time on interest,* as it affords a much better security than can be found in the hands of any private man, and the half-yearly dividends are more than equal to any profit that can be derived from them when put to interest on mortgage, and the punctuality of payment better secured, and the trouble of collection much less.

Such monies as are here intended, are *legacies or any other provision which is made for young children,* to be paid to them with the interest, at their full age; *any provision which a man may wish to make for himself or wife, against old age;* the funds of *public institutions of religion or charity,*

such

fuch as *churches, hofpitals, poor-houfes, widows' fund, fea-captains' fund,* &c. any accumulation of cafh, which a man may choofe to prepare, in order to complete *fome great payment,* or accomplifh *fome great purchafe at a future day,* fuch as a houfe, a farm, &c. &c. And as bank-ftock of a good bank can at any time *be fold for cafh,* the bank becomes the fureft fund to produce the principal cafh repofited in it, when needed, and alfo the intereft in the mean time, which may be ufed, if needed, when it is paid in, or may be added to the principal in the bank.

This will appear to be a very important ufe of a bank, if we attend to the fubject a little, efpecially to the cafe of *orphans and infants,* and fee in how many ways they are *defrauded or fomehow deprived of the cafh, which their parents have carefully laid up for them,* whilft their infancy prevents their taking care of it themfelves.

8. Another great ufe of a good bank is, *that it probably may very much promote economy and induftry,* as particularly in many of the fore-mentioned inftances, viz. when a man is engaged in accumulating any fum of money for any capital purpofe, fuch as making provifion for his infant children, or himfelf in old age, or for a heavy purchafe, or any other defign which lies near his heart, he will be very induftrious, and his economy will be very good, till he has *made up his heap,* or got the *neceffary fum* together, and by that time he may perhaps have acquired fuch habits of induftry and economy, that he may not ftop at the acquirement of the fum firft propofed, but may be induced to keep on and enlarge it beyond the original defign.

The bank gives a fure operation to fuch a fcheme, at leaft in point of fafe keeping and punctual payment. Neighbours may fee the example and its advantages, and fall into it themfelves, and fo on till the inftances of fuch accumulations, and, of courfe, of fuch economy and induftry, may become general among monied men thro' the State, to the great advantage and ftrength of the State, the bank, and themfelves.

Thefe are only *a few of the benefits derived from a bank,* which our fhort experience will enable us clearly to underftand, stand, and which in point of *fact or reality* are demonstrated by the same experience so clearly and fully, as to put the matter beyond a doubt. I do not pretend to comprehend the great subject enough to explain all the infinite uses and advantages which the long experience of the greatest cities of *Europe* has found resulting from banks, or the still greater advantages which a further experience may discover either to them or to us; but these are certainly sufficient to induce every friend to the integrity, wealth, and honor, interest and genuine respectability of his country, to think favorably of the subject, and to exert all proper endeavours to participate of its uses.

But to pursue the matter further—suppose a number of *private citizens* form a bank, each of whom puts in one or more shares, and raise in that way a bank-stock of any proper sum (say, 1,000,000 dollars) for a fund to support a large and extensive credit, for the purpose of *deposits, loans,* and *discounts,* and appoint proper officers to manage the same, and obtain a public establishment by *a charter,* or *other public act* of the government; this will be *a private bank,* because the stock of it is the money of private men, and the officers or directors are appointed by private stockholders; but *it may in some sense be deemed public,* both on account of its *extensive utility and public importance,* and the *public patronage and establishment* it receives from government.

This bank will have a nature and operation similar to the other, and will afford the same kind of convenience to the citizens who choose to be concerned in it, and in both cases the particular profits of the bank will go to the stockholders, *i. e.* to the private stockholders, whose contributions compose the stock, or to the State, as far as the public funds are vested in bank-stock, if it should be thought proper to vest any part of the public treasure in such stock, but the *management* of it would be exclusively under the conduct of its *own stockholders and directors.*

Of this kind is the BANK OF NORTH-AMERICA, and has a much greater capital (about 900,000 dollars) than any *state-bank* can have in the present condition of our finances,

finances, and its operation, effects, and uses are much more extensive, and its accommodations to the citizens, and even to the State, much greater than a state-bank could have; this may afford one answer to an objection which some may raise against the present bank, viz.

That it would be better to discontinue the present bank, and erect a state or public bank in its stead; another answer may be, *that no plan of this sort can be so sure of a proper management under the State, as it would be under the direction of its own proprietors.* A bank is a sort of mercantile institution, or at least has such a close connexion with the whole mercantile interest, that it will more naturally and properly fall under the direction of merchants, than of any other sort of men less acquainted with its nature and principles, and less interested in its success.

Another reason is, that a bank, whose stock is made up by the subscription of private men, and managed by the stockholders, is the *surest antidote or preservative against tyranny in the government, that can be named;* its owners are the *rich men* of the State, who will never be concerned in *needless popular clamors* or *sedition* against the government, but, at the same time, have both *influence* and *inducement* enough to be a *check* and *restraint* on government, when it becomes *oppressive,* and *really verges towards tyranny.*

The rich have an interest in their poor fellow-citizens, and (as some men use their wives) however tyrannical they may be *themselves*, they will not suffer *any body else* to tyrannize over them. Trade and banks cannot flourish in a *despotic government,* and, of course, where they do exist, they will keep *despotism,* as far as possible, *out of the State.* The stockholders are too numerous, too much scattered, of sentiments and connexions too different, to admit any danger of becoming *tyrants themselves.* I never heard an instance of a State whose government was corrupted by a *private* bank.

But a *state-bank*, if we could possibly suppose that it would be *well managed,* and *grow rich, would tend immediately and directly to tyranny in the government,* because it would give the minister or ruler the command of a vast sum of money; and I never knew a *rich treasury* at the command of *a minister*, whose head was not *turned by it,* and the insanity never fails to take *a direction towards tyranny.*

The better way, I should think, would be *to join both together, so as that all the state-revenues may be paid into the bank, and all public payments be made by checks on the bank,* and let the State become *stockholders* as far as they please, and take sums out of the bank to the amount of their stock, whenever it is necessary.*

This will answer every purpose of *the State* as well as a *state-bank,* will increase the stock of the present bank, and, of course, extend the power and energy of it so much, that it will be able to supply the necessities of the State with *any loans of cash,* which (without the most violent convulsions) can ever be necessary; and, at the same time, would be able to afford most ample accommodations to private citizens or companies, to the vast benefit and increase, not only of private fortunes, but of our *trade, manufactures,* and *husbandry* in general.

The present funds of the BANK OF NORTH-AMERICA, or the cash which supports it, is, 1st. *the bank-stock,* or the money paid in by the stock-holders, which is about 900,000 dollars: and, 2d. the *money deposited* by men of all descriptions, who may draw it out by checks on the bank whenever they please.

These

---

* Many advantages would arise from this method:

1. The bank is more responsible for any deficiency than any private man can be.

2. It has *the best convenience and security* for *safe keeping* the cash deposited in it.

3. No minister or other man *can pay away* public money otherwise than by a *check on the bank,* which is in some degree a *matter of notoriety,* and involves a *responsibility.*

4. The receipts and payments would *be settled up* to a shilling (according to the custom of the bank) at least *once a month.*

5. The *commission* or *allowance* to a treasurer for this service *would be saved,* as the bank would be very willing to undertake the business of *receiving* all or any part of the public revenue, and *paying* the same out, without *any commission or salary, i. e.* without any *allowance* or *charge* for the service; this would be a *great saving,* even if the commission allowed to a treasurer was not more than a *real compensation* for the service.

These sums are variable, indeed, but always very considerable, as no person ever draws checks *beyond his deposit*, very few ever draw *quite up*, and very many people have large sums there, because their *cash lies in the bank* not only *more secure*, but is more *convenient* for payments *there*, than it could be in the *keeping* of its owner.

Some objections have been made to the present bank, which it may be proper to consider—

I. *Such vast sums of money are hoarded up in the bank, that cash is become scarce* in town and country. I answer,— This is not true in fact:

1. Because *the bank circulates daily more cash than it has in the bank*, and, of course, makes cash plentier than it would be, if we had no bank. And,

2. *A very great part of the bank-stock, on the strength of which the bank issues and supports the circulation it gives out, belongs not to this State or its neighbourhood, but to people who live in distant parts*, to whom it must be remitted if the bank should be broke up.

II. *Another objection is, that monied men find a greater advantage in purchasing bank-stock than in letting their money on interest to people in the country, as formerly was done, and, of course, tho' the monied men in town may gain by the bank, yet the country-people suffer by it.*—This is a strange sort of sentiment to appear in form of an objection; because the bank enhances the value, or increases the use, of cash or any other property, so that the possessor can be more benefited by it than before; therefore, the bank is hurtful.

The same cause (*i. e.* the bank) raises the price of wheat and flour, to the benefit of the *country farmer*, indeed, but to the damage of the *merchant* in town, who must pay more for them than before; if our country produce was all consumed in the State, these mischiefs and benefits would balance one another; because what one citizen lost, another would gain; but a very considerable part of our produce is exported and paid for by foreigners; and therefore the higher the price, the greater is the benefit to the State.

But this evil complained of *does not originate in the bank*, but in quite *different* causes; many monied men who used to lend money on interest, have lost their money *by the war, by the enemy, or by the depreciation of money, or by evasions of payment* which have been introduced since, and, of course, have *no money* to lend; and all who have any, have found the danger of letting it in the old way so great, that few will venture into it again; and, lastly, the objection is hardly true in fact; *because any man in the country who has credit enough in town to get a good indorser, can have money out of the bank, as well as a merchant of the city.*

III. Another objection to the bank is, *that the discounts of the bank make money of such easy acquirement, that it induces merchants to* over-trade *their stocks, and dissipating young fellows to* spend *their money* faster *than they would do, if it was harder to get it.* I believe this is all true, and not only arises from, but is an actual proof of, the *great convenience* and *public utility* of the bank.

This is just of the nature of all other objections against a *good thing*; because it may be made an *ill use* of; and will prove that a *good farm* is worse than a *bad one*, because it makes the farmer *lazy*, in as much as a little work on good land will raise his bread; *good victuals and drink* are worse than *bad*, because *gluttons* and *drunkards* will eat and drink to *excess*; a *loving wife* is worse than a *cross one*, because her husband will be apt to lie in bed *too long* with her; and *riches* are worse than *poverty*, because they introduce *luxury*, &c. &c. But I cannot be made to believe that blessings ought to be driven out of the State, because some people will make *an ill use* of them.

I shall ever believe that it is easier living in a place where a man can raise a sum of ready cash on any emergency, without delay or difficulty, than where such a thing cannot be obtained without great delay, trouble, or perhaps selling property to great disadvantage for it. Such a facility is an advantage which, I think, is not to be despised or easily parted with.

IV. Another objection is, *that all the benefits of the bank centre in the city and near confines of it, but the country reaps no advantage from it.* I answer,—suppose this was true (which cannot well be admitted) as it costs the country nothing, why do they begrudge the advantages of it to the city? I dare say the inhabitants of the city would all rejoice most heartily to see the country in full enjoyment of every advantage and convenience of life, that could be derived from nature or art.

But it is very evident that the country derives a great advantage from the bank, for *the richer the merchants are, and the greater their trade, the better market they afford for the produce of the country.* This is a particular of capital consequence to the country, for their husbandry is *animated and supported* by their *market;* indeed, the husbandman and the merchant ever *mutually support and benefit* each other: and it is scarcely possible that *either* of them should be benefited or hurt, but the *other* will be affected by it.

V. Another objection is, *that the great wealth of the bank will give it an undue influence on the government.* There is no doubt but wealth creates influence; but it is that sort of influence which has ever been found safe to the State. Our bank is a sort of mercantile institution, and the influence of merchants is the safest of any that can affect a government.

The *parson* lives on the *sins* of the people, the *doctor* on their *diseases*, and the *lawyer* on their *disputes* and *quarrels* (and, I suppose, they all think they ought to *pray* for their *daily bread)* but the merchant lives on the *wealth* of the people. He never wishes for a poor customer or a poor country; the richer his customers are, the more they can purchase, and the better payments they can make to him. The merchant has every inducement to seek and promote the *wealth* of the State.

Wealth rarely begets sedition; that baneful production generally springs from *poverty, vice, and disappointment.* These are the characters which find an interest in fishing in troubled waters. We have, perhaps, no instance of a nation ruined by its merchants. I never heard of a State distressed by a *private bank;* but instances are plenty enough of States *served and saved* by such a bank.

On the whole, I think it absurd to banish wealth from a State, for fear it should gain *too much influence* in government, or *generate faction* in the State; but of all kinds of wealth, *a bank would be the least likely to produce these effects*, because the stock-holders of the bank are made up of *all parties*, and are as likely to balance each other's influence there, as in *any other part of the State*. It would, in my opinion, be much more politic, to make a *levelling act*, to prevent the great wealth of *individuals*, who are much more likely to become dangerous to the State, than any *aggregate bodies* of men, however wealthy they may be.

VI. Another objection is, *that the general benefits of a bank depend on the integrity of the directors, who may, in many ways, by a corrupt or partial management, destroy these uses, or make the whole stock of the bank subservient to the interests of a few favorites, and, of course, the great body of the people must be excluded from the advantages of it.* I answer,—this is an objection that may be made with equal force against every institution on earth; none of which are so good and beneficial, but their uses may be lessened or destroyed by corrupt management; and when our directors are called upon to vindicate themselves against any such charge, it will be time enough to think of an answer: in the mean time, the present internal strength and good condition of our bank demonstrate, that the management of the directors has been conducted with great prudence.

I here beg leave to subjoin *a short history of the Bank of North-America, with an account of some great difficulties it hath had to struggle with from its first commencement (four years ago) down to this time, and to make some remarks on its present state.*

I. I shall attempt to give a short history of our bank.—It being observed that the *finances* of the wisest and best regulated States of *Europe*, have for a long time been *negotiated thro' their banks*, or at least been so *closely connected* with them, as to derive the most *capital benefits* and *assistances* from them, mr *Morris*, in 1781, when our finances were in a crisis almost desperate, I say, mr. *Morris*, being then *Financier-General*, adopted the scheme of forming a

bank

bank in *America*, which was propofed to and approved by Congrefs, to which *a thoufand fhares, of* 400 *dollars* each, were foon fubfcribed, and application was made to Congrefs for *a charter of incorporation*, which was granted by their *public ordinance of December* 31, 1781. It appears by the preamble of faid ordinance, that Congrefs approved and adopted the fcheme *from a conviction of the fupport which the* finances *of the United States would receive from a national bank,* and that *the exigencies of the United States made it indifpenfably neceffary* that fuch a bank fhould be incorporated.

Tho' this act of incorporation paffed in Congrefs, *Dec.* 31, 1781, yet it was *no new or fudden thought;* for the Financier-General had laid the plan of a national bank before them as early as *May* 17, preceding, and on the 26th day of the fame month Congrefs approved the fame, and engaged to grant an act of incorporation, as foon as the fubfcription fhould be full; nor was *the thing new to any of the States,* for the fcheme of the bank, and the refolution of Congrefs of *May* 26, were publifhed in all the States, and fubfcriptions were publicly opened in them all.

In the refolution laft mentioned, Congrefs recommended to all the States to make all neceffary laws *for fupport of the* BANK, and in particular to make it felony to counterfeit the bank-notes, feal of the bank, &c. &c.

All the States *recognifed the act of Congrefs* for incorporating the bank, many of them moft *explicitly*, the reft *implicitly*, as none of them objected to it, but all made ufe of the bank, and participated of the benefits of it, as far as their opportunity and convenience prompted them.

The State of Pennfylvania recognifed not only the faid recommendations, by their act of March 18, 1782, againft counterfeiting bank-bills, &c. but by another act of *April* 1, 1782, counting upon the act of Congrefs incorporating the bank, did grant an act of incorporation to the bank, fimilar to, and in the fame words of, that of Congrefs, enacting THAT THOSE WHO ARE AND THOSE WHO SHALL BECOME SUBSCRIBERS TO THE SAID BANK, BE AND FOR EVER HEREAFTER SHALL BE, A CORPORATION

ration and body politic, by the name and stile of the President, Directors, and Company of the Bank of North-America.

By thefe public acts, the fubfcribers to the bank confider themfelves and their property in the bank *for ever*, under the moft folemn and facred *fanction and protection of the law, and guarantied in the moft effectual manner conceivable by the public faith*, pledged to them both by Congrefs and the State; for it is not poffible that the public faith can be plighted more folemnly and more effectually by any fupreme or fubordinate authority, than by a *formal public act*.

Under this facred fanction of the law, and fully confiding in the honor, juftice, and even contract, of our Legiflature, the Directors, in *January* 1784, refolving to make their inftitution as extenfive and ufeful as poffible, opened their books *for new fubfcriptions*. Under the *inducement and encouragement of thefe firm eftablifhments*, very many perfons, both citizens and foreigners, became fubfcribers, *and placed their money in our bank;* the amount of the new fubfcriptions, after the charter of this State was obtained, was above 500,000 dollars. Old men placed the money defigned for the fupport of their old age in the bank; the money of widows and orphans likewife was lodged there, as well as the monies of the merchants, and every other defcription of men.

The amount of the old and new fubfcriptions arofe up to the vaft fum of 900,000 dollars, which is the prefent amount of the ftock of the bank, a vaft fum indeed for the new beginnings of *America*, tho' fmall when compared with the immenfe ftock of fome *European* banks.—With the depofits and this great capital ftock (which was permanent, and not liable to be withdrawn by the proprietors, as the depofited monies were) with the depofits and the permanent ftock, I fay, the bank was in condition with great fafety *to make fuch extenfive negotiations, as could afford very capital accommodations both to the public and to private citizens*, whenever their occafions and exigencies made the affiftance of the bank neceffary to them.

So

So great was its success, and so amazing were its effects, that it appears by the bank-books, that its cash-account in one year, viz. from *January* 1, 1784, to *January* 1, 1785 (the third year of its operation) amounted to the almost incredible sum of 59,570,000 Mexican dollars; and tho' the attacks upon the bank, and many other difficulties which much diminished its negotiations in the succeeding year, were so great as seemed *almost fatal*, yet such was its *great internal strength*, and the *energy* of its *very nature*, that its transactions from *January* 1, 1785, to *January* 1, 1786, amounted to about 37,000,000 dollars.

II. *I now proceed to give some account of the difficulties which the bank has had to struggle with, from its first beginning down to this time.*

1. *The first difficulties arose from the novelty of the thing.* The Directors were engaged in a business in which they had no experience (nothing of the kind having ever before been practised in *America*) and tho' they acted with the greatest consideration, care, and caution possible, yet all this notwithstanding, it is hardly supposable but *some errors in management must have been committed*. These (if any have happened) by experience will be discovered, and by prudence may be corrected and avoided in future time, but they form no conclusion against the *principles* of the bank or its *natural* utility.

The same novelty of the thing prevented a *general confidence* in the bank at *first* among the people.

It was further unlucky, that the bank was first opened at a time when the people had so often been disappointed and deceived in every species of public propositions and engagements relative to money, that they knew not whom they could trust; they hesitated lest they should be taken in by the bank, as they had often been by very numerous proposals to which their confidence had been courted. But the *fidelity* of the Directors, and the *perfect punctuality of all payments* at the bank, soon got the better of this diffidence, and the bank gained an almost universal *credit* and *confidence* among the people, even among its professed and bitterest enemies.

2. Another

2. Another difficulty with the bank has ever been, that *the balance of foreign trade has been against America, ever since the bank was first established.* This has occasioned such great exportations of cash as render it scarce, and, of course, embarrasses all cash business. This must deeply affect the bank, as it is obvious at first sight to every one.

3. Another sort of difficulties arose *from numerous enemies, who, from different motives, embarrassed the operation of the bank much;* they began with crying up the *public utility* of the institution, and its great profits to the stockholders, and thought that one set of men ought not to monopolize the reputation and opportunity of doing so much good, and engrossing such great profits to themselves, and withal threw out hints, importing that the Directors were *haughty, partial, and not obliging enough, &c.*

To remedy all which, in 1784 they set on foot *a scheme for a new bank, by the name of the Bank of Pennsylvania,* got large subscriptions for a fund to begin with, and petitioned the Assembly of this State for a charter, &c. not a word was heard all this time against the bank, *as an institution hurtful to the States or individuals,* but its *mischiefs* were made to grow out of its *great utility* and *salutary* effects.

The Directors, with much trouble, *put a stop to this plan,* by strongly urging the fatal consequences arising *from two capital banks operating in one city,* which might, perhaps, *act in opposition to each other,* and, of course, destroy each other. They finally persuaded the subscribers to the new bank to relinquish their scheme, and join the old bank, and add their subscriptions to it, which they at last agreed to, and so that difficulty was got over.

But the bank did not rest long, for soon after this last mentioned difficulty subsided, there arose a pretty numerous party in the State who adopted the *scheme of paper money to be issued by our General Assembly.* All the difficulty was to make it pass *equal to hard money,* and they had little hopes of this, unless the *bank* would give it *a currency,* which every body saw plain enough that the Directors

could

could not do. The *bank*, therefore, and the *scheme for paper money*, were confidered as inconfiftent with each other, and one or the other, of courfe, muft fall. The party for paper money determined at once that the *bank muft be facrificed*, and united with all its other enemies to decry it as an inftitution *injurious to the State, and incompatible with the public fafety*.

They raifed (and declaimed upon) many objections to it, the moft material of which (that I heard of) I have confidered already in the foregoing pages of this Effay. The matter was carried fo far, that an act of the Legiflature of this State was obtained, and paffed *September* 13, 1785, repealing the act of *April* 1, 1782, which granted the *ftate-charter* to the bank, and alfo the act of *March* 18, 1782, which made it *felony to counterfeit* the bank-bills, &c. and thus ftands the matter at prefent.

III. I now proceed *to make fome remarks on the prefent ftate of the bank*.

1. Notwithftanding all the difficulties above-mentioned, the bank is now in good condition; its internal ftrength is not weakened; its funds are not diminifhed, tho' its energy and extent of operation has been indeed fomewhat leffened, as was obferved before.

2. The prefent funds or wealth of the bank confifts in, 1ft. *the bank-ftock, about* 900,000 Mexican dollars. 2d. In the *difcounted bills* now in the bank, and payable to it. 3d. The *cafh depofited* in the bank for fafe keeping, and which the owners may draw out whenever they pleafe. 4th. The *furniture and utenfils* of the bank, and any *fmall profits* which may have lain over or arifen fince the laft dividend.

The debts of the bank to be paid out of their ftock are, 1ft. All the *bank-bills now in circulation*. 2d. All the *bank-credits* or balances due to fuch perfons as have depofits in the bank. N. B. *When both thefe are deducted from the ftock, they leave a balance of about* 900,000 *dollars in favor of the bank*.

3. The

3. The *legal* establishment of this bank is derived from the charter of Congress, of *December* 31, 1781; from the charter of the State of *Massachusetts-Bay*, of *March* 9, 1782; from the charter of *Delaware* State, of *February* 2, 1786; from the recognisance of the charter of Congress, publicly made by the State of *Pennsylvania*, in their act of *March* 18, 1782, and their charter of incorporation of the bank, by their act of *April* 1, 1782: but it is to be observed, that *these two last mentioned* acts of the State of *Pennsylvania* were repealed by their act of *September* 13, 1785. This repeal of the said two acts of the Legislature of *Pennsylvania* has given rise to several very important questions.

Question I. *Whether Congress has a right to establish a national bank, so as to make it such a legal institution as the laws of the States of the Union are obliged to acknowledge or recognise?*

1. I answer,—this objection is grounded principally on the second article of the Confederation, viz. "Each State retains its sovereignty, freedom, and independence, and every power, jurisdiction, and right, which is not *expressly* delegated to the United States in Congress assembled." But the answer is easy; for,

1st. A power of incorporating a *national bank* never did exist in any of the States. They might erect banks, or any other corporations, and call them by what *name* they pleased; but their *authority*, like that of all their other laws, must be limited by the bounds of the State, and could not extend beyond them. Nor,

2d. Does this act of Congress *limit the power* of any of the States?—They still retain and may exercise *every power*, jurisdiction, and right of incorporating banks, as fully as ever they had them: for,

3d. The said second article of Confederation does not restrain Congress from having or exercising any sovereignty, power, jurisdiction, or right, whatever; it only restrains them from exercising it in *such manner as to deprive the States of it.* Notwithstanding all the sovereignty and power of Congress, they shall ever be so limited, that each

State

State shall retain its own sovereignty, power, &c. even *concurrent jurisdictions* (if these can be called such) often exist together without the least restraint of each other.

2. The act of Congress incorporating the bank, *is an act of finance;* they considered it most expresly as a means, a very important *means, of finance*, which is a branch of power that most undoubtedly falls within their authority or jurisdiction. They are not *expresly* empowered, indeed, to appoint a *Financier*, give him instructions, receive his plans, or *form a bank*. But, as all those were necessary means of promoting the general interest, the liberties, and general welfare of the States, which are the grand and most acknowledged objects of the Confederation, they are doubtless comprehended within its powers.

3. The Confederation (article 9) empowers Congress to *borrow money* on the credit of the States, and *this certainly implies a power to find or procure somebody who will lend it to them;* and this they effected to a great degree by incorporating the bank, which supplied them to a very large amount.—They owed the bank at one time 400,000 Mexican dollars, for money lent them by the bank; and all the monies lent at different times to Congress, and to the different *departments* under their direction, amounted to above 2,000,000 Mexican dollars; and these loans were of such capital and essential service in that most deranged and weak state of the public finances, that (in the opinion of those best acquainted with the matter) the war could not have been continued without them.

The bank also lent at different times to this State, for its defence and other public purposes, above 130,000 dollars, which certainly proves that the bank was very convenient to the public, and very necessary to the general welfare and general interest of it; and, therefore, must be comprehended in the powers granted to Congress, to manage the general interest, and secure the liberties, defence, and general welfare of the States.

4. *The independence, defence, and almost the very existence, of our present political establishments must depend on the bank, in case of an invasion of an enemy;* for it is very certain, that,

in such case, due and necessary opposition and defence could not be made by a depreciating currency; nor do I think it would be possible for the Congress or States to borrow elsewhere monies sufficient, and in season, for our defence; or to issue paper bills enough for that purpose, which would not depreciate.—I apprehend I shall not be called on for any proof of this.

I therefore go on to infer, that Congress, who are expressly empowered to secure *the defence, liberties, welfare, and general interests* of the States, are, of course, empowered *to institute a bank*, which is so *apparently and essentially necessary to all these great purposes*.—It follows then, that those who oppose the bank, oppose the essential means of our defence, and, of course, lay us open to destruction, the first time any enemy shall invade our country.

5. If we should admit that there was a defect in the powers of Congress to incorporate the bank, yet *that defect is amply supplied by the subsequent recognisance of the States, their acquiescence in the institution, and participation of the benefits of it, for a course of years; for a subsequent consent of the principal* is as good as *a previous order*, to every purpose of establishment or legitimation of any act of *a substitute*.

On the whole, then, I conclude that the Bank of *North-America*, by the ordinance of Congress for its incorporation, is a well-established and *legal* institution, and as such ought to be considered and recognised by all the States, both in their laws and all judicial proceedings, as far as the same may affect the said bank.

Question II. *What is the meaning, energy, and operation of the act of this State of March 18, 1782, making it felony to counterfeit the seal or bills of the bank?*——I answer—

1. It carries in it the strongest *recognisance* or *acknowledgment of the legal establishment of the bank;* and, of course, of the authority and lawful force of the ordinance of Congress for its incorporation, on which alone the legality of the bank then depended; for it is trifling, it is ridiculous, it is infamous, to suppose that the Legislature of this State would, by a most solemn act, make it *felony, i. e.* death,

to counterfeit the seal and bills of any number of men, who had *no legal right* to *make a seal, issue bills,* or *assume* to themselves any other *powers,* liberties, or privileges of *a corporate body.*

2. *That act implies the most solemn consent of this State to the aforesaid ordinance of Congress, and carries in it further the nature and energy of a solemn stipulation and compact* of this State with Congress, *i. e.* with all the States, to support that public measure of the Union, with all the weight and authority which this State could give to it, in all the particulars or clauses mentioned or enacted in the said law.

The *public and vigorous support* of the particular States gives *great force* to an act of Congress, tho' it might be considered as *fully legal* without it, gives confidence in the public measures, and is a good reason and strong inducement to engage the public councils of the particular States, as well as individuals, strongly to exert themselves and risk their fortunes therein. Therefore,

3. *That act cannot, of right, be repealed by this State, without consent of Congress, i. e. of the other States of the Union.* It is a part of *that support* of a public measure of of the Union, on which the *other States* have, and ought to have, *dependence and confidence. Mutual confidence is the end of the Union,* as that alone can produce defence and other exertions for the public welfare; all the States have therefore an interest in *that support,* a very great interest, indeed, and cannot be deprived of it, without a violation of the union; it is a part of that band of union, which holds the States together; to take it away, therefore, is to weaken the union, and, of course, to lessen its power of operation, and the benefits resulting from it.

Indeed, if this State can *repeal* the said act *without consent of the other States,* I do not see why they may not go on to *repeal* all the acts they have ever made *in support of the union,* and all the powers of it, even up to that act of theirs which consented to and adopted the *Confederation* itself.

Question

Queſtion III. *What is the meaning, energy, and effect of the act of this State of April* 1, 1782, *incorporating the bank?* I anſwer,—

1. It carries in it *the moſt public and full acquieſcence and ſatisfaction of our Legiſlature in the act of Congreſs for incorporating the bank;* becauſe it counts upon that act, without the leaſt cenſure, but with moſt apparent approbation of it.

2. It imports their *approbation*, becauſe they ſhow a readineſs to give it all the ſupport which the authority of this State could give, and add to its eſtabliſhment the further ſanction of a charter of this State, conceived in the very words of Congreſs.

3. Tho', as I take it, *this ſtate-charter* did not add any thing to the *legality of the bank's eſtabliſhment under the charter of Congreſs,* yet it ſerved to obviate and ſatisfy the *prejudices of many people,* who had formed an opinion, that it would be ſafer to truſt their property in the bank, *with a* ſtate-charter, than *without* one, and, on that account, *withheld their ſubſcriptions till the ſtate-charter was made.*

I never heard that any body, at that time, diſputed or called in queſtion the *legal authority* of Congreſs to give a charter to the bank; but the public faith, plighted by Congreſs, relating to money, had been at that time ſo *often and recently violated,* that very little confidence was placed by many people in their *public acts* or *reſolutions* of any ſort, who therefore thought themſelves more ſecure under a ſtate-charter, than they ſhould be under a charter of Congreſs, without ſuch ſupport.

This I take to be the true reaſon why the Preſident and Directors of the bank applied to our Aſſembly for a ſtate-charter, which manifeſtly removed many *prejudices* and *obſtacles* which operated againſt the bank, as it was plain that ſubſcriptions to it were offered faſter, and bank-ſtock was more coveted, after the ſtate-charter was obtained than before: therefore, I think it very evident that,

4. This act operated by way of *ſtrong inducement and encouragement to very many citizens, as well as ſtrangers,* to *ſubſcribe to the bank, and truſt their property in it;* and that

the

the act was purposely made with intention that it might have this operation and effect; and therefore ought to *secure the proprietors* from *any disappointment*, as far as the whole force of the act can do it; for certainly it cannot be justifiable in any State *to hold out encouragement* to the people, to draw them into a *snare*, and then leave them in the *lurch*.

5. Whatever might be the effect of this act on the bank, by way of aiding the legality of its establishment, or giving it support as a Continental institution, there is no doubt but it had this one perfect effect, viz. it incorporated the subscribers to the bank into a legal company, and instituted a *complete, established,* and *legal bank* of *Pennsylvania*, tho' by the name of the President, Directors, and Company of the Bank of *North-America;* for any State may give *what name* or *title* they please to their coporations, tho' they cannot extend their *authority* or *privileges* beyond their own jurisdiction.

This act, therefore, undoubtedly brought the bank under the *cognisance* of the laws of *Pennsylvania*, and entitled the Company, and every proprietor of it, to the full *protection* of these laws. Whether this put them into any *better* condition than they were before, made their establishment any more *legal*, or increased their right to the *protection* of the laws of *Pennsylvania*, or not, may be a question; but it can be no question, that very many people were of this opinion, and governed their conduct by it.

It is further certain that this state-charter may eventually prove of most capital service to the stockholders; for it is possible that Congress may repeal their ordinance for incorporating the bank, or, by some other act of sovereignty, may vacate its charter (for strange things happen sometimes) or the union of the Thirteen States may, by some means or other, be dissolved (which, I think, would soon happen, if each State should *withdraw its supports*) and, by that means, the authority of all their acts might cease, and, of course, their charter of the bank might fall with the rest.

Yet,

Yet, I say (all these mishaps notwithstanding) under the charter of *Pennsylvania*, the bank would continue to be a *legal state-establishment*, and might go on with its negotiations, and, in short, pursue the whole business which the great interests of the concern might make necessary.

Question IV. *Can the act of March* 18, 1782 (making it felony to counterfeit bank-bills, &c.) *and that of April* 1, 1782 (incorporating the bank) I say, *can these acts, of right, be repealed by our Legislature, without consent of the parties interested.*—I give my answer in the negative, and for this my opinion I beg the reader's candid attention to the following reasons, which appear to me to deserve great consideration, even by those who may not think them of sufficient force to justify my conclusion.

1. These acts *vest a right, privilege, and interest, i. e. a valuable property in all the stockholders of the bank*, and therefore cannot, of right, be repealed by any act of the Legislature, *without the consent of the stockholders*. These acts are of the nature of *bargains or contracts* between the *Legislature* and the *stockholders*, in which the stipulations were, that in consideration that the stockholders had or should *put their money* into the bank, the Legislature would give such *support* and *legal establishment to the bank*, as should enable them to make and enjoy all the advantages and profits which should result from it, under the *firm protection of the law*.

On this *encouragement*, the stockholders held or placed their fortunes in the bank, and the Legislature passed the said acts in support of it, and so the *bargain was finished*. I take it that when the act of the Legislature vests in or grants to any individual or company of men, on valuable consideration *(i. e.* for which the grantee pays his money) *any valuable right, interest, or property,* the *grantees instantly become legally seized of such right, which thereby becomes as much guarantied or warranted to them by the law of the land,* as is any *other property* whatever which they *may* or *can possess;* and, therefore, they cannot be devested or deprived of it by any act of the Legislature, any more than of their *lands, cattle, furniture,* or any *other estate,* of which they

are

are lawful owners, and which they hold under the full *protection* of the law.

The sort of acts of the Legislature which I here mean (that vest a *right* or *interest* in any *individual* or *company* of men) are such as these, viz. an act granting *a commission of sewers to owners of meadows,* who expend much money in banking and ditching them, to make them useful to the public and their owners; an act granting *toll to persons who shall build a bridge,* for which they contribute their money; an act granting *wild lands to people who will cultivate and improve them,* and who expend their money for that purpose; any acts for *supporting and incorporating the subscribers of a bank,* in consideration of *large sums of money* subscribed or contributed to it, and in prospects of great benefits resulting from it, both to the public and to the stockholders; an act for incorporating *churches, universities, hospitals, schools, &c.* in consideration *of money paid or to be paid* by the contributors, &c. &c.

I conceive that all acts of this kind vest *such rights, privileges, or interests in the grantees* (who thereby gain such *protection* of the laws in the enjoyment of them) *that they cannot be rightfully devested or deprived by any act of repeal of the charters or acts which give their title, or by any other act of the Legislature whatever.*

2. The second great reason of this is, that *the declaration of rights* (which is part of the Constitution of this State) *gives every citizen a right to be protected in the enjoyment of his property.* It knows but two ways by which the subject can be devested of his lawful property; 1st. by *crime and forfeiture;* and, 2d. *by his own contract or consent:* if his property is challenged or demanded of him in either of these ways, or by any other way, let the controversy be of what nature soever, respecting property, he is entitled *to a fair trial by jury.* [See articles 8, 9, and 11.] This can be had no where but in a *judicial court.*

The General Assembly are *not such a court;* they have the *legislative,* but not the *executive* or *judicial,* power of the State; they can neither *empannel a jury,* nor make a judicial decision *without one,* much less can they deprive any individual or company of subjects of any of their legal rights, interests, property, or privileges, *without any trial, summons,* or *examination* at all, by any *act* or *repeal of acts* whatever, which they can make.

3. I take it, *that the declaration of rights is of superior authority to any act which the General Assembly can make, and will control and even render totally null and void any act of the Assembly which infringes it; and will* and ought to be considered so *by the judges of our courts, whenever the same may be pleaded before them:* for when two *contradictory laws* are pleaded before a court, it is impossible but the *one* or the *other* must be judged *void;* and if *one* of these laws appears to be grounded on a *superior* authority to that of the *other*, there can be no doubt but the *superior* authority must control the *lesser*.

I consider the Assembly as *the mere creatures* of their constituents, and acting merely by *a substituted power;* and the declaration of rights I consider as *the capital instructions* which they receive from their *constituents,* by which they are *bound to regulate their conduct, and by which their power and authority are altogether limited.* This doctrine ought to be brought into full view, and to be recognised by every subject, in its whole importance and energy, whenever we see our Assembly *infringing the declaration of rights,* in so capital and alarming an instance, as to make any act whatever, which will, *in its operation, unavoidably and eventually deprive any subject, or number of subjects, of any right, interest, or property, without trial by jury.*

The very persons whose *wishes* or *prejudices* may be gratified by such acts of the Legislature, ought to *tremble* at their consequences, for the *two-edged* sword, which has *one edge* turned against our enemy, has *another* which may be turned against *ourselves, i. e.* it can cut both sides alike, and is equally qualified to wound *both parties,* whenever it may be applied to them.

Charters (or rights of individuals or companies secured by an act of the State) *have ever been considered as a kind of sacred things,* not to be vacated by a bare *holding up a few hands,* and *soiling a page of paper,* without any further previous

vious or subsequent forms or ceremonies; but in all wise States have ever been considered as *securities* of such *capital consequence*, that any attempts to destroy them have ever excited a *general alarm*, and have rarely happened but in times of great *corruption* of government and *dangerous encroachments* of arbitrary power.

I think it, on the whole, very manifest, that a Legislature, which, for valuable consideration paid, has by public act *sold and granted certain valuable rights, privileges, or interests* to any individual or company of men; I say, such Legislature have *no more right by repeal of their act to vacate the title and destroy the estate* of such grantees, and to *release themselves*, than any private contractor has to *release himself, and refuse to execute* his own contract, whenever he grows *sick* of his bargain.

Indeed, I think the sacred force of contracts *binds stronger in an act of state*, than in the *act of an individual*, because the whole goverment is injured and weakened by a violation of the public faith, but the vacillation of a *private man* can produce no more than *private damages*.

But as *public faith* is an old threadbare topic of argument, and is as much *out of fashion* as going to *church* or reading the *bible*, and has been dinned in the ears of some folks, till, like the doctrine of repentance to sinners, it rather manifests than convicts, I will forbear pressing it further at this time, as I wish not to *disgust* but to *persuade*.

4. *The ordinance of Congress for granting the charter of the bank is a measure of the Union*, solemnly recognised by this State (in the two *repealed acts*) in which all the States are interested, and is, therefore, of such *high authority* as controls all the States to such a degree, that any attempts of this State (by an act of repeal, or any other act) to withdraw their support, and thereby weaken and embarrass such measure of the Union, must be void, *ipso facto*, in itself.

For I take it, that every act of Congress appointing or directing any measure of the Union, when recognised by the States, either by their express act of approbation, or by by long acquiescence and practice, is of superior authority to any act of any of the States, nor *does it remain in the power of any particular State to withdraw their support from it, or to release and discharge themselves* from their obligations to it, or to make any act which shall, in its operation, *lessen the energy and effect of it.* But I have touched on this before, and so need not enlarge on it further in this place.

5. The act of repeal *(Sept.* 13, 1785) *deprives a great number of our citizens and strangers of their rights, privileges, and property,* to a vast amount, and to the utter ruin of many families; rights, privileges, and property which were *guarantied and secured* to them *for ever,* by the most *solemn act* of our Legislature, and, of course, by the whole *force and power of the law;* and all this by an act of *mere sovereignty,* without so much as alleging against them *any crime* by which they have *forfeited,* or *contract* by which they have *alienated,* them, and without any *summons,* or *trial,* or *judgment of court,* or *verdict of jury.*

This is so directly in the very face of our *declaration of rights,* as manifestly *infringes* it, and, of course, renders *the act void.* This is, indeed, rather an epitome of what I said before than a new argument, but the immensity of the loss or damage occasioned by the said act of repeal, may, perhaps, engage the reader's attention, and set the subject in a stronger light of importance, than it might appear in, were the consequences *less fatal and ruinous* both to the *Union* in general, to *each of the States,* and *all the individuals* who are concerned in the bank.

But admitting that the act of *Sept.* 13, 1785, for repealing the said acts of *March* 18, 1782, and of *April* 1, 1782, is to all intents and purposes valid in law, and, of course, that the bank is thereby deprived of all the support and legal establishment which it once received from the said laws, when they were in force, there arises another question, viz.

Question V. *In what condition does the said act of repeal leave the bank?* I answer,—

1st. In

1. In point of its *legality, the said act of repeal leaves the bank just where the said repealed acts found it,* when they were first made; the repeal takes away *no more* than the acts themselves *gave,* and, of course, if the bank was a *legal establishment* before these acts were made, it *continues so* still after the repeal of them: therefore,

2. The President, Directors, and Company of the Bank remain a *legal corporate body,* under the charter of *Congress,* and may do all acts as such in *the same manner* as before the said repealed acts of this State were made.

Upon the whole matter, I think it very plain that *the supreme authority* of all States under all forms of government, whether monarchical, oligarchical, or democratical (a theocracy only excepted) *is lodged in the body of the people.*

1st. Because the *rights to be secured by, and which are the sole end of, all civil government, are vested in them:* and,

2d. Because the great *force or strength which must support all civil governments is lodged in them;* and, of course, all *pacta conventa* or capital constitutions established by them, do *bind and control all authorities whatever which act under them,* and, of course, it appears that the Legislature of this State have not an *original* but *a derived* authority, which, of course, is not *absolute* but *limited;* it is limited,

1st. By *the laws of* GOD:

2d. By the *Constitution of this State:* and,

3d. By the *confederation or union of the Thirteen States,* and, of course, by *every legal act of Congress* under that union, for the general welfare of the States: therefore, if our Legislature should make an act to repeal *the ten commandments,* or to infringe *the Constitution,* or to destroy or weaken *the Union, or any legal measures of Congress,* it would, of course, be *ipso facto void.*

Further, I take it that our General Assembly are limited and tied down to *the sort or kind of authority which is given to them;* all acts proper for a *legislative body,* they are empowered to do, *subject to the aforesaid limitations,* but they cannot assume to themselves or exercise the *judicial* or *executive*

cutive powers of government; these powers are totally out of their commission or jurisdiction, and they can no more intrude on, or exercise the *authority of these departments,* than a *sheriff* can obtrude himself on the *judge's seat,* or a *chief justice serve a writ.*

Therefore, it follows that if the Legislature should pass an act, which, by its operation, takes away the *life, liberty, or lawful rights, privileges, or property of any subject, i. e.* such as the subject holds under *the protection and sanction of the law,* it must be *void;* for if any thing of this sort is to be done in the State, or if any controversy or question about it, is to be decided, the Constitution has ordained *a different method, a quite different court or authority, in and by* which it must be done.

It is no objection to this, to say that much and many important things *must* be left to *necessity* and *the discretion* of the Assembly; for such *necessity* must *exist,* before it can *operate, or justify any act grounded on it;* and because much is left to the *discretion* of the Assembly, it does not follow, that they have a right *to throw by all discretion,* and act without any.*

But

---

* There is no doubt but such a combination and concurrence of events may happen, as will make *a departure* not only from the *ordinary course* of administering justice, but even from the *common maxims of justice itself,* necessary.

Such a *necessity* was found in *France,* when a *remedy* was to be provided for the *flagrant mischiefs of the Mississippi scheme.*

The *South-Sea bubble* produced a like *necessity* in *England,* in order to obviate the *enormous and complex mischiefs of that fatal excess of speculation.*

The National Assembly in *France* have found a like *necessity* in order to reduce the *enormous accumulation* of the wealth of the community *into few hands* (viz. of their nobility and clergy) and to liberate the nation from the *distress, weakness,* and *ruin* thence arising.

Perhaps every *cession of territory* from one nation or state to another involves in it some such *necessity.*

And we may probably meet the same *necessity,* if our nation should see fit to *exonerate itself* from the immense *burden of providing about* 30,000,000 *dollars,* to pay *speculators* who never *earned a shilling of it,* nor ever rendered any *services* or *valuable consideration* whatever to the *nation* or any *body else,* for any part of it.

But it is to be here noted with great care, that such *necessity must exist,* before it can *operate,* or be pleaded *in excuse* of the extraordinary measures which it will justify; but a pretence of such necessity, when it does not really *exist,* is not only *ridiculous,* but *very dangerous.* This is arguing on *false position,*

But waving all questions of *law*, I beg to consider the bank one moment in the light of *prudence*. Supposing the bank and all its operations could be broke up and entirely stopped on *March* 1, next, what would be the consequence?

1. The *great* and *usual circulation of cash* (thro' which 37,000,000 dollars were negotiated last year) would at once be *stopped*.

All discounted bills must immediately be paid or sued, which would ruin very many, I think I may say, scores of substantial families; and their failures would occasion,

3. A great *loss to the bank*, and, of course, to the stockholders. And,

4. The *stockholders must lie out of their money* till the bank-accounts could be settled, which would probably be some years.

5. All the monies belonging to subscribers *out of the State*, must be carried *out of it* as fast as they could be collected: and,

6. A most *fatal wound* would be given to *our credit*, as well as to all *our trade*, and every *kind of business* which depends on the circulation of cash.—Who but an *enemy* would wish for such calamities, or promote the means of them?

I will conclude my Essay on this very important and interesting subject, with only observing, that I have *stated the facts* with all care and the best information, and, I believe,

---

position, a sad example of which we have in the troubles of *Charles I.* of *England*.—The King, or rather his court, held out,

1. The *vast powers and prerogatives* of the crown in cases of. *extreme necessity, i. e.* when the country was *invaded*, or *otherwise in imminent danger*; and,

2. That the King, holding the *supreme executive power*, was the *legal and proper judge* of that *necessity*.

On these positions they proceeded to justify the power at that time claimed and practised by the King, of *raising money without act of Parliament*, such as *ship money*, *coal* and *conduit money*, &c. &c. *i. e.* it was only saying that *the King judged* the existing *necessity* sufficient to *warrant* these measures, and the matter was all *legal*; that was the *clincher* that finished the business. I am told, this argument of *necessity and imminent danger* was often called up and urged in the Assembly of *Pennsylvania*, when the *repeal of the charter of the bank* was debated there.

lieve, with exactness and truth; should I have erred, I am ready to submit to better information; *the sentiments and reasonings* are open and obvious to every one, and, I wish, may be received and considered in the same light of importance in which they appear to me. I have no interest in the subject distinct from that of my fellow-citizens, and as I would not be willing to be *misled myself*, so neither do I wish to *lead them into error*. *Magna est veritas et prævalebit*.

STRICTURES

ON THE

NET PRODUCE

OF THE

TAXES OF GREAT-BRITAIN,

In the Year 1784, *as published by Order of their* House of Commons.

[*First published in Philadelphia, Aug.* 4, 1785.]

HAVING by accident met with *a list or detail of the British taxes for* 1784, and the *net produce* of each of them, which lays open in a pretty clear manner the *sources* of the *British* revenues, and points out the *ways and means* by which those immense sums are raised, which are necessary for the current services of the year, payment of the interest of their vast national debt, support of their public credit, &c. and as the attention of the *Thirteen American States* is, or ought to be, much fixed on *a public revenue*, and, of course, on *our trade*, out of which it must grow; I thought the practice and example of so old, so experienced, and successful a people as the *Britons*, might

might be of ufe to us at this time, and therefore procured the account or lift of their revenues above referred to, to be publifhed in the *Pennfylvania Packet* of *Auguft* 4, 1785, and added thefe Strictures on them.

Whether the *Britifh* government has expended the vaft, the immenfe fums produced by their finance for the laft 90 years, for purpofes *falutary* and *beneficial* to the nation, or not, is out of the prefent queftion; but their *fuccefs in raifing thefe vaft fums* is certainly furprifing. Efpecially when we confider that this has been done in fuch a manner, that the nation has not only, *not been impoverifhed thereby*, but has been *increafing rapidly in the moft fubftantial riches*, during the whole time it fupported the immenfe preffure of their taxes.

The *houfes* of *Great-Britain* are now much more valuable than they were 90 years ago; the *live flock* of their farms is greatly increafed; their *lands* are better cultivated, and much more productive; their conveniences for *tranfportation* are greatly increafed by mending *roads*, opening *canals*, and clearing *rivers* for *inland navigation*: their *manufactures* are vaftly increafed, both in quantity and value; the *trading flock* of their merchants, their *fhipping*, and the *exports* of their manufactures, and *produce* of their lands, are vaftly increafed fince the year 1694, when the Bank of *England* was firft inftituted, and the fcheme of funding the public debts had its origin. By *thefe only* the wealth of the nation can be truly eftimated.

This *real wealth*, confidered as national, has very little connexion with the public funds or ftocks; for fhould they all fail, this muft continue, and out of it might always be produced *funds* or *flocks* fufficient for the ufe of the public: *this kind of wealth* muft then be confidered as the *real*, *fubftantial* wealth of the nation; the great *bafis* on which all the fuperftructures of public credit or nominal wealth muft be built, and by which they muft be fupported.

The fact is, then, that this *real wealth* of *Britain* is much *greater* now than it was 90 years ago, notwithftanding the amazing taxes which have been paid during the whole of the laft 90 years, and the vaft debt which now lies on the nation: indeed, this real wealth, as observed before, has *little connexion* with this public debt; but, on the whole, is rather *helped* than *hurt* by it; for it appears very plain, that the national wealth has increased faster under the weight of that debt, than ever it did before the doctrine of creating and funding a national debt was thought of.

It appears, then, that the national *debt*, or the *public credit, may fail*, without destroying the real and substantial wealth of the nation; for if the public credit was to fail, as *our* Continental money, and *their* South-Sea stock, once did, and every person who had any thing in the funds should lose it all, this would not destroy the *houses, fields, cattle, &c.* of the country; it would only produce a *shift of property* from one person to another; would produce infinite injustice and ruin to individuals, indeed, and no degree of punishment would be too great for those, thro' whose mismanagement, fraud, and corruption, such a thing should happen; but it would by no means bring on the *destruction of the nation*.

All that could happen would be, that those who had monies in the stocks would *lose* them; and those who were taxed to support the stocks, would be *liberated* from the burden of tax; but the *fields* would produce the same quantity of *wheat*, and the *meadows* would fatten the *same number* of cattle, as before; and, of course, the bread and the meat would be as plenty as ever, and the more bread and meat the country produced, the richer it certainly would be.

Therefore, a man who buys lands and puts them into high cultivation, or erects mills, shops, &c. for manufactories and conveniencies of life, possesses *most substantial wealth of high independence;* whilst the man who deals in public *securities* and *paper credit*, depends on the humor, the honor, the wisdom, and the justice of the nation, and therefore acquires a wealth ' *which is liable to moth and rust, and which thieves can steal*.'

The long experience of *Great-Britain* affords a most irrefragable proof of fact, that both those kinds of wealth are mutual supports of each other, *i. e.* that public credit

increases

increases the *value* and *produce* of the lands and manufactures, whilst, at the same time, the lands and manufactures produce the *great staple* and extensive commerce, which enable the nation, *by a proper management*, to support the public credit; and, therefore, what *this proper management is, becomes a matter of much importance for us to know, and carefully attend to.*

For *Britain* and *America*, in one great thing, are alike, viz. the source of wealth in both countries is the same; the lands and manufactures are the *first matter* which affords the great staples of *commerce*, as well as the most capital *home-supplies* of the people; therefore, it is probable, that the same management or line of conduct which has proved advantageous to *them*, may be so to *us*.

We see in the account of the taxes of *Britain*, a specimen and a good deal of the detail of this important management,—on which I beg leave to remark—

I. *They are very careful to make their revenues in such form that their produce shall be certain, and their amount capable of pretty exact computation.*

II. To be guarded against all possible delay or disappointment, *they circulate their revenues mostly thro' the bank, or at least keep the exchequer so closely connected with the bank, that they can at all times avail themselves of a bank-credit when they need it:* so that they are always able to satisfy the demands of every creditor of the public funds, without the least delay or trouble: this could not, perhaps, by any possibility, be done in any other method than by the help of the *bank*, and the importance of it will be obvious to any body, who considers that *public credit* can by no possibility be supported in any other way than by *most punctual payments* to the public creditors: the experience of all nations, but especially our own, has taught us that public *promises* and *paper*, or public *laws of regulation* and *tender*, can *do nothing* towards the support of public credit, without *punctual payment* of the public creditors.

III. They have ever made it an object of great care, *to lay and collect the public taxes in such a manner as should be the most easy, the most insensible, and the most advantageous of*

any

any they could devise: this is, indeed, the *materia magna* of the whole subject (which is odious and heavy, under all forms of delicacy and prudence that any administration can devise) as instances of this, it is easy to observe—

1. That *the great burden of their taxes consists in the customs, excise, and stamps;* the net produce of these is above 9,000,000*l.* sterling, in all which, lands, labor, and farmer's stock are not called on, nor is any person compelled to pay any of the taxes, unless he chooses to be concerned in the articles taxed.

2. *The tax is laid in a very great measure on either articles of mere luxury, or such fine and rich goods as are consumed mostly by people of wealth,* e. g. about one half of this tax is on *drinkable liquors* (for under this class I shall doubtless be allowed to rank malt, hops, tea, &c. &c. the sole use of which is to make such liquors) these are mostly articles of luxury, as wines, spirits, strong beer, &c. *Tobacco* and snuff are great articles, as also are *East-India goods, carriages, &c.* most of which are either articles of *mere luxury,* or the consumption of very *wealthy people.* But,

3. *Goods of necessary consumption are not wholly omitted,* as we see in the articles of *hides, tallow, candles, salt, coals, paper, &c.* but in these the heaviest part of the burden falls on the *rich,* as they consume these articles with much greater prodigality and profuseness than the poor.

4. Very poor people have very small use for any papers which pay a stamp-duty, and, of course, those duties are almost wholly paid by people of at least good substance, if not great wealth.

5. *The heaviest and most painful part of said taxes is that on houses and windows,* ranked under the head of incidents; this is said to be paid by the poor tenants, many of whom brick up their windows to avoid the tax.

6. *The land-tax at* 4*s. on the pound* (not mentioned in the account) *produces about* 2,000,000 *a year:* but this, tho' called 4*s.* is really not more than 1*s.* or perhaps not 6*d.* because that tax is laid on *an old assessment* or estimate of the lands of *England,* which sets them at less than a *quarter* of their present value, and some very improved estates are not

estimated

estimated at *one-tenth* of their present value, and, of course, if a man has rents to amount of 100*l.* per annum, his tax may be 5*l.* or perhaps not 40*s.* This, and the tax on *houses* and *windows*, are all which bear any resemblance to *our taxes on polls and estates*, and, in point of *weight and burden*, bear no proportion to ours.

On the mode of the *English* taxes, and the operation of their national debt, the following things may be noted, and deserve our consideration.

I. Their taxes being chiefly on luxuries *are a benefit and saving to the nation;* they lessen the *consumption*, and of course restrain the *excesses*, of luxury, and prevent the vices, expenses, and mischiefs, which would otherwise ensue.

II. *The taxes prevent the exportation of money;* that part of the price of the goods taxed, which goes to pay the duty, cannot *be exported*, but goes into the public treasury, whence it issues in half-yearly payments to the *public creditors all over* the nation.

III. *This produces a great plenty and brisk circulation of cash;* for these payments are all made without the least delay, and in ready cash, and the amount being very large (perhaps, about half the current cash of the nation yearly) makes a very large and brisk circulation of cash, and the frequency of the payments keeps up that circulation into almost an equable flow thro' the year.

IV. From this plenty and quick circulation of cash produced by the taxes, *each individual, or at least the nation at large, derives a benefit which more than compensates the tax which is the purchase of it;* for every one knows the odds of doing business in a place where *cash is plenty* and *briskly circulating*, and in a place where it is *scarce and stagnant;* this will soon produce a difference in the proceeds of any man's business, equal to his share of the tax.

V. *This shows a reason why the British nation increases rapidly in wealth under the pressure of vast taxes*, and has uniformly done so for 90 years past; *i. e.* the benefits resulting from the tax are more than a compensation for the inconvenience of paying it. So that it leaves a balance of profit in favor of the nation or individual who pays it.

VI. This

VI. This benefit refults chiefly from the *great punctuality with which the public creditors are paid*—to a day—to an hour—without the leaft put off or delay. This not only fets the example, but gives the power, of punctual payments, and ftrongly tends to introduce the general practice of it, to the vaft advantage of all trade. This depends on the fame principle as the old adage, viz. " If you would make money faft, pay a high rent;" *i. e.* it is better to have a ftand in a place of *brifk bufinefs*, tho' the *rent is high*, than to fit down in a *dull* place at a *low* rent, or even *rent-free*.

VII. This punctuality of the public payments, which produces fo many vaft advantages, *becomes practicable only by the clofe connexion which fubfifts between the public treafury and the bank;* but thefe advantages are not the whole of the benefits thence derived, the *fame thing enables the treafury* to furnifh any fum of money in an inftant, which any emergency may make neceffary; fo that the nation is never in danger of *lofing the benefit* of any important manœuvre for *want of cafh*.

By this means they have often been enabled to oppofe *foreign enemies,* crufh interior *rebellions,* fupport their great *trading companies* at a hard pufh, give aid to the *bank,* and ever to preferve their *public credit.*

And could that difcerning, fuccefsful people have poffeffed wifdom and gravity of counfel enough to make the beft ufe of their own advantages, *fua fi bona norint,* their happinefs and glory muft have been vaft indeed. Had they in *improvements* of their hufbandry and trade, in *meliorating* and *decorating* their country, fpent the money which they have *wafted* in needlefs *fubfidies* to foreign princes, in *Continental* and *American* wars, and many other fatal policies, their *ftrength,* their *riches,* their *refpectability,* their *happinefs* would have rifen fuperior to that of any nation on the face of the earth.

This is the nation from which we derive our *origin,* and I hope we may refpect the *honors of our parentage,* without imitating the *vices of our anceftors.* And what I have to wifh is, that tho' we are broken off from them, we may have

have wisdom and sound judgment enough to *esteem* and *imitate* those parts of their policy which have *raised* them above the nations round them, whilst their fatal calamities may sufficiently *warn* us to avoid their *mistakes and errors*. It is with this view that I offer these thoughts to my fellow-citizens, which, I doubt not, will be received with candor, as I know they are written with sincerity.

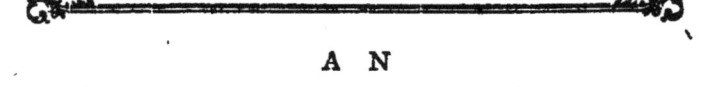

AN ESSAY ON TEST-ACTS

Imposed with Penalties.*

[*First published in Philadelphia, Sept. 12, 1781.*]

TEST-ACTS imposed with penalties, I humbly conceive, are hurtful; because,

I. Their address is to the *hidden things of the heart*, to the *secret sentiments* of the understanding, which are not controllablle

---

* By the act of the Legislature of *Pennsylvania*, *June* 13, 1777, the following oath was required, viz.

" I do swear, or affirm, that I renounce and refuse all allegiance to *George III.* King of *Great-Britain*, his heirs, and successors; and that I will be faithful and bear true allegiance to the Commonwealth of *Pennsylvania*, as a free and independent State; and that I will not at any time do, or cause to be done, any matter or thing that will be prejudicial or injurious to the freedom and independence thereof, as declared by Congress; and also that I will discover and make known to some one justice of peace of the said State, all treasons, or traitorous conspiracies, which I now know or hereafter shall know to be formed against this or any of the United States of *America*."

On which I beg leave to remark,

I. That a very great number of the principal inhabitants of *Pennsylvania*, and as respectable and well-behaved as any in the State, *from scruples of conscience had ever refused to take or subscribe any oath or affirmation of allegiance to any government, either British or American.*

II. Very

controllable by any human authority, nor *amenable* to it; they belong to *God only*, and the *conscience* of the possessor, and

II. Very many very serious and good men, and fast friends to *America* and the *American* cause, thought at that time that the *Declaration of Independence was premature;* and it was a matter of great doubt with all men, whether that independence could be *finally supported;* and, should it fail, many thought,

III. That *abjuring the British government would involve them in perjury*, or, at least, in a *shameful and ridiculous duplicity of conduct*, under the most awful and solemn crisis of deportment.

IV. Many wise men had a great attachment to the *British* government, under which they were *born and educated;* and tho' they *abhorred and condemned* the *demands* and *conduct* of the *British* court as much as any man in Congress, yet did not think that a redress of *American* grievances was *desperate*, or that it was the *real, true interest* of *America* to be *disjoined from the British Empire;* at least, they thought the *American independence* ought to be *settled*, and the *war* should *be over*, and the *disputes* between the contending States should be *adjusted*, before an *oath of allegiance* to the one, or *abjuration* of the other, should be demanded.

V. Many good men thought they did not understand the *nature* and *essential qualities of treasons or treasonable conspiracies*, well enough to be safe in *swearing* to give information of all such as came within their knowledge; or they might *know* such, but not be able to *make proof* of them, and, of course, their information would expose them not only to the *resentment*, but to *real actions of defamation*.

I do not pretend to determine whether any or all of the above objections against taking said oath, were good and proper or not; but they had such weight with *great numbers*, that near half of our most serious people refused taking the oath.

Yet, I conceive, all men will allow that *Pennsylvania* was as *true* to the *American* cause, and *supported* it with as much *effort, zeal, and unanimity* as any State in the Union; and the *few tories* we had, who retained any attachment to the *British* government, *were most effectually converted* by the samples of *British faith, honor, and savageness*, exhibited by General *Howe*, whilst he commanded the *British* army in *Philadelphia* and its neighbourhood.

But be all this as it may, the *extraordinary penalties* with which the oath was enforced, were, in my opinion, equally *useless, absurd*, and *severe;* some of which were as follows, viz.

That every person above the age of eighteen years, refusing or neglecting to take and subscribe the said oath or affirmation, shall, during the time of such neglect or refusal, be *incapable* of holding any *office* or place of trust in this State, *serving on juries, suing* for any *debts, electing* or being *elected, buying, selling*, or *transferring* any *lands, tenements*, or *hereditaments*, and shall be *disarmed*, &c.

—— Travelling out of the city or county where he usually resides, without a certificate of his having taken the oath or affirmation, may be committed to the common gaol to remain without bail or mainprise.

Shall be *disabled* to *sue* or use any *action, bill, plaint*, or *information* in course of *law*, or to *prosecute* any *suit* in *equity* or otherwise howsoever, or to be *guardian* of the *person* or *estate* of any child, or to be *executor* or *administrator* of any person; shall be incapable of any *legacy* or *deed of gift*, or to make *any will* or testament; and shall be compelled to pay double taxes, &c.

All

and no man can be obliged to *confess or divulge* them, more than to *accuse* himself. Test-acts, tho' in a less degree, are of the same nature as *racks and tortures*, are calculated for the same ends, produce the same effects, and are therefore grounded on the same principles, and, of course, are reprobated by the same reasons; their end is to *wring out* those hidden things of the heart, which no man living has a right to demand, and, of course, no man can be under any obligation to *disclose*. It is impossible that any man should have a *higher* and *more exclusive* right to any thing whatever, than to the secrets of his own mind; and, therefore, to *force* them from a man is a direct violation of the most *sacred*, as well as most *delicate, rights* of human nature.

II. Every man *has a right* (in the use of his reason) to form sentiments of *government*, as well as of *religion*, and every thing else which *concerns his well-being*. There can be *no crime* in this, and, therefore, his *sentiments* of government (be they what they may) ought not to subject him to any kind of *punishment* either of *pain or loss*, or deprive him of any one *privilege or benefit* of civil society. It is true, if he *accepts an office* under a government which he

---

All non-juring *trustees, provosts, rectors, professors, masters* and *tutors* of any *college* or *academy*, and all *schoolmasters* and *ushers, merchants* and *traders, sergeants* and *counsellors* at law, *barristers, advocates, attornies, solicitors, proctors, clerks* or *notaries, apothecaries, druggists*, and every person practising *physic*, are disabled in law to use *any of those employments*, and liable to be *fined* 500*l*. for practising in any of them.

Two justices may summon any non-juring person before them, and, on refusal to take the said oath or affirmation, *commit him to the common gaol or house of correction for three months*, unless he pay any sum, with costs, under 10*l*. which they may require, and also become *bound with two sufficient sureties* to appear at the next court of general quarter sessions of the peace; where, if he refuses to take the oath or affirmation, he shall, under the direction of the court, *depart the State in thirty days*, and *forfeit his goods* and *chattels* to the State, and his *lands* and *tenements* to the *persons* who would by law be *entitled to inherit the same*, in case such offender was *dead intestate*, &c. &c.

N. B. By act of Assembly of *March* 29, 1787 the above-mentioned oath, with all the shocking penalties of it, was repealed, after it had done infinite mischief in the State, and had kept the party that made it, in the saddle about ten years (which, by the way, I conceive, was the principal design and use of it) and there was substituted in the stead of it, a very simple oath of allegiance, without any of the exceptionable clauses of the former, by which the rights of our citizens are restored, and a happy peace and general satisfaction of our people have succeeded.

he disapproves, he ought to execute the office faithfully and legally, or he is punishable; if he cannot do this, he ought not to accept the office: he doubtless ought also to be a quiet and peaceable subject of the government which exists, and to use none but lawful means to mend or alter it.

He is supposed to be of a *minor party*, who must be governed by the *major vote*; but such minor party, having no guilt, is entitled to every blessing and benefit of government, as much as any of that party who are most cordial to the present establishment, *i. e.* government ought to hold an even, true, and just balance over every subject, and secure and defend the rights, liberties, property, privileges, &c. of every individual equally. The law is the equal right of every man, and therefore every man has an equal right to all its benefits, protections, securities, privileges, and advantages of every kind, till by some act of guilt he shall forfeit them.

It may be objected here,—shall *the enemies* of the *present Constitution* * enjoy the *same privileges* under it as its *friends*, who have run *every risk*, and made the *strongest exertions*, to introduce and establish it? I answer—*Yes*. It is to be presumed, that the zeal of the patrons of the Constitution has ever been directed in all their exertions with a single eye to the public good, otherwise they certainly deserve no favor; if their design was to introduce a partial government, not equal to all, in which they and their friends could *monopolize the benefits and emoluments* of government to themselves, they must be deemed very execrable, and their plan and administration most pernicious to society.

Government (both in theory and practice, system and administration) is a sort of *public thing*, in which *every individual has an interest*, and this interest is of so high and delicate a kind, that *any violation* of it excites the *highest resentment* in the sufferer. To be thrown *out of the protection of the law*, is a punishment of a very high nature, and

in

---

* The Constitution of *Pensylvania* then newly made (but since abrogated by the late Convention of the State) was greatly opposed by most men of gravity and wisdom, tho' it was carried by a warm party which prevailed at that time, and was propped up by test-acts, &c.

in all good governments pre-supposes a *conviction* of some very *black* and *atrocious crime*, some crime of a very high nature and deep guilt. Wherefore, the *least disfranchisement*, or *deprivation of any one benefit*, which ought to flow from government equally on every subject, must partake of the nature of that high punishment, and, of course, ought never to take place, but where there has preceded a *conviction of such high guilt* as will justify it.

To adopt any *principles* or *administration* of government, which, from their nature, must keep *party resentments alive*, and fret the community with the perpetual *gnawing anguish of continued oppressions*, is the height of absurdity, must keep society in a perpetual ferment, and will for ever prevent the community from cementing in such an union, confidence, and acquiescence in the government, as are essential to the well-being of civil society; for human nature must cease to be what it is, before any part of mankind will acquiesce in an administration which treats them with *distinctions of contempt*, like underlings *cut off from* those *honors or emoluments* of the State, which the government diffuses with equal benevolence on all their neighbours.

If the government be *good* and *properly administered*, it will *prove itself so by practice*; the benefits of it will be diffused thro' the community, and be felt by every one. This will naturally reconcile every opposer to its principles and practice, and it will soon have *all good men* for its friends; and when this is the case, there will be little danger of public disquietude arising from the *wicked* and *guilty part* of the community, who are uneasy with the government only because it restrains their wickedness, follies, or lusts.

It appears, then, that the *test-acts*, which have for their object the *secret thoughts*, *opinions*, *sentiments*, and *designs* of men, have an object which no human authority *can* or *ought to reach*; that the very attempt to do this is a violation of the most sacred rights of the subject; it is an intrusion into the great and exclusive prerogative of the ALMIGHTY, to whom alone *secret things belong;* goes on a supposition that is both useless and impossible, viz. that the secret opinions, sentiments, and designs of all men *can or ought*

ought to be alike; limits the rights, privileges, liberties, and security of the subject, to conditions which are absurd and ridiculous, because they have no connexion with the *virtue* or *vice*, the *merit* or *demerit* of the subject; and is so far from securing the peace, good order, and safety of society, that it cannot fail, on most natural principles, to keep up a perpetual fret and resentment of parties, to plant and keep alive that discord, uneasiness, and revenge, which is of the worst tendency, and generally produces very hurtful, and often very tragical, effects.

In fine, human nature is such, that all mankind have *secret things about them*, which they wish and think they have right to hold secure against the *forcible intrusion* of any body; if they disclose them, it must and ought to be their own voluntary act, to which they ought to be *courted*, not *compelled*; any attempt, therefore, by violence and the force of laws, to *wring such secrets* from the possessor, is against nature, is an insult on the natural feelings of every person living; the absurdity, indecency, and injury of which all men living see fast and clear enough, when it is put in practice by their enemies on themselves or their friends.

But what adds to the absurdity of this ill-fated piece of policy, is, that the *little benefit* which is hoped for and expected from it, *fails entirely in the effects;* and so after all the risks, scandals, cruelties, and mischiefs wrought by it, there remains *no balance of profit* at all, and the measure turns up at last, after all the trouble and pother about it, *ridiculously useless.* For,

III. The benefits expected from it *all fail upon the trial.* It would, indeed, be a fine thing to have a criterion by which we might distinguish our friends from our enemies, to have all our subjects under the strongest voluntary ties to the government, and to have the sacred power of *religion mustered in aid of our civil policy:* but plain fact and the fullest experience prove, that these effects *are not, will not, cannot* be produced by *test-acts.*

Read the history of the *weak reigns* of the bloody Queen *Mary* (the *British* persecutrix) of *James I.* and *Charles I.* of *England;* of *Henry II. Charles IX.* and *Henry III.* of *France;*

France; in which *test-acts greatly abounded* (and, I think, they are ever a sign of a *weak* administration:) in all these we find a cloud of evasions, explanations, mental reservations, &c. which, with infinite variety of operation, never cease till they have totally avoided or obliterated the force of the acts.

For, whatever *obligation* the imposers of these acts may conceive to be in them, or whatever *force* the decisions of divines, civilians, or canonists may give them, it is plain that the general sense and practice of mankind, when harassed with them, give them *mighty little* or *none* at all. It is a well-known maxim, that the construction of any statute obtained by usage and common practice, is of more effect than the words, because such usage always controls the words: and if this rule may be allowed to apply, mighty little binding force will be left in the test-acts.

Indeed, I think it requires but little acquaintance and observation of the world, to see plain enough, that it is matter of general sentiment, that the most of mankind always did and always will believe, that if *rulers* or *robbers* attempt by force to wring from you any secret of your mind, which they neither *have* nor *can have* any right to know, that it is very proper and lawful for you to *deceive them, cheat them, bubble them, and get rid of them any how that you can*, and retain your own secret.

Can any man in his senses expect to get a true answer, were he to demand an oath of each subject of any State, *whether he was or ever would be a traitor or heretic?* and this I take to be the meaning of every test-act and oath of allegiance forcibly imposed on the subject, with this difference (which often makes a notable difficulty) the question sometimes is, not whether you are or will be a traitor *to the State*, but *to some proposition, fact, whim, or system specified in the oath*, and which is not always thought to be the same thing with the true interests of the State.

If any man thinks true answers can be obtained by this method of interrogation, it may not be improper to try the precious expedient in a few other similar cases, viz. try to oblige a woman to answer on oath, whether *she is or ever will*

will be a whore; a clergyman, whether he is or ever will be *a liar, drunkard,* or *heretic;* a merchant, whether he ever *did* or *will* make *false entries* in his books, or *forge* bills of exchange. I am of opinion, that a little practice of such a sweet cue on various subjects, would soon demonstrate the utility or absurdity of this *magical kind of logic,* or method of investigating truth, show how it will suit the ordinary feelings of the human heart, and discover what rare inducements such curious questions must excite in sensible minds, to tell the *truth,* the *whole truth,* and *nothing but the truth.*

But if this unreasonable, indelicate method of investigating truth would always produce it, I have still a pretty cogent reason against the practice of it, viz. that the public would not be *benefited,* but *greatly prejudiced by such a discovery.* I think it is very evident that many sins do *less hurt* while they *lie concealed,* than they would do, *if published;* eaves-droppers rarely hear any good of themselves; jealousy is a low, uneasy passion, and is commonly gratified by an *increase of torment;* and people that are anxiously fond of *fishing* for secrets, rarely fail to *hook in* trouble; and these observations are not less true, and commonly more dangerous, in *state-policy* than in *private life;* but in both equally indicate *weakness of intellects,* disorders of imagination, great ignorance of human nature, and that painful, ridiculous anxiety which generally accompanies irritable nerves, and want of true, sound judgment.

This weakness of human nature is a kind of *womanish imbecillity,* like tears, which appear much more ridiculous in subjects of *dignity and gravity,* than in the *weaker sex,* to which they more properly belong. Government may enjoin a *thousand oaths,* and thereby occasion *ten thousand perjuries,* not one of which can be proved or punished without *overt acts,* and such *overt acts* will have equal effect both of conviction and punishment of all the abjured treason, *without the oaths* as *with them;* and, of course, the oaths are at least useless, if not hurtful.

Dignity and gravity ought always to be most carefully maintained in government; which will ever lose its respectability, when it defcends to *low, pimping* methods of adminiftration. The tree is to be judged by its fruit only.

It is by *overt acts only* that the defigns of the heart can be made *to appear;* within this line of evidence we are limited *by the laws of nature,* as within brazen walls, beyond which the human powers cannot go. Nor does the fafety of human fociety require this to be exceeded; for I am fully perfuaded, if the well-being of mankind had required any other or better way of *difcovering the fecrets of the heart,* the *great Governor* of the world would have communicated to men fome *other way* in which it could be done.

I have on the whole no opinion that *teft-acts* or even *oaths of allegiance* afford any kind of fecurity to the State; nor have I any very high opinion of *oaths of office,* but I do greatly object to *any oaths being tacked to an office,* more than the fimple *adjuration to execute the office legally and faithfully;* and I equally object to municipal rights and privileges being made dependent on teft-oaths or folemn declarations of fecret opinions or fentiments.

I have candidly given my reafons for my opinion, which I hope will be candidly confidered; and beg leave to move, with fome hope and great humility, that *all acts which enjoin fuch oaths,* efpecially *the teft-acts,* may be repealed by the proper authority. But if a repeal of thofe acts fhould be thought too much, I beg leave to recommend the removal of fome of the feverities which are impofed by thefe acts on the non-jurors; particularly their *double tax,* and the demand of that part of their tax in *hard money,* which the jurors are allowed to pay in *paper of about one-third the value of hard money.*

As a reafon for this, I humbly urge, over and above the capital arguments drawn from the juftice of government, and the equality and impartiality with which it ought to be adminiftered to all orders and ranks of people, I fay, befides this, I wifh to urge the neceffity of convincing all our people, *by the equity and impartiality of our government,* that it is a *fafe and fure protection* of perfon and property; that

the

the *burdens* of it are *equally laid*, so that no *one part* of the community is *oppressed or burdened more than the rest*.

This will give a practical proof that our government carries in it the most characteristic marks of a *free, just, and gentle policy*, which is directly opposed *to tyranny*, the essence of which consists in a *denial or partial distribution of justice*, and laying *unequal* burdens on *one part* of the community, in *favor of other parts*. This will soon gain the approbation and confidence of all people of serious and cool reflexion; the *violent ravings* of passion and prejudice will soon *spend their own strength*, and subside of course, when all *real ground* of complaint is taken away.

The non-jurors are very numerous; our business and interest is to get them reconciled, not exterminated. Mankind will ever like that government best, where they can enjoy most security, justice, and peace. Our political character, both among neighbours and foreign nations, requires this; if great numbers of *our own people* have a strong aversion to *our* government, it will afford a presumption to strangers, that either our people or our government must be *very bad*. Either of which will lessen our dignity and weight, and injure our public character abroad, and discourage that accession of foreigners, which is necessary to increase our population, trade, and husbandry.

Rigor and *force* can never govern any people longer than till they can find an opportunity of *avoiding* or *revenging* it. The understandings of the people must be convinced and courted, and the cements of society cannot be long wanting. We may, by perpetual, galling, and odious distinctions, keep up the *heat and virulencies* of parties, as long as those of the *Guelphs* and *Gibbelines* lasted in *Italy*, and to about as much advantage, *i. e.* till the peace, wealth, and morality of the country are all ruined.

We may, if we please, with more ease, like *Henry IV.* of *France*, by giving equal justice, benefit, and favor to all, soon convince all, that the government is their *best friend* and *surest protection;* then they will love and trust it for their own sakes, and when *interest* and *allegiance* conspire

spire together, and mutually support each other, the government has the highest possible security of good order, public peace, and social happiness.

Sundry other reasons and observations might be added on this subject, which I can only hint at here, and leave the reader to enlarge on them as he pleases.

I. A great *multiplicity* of oaths makes them *common* and *familiar*, and thereby *lessens* their solemnity and practical force.

II. It cannot be expected that they will be *sincerely taken and kept;* and, therefore, they will introduce many *perjuries, evasions, &c.* which naturally tend to eradicate from the mind the high obligation of such awful appeals to the ALMIGHTY, and that *solemn sense of truth*, which most effectually secures the benefits of an oath.

III. It is presumed that very few of the present non-jurors refuse the oaths because they wish to return to the *English government*, or because they are averse to the *American independency;* but for a great variety of other reasons, which might be easily mentioned; and for the truth of this I appeal to the non-jurors themselves, who can best explain their own opinions and sentiments.

IV. Some of the enjoined oaths contain *facts* which many do not believe to be true, and *contradictions* which cannot be reconciled.

V. People of the most delicate sentiments of religion and truth only, *i. e.* the *best people* in the world, may be *governed* and perhaps *hurt* by them; whilst people of a *contrary* character will all avail themselves of some *shift or other* to avoid their whole effects.

VI. The experience of ages and nations proves that this measure has ever *failed of producing the effects proposed and intended* by it. Have we secured the obedience and good-will of one *American* subject by it? We have seen, with indignation and contempt, the *British generals* rigidly imposing *their* oath of allegiance wherever they gained footing, and hanging such as have relapsed; the consequence is, they have *disaffected* and *lost* all their friends in the southern

southern governments lately, and in all the rest long ago; the revolts against them are nearly universal.

VII. The real object of these tests is not always the *safety of the State;* they are *too often* made use of as *engines of a ruling party,* to entrap and punish such people as they suppose inimical to *themselves,* and whose conduct is so prudent and inoffensive, that they are not liable to punishment, but by some law which creates a crime which can be proved and punished *without the evidence of overt acts.* This is the height of *abomination,* a most execrable corruption and abuse of the most sacred rights of law.

VIII. When, by such wicked tricks, numbers of our freemen are excluded from their *right of election,* and bearing their part in the government of the State, the *essential principle* on which the government of the United States is founded, *is violated.* This principle is, *that all right of government lies in the people,* and that *our government* is a government of *the people;* which cannot be the case where numbers of the *people,* who have a right to a share in it, *are excluded.*

It is easy enough for any party which gets into the saddle, to keep their places there, by imposing some *condition* which is either *impossible* or *impracticable,* on all the people of *different* sentiments from themselves, *e. g.* they may make the very *point in question* between the two parties a *term* of admission or exclusion of the civil privileges and franchises of the people.

This is a short way of cutting down opposing parties, and destroying their weight in society, and changing the very essence of the Constitution from being the government of *the people,* to that of being a government of *part* of the people *only:* for there is a very wide difference between a government by major vote of *all the people,* and a government by a major vote of *part of the people,* whilst the *other part* are *excluded* from voting at all; for by this method of proceeding, the governing or voting part may, by repeated exclusions, reduce the government to a *very small number,* a mere *junto of a few,* from which the *main body of the people* may be excluded; which is not the free

government

government of the people intended by our Conſtitution, but a mere unchecked *tyranny of a few.*

To effect all which, nothing more is neceſſary than this, viz. whenever there ariſes an oppoſition to any point carried by a majority, for that ſame majority to require *an oath approving the very point in diſpute*, and impoſing a *penalty* of excluſion from *all right of voting*, on ſuch as refuſe the oath, and ſo go on *toties quoties*, whenever an oppoſition ariſes. This will effectually exclude the oppoſition from future voting; for men will often *conform* to a matter carried by a majority againſt them, who would by no means *ſwear an approbation* of it.

This may be repeated till there are but two voters left in the whole State, and then one of them has nothing more to do than to kill the other, and he will be *ſole tyrant*, and will be very ſafe, if he can get a ſtanding army to ſupport him: and this will not be difficult, if he has money enough: and this too will be eaſy; for the voting part of the community can always lay *what taxes* and *raiſe what money they pleaſe*, and the army which is to receive that money, can eaſily *enforce the collection* or payment of it.

Nor is this any very unnatural, ſtrained, or extravagant ſuppoſition; for we have often ſeen *Commonwealths*, by the *fatal errors* of their policy, run into a *monarchical* and *deſpotic tyranny:* and the only ſure way to avoid the fatal conſequences of ſuch errors, is to *nip them in the bud; obſtare principiis*, to detect their principles, and reſtrain and correct the firſt beginnings of them, before they gain ſuch ſtrength as to be irreſiſtible. I am here almoſt compelled to offer to public conſideration one more propoſal, viz.

To take off all *diſfranchiſements and diſabilities* created by any of our ſtatutes, for no other cauſe than *neglecting the teſt-acts, oath of allegiance,** &c.

I write

---

* *Teſt-acts*, at the time this Eſſay was written, were deemed ſo *important*, that any objection to them, or doubt of their uſe, was cried out upon and reprobated by the violent party which then prevailed in the State, as *malignancy* againſt the *American independence*, *diſaffection to the government*, and *a ſort of treaſon.* I was *inſulted* and *much threatened* for writing this Eſſay. A very angry writer, under the ſignature of *A Conſtitutionaliſt*, in the *Freeman's*

I write under a moſt ſerious conviction of the importance of my ſubject, and truth of my arguments, and really myſelf mean to be as open as I wiſh my readers to be, to the conviction of ſound reaſon, and the dictates of true policy, and therefore think I have a right to hope for indulgence, even where my ſentiments cannot obtain approbation.

man's Journal of *Sept.* 28, 1781, undertook to blacken it moſt effectually; then went on to defend teſt-acts, and anſwer my Eſſay. After applying pretty liberally all the hard words he could think of, he gives the character of it as follows:—" Of all publications hitherto exhibited in print, ſince the eſtabliſhment of our independence, this Eſſay is foremoſt in barefaced and undiſguiſed principles, to *toryiſm favorable;* to our *Revolution inimical;* and of our *Conſtitution ſubverſive*:" and then goes on to obſerve, that every independent State ought to be guarded by ſome criterion, by which *good citizens* may be diſtinguiſhed from *bad* ones; and that all ſuch States have good right and authority to adopt any ſuch criterion or term of citizenſhip, which they think proper; and that teſt-acts are of this kind, &c.

In my reply, publiſhed in the ſame *Journal, Oct.* 5, 1781, I urge that teſt-acts have no more connexion with the *independent government of the Union,* or the *Conſtitution of this State*, than with *all other governments;* but they may be neceſſary to *toryiſm*, as they have been generally moſt *adopted* and *preſſed* in the *weakeſt* and *worſt governments;*—that I do not diſpute the *authority* of any independent State to make teſt-acts; it is the *expediency* only of making them which I object to—that very many *good* men will *refuſe* them, and many *bad* men will *take* them—that the merits and qualities of citizens ought to be taken and eſtimated by their *conduct* or *overt acts,* not by the *ſecrets of their hearts,* which are cogniſable by God *alone*, not by the *State,* till *by overt acts* they are made *known:* the *Conſtitutionaliſt* ſays, that non-jurors are *aliens,* not *citizens;* this I denied; for were they *aliens,* they could not be *holden* to any *municipal obedience* or *duties,* ſuch as taxes, ſervices, &c. or be *capable of treaſons,* or *crimes* againſt the *State,* to which (if aliens) they could owe *no allegiance*—I further urged, that teſt-acts, where the moſt that could be, was made of them, amounted to no more than *a man's teſtimony in his own caſe,* which was not admitted in matters of the ſmalleſt moment, and, of courſe, the moſt important of all intereſts ought not to be controlled or limited by it—that preſſing teſt-acts was a ſure way to keep alive the moſt galling *fretts* and *diſcontents* in a State, and was very bad policy even in a *ruling party,* becauſe the ſame meaſures might be *retorted* upon themſelves, if they ſhould happen to ſlip *out of* the ſaddle, and their *opponents* ſhould get *into* it.——

On the whole I much prefer a government which ſecures to every man the ſecrets of his own mind, and makes him amenable for his conduct and overt acts only, rather than one which intrudes on ſuch ſecrets, and makes the diſcovery of them on oath a term of the richeſt and nobleſt benefits and privileges of ſociety.

If any body may wiſh to ſee more of this matter, I refer him to the pieces at large, which are preſerved in the *Freeman's Journal,* as quoted above.

AN

AN ESSAY

ON THE

EXTENT AND VALUE

OF OUR

WESTERN UNLOCATED LANDS,

AND THE

PROPER METHOD

Of disposing of them, so as to gain the greatest possible Advantage from them.

[*First published in Philadelphia, April 25, 1781.*]

IN my several treatises on *finance*, I have all along endeavoured to open and explain the great general principles of the subject, viz. *improvement* of the revenue, and *economy* in the expenditures. In this Essay I mean to confine myself to *one particular source or object of public wealth*, out of which *great revenue* may be obtained by proper and timely wisdom and care, I mean, our *vacant, unsettled lands*. I will endeavour to arrange, as clearly as I can, what I have to say on this subject, under the following heads, viz.

I. *The whole territory or extent of the Thirteen States is the aggregate of them all,* i. e. the territory or extent of each of the States added together, make the whole territory or extent of right and dominion of the United States; and, of course, whatever is comprehended within the boundaries of each State, now makes a part of our Commonwealth.

This is to be considered as our *present possession*, our present decided right, which is guarantied to us by the treaty with *France* (Article XI.) together with any ' additions or conquests, which our Confederation may obtain during the war, from any of the dominions now or heretofore possessed by *Great-Britain* in *North-America*;' so that by conquest we may extend our dominion further, if we can; and, in this case, we shall have the guarantee of the treaty aforesaid for our security; but if this cannot be done, our present possessions are absolutely and unconditionally guarantied to us, with liberty, sovereignty, and independence, absolute and unlimited, in and over the same.

And as the great interests of *France* and our Commonwealth will always make the *perpetual union* of them necessary, so these powers united will be able to afford such a sure mutual protection to the whole dominions of each other, as will render them wholly secure and free of danger from any other powers whatever; so that we may safely compute on all the advantages of our present possessions, and turn our thoughts on the ways and means of making the best of them; while, at the same time, we have a rich and valuable chance of acquiring by conquest new dominions, and, having, of course, such new acquisitions covered by the same guarantee which now secures our present possessions.

Nobody can pretend to deny that our present possessions comprehend *all the lands included within the boundaries of the Thirteen States, as the same existed at the time our independence first began;* but it will be strongly urged that they cannot extend *beyond them,* so as to cover any lands not included within the bounds of *some one* of the States, unless we can make a claim to a further extent *by conquest;* indeed, I do not see how we can *otherwise* support a claim to independence, sovereignty, and dominion over any thing which was *not within our bounds* at that time: therefore, it follows,

1. That wherever we fix the *exterior limit or bounds of any one of the States,* there we fix the *bounds of our Commonwealth;* and it will be urged against us, that all beyond is not our territory, our right, or dominion: and, therefore,

2. It

2. It is our interest *to extend the exterior boundary of each of our States* as far as we *fairly can;* and, of course, any attempt (arising from envy or any little disputes) to *abridge or reduce the limits of any of the States* to lines short of their true extent, and so prevent their *covering the whole territory to* which their original charters, or usual prescriptive titles, give them right, is the *height of folly* and *absurd policy*, and operates directly against the great interests of the Commonwealth.

And here I cannot but take notice of the madness, short-sighted policy, and *public mischief*, of a late pamphlet, entitled *Public Good*, which, by very weak and trifling arguments, attempts to limit the territory of *Virginia* to a very inconsiderable part of its original and true extent. I think some note of disapprobation should be fixed on that treatise, lest it should be produced in future debates, as a proof of the general sense of the States at this time.

There is, indeed, as is well known, some *obscurity of description* to be found in all the *ancient charters* of these States, which, by that means, admit of a latitude of construction; but most of these are reduced to a determinate certainty by *subsequent acts, decisions, usages, &c.* and, I conceive, that for most obvious reasons.

II. *The boundaries of the several States are to be taken and ascertained from their original charters, with such construction as has obtained by subsequent usage, judicial decisions, or any other acts of the crown or the inhabitants, which tend to give them a determinate and fixed definition.* If, in any case, no light can be drawn from such usage or subsequent acts, the particular boundaries must depend on the words of the charters, with such reasonable construction as shall give them their *greatest effect*, and be *most adequate to the original intention* of them, or, in law language, so *ut res magis valeat quam pereat;* by which rule of construction, there can be no doubt but *Virginia*, having boundaries sufficiently fixed on the sea-coast, is *to extend west,* and *carry her breadth to the South-Sea,* or at least as far as the *dominion of the crown extended,* at the time when American independence first began.

Two

Two things are sufficiently clear,

1st. That all the States are so bounded on each other, that there are *no strips of land lying between any two of them;* and,

2d. That their western boundary is *the South-Sea,* or at least the *western boundary of the dominions of the crown,* at the commencement of our Commonwealth.

So that the country or territory of the Thirteen States, is clearly bounded on *the west* as aforesaid; on the *south,* by the south line of *Georgia* (about N. lat. 30° 22″) on *the east,* by the sea, including the islands lying in the offing of the coast; and *north,* by the north line of the Province of *Maine, New-Hampshire,* and *the Massachusetts State* (about N. lat. 45). its *length,* north and south, is about 1000 *miles;* and its *breadth,* east and west (if it extends no farther than the *Mississippi* river) about 600 *miles* on the *southern* part, and 1250 *miles* on the *northern* part.

The contents of which are somewhat more than 810,000 *square miles;* more than equal to those of *France, Spain, Germany,* and *Italy,* and much more valuable in respect of air, climate, soil, timber, fossils, fisheries, harbors, rivers, &c. with all conveniency for transportation, both by maritime and inland navigation.

It is further to be noted here, that with respect to *Virginia,* and some other governments, which either never had any charters, or whose charters have been surrendered to the crown, that the *soil and jurisdiction* of them were *both in the crown,* and therefore the King *ever* claimed right to make new grants of soil, and carve out and establish any new jurisdictions or governments which he thought expedient, and on this principle actually did carve *Maryland* and part of *Pennsylvania* out of *Virginia;* how justly I am not to say; but this does not hinder *Virginia* from taking her departure from her true eastern boundary on the sea-coast, and covering all the lands within her limits (not included in these *carvatures*) to her utmost western boundary.

It is, indeed, to be observed here, that ascertaining the boundaries of any State, does not prove the *title or right of such State to all lands* included within such boundaries.

There

There is a distinction to be made between those lands which have been *alienated by the crown*, the title of which, at the date of our independence, was not in the crown, but vested in particular persons, either sole or aggregate, and those which *remained in the crown*, the title of which the crown then held in right of its sovereignty, which was a right vested in the supreme authority, in nature of a trust for the use of the public.

There is no doubt but every right and title of all persons and bodies politic are as effectually secured and confirmed to the owners, to all intents and purposes, under the *Commonwealth*, as they were formerly *under the crown*; but it cannot be admitted that any individual or bodies politic should acquire *new rights* by the Revolution, to which they were not entitled under the crown, *i. e.* each State has right to claim, hold, or alienate whatever property or estate it had right to obtain, hold, or alienate, whilst it was a colony under the crown; but cannot have right to claim, hold, or alienate any estate, the claim, tenure, or alienation of which was then the right of the crown.

But every such estate being then held by the crown in right of sovereignty, or its supreme power, in trust for the use of the whole community or body politic, of which it was the supreme power, must pass, by the Revolution, into the supreme power of our Commonwealth, *i. e.* into the Congress, and be vested in them in trust for the public use of the body politic, of which they are the supreme power; and the right of tenure and alienation must be vested in them alone.

Indeed, in all revolutions of government which have ever happened in *Europe*, and perhaps in the whole world, all *crown-lands, jewels*, and *all other state* which belonged to the supreme power which *lost* the government, ever passed by the revolution into the supreme power which *gained* it; and all such estate always became vested in the *latter* occupant, in the same condition and under the same limitations to which it was subject under the tenure of the *former* occupant.

Nor can I see the least pretence of reason, why we should depart from a rule of right grounded on the most plain and natural fitness, adopted by every nation in the world under like circumstances, and justified and confirmed by the experience and sanction of ages. I think that nothing but our unacquaintedness with the heights to which we are risen, the high sphere in which we now move, and an incapacity of viewing and judging of things on a great scale, could give rise to so extravagant an idea, as that *one State* should be *more entitled than another* to the *crown-lands*, or any other property of the crown, which ever was in its nature public, and ought to continue so, or be disposed of for the use and benefit of the whole public community; or that one State should acquire more right, or property, or estate than another, by that Revolution which was the *joint act*, procured and perfected by the *joint effort* and *expense*, of the whole. We have too long and too ridiculously set up to be wiser than all the world besides, and too long refused to be instructed by the experience of other nations.

III. The vast territory of the Thirteen States above described, and containing something more than 500,000,000 *acres of land*, is mostly wild and uncultivated; a strip only adjoining to the sea, and not containing more than *one-third*, or at most *two-fifths*, of the whole, and that by far the poorest part of the soil is any how become private property and settled; the rest remains a large extent of the richest wild lands in the world, to be disposed of and cultivated in future time; and the part which I call settled, is so far from being filled with inhabitants, that it does not contain more than *one-tenth part* of the people which the soil, in a state of perfect cultivation, would support; the frontiers are every where thinly settled, and, of course, very liable to the inroads of the enemy, and very difficult to defend.

IV. Six only of the States have a large *western extent* of unsettled lands, viz. *Massachusetts, Connecticut, Virginia, North* and *South-Carolina,* and *Georgia*; the other seven are limited within *much narrower* bounds.

V. Tho'

V. Tho' the *title* and *right* of the said six States to their *whole western extent* should be indisputable, yet the *preservation* and *use* of it *are secured* to them, and the whole must for ever *be defended*, by *the arms* and at the *expense* of the States-general. The *quotas* of this expense ought to be *proportioned* to the value and extent of the thing secured and defended by it; *qui sentit commodum, sentire debet quoque onus:* but if the quotas of the said six States should be *increased* in proportion to the great *extent* of their territory, or even the *value* of the same, it would bring such a very *pressing weight* on the present inhabitants, as might be beyond their strength, or at least very inconvenient to them.

For here it is to be considered, that the expense of the war is not to be estimated merely by the *cash* it has cost; but the *devastations* of the enemy, the loss of *lives, &c.* are to be brought into the account; and when the estimate comes to be made on these principles, it will rise very high on such parts of the interest defended as could lose *no lives,* because it had *no inhabitants;* and was incapable of *devastation*, because it had *no improvements* which could be destroyed.

Besides, as all the States have exerted themselves with *equal ardor, danger,* and *effort* in carrying on the war, it is but reasonable they should all share *alike* in the *advantages* resulting from it. To these might be added many more strong reasons why the said six States should cede or grant their western uncultivated lands to the States-general, to remain a common stock, till they can be disposed of for the good of the whole.

But I deem it needless to urge this matter farther, because I am informed that a general conviction of the expediency of this measure prevails thro' all the States, and that it is freely agreed on the part of the said six States, to make such a *cession* or *grant* to the States-general, as above mentioned, and that the same will soon be done.*

We

---

* The foregoing ideas and arguments were such as were suggested at the time when this Essay was first published, and were matters of much
conversation

[492]

We will suppose, then, that this is done, and the right and title of these western uncultivated lands vested in the States-general; what is to be done with them? i. e. how are they to be managed, in order to obtain the greatest national benefit possible from them?

Some people think we ought to *sell* or *mortgage them to foreign States*, for money in our present distress. But I have many reasons against this method. The first is,

That it is capable of the most demonstrative proof, that *no importation of money* can help us, even if it *was given to us*, much less if our lands are to be *mortgaged* for it. We are in much more danger from *the plenty* of money coming from all quarters in upon us, than from any *scarcity of it*; our salvation must arise from the *wealth* and *virtue* which abounds *in the country*, not in hunting *abroad for money*.

Besides, I abhor the very idea of *strangers* having their *paw on any of our lands* in any shape whatever: and,

Further, they would bring *mighty little in* this way, i. e. very little *present* benefit, tho' enough of *future trouble*; it would be like killing the goose that laid an egg every day, in order to tear out at once all that was in her belly. But every idea of this sort is painful to me; I wish not to dwell longer on it, but beg leave to propose a method which appears to me more for our advantage.

I. Let the *ceded territory* be divided from the *unceded* by the plainest lines, and let it be kept in its present uncultivated state, and preserved from the *intrusion of any settlers* whatever, by the most rigid and effectual prohibitions, till the *lands adjoining* are *fully settled*: then,

II. Survey

---

conversation and discussion both in and out of Congress, but have all been long since adjusted and settled.

The boundaries of the Union were defined in the treaty of peace with *Great-Britain*, in *Feb.* 1783, and extended much beyond the limits here proposed.

And the affair of the great western extent of the six States was accommodated to general satisfaction, by *cessions* of such parts of them to Congress as lay beyond their settlements, since which the lands so ceded have been considered as public property, and as such subject to the disposal of Congress, for the benefit of the whole Union.

II. *Survey out townships of six, eight, or ten miles square,* contiguous to the settled country, and sell the lands at vendue to the highest bidder, on the following conditions:

1. That none be sold at less than a *Spanish* dollar per acre.

2. That every purchaser be obliged to settle and improve his purchase within two or three years, or forfeit his lands; the particular regulations of which should be published at the time of sale, and be rigidly executed; and when the *first course or tier* of townships are sold, and the *settlement of them secured*, lay out *another tier*; sell them in like manner, and so on thro' the whole. This method will have the following advantages, viz.

1. All the lands sold will bring at least a dollar per acre; and if we admit, as above computed, those 300,000,000 acres of our western territory to become the public property of the States-general, and allow 100,000,000 acres for lakes, ponds, beds of rivers, barrens, &c. there will remain 200,000,000 acres of good land to be sold; which, at a dollar per acre, will produce 200,000,000 *hard dollars* for the treasury of the United States; the annual interest of which, at 5 per cent. will be 10,000,000 dollars *per annum*; a sum much more than sufficient to defray the whole public expenses of the Thirteen States, in a time of peace, and, of course, a large surplus to be expended on a navy, roads, canals, and many other improvements of our country, with a sufficient sum to be laid up for a time of war.

2. This method will push our settlements out in close columns, much less assailable by the enemy, and more easily defended, than extensive, thin populations; there will be people here for defence *near the frontiers;* they will have the inducements of a *near interest* to animate them to the service; their course of life and acquaintance with the country will render them much *more fit* for the service, than people drawn from the interior parts of the country; and the necessary force may be collected and put into action *much quicker*, and with much *less expense*, than if the same was drawn from distant parts.

These

These and many more and great advantages will naturally result from our pushing out our settlements in close columns, which cannot be expected or hoped for from a vastly extended frontier thinly inhabited.

Add to this, that every new beginner makes his first improvement *in company of near neighbours, and at but small distance* from *older settlements*, much *more easily* than he could do alone in a wilderness, where he could receive *no helps from neighbours*, let his necessity be ever so great.

3. This method would obviate one abuse very hurtful to new settlements, most injurious to the individuals who first migrate and bear the hardships of first cultivation, and which greatly retards the population and improvement of a new country, viz. *large quantities of land lying unimproved in the hands of non-residents or absentees*, who neither dwell on the land, nor cause it to be cultivated at all, but their land lies in its wild state, a *refuge for bears, wolves*, and *other beasts* of prey, ready to *devour* the produce of the neighbouring farmers, bears no part of the *burden of first cultivation*, and keeps the settlers at an *inconvenient distance* from each other, and *obstructs* the growth and riches of the townships in which it lies; whilst the owner, by the *rise of the land*, makes a *fortune* out of the *labor* and *toils* of the neighbouring cultivators. This is a most *cruel way of enriching one man by the labor of another*, and so very hurtful to the cultivation of the country, that it ought to be restrained by the most decisive measures.

4. This method will give every inhabitant of the Thirteen States an equal chance of availing himself of any advantage of *procuring lands for the accommodation of himself or family;* whilst, at the same time, the ceding State will reap great benefit from the *produce* and *trade* of the adjoining settlements, which will, at the same time, become a *secure barrier* to their frontiers, against the incursions of an enemy on that side.

5. In this method we can *extend our laws, customs*, and *civil police* as *fast* and as *far* as we extend our *settlements;* of course, our frontier people will enjoy every benefit of civil society and regular administration of justice; which
cannot

cannot take place with equal perfection in the great extent of a thin settled frontier.

6. Another thing very necessary to be observed in the whole management of this affair is, *to cultivate a good and friendly correspondence with the Indian natives, by a careful practice of justice and benevolence towards them.* They are an innumerable race of people, probably extending over a vast country to the west seas, and very great advantages may be derived from their trade, if we can gain and preserve their confidence.

Whereas nobody ever yet gained any thing by an *Indian war*. Their spoils are of no value; but their revenge and depredations are terrible. It is much cheaper to purchase their lands, than to dispossess them by force; and justice in all cases is more profitable than violence and wrong.

It may be noted here, that many inhabitants are already on the lands supposed to be ceded. What is to be done with them? I answer—if their continuance is matter of *uneasiness to the Indians*, and is likely to produce broils with them, they are by all means to be *removed*. For it is unreasonable that the public tranquillity should be endangered for the sake of the convenience of a few people, who, *without the least pretence of right*, have fixed themselves down on lands *not their own*.

But notwithstanding this, if their continuance will not endanger the public security, let them keep their possessions on express condition, viz. that, when the townships in which their possessions shall be included when the future surveys shall be made, shall be sold, they shall pay as much for their lands as the other purchasers of the same township pay on an average for theirs, excluding every idea of favor, to which they may think themselves entitled for their *first migration* and *cultivation*. For I esteem all this very wrong and injurious to the public, which rather deserves punishment than reward.

But there is another objection more forcible, which, I suppose, will be pretty readily made to my scheme, viz. all the benefits of this scheme are *future*, are a great *way off;* but we want *present* supplies, to relieve the present necessities
of

of our country. This was Esau's argument, which he sold his birthright for a mess of pottage, and is certainly a very good one, when really grounded on fact; for no doubt a man had better give his whole fortune for *one meal* of victuals, than *starve to death* for want of it; but I think wise men will examine this fact very closely, and be very decidedly convinced, that the *supposed* present necessity is really great enough to induce us to forego all the fore-mentioned advantages for the sake of the pittance, the trifle of money which those lands would now bring, if sold or mortgaged at present for the utmost they would bring, attended with all the shocking and mortifying disadvantages of giving any foreigners a footing in our country, and a claim upon our most essential and central interests.

But I think the objection itself is grounded on an error; for I think the present advantages resulting from my plan greater than could arise from any kind of mortgage or alienation of these lands; for I consider them like a *rich, valuable, and sure reversion*, which never fails to give the owner a great estimation, credit, and respectability in the eyes of his neighbours, tho' he receives no pecuniary of present profits; but if this reversion was sold or mortgaged for a trifle, and soon dissipated (as doubtless would be our case) the owner would appear in a light more contemptible, and in every view much more disadvantageous, than if he had never owned the right.

It cannot be too often repeated, that *we are not capable of being saved, or even helped, by the importation of foreign money*; it will destroy our *industry*, it will introduce *luxury*; the increase of *quantity* and *ease of acquirement will depreciate it*, and thereby defeat its own uses.

This is as true as the diurnal rotation of the earth, but, like it, not obvious to the perceptions of every mind. Unhappy for us! the *nature of money*, and the *radical essence* of the *public finance*, depend on principles *too latent* for easy comprehension; and what makes the matter more dangerous, like many delusive appearances in the natural world, is, they seem to be perfectly easy and obvious, when they are least understood; and therefore it has been observed in all

all ages, that they work like *magic* under the direction of unskilful men, ever producing *effects* the *least expected*, as well as failing of those *most sanguinely* computed upon.

Their operations, like other doctrines which depend on an infinity of relations, are governed by so many co-operating causes, that their delineation is very difficult, and their demonstration intricate, and not to be understood without a long and deep attention.

They make a part of the *great law of proportions*, which nature never fails to regulate and adjust with perfect exactness, but which the greatest and strongest intellects, with the most nervous attention, can but *imperfectly comprehend*.

Therefore, in this, as in all other branches of physical knowledge, our safest cue and surest principles must be drawn from experiment. But to return to my subject—

I do not apprehend the actual pernancy of profits from our western lands, when disposed of according to my plan, so very distant as many may imagine. The argument of analogy, from what has been to what will be, is generally allowed to be a good one. If, therefore, upon this rule of reasoning, we may suppose that the increase of population in our country shall continue the same in time to come as we have experienced in time past, viz. that the number of souls double once in 25 years, it will appear very probable that our own eyes may live to see the commencement of a great demand and rapid sale of our western territory. The number of souls in the Thirteen States in 1775, was generally computed at 3,000,000. [Some people of great observation were of opinion, this number was much exceeded.] On the aforesaid scale of computation, the number of souls in these States, at the end of the next century, will amount to 96,000,000 ; enough to extend over the whole territory of our Commonwealth, and more than *Spain, France, Germany,* and *Italy* now contain.

7. I will here subjoin one thing more, which may perhaps be thought worthy of some consideration, viz. that in surveying and granting the western lands, all saltlicks, and mines of metallic ores, coals, minerals, and all other valuable

valuable fossils (in all which the country greatly abounds) may be reserved and sequestered for public use: a great revenue may grow out of them; and it seems unreasonable that those vast sources of wealth should be engrossed and monopolized by any individuals. I think they ought to be improved to the best public advantage, but in such manner, that the vast profits issuing from them should flow into the public treasury, and thereby inure to the equal advantage of the whole community.

The foregoing considerations open to view such great objects, such prospects of vast population and national wealth, as may at first sight appear chimerical, illusory, and incredible. A great minister of state was formerly so astonished at the very mention of the vast supplies predicted by the prophet *Elisha*, that he, with amazement mixed with unbelief, exclaimed, " *If the Lord would make windows in heaven, might this thing be!*" But I mean to subject this Essay to the most rigid examination. Please to review every proposition, and closely examine every argument and inference I make, and if they do not justify the conclusion, reject them; but if you find the facts alleged, true, the propositions just, and the inferences fairly drawn, do not start at your own good fortune, or shrink from the blessings which Heaven pours on your country. The boundaries herein described, by which the contents of our territories are computed, are taken from *Mitchel*'s map, published in 1755, at the request of the Lords Commissioners of Trade and Plantations, and is chiefly composed from draughts, charts, and actual surveys of different parts of the *English* colonies and plantations in *America*, great part of which have been lately taken by their Lordships' orders, and transmitted to the plantation-office, as is certified by *John Pownal*, secretary of said office, and is perhaps a map of the best authority and greatest accuracy of any extant. The facts are of public notoriety. The computations are all made on obvious principles, and may be corrected by any body, if wrong. The sentiments are my own, and are cheerfully submitted to the most rigorous scrutiny that can consist with truth and candor. The subject

ject is very large; I do not pretend to exhaust it, or that this Essay is a finished piece; it is a sketch only, a draught of outlines, which, I hope, will be allowed to deserve at least a candid attention. I wish it might be sufficient to produce a full conviction, that it cannot be the interest of the United States either, 1st. to suffer such vast and valuable blessings to be ravished from us by our enemies; or, 2d. to consent to their being sold and alienated to foreigners, for any little, trifling present considerations; such foolish bargains must originate in very narrow views of the subject, and terminate in shame and loss, and in every stage be marked with mortification, disputes, and embarrassment.

I will conclude by just observing, that this Essay is wholly confined to one branch only, to one single resource, of our public revenue; only one item of our national wealth: an income vast indeed, not drawn at all from the purses of the people, but capable of being so conducted, that every individual who chooses to be interested in it, may find a good profit resulting from the concern. I do not doubt but if the whole great subject was properly surveyed by a mind capable of such reflections, many other sources of revenue might be found, of vast utility to the public, and in no sense injurious, but highly profitable, to individuals. So to graft the revenue on the public stock, so to unite and combine public and private interests, that they may mutually support, feed, and quicken each other, is the secret art, the true spirit of financiering; but we must never lose sight of this one great truth, viz. that all resources of public wealth and safety are only materials put into our hands for improvement, and will prove either profitable or hurtful according to the wisdom or folly with which they are managed. Ruin may grow out of national wealth, as well as from national poverty. Perhaps it may require more great and good talents to support an affluent fortune than a narrow one. Affluence has at least as many dangers as indigence. All depends on the characters of the men who manage them. The happiness and wretchedness of nations depend on the abilities and virtue of the men employed

ployed in the direction of their public affairs. And I pray God to imprefs a due fenfe of this great and moſt important doctrine on the minds of all electors, and others concerned in the appointment of public officers.*

---

* It may be worth notice here (tho' it does not immediately belong to the fubject of the foregoing Effay)

1ſt. That the firſt Congreſs under the New Conſtitution met at *New-York*, March 4, 1788; and, after two long feſſions, adjourned to *Philadelphia*. The firſt feſſion which was held there was on *Dec.* 4, 1790; and the feſſion concluded on *March* 3, 1791.

2d. That *eleven States only* had adopted the New Conſtitution at the time of the firſt feſſion of Congreſs under it; but the two deliberating States, viz. *North-Carolina* and *Rhode-Iſland*, foon acceded, and their delegates were admitted in Congreſs.

3d. That two new States, viz. *Kentucky* and *Vermont*, were admitted into the Union in *Feb.* 1791: fo that the *American* Union now confiſts of *fifteen* States.

SCALES

[502]

SCALES of DEPRECIATION of Continental Money.

	Of Congress.			Of Pennsylvania, by act of Assembly.	From the merchants' books: For Philadelphia.	For Virginia.
1777.						
January				1 1-2	1 1-4	1 1-4
February	*Value of 100 Continen. dollars in specie.*			1 1-2	1 1-2	1 1-4
March				2	2	2
April				2 1-2	2	2
May				2 1-2	2 1-2	2
June				2 1-2	2 1-2	2
July	Dollars.	90ths.	8ths.	3	3	3
August				3	3	3
September	100	00	0	3	3	3
October	90	77	3	3	3	3
November	82	73	0	3	3	3
December	74	70	0	4	4	4
1778.						
January	67	85	0	4	4	4
February	61	83	2	5	5	5
March	56	79	6	5	5	5
April	48	74	4	6	6	5
May	42	77	5	5	5	5
June	36	86	1	4	4	5
July	32	79	3	4	4	5
August	27	87	3	5	5	5
September	24	78	5	5	5	5
October	20	84	5	5	5	5
November	17	88	0	6	6	6
December	14	89	2	6	6	6
1779.						
January	12	85	1	8	7 8 9	8
February	10	85	6	10	10	10
March	9	87	1	10 1-2	10 11	10
April	8	89	7	17	12½ 14 16 22	16
May	7	89	5	24	22 24	20
June	6	89	2	20	22 20 18	20
July	6	40	0	19	18 19 20	21
August	5	89	6	20	20	22
September	4	88	5	24	20 28	24
October				30	30	28
November	3	89	6	38 1-2	32 45	36
December	3	30	0	41 1-2	45 38	40

SCALES

Scales of Depreciation of Continental Money.

	Of Congress.	Of Pennsylvania, by act of Assembly.	From the merchants' books: For Philadelphia.	For Virginia.
1780.				
January	3 40 b	40 1-2	40 45	42
February	2 89 b	47 1-2	45 55	45
March	2 45 b	61 1-2	60 65	50
April	2 45 b	61 1-2	60	60
May	2 45 b	59	60	60
June	2 45 b	61 1-2	60	65
July	2 45 b	64 1-2	60 65	65
August	2 45 b	70	65 75	70
September	2 45 b	72	75	72
October	2 45 b	73	75 80	73
November	2 45 b	74	80 100	74
December	2 45 b	75	100	75
1781.				
January	2 45 b	75	100	75
February	2 45 b	75	100 120	80
March	2 45 b	75	120 135	90
April	2 45 b	75	135 200	100
May	2 45 b	75	200 500	150

May 31, 1781, Continental money ceased to pass as currency, but was afterwards bought and sold as an article of speculation, at very uncertain and desultory prices, from 500 to 1000 to 1.

The exchange of State-money of *Pennsylvania*, in *May* 1781, was 2½, 6, 7, 5, and 4, to 1 hard Money.

A CHRO-

A

CHRONOLOGICAL TABLE

OF

REMARKABLE EVENTS.

AMERICA first discovered by Columbus in the year of our Lord, - - 1492
North-America discovered by Cabot, - 1499
Penn's charter for Pennsylvania, - - 1680
American Philosophical Society established, - 1762
Tea destroyed at Boston, - - Dec. 16, 1773
Boston port shut, - - - June 1, 1774
First Congress met at Philadelphia, - Sept. 5, ———
Battle of Lexington, - - April 19, 1775
First emission of Continental money, - May 10, ———
Gen. Washington appointed, - - June, ———
Battle at Bunker's-hill, - - June 17, ———
Charlestown (Massachusetts) burnt, - June 17, ———
Falmouth burnt, - - - Oct. 18, ———
Canada invaded by the Americans, - - ———
Gen. Montgomery fell, - - Dec. 31, ———
Norfolk burnt, - - - Jan. 1776
Boston evacuated by the British, - March 17, ———
Siege of Quebec raised, - - May, ———
Battle at Sulivan's Island, - June 28, ———
Declaration of independence, - July 4, ———
Canada evacuated by the Americans, - - ———
Battle on Long-Island, - - Aug. 27, ———
New-York taken by the British, - Sept. 15, ———
Battle of White-plains, - Oct. 28, ———
New-Jersey over-run by the British, - Dec. 14, ———
General Washington took 900 Hessians at Trenton,
    Dec. 26, ———
Battle of Princeton, - - - Jan. 3, 1777
Battle of Brandywine, - - Sept. 11, ———
Wilmington (Delaware) taken, - Sept. 19, ———
Battle of Benington, - - Sept. ———

Philadelphia

Philadelphia taken,	Sept. 27,	1777
Battle of Germantown,	Oct. 4,	
Burgoyne taken by Gen. Gates,	Oct. 17,	
Esopus burnt,	Oct.	
Treaty with France,	Feb. 6,	1778
The British commence hostilities with France,	June 17,	
Philadelphia evacuated by the British,	June 18,	
Battle of Monmouth,	June 28,	
Savanna taken,	Sept. 29,	
Stony-point taken by Gen. Wayne,	July 16,	1779
New-Haven taken,	July	
Spain begins a war with Britain,	July 16,	
Fairfield burnt,	July	
Charlestown (S. Carolina) taken,	May 12,	1780
French army arrives at Rhode-Island,	July 10,	
Battle of Camden,	Aug. 16,	
Britain declares war against Holland,	Dec. 20,	
Wilmington (N. Carolina) taken,	Jan.	1781
Articles of Confederation finally ratified,	Mar. 1,	
Continental money ceased to circulate as cash,	May	
Battle of Eutaw Springs,	Sept. 8,	
New-London burnt,	Sept. 13,	
Wilmington (N. Carolina) evacuated,	Oct.	
Cornwallis surrendered,	Oct. 19,	
Savanna evacuated,	July 11,	1782
Charlestown (S. Carolina) evacuated,	Dec. 14,	
Preliminary treaty signed,	Jan. 20,	1783
Treaty with Sweden,	April 3,	
The first air-balloon let off by M. Montgolfier at Paris,	Aug. 27,	
Definitive treaty of peace ratified,	Sept. 3,	
New-York evacuated,	Nov. 25,	
The American army disbanded: Gen. Washington resigns his commission,	Dec.	
Convention met for revising the Federal Government of the United States of America,	May 25,	1787
Finished their deliberations on a plan of government for the United States of America, and published the same,	Sept. 17,	
First Congress under the New Constitution met at New-York,	Mar. 4,	1788
And, after two long sessions, adjourned to Philadelphia; the first session at which place was,	Dec. 4,	1790

F I N I S.

CPSIA information can be obtained
at www.ICGtesting.com
Printed in the USA
BVHW04s2152150918
527529BV00029B/188/P